WAR AND WELFARE

EUROPE AND THE UNITED STATES, 1945 TO THE PRESENT

Jytte Klausen

D1569186

palgrave

WAR AND WELFARE
Copyright © Jytte Klausen, 1998.

First published in hardcover in 1998 by St. Martin's Press
First PALGRAVE™ edition: March 2001
175 Fifth Avenue, New York, N.Y. 10010 and
Houndmills, Basingstoke, Hampshire, England RG21 6XS
Companies and representatives throughout the world.

PALGRAVE is the new global publishing imprint of St. Martin's Press LLC Scholarly and Reference Division and Palgrave Publishers Ltd (formerly Macmillan Press Ltd).

ISBN 0–312–21033–7 hardcover
ISBN 0–312–23883–5 paperback

Library of Congress Cataloging-in-Publication Data
Klausen, Jytte.
War and welfare: Europe and the United State, 1945 to the present / by Jytte Klausen.
     p.   cm.
  Included bibliographical references and index.
  ISBN 0–312–23883–5
  1. Europe—Economic conditions—1945– 2. Capitalism—Europe—History. 3. Welfare state—Europe—History. 4. Central planning—Europe—History. I. Title.
HC240.K531998
338.94'009'045—dc21   98–3792
                                                                CIP

A catalogue record for this book is available from the British Library.

Internal design and typesetting by Letra Libre

First paperback edition: March 2001
10 9 8 7 6 5 4 3 2 1

Printed in the United States of America

CONTENTS

Acknowledgments

This book has taken a long time to write, and I have accumulated many moral debts. The largest one goes to my family, to my husband Alan and my three children, Rebekka, Jan, and Andreas. I do not think there has been any wife and mother who has had a more supportive family than I have.

I extend my thanks for support to Brandeis University, the Mazer Fund and the Marver Bernstein Fund, which have supported me financially at various stages. Thanks to the Bunting Institute at Radcliffe College and the Minda de Gunzburg Center for European Studies, Harvard University, which have housed me. I am grateful to my colleagues in the Department of Politics at Brandeis, who supported me with special thanks to Sid Milkis, Mark Hulliung, George Ross, and Steve Burg. John D. Stephens, Robert O. Keohane, Carl Strikwerda, Cathie Jo Martin, and an anonymous reader, whose comments on the manuscript helped me greatly, have also earned my gratitude. Loren Cass and Susan Schantz, my graduate student assistants at Brandeis, helped me with a cheerful competence that helped keep me sane. My two Radcliffe Research Partnership associates, Lucia Bigelow and Margaret Schotte, did a wonderful job burrowing for arcane materials at the Widener Libraries. I wish partners never had to part but sometimes they do, and I am grateful for the time it lasted. In addition, I owe thanks to my editor, Karen Wolny, whose enthusiasm for the book pushed me to work harder.

ONE

Reconstruction and Capitalist Reform

· Politics in the Aftermath of War

World War II reshaped capitalism and liberal democracy by reordering both the domestic and the international order. This book is about the domestic legacy of the war. In belligerent and neutral countries alike, the war years engendered an expansion of state capacities that permanently changed the balance between state and society. When the war ended in 1945, the reconstruction process rested on piecemeal government decisions to remove or retain wartime controls over society and the economy. In the process of making those decisions, governments shaped society and markets in their own image.

The expansion of the state that accompanied war mobilization and economic shortages between 1939 and 1945 was critical to the creation of the postwar welfare state. Wartime expansion of the state machinery for directing the economy assumed roughly similar forms in different countries and led to a wholly new conception of the possibilities inherent in economic policies. In *War, Economy, and Society, 1939–1945,* Alan Milward (1979) described the convergence of the resource mobilization policies of the belligerent countries. Milward, however, concluded that "There was practically no economic planning during the war in the sense in which that phrase is now used" (130). In his view, the chief legacy of the war was a new consciousness with respect to the government's role in directing the economy.

The thesis of this book is that significant continuities existed between the warfare and the welfare states, but also concurs with Milward that postwar planning quickly assumed forms quite different from those used during the war years. Continuity persisted amidst change, as postwar planning failed first and then succeeded. Wartime planning policies rested mainly on direct controls, rationing, and corporatist purchasers' and suppliers' cartels.

They were coercive controls that were incompatible with democratic constraints on executive power and with interest group autonomy. Planners and reformers, who in the reconstruction debates held high expectations for what planning would accomplish in the future, in many cases underestimated the difference between wartime and peacetime planning, particularly the implications of associational autonomy. The shortcomings of planning theory should not overshadow the importance of the institutional and technological innovations in state capacities for planning made during the war, innovations that in many cases not only survived but were amplified in its aftermath.

The warfare-to-welfare state thesis rethinks the origins of the welfare state by stressing institutional continuity and the unprecedented state expansion caused by war mobilization as causal variables for the permanent reordering of state-society relations that the postwar welfare state represented. It does not explain subsequent changes in economic policy, nor does it address why the postwar commitment to full employment has been abandoned in recent decades. It does, however, suggest a new perspective on how and when states can plan. The state was central to postwar growth strategies in part because wartime state building had radically extended the state's reach and capacities. States are both formal-legal constructions of authority and a social fact.

European states re-entered global trade after 1945 with a slow crawl out of economic autarky. (The term *autarky* means "self-sufficiency" and is used to describe an economic condition of radical insularity. *Autarchy* means self-government or totalitarianism. The terms are sometimes used interchangingly and, in practice, one sometimes follows the other; fascist and communist political theory embraced both, for example. We are in this book concerned only with the economic condition of autarky and its consequences for policy.) Planning was necessary to bridge the gap between scarcity and national economic development. It also helped governments keep promises made during the war years to citizens in return for support for the war effort—promises that are best epitomized by the popularity of the "Beveridge Report" and President Roosevelt's "Second Bill of Rights."

Economic Planning: A New Public Philosophy

Planning and ideas about economic management predate the war. Socialists (and communists) had long argued for state control of economic activity. European and U.S. business and industry groups were engaged in wide-ranging plans for self-government in response to the deflation in the 1920s (Chandler 1990). The publication of J. M. Keynes' *General Theory* in 1936 also summarized a new perspective on the government's obligations for national economic development. Yet prior to the war, liberal democracy had not become reconciled with planning. Business planning had not been effective in arresting deflation and the Great Depression. The Roosevelt administration's National Recovery Administration and Code Authorities had been found unconstitutional. Leon Blum's "little New Deal" had not had produced a turn-around in the French economy. In Germany, Hjalmar Schacht's protectionist program had been used to sustain unheard-of military aggression. Only in Sweden had a positive (but very cautious) beginning been made before the war.

War mobilization put an end to unemployment. The war controls created a functional template for cartelization and for industry-state collaboration. Trade unions were brought into the administration of wage control policies. Economists applied Keynesian formulas to the calculation of the national income and for forward planning of incomes and taxes, proving that it could be done. The war provided a deadly blow to liberal capitalism, for the war economy showed that full employment was possible within the confines of a capitalist economy. Postwar planners widely assumed that controls would have to be continued in order to prevent deflation and a slump similar to the one that had followed after the prior war in 1920–1921. This, it would turn out, was a key mistaken assumption, one that caused unions and planners to be ill prepared for dealing with wage inflation when that proved to be the greater threat to economic stability.

Planning and the Welfare State

Current terminology increasingly identifies the "welfare state" with social policy. That was not the way the term was used 50 years ago when full employment was given first priority, and social policy was regarded as a stop-gap measure at best. This book speaks of the "welfare state" in its original sense, namely state responsible for maintaining growth and for social and economic fairness. In postwar debates, the welfare state was seen to have two pillars, full employment and inclusive social policies (Marshall 1950). Economic planning was needed to guarantee full employment, and social policy was necessary to provide for those who were unable to work. It was widely assumed that, with full employment, "need" could be eliminated (Beveridge 1942). Thus social policy became an adjunct to economic policy.

A subcommittee under the postwar planning committee set up by the Swedish economist Gunnar Myrdal that had been created to deliberate on issues related to social policy, family policy, and the position of women, illustrated the extent to which postwar planners prioritized economic policy over social policy. In a report on the economic consequences of social policy, the subcommittee concluded that social policy was indistinct from economic policy, concerned as it was with "the formation of the national income, its distribution, and use" (Sweden 1945, 7). The report spent more pages discussing capital formation and income distribution than social policy, narrowly understood. If social policy had the same aims as economic policy, it followed that it was the least effective means of the two, useful only for "plugging the holes."[1]

Some believed that the core of planning was the creation of a "Plan." However, this proved to be too narrow a view. Planning is, strictly speaking, a matter of coordination and can be accomplished by many means. In practice, planning objectives could be piggybacked onto other policies. Consequently, planning can be viewed as a mind-set or an aspect of various policies. Fiscal policy aims to raise enough revenues to pay for government outlays but also can be enlisted for purposes related to the full employment goal. Penalties or tax rebates can be applied to encourage industry to reinvest earnings and create new jobs, for example. The existence of a government document designated as a "Plan" is by no means the only indicator that planning took place. While one version of planning, which we can call *dirigism* in deference to the French application of this version (it is sometimes also referred to as *planification*), was wedded to the idea of a formal "Plan" to be fixed and administered primarily by government officials; another version focused on the creation of a "Social Pact" between the main economic actors, unions and employers, the designated "Social Partners."

Another complication is that different people have different ideas about the objectives of planning. Aside from full employment, any number of additional beneficial outcomes often were attributed to planning, including greater efficiency, social fairness, higher growth, and economic democracy. The diverse meanings make it hard to come up with a fixed definition, but we are here concerned with the social dimensions to economic development and planning rather than, for example, the rationalization of production. This focus is well in tune with postwar debates on economic policy, which invariably stressed the social obligations of capitalists and made social fairness a primary objective for economic policy. Broadly conceived, the definition of planning used in this book designates the public direction of the allocation of nongovernment economic resources to specific purposes whether exercised through public and private actors. Even when planning was done by interest groups—the confederations of labor and employers in the case of wage policy, for example—"state direction" still was involved. The erasure of a clear distinction between public and private interests was an important aspect of postwar planning.

Postwar planners were far from neutral on the question of who should do the planning. High regard for civil servants and planners was a conspicuous aspects of reconstruction debates on planning. Jean Monnet, the architect of the French planning system, explained in his memoirs that he had studied Stafford Cripps' 1945 "Working Parties" for British industry but concluded that they were handicapped by the absence of a strong presence of civil servants representing the public interest (Monnet 1978, 237). Evan Durbin, a Labour Party intellectual, called for the creation of "some kind of Central Authority with power over industry and finance" to act as a "Supreme Economic Authority" (1949, 52–53). Despite Monnet's criticism, Cripps had very high regard for civil servants. The benefits of public control would be twofold. Economies of scale would produce an efficiency gain in themselves—by eliminating "wasteful" competition—which would pay for social reform. Civil servants would make fairer decisions than businessmen. The latter were motivated by self-interest, the former by the national interests. (See chapter 3.)

Planners agreed that Western planning would differ from Soviet planning by showing greater respect for liberty, but they remained bedeviled by the questions of compliance. How could meaningful planning take place without crossing over into a command economy, and how could planners ensure that planning amounted to more than forecasting? There were two answers to the questions. One was to substitute interest-group negotiation for government dictate and plan by corporatist coordination. This was the road preferred by the Swedish Social Democrats. Another was to rely on the bureaucratic apparatus of the state in what was called central planning. In actuality, there were many stops on the road between the extremes.

The Dutch economist and planner Jan Tinbergen (1956, 1964), who was an ardent advocate of central economic planning, had an answer: Expand the bureaucracy. Planners would prevail by the sheer weight of presence binding private actors to the "plan." Planning, in his view, was a "general rehearsal" of real economic life. Tinbergen (1964, 77–78) predicted that a convergence between communism and capitalism would take place as Western welfare states worked to give "a decreasing weight" to the interests of the owners of the means of production, and in both East and West planning worked to equalize "the weights given to the interests of the various groups of the population." He suggested an elaborate typology for the successive "stages" of economic planning, reaching from central planning boards to "instruction to cells" (88–89). Planners could compensate for their lack of power to command compliance to the "plan" by increasing the size of their organization. The advocacy of central planning without communism seems particularly bizarre given the historical failures of

Soviet planning. While few had illusions about the oppressive political system of the Soviet Union, many continued to believe that it was an economically viable alternative to capitalism.[2]

Gunnar Myrdal represented a somewhat different perspective, although he too took for granted that civil servants (and economists) would make better decisions. Planning was a fact of life and grew naturally out of the expansion of government responsibilities. But Myrdal emphasized planning as an open-ended process of interest coordination between different parts of the government and between government and private actors (1960, 19). He was agnostic about the exact means and methods for planning, but believed firmly that the welfare state required national economic planning. Myrdal accurately perceived that significant cross-national variation would exist with respect to how planning was done.

By 1947 a new conception of planning had begun to emerge, one that substituted group coordination for government dictate. A distinct functional advantage of the corporatist conception of planning was that it avoided tricky questions about the public-private distinction by turning planning into a question of self-regulation. It also accommodated Keynesian macroeconomic theory. The British economist Alec Cairncross (1978) once noted that Keynes spoke of planning as road rules, or rules of conduct that applied to everybody in equal measure. In this conception, an agreement, for example, to deferred pay matched with some other measure alleviating the sacrifice or spreading sacrifice equally across the classes qualifies as planning. But this was not what most planning advocates considered to be "real" planning.

Some planning advocates believed that states needed to step in to compensate for the failings of capitalism, while others thought that the need for planning arose because liberal capitalism could not cope with the rise of organized labor. The latter view was taken by two U.S. political scientists, Robert A. Dahl and Charles Lindblom, who argued that wage rigidity caused by trade union wage control necessitated planning (1953, 1976). In practice most postwar efforts to plan income formation arose precisely from the need to control inflation. Yet the view that planning was needed to further union control continued to hold sway, too. In an study that resonated with Durbin's argument made three decades earlier, Stephen Cohen, also an American political scientist, held in a study of French planning policies that planning should be regarded as a political exercise rather than an economic one because planning "could only be democratic when workers, through their trade union representatives, had sufficient power in the planning process to make working-class priorities prevail" (1977, 203). Durbin and Cohen were emblematic of roughly four decades of left-wing enthusiasm for planning, one marking the dawn, the other the sunset of an outlook on economic policy that was spawned by the war experience. To them, the war years had shown that capitalism and planning were compatible, and that economic reform could succeed without a political revolution. For many on the left, planning was a way of reconciling labor's economic strength with its political weakness.

The left's desire for a "Supreme Economic Authority" sprang from a wish to circumvent electoral politics and to use planning as a correction to liberal democracy. The alliance between state and labor was a way to thwart capitalism, using public power against private ownership. The intellectual elites' distrust of electoral democracy as a vehicle for enduring control of the economy was matched by the unions' abiding distrust of the state. Once wages and trade unions became the central object of planning, the left was deeply divided. Trade unions liked the idea of the state preempting their organizational prerogative to negotiate wages and represent workers no more than business liked the idea of the state setting production targets and deciding who could trade with whom.

High Hopes and Some Disappointment

Some economists argued then, as did the Austrian economist and émigré Friedrich A. von Hayek in his 1944 book, *The Road to Serfdom,* that all planning was incompatible with liberty. But even those who were critical of planning fully expected it to prevail. With regrets, Joseph Schumpeter (1950, 375), also an Austrian émigré, pointed out at the time that the planners had already won the debate at war's end. The war controls had made planning a fact, and privatization was barely on the agenda for reconstruction. The mystery, in retrospect, is why Schumpeter's dire prediction did not come to pass.

In *Modern Capitalism: The Changing Balance of Public and Private Power* (1965), Andrew Shonfield concluded that postwar economic planning had worked to scale back private power. Now, reconsidering the same events three decades later, it appears that his perspective was distorted by the closeness of his object of study. Beginning with demobilization, the thread of history running from 1945 to the present is one of disappointment for planners and their ambitions regarding public control. On balance, we have witnessed a gradual restoration of private power, not vice versa. The planning optimism that dominated the reconstruction debates can seem both naive and puzzling in retrospect. Planners and planning have gone from being regarded as the key to social welfare and economic growth to being considered an obstacle and even a deterrent to growth. Part of the transformation in attitudes and expectations has to do with the failure of the planned economies and the injustices of bureaucratic rule, which over the years have been increasingly widely perceived.

The reversals in our ideas about planning are, at times, almost startling when compared against the backdrop of postwar debates. The collapse of the Soviet Union and the bankruptcy of the East European economies eliminated whatever sympathy remained on the left for state-centered planning. The British Labour Party finally decided to remove the infamous Clause Four from the party constitution at its 1995 annual Conference. The clause dated back to the party's 1918 constitution and declared the party's objective to be "the common ownership of the means of production." Labour's stunning 1997 electoral victory on a liberal platform completed its rebirth as a middle-class party.[3] The conversion of a British Marxist, Andrew Gamble (1996, 192), to the view that Hayek was "more right than wrong" is another sign, albeit on a smaller scale, of the disintegration of an intellectual paradigm that can be traced back to the origins of electoral Marxism.[4]

War Mobilization and the Citizenship State

The convergence of social and economic policy was itself a product of war mobilization. Nineteenth-century wars were fought by lining soldiers up along military front lines. In 1914 the United Kingdom started out fighting as it had fought the Napoleonic Wars, by paying for what was needed: soldiers, ships, and provisions. Men went off to war, and meanwhile life continued. But in the twentieth century, bombing exposed civilian populations directly to destruction and dislocation. Conscription and rationing put the national economy in the service of the war. The feeding and protection of civilians became a matter of concern for states on par with that of providing for soldiers. Planning aimed to balance military and economic needs. During World War II, the crisis was international. Neutral countries, one of which—Sweden—is discussed herein, were drawn in by submarine warfare and the claims made on international shipping tonnage by the joint Anglo-American war effort. The economic effects of the war were many and diverse, but most important for countries not drawn directly into the war was the fact that world trade was brought to a halt. In belligerent and nonbelligerent countries alike, emergency legislation suspended electoral democracy and imposed restrictions on free speech and political activity.

Between 1939 and 1945, society and markets became subordinated to states in ways that endured beyond the cessation of war. State-society relations were permanently altered. When the time came to decide on postwar reconstruction, reform and reconstruction became indistinguishable.

Economic and political development were intimately tied due to the pervasive state presence. Reconstruction was as much a matter of restoring trade and rebuilding housing as it was a matter of intense group competition for control of the state, for shares of the national product, and for the moral and political authority to define the aims of reconstruction.

The state's omnipresence caused a dilemma for those who were reluctant to embrace the state; even the transfer of functions from the state to society required state action. The process required governments to become overseers of reform. Irrespective of ideology, postwar governments became reform governments. Governments and parties that failed to embrace the state with an affirmative program for how to use government to shape society and markets, either because they distrusted the state or were principally opposed to strong states, gave way to those that had no such objections.

The Postwar Consensus

The shift to a new epistemology of government responsibility for shaping socially responsible capitalism encompassed both left and right. In his book on agrarian socialism in Canada, the political scientist Seymour Martin Lipset (1959) argued that reform movements succeed when the entire spectrum of politics shifts in favor of reform. This holds for postwar Europe. But Lipset also traced the shift to popular mobilization, a connection that is much more ambiguous in the case of postwar Europe. There, elites and the public too embraced a new public consciousness, but reform was not the result of popular mobilization for new state action as much as it was in defense of preserving the state. State-expansion often preceded electoral mobilization in favor of the state and postwar elections and changing party alignments ratified a process of change that had started early on in the war, at a time when partisan competition was suspended and unprecedented executive powers founded on emergency legislation allowed governments to act without constitutional constraints.

In France, reconstruction debates took place in Algiers, where the "Free French," the French resistance forces, were located, and in Washington, D.C. In Germany, they took place among displaced and suppressed groups of survivors and, most important, among Allied policymakers. In Sweden and the United Kingdom, displacement and the suspension of partisan activities that accompanied national emergency governments reduced political activity while government-sponsored agencies cranked out "war aims" platforms that promised the attainment of social justice as the reward for shared sacrifice during hard times.

The impulse for a new public philosophy derived in the first place from the functional and institutional changes in the state caused by the war, rather than from popular political mobilization. Adjustment to the "new" state occasioned large-scale changes to national party alignments. In Britain, the Labour Party assumed power in 1945 backed by an election that was a vote for continuity and for change. Voters correctly saw the party as one the more likely to carry on the aspects of wartime policies that they supported.

"War Socialism" and the Political Parties

The left recognized that the war controls on the civilian economy were a gift of power. The embrace of war controls as a means for peacetime planning was expressed with great clarity in a 1944 report, *Full Employment and Financial Policy*, from the British Labour Party's National Executive Committee. It listed a range of controls that should be kept—from state trading to foreign exchange controls—and observed what great benefits the controls had brought to the people. "We must not let this Socialist advance be halted or turned back," it concluded (7).

The party leader of the German Social Democrats, Kurt Schumacher, whose orthodox positions eventually worked to alienate the party from the reconstruction process, adamantly held to the belief that capitalism and democracy could not coexist in Germany. He fully expected a proletarian revolution to be around the corner in 1945, suppressed only by the presence of Allied military forces. In a public speech in October of that year, Schumacher announced that "the crucial point on the agenda is the abolition of capitalist exploitation and the transfer of the means of production" (Scholz and Oschilewski 1953, 36–50).

In the United States, Walter Reuther, the president of the United Autoworkers Union (UAW) and a self-described social democrat, suggested that the War Production Board, the central planning agency for the direction of the civilian war economy, be turned it to the "Peace Production Board" and made permanent. Philip Murray, president of the Congress of Industrial Organizations (known as the Committee for Industrial Organization until the name change in 1939), who before the re-creation of a joint confederation in the AFL-CIO represented the fast-growing industrial unions, proposed a "Labor-Management Charter" that would have made aspects of wartime planning policies permanent (Lichtenstein 1995, 225).

A decade later socialist parties had changed their programs. By the 1952 congress of the Swedish Social Democratic Party, the party leadership already had decided to scrap most of the postwar program and to aim for shared growth rather than economic planning. In its 1959 Bad Godesberg program, the German Social Democratic Party erased its Marxist heritage and declared itself a "people's party." In Britain, Anthony Crosland launched the idea, in *The Future of Socialism* (1956), that macroeconomic policy had already caused a transfer of power from management to labor and that the goals now should be to enhance opportunity for the working class through improved education and social services and to attain a higher standard of living through economic growth and redistribution. The controls remained, but not principally as part of the left's program for reform. They were needed as part of a program for macroeconomic stabilization and economic parity between various kinds of incomes—wage incomes, farm incomes, or profit—that both the left and right embraced.

Ralf Dahrendorf (1967, 1980a, b), a sociologist and German statesman, has argued that the new public philosophy that emerged after 1945 was inherently nonliberal. It was nevertheless one to which nonsocialist governments also conformed. By 1950–1951 the British Conservative Party had espoused planning and the welfare state, a change that was signified by the party passage of a new program, *The Industrial Charter* (Conservative Party 1947). The German Christian Democrats' embrace of responsibility for generous social welfare programs (first proposed by the Social Democrats), as in the case of the 1957 *Rentenreform,* is another example.

The nonliberal bias of postwar policymaking derived from the strategic position of the state and from the advantage that prostatist parties and programs derived from that fact. It was a bias that socialist and social democratic parties could mobilize to their advantage, but only if they gave up their traditional hostilities to the capitalist state. The Swedish Social Democrats did this, but not without difficulties that easily matched those facing right-wing and center parties. A "window of opportunity" was created in 1945 for a socially inclusive strategy for national economic development. The capacity to mobilize that bias for partisan advantage hinged on the dynamic of party competition, the flexibility of elites, and the sociology of class.

The Citizenship State

The tectonic shift of postwar politics to new ground based on state-centered economic and social planning raises questions about the historical meaning of war.[5] We have so far stressed the development of new institutional capacities and the fact of state-control of the economy in 1945 as precedence-setting phenomena. This discussion has left out the question of legitimation. The state was not only there, it was mostly also very much wanted. Even the United States, not generally regarded as a strong case of welfare state capitalism, conformed to the warfare-to-welfare state thesis in this respect.

With the attack on Pearl Harbor on December 7, 1941, the United States was brought into the war, and many of the features of the warfare state that consumed and transformed European states were applied on U.S. ground as well. Congressional resistance to the Victory Program, a war productions program that put industrial production under unified centralized direction, melted away.[6] The legacy of the apparatus created to manage this program inspired postwar planners. But politically, promises such as those made by Franklin Delano Roosevelt in his message to Congress on January 11, 1944 changed postwar history.

The message began by listing the control policies still needed to sustain the war economy: industrial conscription, increased taxes, minimum agricultural pricing combined with maximum consumer prices, and an extension of the Stabilization Statute from October 1942, which gave the president extraordinary economic powers. Roosevelt linked control policies with citizenship, promising a "Second Bill of Rights under which a new basis of security and prosperity can be established for all regardless of station, race or creed" (Ausubel 1945, 27). What are we to make of the link among wartime state expansion, coercive planning, and the promise of postwar citizenship? FDR's guarantees echoed promises made to British subjects by William Beveridge, the unofficial author of the postwar welfare state, in his 1942 report, *Social Insurance and Allied Forces*. The U.S. postwar welfare state never did reach the standard set by Roosevelt (or Beveridge), but the statement nevertheless makes the linkage between citizenship and war mobilization plain.

Historical sociology has put the spotlight on the crucial importance of wars in early European state formation. Brian Downing (1992) has linked medieval constitutionalism to the shift in military technology signaled by the rise of peasant armies, and Charles Tilly (1975, 1989) has demonstrated how modern nation-states were the product of the internal and external coercion associated with military mobilization. Michael Mann has explicitly described the history of citizenship—including T. H. Marshall's famous "social citizenship"—and the welfare state as a ruling class strategy for national survival in the age of Total War. Mann writes that "[b]ut for the logics of geo-politics and war—including the sacrifices of my own generation—it might have been a very different and infinitely more depressing picture in Europe" (1988, 206). Comparative studies of the welfare state have nevertheless not been attentive to the central role of war mobilization and its institutional and political legacy in shaping the postwar welfare states.

An emphasis on the importance of wartime institutions in shaping postwar policy and on state capacities as central to the understanding of "Golden Age" welfare capitalism nevertheless fits with Alan Milward's argument in *The European Rescue of the Nation-State* (1992) and Barry Eichengreen's in *Restructuring Europe's Trade and Payments* (1993). Both see postwar international institutions like the European Coal and Steel Community (ECSC), the European Payments Union (EPU), and the Marshall Plan, as instruments for national economic development and as accommodating national interests rather than as instruments of international trade liberalism that traditional historiography has made them out to be. This work points to a new departure for the understanding of domestic policy.

The Indictment of Liberalism

If we consider per-capita growth across various countries in the decades preceding the World War II, the assumption that liberalism was a flawed economic system and capitalism a failure seems a reasonable one. The only countries to see substantial economic growth return in the late 1930s were Germany and Sweden, both of which had embraced some kind of economic planning in the wake of the Great Depression. In the countries that stuck to liberal prescriptions, the recovery never materialized. (See Table 1.1.) France stayed in the slump throughout the interwar years, and Britain experienced only a very moderate recovery.

The conclusion that capitalism had failed was justified, if we look at the interwar economic system from the perspective of workers. Of two evils, inflation and deflation, workers had learned to fear the latter more than the former. Brief hyperinflation in the wake of World War I was replaced by a grinding, decade-long erosion of incomes from deflationary policies. From 1920 to 1938 unemployment and stagnating or declining real wages were the rule. (See Table 1.2.) In Germany the war settlement led to disastrous economic policies and hyperinflation, culminating in a currency crisis in 1923. Real per-capita income declined by about 14 percent between 1925, when inflation was stabilized, and 1932, the Weimar Republic's last year. In Austria a weak recovery following the hyperinflation of the early 1920s evaporated quickly in the depression, and despite a second recovery after the 1934 collapse of the First Austrian Republic, the interwar years were a period of economic decline that did not come to an end until *Anschluss* in 1938. In France the decline was less harsh but the economy still lagged behind the improvements in growth brought by national socialism or social democracy.

In Sweden prices increased by close to 40 percent in 1917–1918, but inflation tapered off in the following years and was replaced by declining prices in 1921–1922. A 1933 crisis program, put together by a Social Democratic minority government supported by a small agrarian party, tagged

**Table 1.1   Average Annual Economic Growth. Select Periods 1900–1994
(Constant prices, percent)**

Country	Years	Average Annual Growth Rates	Base Year
Austria	1900–1913	N.A.	
	1920–1933	1.75	1937
	1933–1937	2.90	1937
	1937–1948 (est.)	−.89	1954
	1950–1972	10.04	1970
	1973–1994	2.98	1970
France	1901–1913	3.06	1938
	1920–1938	2.26	1938
	1939–1945	−8.19	1938
	1952–1972	8.61	1970
	1973–1994		
Germany[1]	1900–1913	2.85	1900
	1925–1932	−.69	1900
	1933–1938[2]	12.33	1900
	1938–1950	−3.26	1900
	1951–1972	11.90	1970
	1973–1994[3]	2.62	1970
Sweden	1900–1913	3.53	1908/1909
	1920–1938	4.19	1908/1909
	1939–1945	1.77	1908/1909
	1949–1972	6.15	1970
	1973–1994	1.61	1970
United Kingdom	1900–1913	1.55	1900
	1920–1938	2.19	1900
	1939–1945	2.37	1900
	1950–1972	3.92	1970
	1973–1994	2.37	1970

Sources: For figures until 1950, see Flora (1987). For 1950 to 1994, see International Monetary Fund's *International Financial Statistics Yearbook* (various years).
Notes: [1]Postwar figures, Federal Republic only.
[2]Adolf Hitler appointed chancellor on January 30, 1933.
[3]Western Länder only.

agricultural prices and wage increases and set off sustained growth in the 1930s. In Germany the National Socialists' economic planning and war mobilization provided citizens with improved living standards. As political scientist Gregory Luebbert (1991) pointed out, the many reasons for disapproving of national socialism should not blind us to the fact that between 1933 and 1938, the economic program of the German National

Table 1.2 Wage Growth, 1914–1975 (Current prices, percent)

Period	Austria	Germany	Sweden	United Kingdom
War years, 1914–1918	NA	890.0	209.5	184.9
Boom, ca. 1920–1922	NA	8 mill.[3]	46.6	98.7
Recovery, ca. 1923–1928	NA	85.2	4.2	−31.5
Depression, ca. 1929–1934	−4.1[1]	−7.6[4]	6.9	6.1
War years, 1939–1945	NA	NA	32.3	46.1
Reconstruction, 1945–1950	215.9	NA	41.9	15.3
1950–1959	50.1[2]	78.6	116.9	77.9
1960–1969	91.8	92.0	103.7	71.5
1970–1979	87.5	46.5	51.3	111.9

Source: Mitchell (1980).
Notes: [1]1927–1934.
[2]9 years only, 1952–1960.
[3]1920–1923.
[4]1930–1938

Socialist Workers' Party (NSDAP) stemmed the depression and brought real improvements in economic welfare to many Germans. On balance, the nonliberal programs for fixing the economy had proven the most efficient in the prewar years. The enthusiasm for economic planning rested on solid empirical grounds. That does not mean that planning was all about reason and facts and that ideology and political competition played no role in shaping the postwar debates on it. In Britain the indictment of competitive capitalism was also widely agreed upon, also outside Labour Party circles. In 1945, four months after the election that produced the Labour government, the historian A. J. P. Taylor concluded in a radio broadcast that "nobody in Europe believes in the American way of life—that is, in private enterprise" (quoted in Howarth 1985, 15).

The failure of interwar economic theory caused postwar planners to make a critical mistake. It was widely assumed that the key problem facing policymakers after the conclusion of war would be to counteract deflationary pressures and to keep prices and wages up. History showed the way. A brief boom following the conclusion of hostilities lasted roughly 18 months from 1918 to 1920 and was followed by a prolonged bust. British real wages declined by 38 percent between January 1921 and December 1922. From 1913 to 1939, one last prewar year to another, money wages increased by close to 1 percent in Great Britain and by 0.1 percent in Germany (Scholliers 1989, 232). British unions had good reasons to fear postwar deflation, so good that it is understandable that they sometimes closed their eyes to early warnings that inflation might be an obstacle to raising living standards. Only in Sweden and Germany did robust memories of inflation work to make the unions more amendable to restraint.

The Control Economy

The civilian war economy that was set up between 1939 and 1945 ushered in a range of new planning technologies. After demobilization, government controls over the economy were still conspicuous. The exception was the United States, where the War Productions Board (WPB) revoked a large number of orders and schedules related to the control economy upon the Japanese surrender. On August 20 alone, the WPB removed 210 individual controls related to the consumer goods and construction industries (Industrial Mobilization for War 1969, 950). Its actions caused accusations of "cavalier" disregard by other agencies including the WPB's successor organization, the Civilian Production Administration. Once created, controls were in place until lifted. In some cases, control expired automatically when the temporary emergency legislation that authorized their creation expired. But even in that case, the actual dismantlement of the controls required deliberate action; people had to be laid-off, offices closed, forms and regulations retired. This is not a trivial point; inertia worked in favor of the planners' ambitions. In the European context, a number of factors worked to prolong the life of controls. Continued shortages were an important cause of postwar controls. Political support from interest groups and trade associations that had grown to national prominence on the backs of the controls was another, as well as the widely held belief (outside the Federal Republic of Germany) that the controls were a fair solution to the problem of shortages.

In some countries, controls were lifted in 1945 only to be reimposed in 1947 in response to a looming international crisis. The precipitating event was a sterling crisis, but the underlying cause was the imbalance between unmet European needs and a demand for U.S. consumer goods that could not be matched by dollar earnings in the importing countries. The crisis was the result of a miscalculation. Currency convertibility had been made a key criterion of the new order by American policymakers who insisted on multilateralism and free access for American goods to European markets as a precondition for providing support for European reconstruction (Gardner 1969). The presumption that a quick return to convertibility and liberalization was possible informed the 1944 Bretton Woods agreement, the Anglo-American loan agreement, and the 1946 plans for the failed International Trade Organization.

When convertibility drained British currency reserves at an unanticipated rate, the full implications of the European reconstruction crisis and the fundamental imbalance between the European and U.S. economies became apparent. The next step was one of retreat, the creation of the European Payments Union (EPU), which allowed for multilateralism in place of immediate convertibility and a slow retirement of physical controls on foreign trade and the multitude of bilateral trade agreements—often bordering on barter—that "dollar shortages" had propagated (Eichengreen 1993).[7]

The reorganization of international trade depended on the position of the U.S. dollar as the currency of last resort against which the value of all other currencies was measured. The system imposed a coordination problem on states, the "external constraint" of matching domestic economic demand with foreign trade. Readers are directed to the technical literature (see Dornbusch and Fischer 1994; Kindleberger 1993), since the system plays a part of some importance in what follows, some explanation is called for.

The External Constraint

A country's balance of payment is a measure of foreign economic transactions. It is made up of the current account and the capital account. The current account equals the net balance of trade in goods and services with foreign countries and net income from foreign assets. The capital account equals the net capital inflow into the country of bonds and stocks. The balance of payment is like a ledger; it *must* balance. This means that any deficit on one account must be made up on the other. Postwar imbalance problems derived from two distinct sources: Europeans buying more from the United States than they were selling or American investments in Europe unmatched by European investment in the United States. From one perspective this was a good thing—imports allowed European consumers and industries to get hold of much needed goods, U.S. investments helped rebuild Europe—but the structural constraint put policymakers in the awkward position of having to ration growth.

Corrective policies tended to converge on the current account rather than the capital account since such policies were more likely to show results on the former account. Charles Kindleberger (1966, 18), an economist and participant in the U.S. State Department's deliberation on postwar German reconstruction, espoused American views on the matter when he wrote about "Europe's gripes" that, "we [the U.S.] are providing Europe with liquidity it cannot or will not provide for itself." That did not mean that Europeans forsook capital controls, banking controls, and a range of other policies design to prevent a negative capital balance from occurring. European resistance against automatic convertibility with dollars also points to the conclusion that, rightly or wrongly, European policymakers thought the costs of liberalization too high.

The functional requirement that the balance of payment current account approach near-equilibrium imposed certain constraints on economic policy that worked to sustain both government responsibility for economic management and stabilization policy focused on income adjustment, often along parity principles similar to those that informed wartime incomes policies. The balance requirement coupled foreign and domestic economic policies by obligating states to seek to bring domestic economic development into proximate harmony with that of its main trading partners. Wartime indexation policies subsequently provided the model for decades of anti-inflationary measures (Brown 1985). In the 1960s and again in the 1970s, unions and governments returned to the parity paradigm established during the war years for wage and price indexation and "social contracts" tying incomes to a common norm.[8]

Typically, a trade deficit caused by domestic demand for foreign goods—traded in dollars—in excess of exports brought on a panoply of corrective policies that replayed wartime stabilization policies, ranging from physical controls on imports, wage restraint, or various contractive measures, such as higher interest rates or higher taxes. The problem with general income restraint was that it did not discriminate, and it dampened both domestic and foreign demand. For that reason, governments preferred policies that discriminated against foreign consumer goods whenever possible.

Depressing domestic demand worked only as medium-term policy and came with some costs that made governments reluctant to take this route. An immediate crisis called for other corrective measures, such as the 1947 sterling devaluation. A devaluation brings down the exchange rate between a weak currency (sterling) and a strong one (dollars), causing goods priced in dollars to become more expensive in sterling and those priced in sterling to become cheaper in dollars. Devaluation was rare, but it was still one tool among several in the toolbox for stabilization policy (Carlin and Soskice 1990, 295). A system of flexible exchange rates seems at first glance to make sense. Repeat attempts in the early 1950s to switch Britain on to a scheme of flexible exchange rates known as "Robot" seem to support this view. The reason for the failure of flexible currency policy was domestic rather than international; British policymakers thought that the social and political costs of abandoning fixed exchange rates would be too high (Krugman 1992).

National Reconstruction and Trade Liberalization

Scholars today disagree over whether, in the 1950s, sustainable equilibrium rates existed that would have come at a cost acceptable to domestic policymakers. The critical issue was wage discipline and the consequences of variation in unit labor costs for differences between U.S. and European producers with respect to productivity (Eichengreen 1993, 61). Floating (or flexible) exchange rates and unrestricted convertibility would have implied radical price increases on imported goods and lower prices for exported goods.[9] A fully liberalized international trade order would jeopardize national economic development, full employment and higher wages in particular.

Scholars recognized the tensions between the liberal and nonliberal elements in the postwar order. The sections in Keynes' *General Theory* that outlined his theory of demand-led economic growth assumed a closed economy. Myrdal held that the welfare state and international liberalism were antinomies. Of the two, Myrdal believed, it was the welfare state that represented the future. "It cannot be helped," he said, "that everywhere national integration [in the welfare state] is now bought at the cost of international disintegration" (1960, 131). The welfare state is both nationalistic and protectionist, he argued, because no nation could reasonably be asked to compromise national economic development in order to sustain the realization of liberal ideals regarding internationalization and free trade.

Focus, Method, and Organization of this Book

The approach of this book is historical-institutionalist because of its emphasis on the reactive nature of policymaking and the importance of institutional constraints in shaping the articulation of interests and policies (Weir 1992). Yet the divergent trajectories of national planning policies after 1945 present us with some important questions about the limits of institutionalist explanations.

Explaining the Welfare State

Debates among comparativists have in recent years centered around questions regarding the balance among institutions, politics, and social structure. Comparativists readily agree that all three matter, but not which comes first. Jonas Pontusson (1995) has argued that we need to "take interests seriously" and "put institutions in their place." This admonition is a response to a literature that has stressed the causal importance of states, or rather their role as "autonomous actors," as Theda Skocpol (1985, 5) famously put it. The institutionalist perspective has not implied that interests or electoral mobilization played no role but simply that interests are malleable and therefore to some degree "dependent" variables. As Kathleen Thelen and Sven Steinmo (1992) state that interests are "refracted" by domestic political institutions. The institutionalist school of thought was a reaction against theories that regarded the political mobilization of the working class as the primary source of social and economic reform. Institutionalists in turn reacted against the Marxist account that tended to regard the capitalist state as immutable and a proxy for capitalist interests.

Some of the first comparativists to argue that states were susceptible to the interests of the popular classes were Walter Korpi (1983), Gøsta Esping-Andersen (1985), and John D. Stephens (1986). Responding to accusations of being "Swedo-centric," Esping-Andersen (1990) subsequently argued that there were three distinct class-based paths to welfare state formation or welfare state regimes. In collaboration with Dietrich Rueschmeyer and Evelyne Huber Stephens, Stephens (1992) expanded his perspective to include Swedish state development under an umbrella of path-dependent trajectories to variations of capitalism that resonate with the earlier works of Stein Rokkan and Seymour Martin Lipset.

Speaking for the structuralist camp, Jonas Pontusson and Peter Swenson have argued for a theory of state expansion that recognizes that political power does not arise from the electoral channel only but also from businesses' control over the economy. They have, in their own words, "challenged the conventional image of Sweden as the land where labor rules" and argued that even the most heralded aspects of the Swedish welfare state were possible only with capital's support (1996, 223–250). Swenson (1991, 69–96) has argued that Swedish wage policy was subordinated to the interests of Swedish export industries already in the 1930s (1991, 69–96). If the primacy-of-business thesis holds even against the "hard" test case that Swedish social democracy presents us with, Swenson (1997) and Pontusson (1992, 1995) argue that it is fair to expect the thesis holds elsewhere too.

This study does not support the primacy-of-business thesis, nor for that matter a primacy-of-labor thesis. In chapter 5 it is shown for example, that the interests of Swedish export industries began shaping wage policy three decades later than claimed by Swenson, and when export industries finally prevailed, it was in concert with other group interests.[10] It is nevertheless also plainly true that Social Democratic economic policies aimed to reconcile trade union interests with a growth-oriented development strategy that allowed room for private industry. The conspicuous circularity of the debate suggests that the difficult part is to decide at what point and in which way institutions, class structure, and political mobilization matters.

Logic of Comparative Inference

Standard wisdom is that comparative generalization is best served by a "same-case" method that allows for variations on the dependent variable

(Lijphart 1975). Good theory should explain divergent outcomes. The comparative method presupposes that we can discuss, in a meaningful way, that particular cases are "instances of the same" or "instances of difference," the terms used by John Stuart Mill in his *A System of Logic* (1843/1949). That in turn presupposes that distinctive and historically contingent and contextualized institutions and events can be regarded as functionally equivalent, despite differences in context. Causal inference hinges on the capacity to clearly distinguish analytically between dependent and independent variables. In truth, we are engaged in an exercise of "make-believe." We can approximate the logic of inference, but we cannot take our units of analysis into a laboratory and demonstrate cause and effect by replicating them.

Complex systems cannot be compared as "wholes" but only their functionally equivalent parts. This fact implies that we make assumptions about boundaries of the parts of systems and compare those, subject to the assumptions involved in framing the mental matrix of comparative inference (Przeworski and Teune 1970). Planning is, as we have seen, a fuzzy variable. We are, in effect, comparing the contested role of the state in directing the economy; the outcome, which this book seeks to explain, is the continuation (or discontinuation) of planning after the war. The legacy of the war had two components, an institutional one and a new public philosophy of citizenship. The dualism implies a problem that here is addressed by the inclusion of the Federal Republic of Germany, a case that presents a test of its own. In this belligerent but defeated country, the legitimating influence of promises of citizenship in exchange for support for the war effort was not a factor in postwar policies. Allied military occupation and the beginning of another war, the Cold War, instead influenced the construction of postwar Germany in unanticipated ways, sometimes providing West German citizens with accidental benefits. The Western Allies played a critical role, for example, in instituting codetermination laws providing German unions with rights that their own Christian Democratic government was unwilling to permit. (See chapter 6.) The Allies' motives were mixed, but the desire to provide German industry and employers with the check of an effective trade union opposition was a primary one. The inclusion of a neutral country, Sweden, in our discussion also allows us to control for one of the causal variables, and to test the causal importance of the war effort itself (in contrast to economic shortages) for state expansion and citizenship.

The logic rules of comparative inference are not easily reconciled with the real-life complexities of history. Interdependence is one such problem; to what extent were national policymakers acting or acted upon by U.S. interests, by the emerging new world order, et cetera, when they went about retrofitting the wartime state for peacetime purposes? In practice, we can recognize the fact of interdependence; in theory, we need to distinguish between dependent and independent variables. In this book, I treat national policymakers as sovereign actors who are cognizant of limits and extraneously fixed cost-benefit tradeoffs.

The global reach of the international crisis in 1940 to 1945—and the one that followed, the Cold War—implies that every country was affected by aspects of the war. In the case of neutral countries such as Sweden, which were spared direct involvement, economic autarky and proximity to military action led to emergency state powers and economic shortages caused planning. In a broad sense, nearly any country would present us with a "comparable-case" scenario. Variations in the involvement in the war—belligerency versus neutrality, victory versus defeat—represent aspects of the war experience that are plainly relevant to our thesis. More realistically, the case selection method presents us with what in the technical language of comparative methodology can be called a mixed-selection procedure, allowing for different values on both the dependent and independent variables (Keohane, King and Verba 1994, 144). The inclusion of the United States, in turn, presents a test of a different kind. In this case, belligerency went hand in hand with promises of citizenship—as the quotes from Roosevelt's 1941 message to Congress illustrate—but planners widely regarded postwar planning as a disappointment.

The rulebook for causal inference also presumes unit homogeneity between variables. This assumption implies that the variables should in some significant sense be alike or "functionally equivalent." Keohane, King, and Verba acknowledge that it can involve problems: "Attaining unit homogeneity is often impossible; congressional elections, not to speak of revolutions, are hardly close analogies to light switches" (1994, 93). It is common to construct the Anglo-Swedish comparison as a paired comparison based on approximate similitude (Fulcher 1991). Still, the comparison presumes some near-heroic assumptions regarding variable independence. We presume, for example, that differences in size, economic development, and international obligations were of marginal importance to our object of study. The argument used here is that economic contexts provided governments in both countries with different but equally compelling reasons to engage in planning.

It makes little sense to take a binary approach to the analysis of postwar planning. We are talking, more or less, about planning rather than planning or no planning. Variations on the dependent variable—the degree to which the planners' designs were realized—suggest that endogenous variables, divergent institutional frameworks, and variations in group interests, for example, worked to shape unique national adjustment paths. We often speak of national roads of political development in cases were circumstances of broadly similar points of departure interact with domestic sociology and political systems to produce divergent outcomes (Luebbert 1991).

Some basic facts suggest that the capacities of postwar reform governments were contingent on constitutional variables, electoral rules in particular. In 1945 unencumbered government control gave, for the first time, the British and Swedish labor parties a chance to use the reconstruction process to attempt to realize similar objectives. In Britain, Labour received 47.8 percent of the vote in the 1945 election and 46.1 percent in 1950. The Swedish Social Democrats got close to 42 percent of the vote in the 1932 election and 45.9 percent in 1936. In 1944 they got 46.7 percent, after getting 53.8 percent in 1940. The similarity with respect to electoral support means that the two cases can be treated as a "same-case" scenario in this respect; in other words, variations in electoral support can not explain divergent outcomes. A match of the Labour governments of 1945 to 1951 with the 1932 to 1936 and the postwar Social Democratic governments creates a sample of left-wing reform governments, which repeatedly has tempted comparativists to theory building (Ingham 1974; Weir and Skocpol 1985; Pontusson 1988; Fulcher 1991).

Organization

Chapters 2 to 7 are taken up with country studies following the comparative matrix just specified. In chapter 8, the comparative perspective is enlarged to included Austria and briefly also France. It also addresses the role of states in shaping divergent national growth strategies in the postwar period. Chapter 2 discusses the evolution of civilian controls and the reordering of society-state relations in the United Kingdom during the war years. The important contributions of Stafford Cripps and William Beveridge to the growth of pro-planning sentiments are also discussed. Chapter 3 turns to the articulation of class interests in Britain with respect to economic planning and the breach between the unions and the Labour government over wage policy. Chapters 4 and 5 present a parallel account of the development of a control economy in Sweden and the postwar adjustment process. Chapter 6 discusses Allied policies in the Western occupation zones of Germany in 1945 to 1949. The chapter challenges the view that Christian Democratic policies conformed to a neoliberal template and points to elements of continuity between occupational policies and postwar economic policy. Chapter 7 contains the American case study, which helps clarify the causal importance of constitutional frameworks in molding policy responses. Like the dog that did not bark, the U.S. case study also helped underline the significance of economic shortages, including "dollar-shortages" in shaping divergent economic policies elsewhere. The final chapter returns to comparative theory and the warfare-to-welfare state thesis. It argues that no one adjustment path exists. The war years and the reconstruction of the international order after 1945 brought strong converging pressures to bear on national policy, but divergence has increased as these pressures have waned. A number of new puzzles and questions arise from the conclusion—for example, the suggestion that internationalization is not associated with a new convergence to capitalist sameness but with an increase in national variation.

TWO

Great Britain: Labour's Spoils of War

Postwar Reform and British Liberalism

The postwar Labour governments (1945 to 1950 and 1950 to 1951) of Great Britain have long generated scholarly controversy. The 1945 election has been regarded as a mandate to radical change, even socialism, and some scholars have castigated Labour leaders for failing to carry out policies commensurate with the mandate (Miliband 1961). In recent years scholars have lowered their expectations with respect to what might have been accomplished and have tended instead to see Labour's policies as "genuinely consensual" (Fielding, Thompson, and Tiratsoo 1995, 2) or even pandering to naive expectations regarding a "New Jerusalem" and a postwar restoration of British superiority (Barnett 1995).

A different tack is taken here. This chapter describes elements of state expansion during the war that anticipated the British post-1945 welfare state. The argument implies that significant policy continuity existed during the war years and after. The discovery of this continuity between Labour's conception of economic and social reform and wartime policies is puzzling, for comparative literature on the postwar welfare state pegs Britain as an instance of liberal "exceptionalism" (Esping-Andersen 1990). Yet, wartime state expansion, the emergence of a control economy, and the development of corporatist coordination in conjunction with the control economy put British policymaking on a path convergent with that of other nations relying on the state to run the economy in support of war mobilization (Milward 1979, 1984). It follows that we need look to post-1945 developments for the sources of British postwar exceptionalism, by which I mean the absence of a planned approach to national economic development of either dirigiste or corporatist bent.

This chapter concentrates on a description of wartime policies. Chapter 3 describes the mainsprings of opposition and support for planning after 1945.

Majority Government and Reform Policy

The central puzzle confronting us is why broad support among elites and the public for economic planning and enthusiasm for the apparent success of the control economy created between 1940 and 1945 did not produce lasting planning institutions. The puzzle has an additional political dimension. Although the Labour Party was credited with the implementation of the welfare state, the party was not returned to power until 1964. After the 1997 election, which invites comparison with the 1945 election because it provided Labour with a majority greater than that obtained in 1945 (1945: 146 seats; 1997: 179 seats), Tony Blair, the party leader and new prime minister, warned party members of the party's history of inability to get reelected. This is nearly true. Labour was returned to power in February 1950 with a majority of five seats. The government lasted until October 1950, when a new election boosted Labour's share of the vote to 48.8 percent but nevertheless produced a Conservative majority. (The incongruity was explained by inequitably drawn constituency boundaries that, coupled with the bias of plurality elections, produced a Conservative majority where none existed.) The Swedish-British comparison points to some important questions. If the example of the Swedish Social Democrats showed that reform governments can use policy and state power to put in place policies that generate new support for further reform and perpetuate left control of government (Esping-Andersen 1985, 10), why did this not happen in Britain? In this view, Labour's failure to get reelected points to a much larger failure to conceive of reform policy as a means for political control and for coalition-building.

Labour's difficulties cannot be discussed without considering the consequences of an electoral system that exaggerates electoral gains as well as losses and majoritarian government that discourages consensual policy-making. The 1945 election result was at the time heralded as a social revolution through the ballot box but scholars have subsequently disagreed about its nature, alternately portraying it as an unanticipated surprise or as an entirely predictable consequence of electoral shifts during the war years (Addison 1982, 248; Fyrth 1995). It was hardly a typical election. Turnout was relatively low, in part due to low turnout in the armed services. Electoral rolls had not been updated since November 1939, so younger voters were prevented from voting. Labour received 48.3 percent of the national vote, but the bias of the "winner-takes-all" system of counting votes

awarded the party control of 61.4 percent of the seats in Parliament.[1] Plurality elections introduce elements of unpredictability, even unfairness.
Labour's 1945 victory was not as massive as it seemed, and the defeat in
1951 was actually a gain. The Swedish electoral system is based on the proportional principle that, on one hand, denied the Social Democrats
Labour's experience of one-party majority, but also sustained their claim
to power as the largest party even during periods of electoral setbacks. The
Social Democrats' unique position as the party of government for an uninterrupted 44 years (1932 to 1976) and for all but 10 of the last 64 years
owed much to the historical fact of a divided center-right and to a constitutional system that favors coalitional policymaking, which almost inevitably awarded the Social Democrats a secure place in government.

Electoral rules bear directly on the competitive conditions for articulating party appeals and indirectly on government formation. The political
scientist Arend Lijphart's work (1975, 1977) on plurality and proportional
systems catalogs the systemic implications of the two ways of counting
votes. His conclusion that majoritarian systems are prone to adversarialism
and proportional systems to consensual policymaking has been sustained
by other comparativists (Stepan and Skach 1993) and by political theorists
who find that deadlocked government promotes inclusive policymaking
(Goodin 1996). The Swedish-British comparison does not neatly conform
to theory for a number of reasons. Elements of a postwar economic policy consensus emerged despite changing governments, epitomized by the
phenomenon of "Butskellism," named after the Conservative chancellor of
the Exchequer, R. A. Butler, and his Labour counterpart, Hugh Gaitskell
(Worswick and Ady 1962, 15). The presumption that plurality systems produce little motivation to coalition building is dubious. In proportional systems with their propensity for coalition government, compromise is part
and parcel of government formation based on the need to contract with
other parties to create a governing majority. In plurality systems, the compulsion to build coalitions lies elsewhere. Party choice may be restricted
but the parties are themselves "big houses" for many interests, all making
claims to determine policy. Conversely, no guarantee exists that the diffusion of power in multiparty systems actually leads to conciliation between
the major political actors. Swedish opposition politicians are unlikely to
accept that the Swedish experience with one-party domination is more
"inclusive" than the British system with government alternating between
the two main parties. The more important constitutional variable to be discussed turns out to be related to party constitutions, more specifically the
constitutional nature of party-union relations. In the case of Labour, the
unions dominated the party organization; in the case of the Social Democrats, the party held sway over the unions.

Constitutional variables are obviously important, since they affect policy-making procedures, the nature of government formation, and the process of interest articulation, but it is often difficult to predict the effect on particular policies. Although they clearly impinge on the Swedish-British comparison, as when proximate shares of the national vote in one case result in the loss of power and in the other become a mandate for further reform, the degree of internal discipline and cohesion was nevertheless the critical variable setting the two reform governments apart. Partisan differences notwithstanding, the critical cleavage lines on how to do planning ran within the Labour Party rather than between the parties. (Chapter 5 describes how a consensus on planning evolved in Sweden.)

Another question is how much policy consensus mattered. Thirty years after the first postwar Labour government embarked on its ambitious program for planning, a comprehensive study of British economic policy lamented that policymakers continued not to act on two essential areas: national planning and modification of collective bargaining practices (Meadows 1978, 412). Both parties share responsibility for the failure to settle the issue between 1945 and 1955, a failure that looms large in the explanation of both puzzles. Policy failure has frequently been offered as the explanation of Britain's lagging postwar economic performance. Low investment, uncooperative unions, and bad government policies, have been fitted for the role as main culprit. Economists trying to explain the absence of a broad economic strategy in British economic policies frequently reach the conclusion that "politicians are creatures of the short run" (Alford 1995, 86). This kind of explanation is unsatisfactory, however, particularly in view of evidence that long-term strategies for economic development did emerge in other countries: the Federal Republic, Sweden, and France are examples. Andrew Shonfield (1965, 93) professed puzzlement and commented on what he saw as a curious lack of understanding on the part of British policymakers as to what it would actually take to do planning.

While it is fair to expect that "policy matters," we cannot presume that the "right" policy would have fixed all ailments. Accepting that policy matters a lot, where do we put the blame for failure? Political scientists, historians, and economists have pointed to shortcomings on the part of nearly all actors involved. Some have blamed trade union opposition to wage planning as the central cause of failed policy (Beer 1965; Middlemas 1986, 1990; Brown 1986). Corelli Barnett (1986, 1995) accused the postwar Labour governments for naivete, and worse, with respect to Britain's international and national capacities in the postwar years. Countering accusations of "spendthrift policies," Alec Cairncross (1992, 5), an economist and participant in the determination of wartime and postwar economic policy, noted that social programs were devised as fully funded insurance programs. He pointed to agricultural subsidies and rearmament as the real drains on postwar budgets, and in doing so joined another distinct camp in the discussion that has pointed to bad luck and American policies as the real source of policy failure. In a much-quoted economic history of post-war policies, the economist J. C. R. Dow (1970) listed a litany of miscalculations, mistaken assumptions, and misfired policies, and more or less concluded that U.S. policymakers were responsible for British troubles.

The economists' defense of extenuating circumstances fails to take into account the fact that planning failed to do for Labour what the party thought it would, in other words, planning's failure was a political failure in addition to the economic shortcomings it may have caused. Tomlinson (1991, 1992, 1994a), a British economic historian, instead emphasizes the organizational legacy of the wartime coalition government for postwar policy and the tensions between different strands of thinking about planning. He too castigates Barnett for excessive criticism of Labour but acknowledges that the government in practice gave highest priority to the perpetuation of Britain's imperial ties (1990, 222; 1994b). In this, as in the attempts to protect sterling, the Labour government acted within a national consensus and with the support of unions and business (Strange 1971). Greater consensus existed on matters of economic policy between the parties than Barnett's criticism of Labour lets on.

Some of the older historiography supports the view that continuity held between the warfare and welfare state, and that critical aspects of postwar policy were decided well ahead of the 1945 election. A small but important collection of essays entitled *Lessons of the British War Economy* put together by D. N. Chester (1951/1972) brought attention to the radical innovations and the pathbreaking experiences of wartime planners and their precedence for postwar policies. In his three-volume study of the British state, Keith Middlemas (1986, 1990, 1991) also stressed the role of wartime state expansion in shaping subsequent policymaking and for state-society relations. In his view, however, the origins of "the corporate bias"—by which he understood a conflict resolution system outside the formal channels of liberal democracy based on the representation of class—derived from British elites' wartime fears that the eruption of domestic class conflict would put national interests at risk, rather than from the development of new state institutions in response to the functional requirements of war mobilization per se. All of these authors assumed that they were studying uniquely British developments.

Fighting the Good War

British war preparations did not begin in earnest until 1939. As it became clear that appeasement could not prevent British involvement in another

European war, the Chamberlain government began to mobilize. After the German invasion of Poland on September 3, 1939, Britain declared war against Germany. On August 24, 1939, Parliament passed emergency powers legislation granting the government the power to issue, by administrative order, all necessary legislation to protect public safety, national defense, the maintenance of public order, the efficient prosecution of war, and the maintenance of the supplies and services essential to the life of the community. A Food Department had been created already in 1936 under the Board of Trade. Once it was set up separately, the Ministry of Food quickly became the largest wartime service ministry. Another important new department was the Ministry of Labour and National Service in charge of manpower planning, including conscription, resided with the department. By September 1, 1939, five new control ministries were created, and a sixth (Aircraft) was added later for a total of seven new wartime departments. Two additional emergency power acts were passed in May and July 1940. The first act expanded the 1939 act to include industrial conscription, by allowing the state to seize not only property but also manpower for the war effort. The second act was passed in anticipation of an invasion and partial occupation of the British Isles and allowed for the creation of special war zone courts on British ground. It was never used.

The Nazi occupation of Denmark and Norway in April 1940 produced a crisis in the Conservative Party that lead to Neville Chamberlain's resignation and the formation of a National Unity government among the Conservative, Liberal, and Labour parties under Winston Churchill's leadership. Campaigning in by-elections and local elections were suspended, and the life of the sitting Parliament extended by special legislation. A War Cabinet was set up as "the organ of Supreme Control," a government within the government consisting of a small number of key people acting with Churchill as chair (Hancock and Gowing 1949, 90–95). During the course of the war, the War Cabinet acquired specialized staffs, including an Economic Section and a Central Statistical Office. Control over economic policy and the attached planning capacities shifted from the Treasury to the War Cabinet's Economic Secretariat. Wartime planning involved, at the same time, a diffusion of power over a vastly expanded government control machinery and the centralization of power within the government in offices linked directly to the War Cabinet. The collaboration between Labour and the Conservatives strained both parties but held until 1945.

The regulation of the civilian war economy rested on collaboration between state and industry. Trade associations, unions, and farm organizations were deputized to carry out the administrative and organizational functions associated with the control economy and participated in a myriad of newly created control boards. The new responsibilities of interest organizations spawned both national centralization and organizational diffusion to previously less organized areas. Where no organization existed, the state often stepped in and created an associational framework for the purpose of administrating the controls. Between 1939 and 1945, a wholly new and comprehensive machinery for managing the civilian economy was put in place.

The lessons of World War I shaped preparations for the next one, in politics and in practical administration.[2] In 1914 to 1916 the government relied on the same means for resource mobilization that it had used a century earlier in the Napoleonic wars. On Gladstonian principles, the government paid for whatever it needed for the war effort by raising taxes and public borrowing. State controls, conscription, and even the sense that the government was responsible for balancing military and civilian needs were absent (Hancock and Gowing 1949, 20). But in 1916 a change took place as the inadequacy of the old methods became clear. A new Ministry of Food assumed control over the production and distribution of food. Munitions industries were put under the control of the Ministry of Munitions. By the last two years of the war, voluntarism and private arrangements were replaced by conscription and state controls. The outlines of the twentieth-century warfare state began to emerge, and also within it a template for the administrative apparatuses of the modern welfare state.

The experience of wartime planning inspired much positive thinking about the uses of planning in peacetime. The Federation of British Industries (FBI) had been created in 1916 and inspired ideas about industrial self-regulation. The Labour Party's 1918 Reconstruction Program, Labour and the New Social Order, held that "People will be extremely foolish if they ever allow their indispensable industries to slip back into the unfettered control of private capitalists. . . ." (15). Despite much enthusiasm for various aspects of planning broadly understood, the war machinery was dismantled between 1919 and 1922 (Ritschel 1997). The decision to restore the gold standard at the prewar rate of exchange imposed a rigid set of constraints on economic policy, leading to a steady deflation. The elimination of agricultural protectionism was another important decision. The critical elements that sustained continuity between the warfare and the welfare state in 1945, including the direct involvement of the Labour Party and the trade unions in the administration of war control, were missing in 1919.

Wartime Innovations in the Machinery of Government

In 1939 to 1945 the war experience gave rise to innovation not just in the machinery of the state but also in the purposes of state action. These were wholly or partially carried on after the war and used to undergird the welfare state. In 1945 the "peace dividend" included a range of new state capacities and an enlarged machinery for state-centered direction of economic activity. The reconstruction process altered the balance between departments but did not lead to any significant release of manpower from the public sector. The administrative transition from warfare to welfare regulation is illustrated in a small way by the shifts in government staffing. Between July 1 and October 1, 1946, the number of government employees increased by more than 4,000, despite a decrease of 9,500 employees in the four defense departments.[3] The Ministry of Supply showed only a small reduction in employees, for example, because of new commitments in civil aviation and housing, industries that had been given a role in the Labour government's reconstruction plans. Aside from the Ministry of Food, which had been largely concerned with the administration of food controls, other civil departments either retained or increased their staffing levels. Expansion was marked in the Ministry of Works, Inland Revenue (in charge of collecting taxes), and the postal service (Great Britain 1947b). The increases reflected new commitments to higher service levels. Between 1946 and 1948 total government employment increased by 3.4 percent, a small but surprising increase because it came on the heels of the wartime expansion. It reflected more than a 50 percent increase since 1939 (Great Britain 1949, 31). In addition, the postwar government's nationalization program soon added another two and half million employees to the public sector.

The war brought hardships but also some benefits for the general population. Income redistribution and government responsibility for the needy ranked high among the latter. The halt to international trade meant increased consumption of domestic products, which benefited British agriculture in particular. Farm programs designed to boost production also boosted farmers' incomes, which by one estimate increased seven and a half times between 1938 and 1949 (Milward 1984, 30). Munitions industries brought economic growth to the country's habitually depressed regions. Full employment and middle-class exposure to the exigencies of war helped bridge the gap between the classes, in turn sustaining support for new social programs. Where social policy previously had been concerned with the amelioration of social misfortunes among particular groups or segments of society, for the first time wartime social policy addressed the needs of the entire population.

The war economy tested Keynes' ideas about forward planning of incomes and income stabilization, which had been regarded with some skepticism before (Stone 1951/1972).[4] The calculation of "the inflationary gap"—the difference between actual output and aggregate purchasing power—required the development of new forecasting techniques and improved government information gathering, leading to the creation of a new Statistical Office. By taxing the excess purchasing power created by government outlays, the government could harness the growth potential of the war effort. Keynesian principles guided the 1941 budget speech by the Conservative chancellor of the Exchequer, Kingsley Wood, and subsequent wartime budgets with their mix of expansive and contractive measures designed to stimulate war production and sterilize their inflationary effects.[5] The war budget anticipated theoretically and practically the development of postwar macroeconomic stabilization policies. A new trust in the capacities of government grew. National budgets evolved from statements accounting for government receipts and expenditures into comprehensive planning documents, typified by the *1947 Economic Survey,* which is discussed later. In the process, the state acquired new technologies and capacities needed for economic planning, ranging from the statistical tools for forecasting the national income, the use of a cost-of-living index from 1942 onwards for measuring inflationary tendencies and calibrating policy, and a manpower budget for the allocation of employment between industries and between military and civilian employment.[6] When we add the deliberate, if not always successful, attempts to apply a parity norm to civilian wage increases and those of servicemen, the core aspects of Keynesian incomes policy were in place.

Central features of postwar social programs also were anticipated in the war years, long before the election of the postwar Labour government. The creation of a national health service was proposed in February 1944, in part because the government already was providing health service to a large share of the population connected to what was imprecisely defined as "the war effort" and in part because the job of sorting out who was entitled to what and who should pay had become so complicated. In September of that year, all restrictions on the admission of civilians to emergency medical service hospitals were lifted, and a system of national health service was, in effect, initiated as patients were shuttled around to different areas of the country and middle-class patients were sent to public assistance hospitals (Titmuss 1950, 466 and 501). The state stepped in as surrogate provider to compensate for the hardships imposed by the conscription of fathers and sons, providing allowances for dependents, responsibility for immunization and clothing of evacuated children, communal feeding, and even a National Milk Scheme for children and nursing mothers. In some instances the links between social reform and the war effort were attenuated, as in the case of the 1944 Education Act (Titmuss 1950, 114).

War Mobilization and the New Social Contract

Trade union hostility and the courts' willingness to strike down government war regulation during World War I critically influenced the government's approach to war mobilization in preparation for the second. The new emergency powers legislation aimed to efface court opposition. The inclusion of the Labour Party into the government was meant to secure union cooperation. When, on May 10, 1940, the Labour Party joined the Conservative Party in a coalition government, the warfare state was legitimized by a new construct: the inclusive "citizenship" state. W. K. Hancock, editor of the mammoth *History of the Second World War,* concluded: "There existed . . . an implicit contract between Government and people; the people refused none of the sacrifices that the Government demanded from them for winning the war; in return, they expected that the Government should show imagination and seriousness in preparing for the restoration and improvement of the nation's well-being when the war had been won" (Hancock and Gowing 1949, 541). The compulsion and coercion of conscription and economic control, as well as certain abrogations of political freedom were legitimized by a widely postulated norm of equivalence between the classes and different sectors of society and just cause.[7]

The creation of a coalition government represented an important step toward the integration of the working class into political power and made the Labour Party and the trade unions a "partner" with business and the old elite in the war effort. Labour's inclusion in the government represented a significant political gain to the party and its leaders. In 1940 the party had only 154 members in Parliament, and Labour had not yet recovered from the split in 1931 when the prime minister (and party leader), Ramsey MacDonald, left with a small group of prominent members to form a new government with Conservatives and Liberals. This split ensued after conflict with unions over reductions in unemployment benefits made in response to orthodox economic theories that held that wage reductions were needed to produce an economic recovery. (The split left Labour with only 52 seats in 1931.) In 1935, in the last prewar election, Labour received only 37.9 percent of the vote. The Conservative Party was elected to government with 53.7 percent.

Labour's postwar leaders were drawn largely from the wartime government. Clement Attlee (1883–1967), Labour's leader since 1935 and future prime minister, was made Lord Privy Seal and then in 1942 deputy prime minister. Attlee, Herbert Morrison, and Ernest Bevin represented Labour in the War Cabinet. Attlee was first elected to Parliament in 1922. He was one of the few Labour members to survive the 1931 election disaster, a fact that smoothed his rise to the party leadership.[8] Herbert Morrison

(1888–1965) became home secretary and minister of home security. The appointment of Ernest Bevin (1881–1951), a trade unionist, to Minister of Labour and National Service was a particularly important step toward the inclusion of organized labor in the national leadership.[9] As a child Bevin had been a farmhand and had worked in various low-skill jobs. He became a union organizer in 1910 and general secretary of the Transport and General Workers Union (TGWU), which he had founded in 1922 (Bullock 1960). Bevin continued to work closely with his successor, Arthur Deakin, even after he became foreign minister. Attlee and Bevin shared a background in the Toynbee Hall settlement movement. Hugh Dalton (1887–1962) was put in charge of the Ministry of Economic Warfare and was made president of the Board of Trade. He headed the Treasury until his resignation in November 1947 after an infraction of parliamentary etiquette. Dalton was Fabian socialist and an academic economist who nurtured the careers a number of young economists, including Evan Durbin, James Meade, Michael Young, Hugh Gaitskell, and Douglas Jay.

The creation of a coalition government did not insulate fully the government against political opposition. Aneurin Bevan (1897–1963), who as Minister of Health from 1945 to 1951 was responsible for the creation and implementation of the 1946 National Health Service Act, incurred the wrath of party leaders by pretending to the position of leader of the opposition and orchestrating several embarrassing anti-government votes in Parliament during the war years (Addison 1977). Emanuel Shinwell, who as Minister of Fuel and Power from 1945 to 1947 was put in charge of coal nationalization, was another left-wing critic. A spat in 1942 over the coalition government's failure to completely eliminate means testing nearly caused Bevan's expulsion from the party (Brooke 1992, 76). A third left "critic" was Harold Laski (1893–1950), who as vice-chair and later chair of the party's National Executive Committee (NEC) steadily reminded Labour's government members of the party's long-term objectives and tried to unseat Attlee as party leader. Ellen Wilkinson (1891–1947) was a junior minister during the war, briefly chair of NEC, and Minister of Education from 1945 to 1947.

Stafford Cripps (1889–1952) was a Christian Socialist and had worked for the World Alliance of Churches in the 1920s until he was elected as a Labour member of Parliament. The Labour Party expelled him in 1939 for his advocacy of a "people's front" with the communists. He was ambassador to Moscow from 1940 to 1942. Churchill appointed him leader of the House of Commons in 1942 and then minister of aircraft production until the war's end. Cripps rejoined the Labour Party in 1945 in time to become President of the Board of Trade from 1945 to 1947. There he oversaw initiatives associated with economic planning of private industry.

In 1947 Cripps was named Minister of Economic Affairs but became economic "overlord" upon Dalton's resignation as head of the Treasury when the two offices were combined. Cripps was often at odds with both the party and the unions; nevertheless, he was one of the most important people in the postwar government.[10] Cripps' move from the fringe of the party to its center illustrates the changed outlook that the party underwent in the war years.

Participation in the 1940 to 1945 coalition government and in the administration of the war economy propelled Labour leaders to national prominence and produced a new generation of party leaders. It helped Labour and the trade unions overcome the legacy of 1931. Labour moved from the opposition benches to become a respected government partner in times of extreme hardship. The unions became integrated with the new machinery of government that in many respects anticipated the characteristic intimacy of postwar social democracy. Between June 1935 and July 1945, no general election took place. Yet Labour ran as a party of government in 1945, having already demonstrated to the voters its capacity to do good. The disadvantage to Labour's unusual road to power was that it was not accompanied by the concomitant programmatic adjustment to the dilemmas associated with socialist reform in liberal societies that socialist and social democratic parties went through in other countries, illustrated by the experience of the 1932 to 1936 Swedish "Crisis Government" (discussed in chapter 4). Labour rose to government power because of the functional and political requirements of war mobilization. The 1945 election produced a state of ecstacy among Labour members and alarm among Conservatives.[11] Nevertheless, the Conservative Party dominated government in the postwar period. Between 1945 and Labour's second landslide election in 1997, Labour held government power for only 17 years out of 50: from 1945 to 1951, 1964 to 1970, and 1974 to 1979.

Economic Policy and the Warfare State

The 1940 Emergency Powers (Defense) Act allowed for military and industrial conscription, but, in spite of repeated demands for the full application of these powers against industry (from the left) or against workers (from the right), on most issues the War Cabinet forged a corporatist approach to resource mobilization instead of using coercion. Still, the state's coercive powers always lurked in the background as an alternative when cooperation failed. The broad range of economic powers provided by emergency legislation included the capacity to determine wages and prices, allocate resources, ban strikes, and coerce industry cartelization. The 1940 act allowed the home secretary, Herbert Morrison, to detain persons of "hostile origins or association." In this position, Morrison was also in charge of press censorship, and responsible for briefly banning the *Daily Worker,* a Communist paper (Brooke 1992, 66). Oswald Mosley, a British fascist, was detained for a time. The extent of censorship is difficult to assess. One recent study of trade union organizing during the war noted that thick ministry files on labor disputes only translated into brief notices in the papers (Croucher 1982). Some cases of censorship were publicly noted, as when in 1941 Morrison squelched a radio script critical of the war effort written by an *Economist* writer. But as any perusal of the magazine shows, censorship rules did not preclude critical reporting. Conservatives frequently complained about the left-wing bias of the BBC, particularly broadcasts by J. B. Priestley, a playwright and novelist prone to hyperbole.

The Labour Party seized the opportunities for economic reform provided by the 1940 Emergency Powers Act. Some considered nationalization of certain industries to be the price of Labour's collaboration. Aneurin Bevan complained in January 1941 that the Emergency Powers Act had been inequitably applied against workers, and industry was given the lighter burden. The Labour Party's National Executive Committee reproached the party's leaders for not proceeding with transport nationalization. Attlee and Bevin, who wanted to nationalize the railroads, were in apparent agreement with this even as they strove to defend the government and protect the coalition (Brooke 1992, 80–81). The nationalization issue caused a split within the Labour Party, which was brought to a head in December 1941 when a faction including both Bevan and Shinwell proposed an amendment demanding public ownership and control of the munitions industries, and other essential war industries, including transport and coal.[12] Coal industry problems caused nationalization to be considered also by others outside the Labour left wing and to be supported by a White Paper entitled *Coal* (Great Britain 1942). The industry was put under public control but, in the end, actual nationalization was forestalled by fears that it would not help to increase output.

The coalition government undertook a number of steps toward social reform. The 1941 Determination of Needs Act abolished the household means test. In 1942 and 1943 old-age pensions were improved, as were widows' pensions. Two White Papers on social insurance from 1944, *Social Insurance I-II* (Great Britain 1994d-e), committed the government to most of the principles laid out by the 1942 Beveridge report. The wartime Emergency Medical Service persuaded many in the medical professions to the need for a national health service, even if the British Medical Association often was critical of many aspects of the national health service reform. A number of proposals on how to create a national health service were produced, including a government White Paper, *A National Health Service,* which articulated a compromise between the government parties (Great Britain 1944a). The proposed nationalization of hospitals evoked little contention, but the prospect of doctors on full-time government salaries struck fear in the hearts of the general practitioners that the British Medical Association represented. (Between the time a bill was introduced in May 1946 and the passage of the final act two years later, the general practitioners successfully modified the scheme.) Also, both parties supported the 1944 Education reform. The Town and Country Act, which would have allowed for public planning of land use, would have garnered the support of both parties had it not been for a rebellion by landowners that divided the Conservative Party (Woolton 1959, 292). The list of joint wartime initiatives contains much of the postwar Labour government's first wave of social and economic reforms, which generally were propelled by practical difficulties and administrative problems made apparent by the war effort.

War mobilization and the administration of economic controls produced an extraordinary surge in administrative capacities. The regulatory machinery was developed by accretion in response to particular problems and mostly by means of administrative rule making. No master plan existed and when something did not work, new rules were added, as in the case of Order 1AA promulgated in April 1944, which duplicated existing prohibitions on striking (Clegg 1994, 255). Palpable fears of trade union resistance produced policies that were both hostile to and accommodating of organized labor. When the unions failed to cooperate, as in the case of illegal striking, the government was noticeably reluctant to use the coercive apparatus on the books. Wartime economic policies were statist, corporatist, and chaotic at the same time. The appointment of Bevin to oversee labor policies implied that the unions assumed responsibility for self-regulation in support of the war effort. On May 25, 1940, Bevin laid out the framework for wage determination during the war and for the trade unions' role in a speech to a special conference of trade union executives. He listed the immediate tasks regarding manpower and war production and promised fair compensation. He then appealed to the unions for collaboration. Their reward would be socialism, not just at home but "throughout the world." As he put it:

> I have to ask you virtually to place yourselves at the disposal of the State. We are Socialists, and this is the test of our Socialism. It is the test weather we have meant the resolutions which we have so often passed . . . But this I am convinced of: if our Movement and our class rise with all their energy now and save the people of this country from disaster, the country will always turn with confidence forever to the people who saved them. (Bevin 1941, 51)

The promise of socialism seems peculiar but such assurances of just rewards were common. Bevin's pledge was made at what was perhaps the darkest moment of the war. Nine British divisions had been trapped in France when the Germans invaded. Coastal and beach defenses had been set up on the British southern coastline in preparation for a German invasion. In the tense period from the German invasions of France and northern Europe, in April and May 1940, to the entry of the United State into the war in December 1941 after Pearl Harbor, it looked as if Britain might fight alone. Bevin's promise of socialist internationalism can be interpreted as a rhetorical ploy aiming to forestall a replay of the political strikes and protests against conscription that had marred the previous war. More likely it reflected the genuine beliefs of a man steeped in late nineteenth-century thought about the innate righteousness of the British working man. Bevin's motives may pique our interest but are finally beside the point. Promises bind irrespective of motives. Bevin's approach implied a new form of cross-class constitutionalism based on parity representation of industry and the trade unions in government controls.

Labor Controls

Economic policymaking rested on a potent mix of compulsion and consent, which made planning possible (Robbins 1947). Official histories of wartime policies agree that prior to May 1940, feeble policies retarded war mobilization. Armament industries suffered from labor shortage despite vestiges of unemployment. Wage inflation was an issue (Inman 1957; Parker 1957). Wage policy was based on a Fair Wages Resolution stemming from 1891, which compelled government and government-controlled establishments to pay prevailing wages. Under circumstances of wage inflation the resolution kept a lid on inflation, with the unintended consequence of making it difficult for armament industries to attract labor. In May 1940 Bevin consulted with union and employer representatives and outlined three alternative wage policies, including the possibility of a statutory wage freeze with a quarterly cost-of-living adjustment to be decided by an Arbitration Tribunal (Inman 1957, 316). At the same time William Beveridge, a persistent critic of the administration of the war effort, was calling for the creation of an Economic General Staff and central control of wages in order to ensure "equality of sacrifice" (Harris 1977, 366). Bevin, ever concerned that the unions should not be put at a disadvantage, opposed central wage control in the absence of comprehensive nationalization. Not surprisingly, unions and employers agreed to oppose central control and agreed with Bevin to maintain the existing machinery for the determination of wages. They also agreed to compulsory and binding arbitration and to a ban on striking. Formally the "voluntary" system was protected, but the possibility of coercion undoubtedly acted as a lever for collaboration.

The corporatist machinery for the determination of wages grew up in place of direct controls. Elements of the framework predated both Bevin's appointment and the 1940 emergency acts but it became effective only in Bevin's hands. At the apex was the National Joint Advisory Council (NJAC) but during the war a smaller executive committee, the Joint Consultative Committee (JCC), consisting of three representatives from unions and industry each substituted for the larger main committee. A parity norm was applied to all decision making in conjunction with Bevin's ministry, which meant that the Trades Union Congress (TUC) in effect got to approve all administrative orders issued by it (Middlemas 1986, 20). A tangle of executive orders and corporatist boards and committees developed.[13] Bevin heavily relied on the JCC, which he allowed to screen policy. Employers and the TUC were allowed to bargain over content in exchange for collaboration in policymaking. In 1941 Bevin praised the system, which he said "has produced the beginnings of an industrial democracy," and predicted its usefulness, also in peacetime, because of the way in which it had brought "problems of inflation, deflation, costs, future of industry, problems of management . . . within the realm of discussion" (Bevin 1941, 66).

The Ministry of Labour was also instrumental in the development of a system for plant-level codetermination on the production side. The structure of the NJAC was mirrored in the National Production Advisory Council on Industry (NPACI) with Joint Production Councils (JPC) at plant levels creating a vertical organization for line management running from the industry level to each firm. The Ministry of Labour and National Service took a strong interest in the codetermination system and encouraged its development, particularly in the war production ministries, and apparently expected them to constitute the beginnings of a comprehensive national system for planning. One estimate is that some 2.6 million workers were represented by productivity councils by 1944 (Tomlinson 1994a, 144). Clegg (1994, 235) takes a somewhat different view, concluding that "the outstanding feature" of the introduction of JPCs in the engineering trades "was a growth in the numbers of shop stewards and works committees." He suggests that, rather than further centralization, the JPCs sowed the seed for industrial relations decentralization. Clegg estimates that membership in the Engineering Employers' Federation grew from roughly 2,000 to 3,500 firms during the war. Members were compelled by the federation's agreement with the government and the unions to recognize shop stewards.

In return for industrial conscription, the prime minister directed all government departments to consult with the TUC before doing anything that touched on labor's interests. Bevin's ministry was nevertheless the central instrument of trade union influence, extending its oversight of a complicated mix of statutory controls and corporatist private agreements into the war production ministries, the Supply Ministries (munitions, agriculture, food), the Admiralty, and the Ministry of Air Crafts.

State-Sponsored Voluntarism

Labor policies were based on a delicate balance of administrative orders and corporatist negotiation. The primary aim was to facilitate increased war production without jeopardizing trade union authority and discipline. We recognize in this balance a basic recipe for growth-oriented industrial trade unionism. A partial list of the main administrative orders illustrates the extent to which the machinery anticipated the thrust of postwar industrial relations policies.

The 1941 Essential Works Order allowed the Ministry of Labour (represented by a local national service officer) to transfer workers to essential occupations and relieve labor shortages in armament industries. A primary tool for manpower planning, the order also established guaranteed minimum working conditions. The Registration for Employment Order created labor exchanges and required men and women of certain ages to register with the exchanges. It was supplemented by an order establishing a classification of priority occupations (coal, agriculture) to which workers could be assigned or prohibited from leaving. The exchanges constituted the practical backbone for manpower planning and the allocation of resources between the various sectors of the economy (Hancock and Gowing 1949, 452). The order was particularly important for the recruitment of women and the transfer of unskilled or semiskilled workers. Order 1305, or the Conditions of Employment and National Arbitration Order as it was also known, prohibited striking and mandated the creation of compulsory and binding arbitration. Under the order a National Arbitration Tribunal was created. The effectiveness of the order can be questioned, since strikes increased during the war. (The number of disputes tripled from 1938 to 1945, Parker 1957, 504). This is not surprising considering that significant unemployment still existed in 1938, but it is surprising considering that striking was, after all, illegal in 1945. Notably, half of all the disputes took place in the troubled coal industry and a large share of those remaining occurred in the engineering trades. By one estimate (Flanders 1952, 65) 17,000 work stoppages took place between 1941 and 1950, the last year Order 1305 was in effect. Most conflicts were local and limited in scope.

Surprisingly, V. L. Allen (1960, 83) found that 1.5 million workers had been on strike between 1940 and January 1944 but only 5,000 of them had been prosecuted under the order and only 2,000 actually convicted.

Union opposition to "dilution," by which was meant the replacement of skilled workers by unskilled or semiskilled workers—presented obstacles to manpower planning and expansion of production. Dilution takes place both when innovations, as in the case of assembly-line riveting, make crafts workers redundant or when unskilled workers are trained to fill the position of a crafts worker without the requisite apprenticeship. The shortage of skilled workers meant that production increases in the armament industries necessarily implied elements of dilution. The passage of the Restoration of Pre-War Trade Practices Act in February 1942 aimed to reassure the unions, but since job control in practice belonged to unions, the real problem was that they had to allow jobs previously held by members to be filled by nonmembers, often women, or to allow new workers and women to join the unions. Clegg (1994, 215) writes that the "acceptance of women dilutees in the engineering industry was probably facilitated by the decision of the Engineers to admit women into their union from January 1 1943." (For a discussion of the Engineering Union's resistance to allowing women members, see Croucher 1982, 273.) The woodworkers' union, no less unwelcoming to women, opted to allow women to pay union dues but still did not allow them into the union. The general workers' union, the TGWU, scooped up most of the new members. By the end war roughly 1.5 million women worked in the metal industries, taking up 39 percent of engineering jobs (Parker 1957, 482; Inman 1957, 79). The promise to restore the prewar staffing norm implied that most of the new workers would have to give up their jobs when the war ended. In this case, the wartime compact between government and unions worked to produce a reaffirmation of union rights at the cost of inclusive unionism and an opportunity to confront the "machine question," trade union opposition to technological advances, and productivity improvements that reduced the need for labor was lost. The wartime legacy was not also always on the side of new opportunity and social and economic development.

A dual system evolved for the determination of wages. On one hand, the Labour Ministry acted to expand the scope of private collective bargaining, particularly by encouraging of the formation of Joint Industrial Councils (JIC). Clegg (1994, 221) reports that by the end of the war, 55 national JICs had been created. In 1944 the ministry published and distributed the *Industrial Relations Handbook,* which included a model constitution for joint councils. Their stated purpose was, "to secure the largest possible measure of joint action between employers and workpeople for the development of industry as part of national life and for the improvement of the condition of all engaged in that industry" (Great Britain 1944c, 235). The ministry had moved beyond the war effort to longer-term objectives.

The ministry also took the initiative to provide rules for guaranteed wages, ranging from "pool pay" for idle dock workers and casual labor to statutory minimum wages in troubled and weakly organized industries such as by retail and catering industries. Trade boards (or wage boards) had been created first by a 1909 that aimed to regulate what was called "sweated" industries, industries with substandard labor conditions. The boards set industrywide minimum wages and working conditions. The number of boards was expanded and their role enhanced during the war. The initiatives amounted to the creation of a nascent comprehensive system for industrywide wage settlements based on collective bargaining supported by government policy. There was nothing coincidental about this; Bevin, the minister of labor and former trade unionist, clearly intended to put in place rules that the unions could use to their benefit after the war (Parker 1957, 439). In 1945 the Wage Councils Act converted the boards to wage councils and enlarged their powers. Some 60 trades and industries had wage councils in 1945; all were industries with small or medium-size firms and often predominantly employed women (Grove 1962, 201).[14]

Actual wages were largely determined by a jumble of payment-for-performance systems, including bonus pay and piecework set by local agreements negotiated by shop stewards. A comprehensive assessment of the relative importance of the different wage systems probably cannot be made. Inman (1957, 320 and 325) reported variations in local piecework rates ranging from 25 percent to 400 percent of time rates. The increased use of performance pay ran counter to the manifest egalitarian thrust of official wage policy. The inflationary implications were not lost on the Treasury. Wage stabilization by means of tying wages to the cost-of-living index was reconsidered in a White Paper, *Price Stabilization and Industrial Policy*, but recognition of the greater benefit of labor peace precluded further action (Parker 1957, 429).

Wartime Wage Policy: New Constraints and New Opportunities

The dualist wage system for determining wages reflected the difficult trade-off between productivity-enhancing pay schemes and equity norms, which were from a dual concern with social solidarity and inflation control. The emphasis on performance pay despite inflation concerns reflected the primacy of war production and increased output over stabilization. British wage policy deviated on this score from Swedish policies during the war years. The deviation can be explained by the fact that Sweden was not engaged in an arms race and instead was primarily concerned with inflation control. Inman (1958, 351) concludes in his official history of labor policy in the armament industries that by the end of the war, the government's reliance on bonus pay and piecework had "transformed the wage structures in establishments." Skilled workers, engineers in particular, had in the course of the war moved away from the crafts unions' traditional emphasis on hourly pay and "quality work" to espouse performance pay and bonuses.

The unions reaped many benefits from wartime labor policies. Average weekly earnings doubled between 1938 and 1945 (Parker 1957, 436). Four million trade union members lost during the Great Depression years were regained, and another million added to a total of 9.3 million members, or close to 45 percent of the workforce (Clegg 1994, 410). Organizational consolidation was another issue. Out of 700 trade unions, more than half had less than 1,000 members in 1949. But the picture changes somewhat when we consider that the 17 largest unions represented two-thirds of all union members and among the largest unions, only two white-collar unions did not belong to the TUC.[15] Eight million members belonged to TUC-affiliated unions.

The TUC often is portrayed as a weak organization, lacking coordinating capacities and unable to live up to the demands of national wage coordination. Yet during the war the TUC had done exactly that. The question is, how could these capacities be transposed to peacetime purposes? In comparative perspective, the TUC benefited by the lack of competing confederations, communist or christian democratic, even as the presence of communists in some unions, particularly the engineering union and the electricians' union, began causing trouble from 1947 onward. Ultimately, the problem was not so much fragmentation but rather the predominance of a small number of large unions.

The inclusion of the unions into the government machinery had consequences for internal trade union affairs. Participation in the regulatory machinery worked to enhance the national confederations' power over affiliates and awarded the daily TUC leadership, represented in the General Council, a near monopoly on the representation of labor interests to the government and to employers. In the course of the war, trade union representation increased from below 10 to some 60 government committees and commissions (Allen 1960, appendix). The change upgraded the importance of an organization that in earlier years had functioned as little more than a political lobby for affiliated unions. This extraordinary expansion of trade union influence through joint consultation on matters of wages, production matters, and manpower planning formed an infrastructure for societal coordination and planning that could be put to peacetime use. In some respects, the regulatory machinery allowed Britain to catch up with labor legislation long implemented in other countries. Arbitration rules and a formal legal framework for conflict resolution had been established in Sweden already in the 1920s and 1930s, for example. Other cases, as in the codetermination framework created by the JPCs, anticipated the system of *Mitbestimmung* that the British occupational authorities played a strong role in developing through their policies toward unions in postwar Germany.

Industry Controls and the
Organization of Business Interests

Business and industry also were mobilized to support the war effort. Firms and industries were corraled into cohesive national and regional organizations for the purpose of self-government and disciplined responses to scarcities, government quotas, and cumbersome administrative controls. The inclusion of trade associations in the administration and determination of various controls helped consolidate and integrate small and medium-size businesses, ranging from fish fryers to rubber manufacturers, in trade associations.

By the end of the war, most industries had acquired a national or regional framework for economic activity coordination. Aside from small and very regional industries, the war controls produced both centralization and diffusion of interest organizations, including trade unions and the farmers' organizations as well as industry and business. Alan Milward treats British control cartels as the functional equivalents of the infamous Nazi cartels created by Albert Speer in conjunction with the formation of *Zentrale Planung,* the central planning agency. He points out that one industry cartel, *Fachgruppe Werkzuge,* was identical to the old machine-tool manufacturers' association (Milward 1979, 124). According to Milward, German planning also suffered from many of the same ailments that afflicted British wartime planning, with cartelistic practices and industry competition for resources compromising the optimal allocation of resources for the purpose of the war effort.

In a broad comparative and historical perspective that runs from the Code Authorities under the U.S. National Recovery Administration (1933 to 1935) to British and U.S. war controls and prewar and postwar German or Austrian chambers, cartels are a basic means for industrial self-regulation and planning. They represent an endlessly transmutable form of economic organization compatible with different political regimes and historical circumstances (Williamson 1985). Yet business and industry have been incapable of staple organization drives without assistance from the state. In this respect, the war economy accomplished what the Great Depression had failed to do in liberal democracies.

The evidence indicates the pervasive importance of wartime organization in promoting national integration of interest groups, even in cases where previous organization efforts had been undertaken during the depression era. Some well-established associations dated back to prewar attempts to regulate particular industries: for example, the British Iron and Steel Federation or the Lancashire Cotton Manufacturers' Association. Older organizations, such as the British Chambers of Commerce, the National Union of Manufacturers, and the British Employers' Confederation, all assumed new political roles in the context of the wartime control machinery. A fixed system of national trade associations emerged first with the imposition of controls during World War I. The National Union of Manufacturers and the Federation of British Industries, for example, were created in 1915 and 1916 respectively. These organizations subsequently became engaged in the representation of business interests to the Labour government after 1945.

In 1940 to 1945, the war controls spawned new business organizations and integration of preexisting ones. A 1944 study found about 1,400 trade associations of various kinds: wholesalers, retailers, and manufacturers. A follow-up study from 1957 found 1,300 manufacturer's associations of which some 250 were incorporated between 1892 and 1955 (Political and Economic Planning [hereafter PEP] 1945). Major bursts of incorporation took place in connection with the imposition of government controls toward the end of World War I (1916 to 1918). A second wave took place in the early 1920s, when industry tried to avert deflation through self-regulation, and a third occurred in response to the controls imposed during World War II and postwar trade restrictions. Forty new trade associations were formed between 1940 and 1945, and another 30 from 1945 to 1948. The corporatist consultative system brought about centralization and organizational expansion also at the level of peak organizations. According to its 1947 annual report, the FBI was represented on 37 committees in 10 ministries and departments by 87 representatives. The list included 37 regional industry boards, the important Census of Production Committee under the Board of Trade and the Economic Planning Board as well as the National Production Advisory Council on Industry (cited from Rogow 1955, 191).

Large companies tended to prefer to work directly with the government. During the war large firms took over the administration of particular industry controls (Rogow 1955); but they also joined the trade associations (Lever Brothers apparently joined 50; see Grove 1962, 128). Lever Brothers and Unilever Ltd. took care of the control schemes for oils and fat. Fuel controls were administered by a board consisting of representatives from the Fuel Suppliers' and Merchants' Associations. Where no trade association existed, government policy worked to create one. In contrast to continental practices, the British associational tradition entirely rested on voluntary principles. The war controls broke with the voluntary principle by making organizational membership a prerequisite for participation in importers' and suppliers' cartels and other industry rings responsible for the allocation of scarce resources or the fulfillment of government quotas for production. As the war came to an end, the specter of involuntary cartelization reappeared. Another fear was that incorporation within the state's planning apparatus would encroach on organizational autonomy. Industry and business could agree to self-regulation in the face of the national emergency, but doing so in peacetime was much more difficult.

British Corporatism

From 1940 to 1945 the FBI had emerged as the strongest of the national organizations of business interests. With its well-established contacts directly to the government and to ministries, the FBI held on to its position of preeminence after the war. Above all, the organization represented all large industries. Many of the FBI's appointees to committees and other contact points with the government were drawn from its Grand Council of 500 large industrialists, not from the general membership. Smaller industries and small businesses belonged to the National Union of Manufacturers, but some belonged to FBI as well. A study from 1957 found that 40 percent of the FBI's membership derived from firms with less than 100 employees (PEP 1957, 46). Yet it is commonly argued that British industry lacks corporatist capacities. The British political scientist Colin Crouch (1977; 1993, 347), who once believed that corporatism was a tool for the suppression of labor, now finds that nineteenth-century liberal proclivities inhibited twentieth-century corporatism. In his widely cited book, *Trust* (1995), the American political scientist Francis Fukuyama also cites Britain as a case of growth-impeding liberalism. Pointing his finger specifically at business and industry, the British labor historian Henry Phelps Brown (1986, 131) concluded in a similar vein that "the British people would have been more prosperous since the Second World War if employers' associations had been stronger." In view of the wartime experience with corporatism, it is difficult nevertheless to accept that organizational weakness prevented employers from acting as a countervailing force. When we consider both the presence during the early postwar years of a regulatory system derived from the war years, and comparative evidence of the general importance of sectionalism as an obstacle to cohesive industry organization in other countries, including corporatist Sweden, the picture of British industry and business as preternaturally lacking in organizational capacity seems a simplification. "Weak" is not the term that comes first to mind when discussing British employers. Samuel Beer (1965, 333) estimated that by the 1950s, the BEC represented 270 affiliates, which negotiated wages with 70 percent of the employed population.[16] The lacking element was less capacity than intent. All of the above suggest that employer strategies with respect to wage policy should not be seen exclusively as a matter of economic interest.

The robustness of wartime and postwar trade associations dealing with industry interests in connection with government controls, purchasing pools, and the myriad of trade regulations, suggests the capacity of British business to organize in response to state action. From this perspective, employer strategies with respect to unions and wage determination stand out as reactive and contingent political decisions.

Industry political action and organization is often reflexive and defensive. The British political scientist Wyn Grant (1995, 23) has concluded that, "the state sets the rules of the game for pressure group activity." The implication is that had postwar British governments pursued a national wage policy, organizational patterns would change accordingly. If industry and business had seen it as politically (rather than simply economically) advantageous to cooperate with such policy, they would have. Two PEP studies (1945, 1957) and one by A. A. Rogow (1955) reported, for example, that trade associations often sprouted employer organizations to deal with wage regulation carried out by the newly established wage boards. Since the boards were local and regional organizations, their activities also stimulated local incorporation of employers. (The wage boards determined wages in competitive and fragmented industries, which generally did not involve large employers.) The government's decision to refrain from national wage policy had the indirect consequence of stimulating a decentralized system of representation for employer interests. All of the above points to the conclusion that the source of corporatist failure has to be found in the postwar years, and cannot be reduced to a question of state tradition or national cultural predilections for liberalism over planning.

High Hopes: Planning for Peace

Plans were made for peacetime reconstruction long before anyone knew that Labour would win the first postwar election. The victory allowed Labour to assume credit for reforms that the Conservative Party would have claimed, had it won the election. Propaganda purposes played no small role in early pronouncements on reconstruction policy. In 1940 a "war aims" committee was created under the War Cabinet and charged with producing declarations of purpose. The statements were broadcast by the BBC at home and to occupied territories.[17] The origin of the initial reconstruction programs explains why the plans employed exalted language and exaggerated rhetoric; they were more propaganda than policy proposals. The "war aims" debate produced a clamor for what was known as the "New Jerusalem," named after a poem, "Jerusalem," by William Blake (1751–1827), which blended national revival with social reform and Christianity.[18]

As the war wore on, utopian invocations gave way to discussions of social reform. By the time the end of the war was in sight, questions of reform became entangled with the practical realities and difficulties associated with a return to peacetime activities. The war aims committee was folded into the Ministry of Reconstruction, which was created in 1943. With creation of a ministry proper, groups and organizations ranging from trade unions and business associations to the political parties got involved in preparing their own programs for reconstruction. Even the Federation of British Industries, normally a bulwark of conservatism, called for comprehensive social reform, economic planning, and full employment (FBI 1944b, 1945). The Archbishop of Canterbury, William Temple, a former president of the Workers' Educational Foundation, charted out metaphysical reasons for social reform. J. B. Priestly (1941), a popular novelist much disliked by Conservatives, assumed the voice of "unofficial" Britain in weekly radio broadcasts making the point again and again that the government cannot ask the people to fight a war unless it is a war for "a people's Britain." In the debate, the role of the many economists who had left their universities to take charge of wartime planning was apparent.[19] It was a situation that called for high hopes and grand designs, and both were produced in great quantity. The social experience of the war machinery, which was largely considered a success, perhaps because the press was restrained from pointing out its shortcomings or because people needed to believe it was a success (Fielding et al. 1995), fueled enthusiasm for planning.

Important statements of postwar objectives included a 1944 government White Paper, *Employment* (Great Britain 1994b), and the Labour Party's 1945 electoral manifesto, *Let Us Face the Future*. The manifesto included parts, but not all of the points listed in the *Interim Report on Post-War Reconstruction,* published by the Trades Union Congress in 1944. In addition, it included William Beveridge's two reports, one on social insurance from 1942 and the other on the preconditions for full employment, which was finished in 1944 but was not published until 1945. The four statements anticipated principal aspects of postwar policy.

The Beveridge Phenomenon

Beveridge was put in charge, in June 1941, of preparing an official report on the consolidation of various insurance programs in part because the government had nowhere else to put him and in part because it wanted to get rid of him (Harris 1977, 376). The report, *Social Insurance and Allied Services*, known as the "Beveridge Report," was published in December 1942. Despite being written in turgid "officialese," it sold half a million copies and was distributed among the Armed Services. The report worked to raise high hopes about social reform as a reward for the war effort.[20] Beveridge, never one to downplay his role, waxed enthusiastically about "a revolutionary moment" and "victories for truth" encompassing his own "plan" and victory in war in one scoop (Beveridge 1942, 6 and 172).

Beveridge identified five obstacles on the road to reconstruction—"Want, Disease, Ignorance, Squalor, and Idleness"—and promised that "freedom from want" was possible. His proposals for reform embraced some core principles that subsequently were elevated by the British sociologist T. H. Marshall (1950) as criteria for the "social citizenship" welfare state required by advanced democracy. One principle was that benefits should be adequate to meet a social minimum criteria; another that both contributions and benefits should be flat-rate and not income dependent. Benefits should be a matter of right, not charity, and should be available to all. The catchwords were "comprehensive" and "universal." A primary objective was to eliminate the highly criticized means test, which encouraged "idleness." In practice, universalism was compromised on several scores. The position of women caused Beveridge many tribulations because of worries of abuse. Although in principle committed to a flat-rate and universalist payment scheme, he ended up proposing variable payments reflecting categories of need largely defined to reflect employment experience, a decision that affected women in particular adversely. Despite difficulties with working out the payment schemes and initial government resistance, Beveridge nevertheless had provided the blueprints for the 1945 Family Allowances Act, the 1946 National Insurance Act and National Health Service Act, and the 1948 National Assistance Act. The 1944 Education Act also can be seen as part of the package.

After the publication of the 1942 report, Beveridge began a campaign for postwar social reform and national planning in print and radio broadcasts as well as meetings with industry groups and trade unions that attracted much public attention (Abel-Smith 1994, 12). The broad scope of his ambitions reached beyond social insurance to employment policy and matters of general economic planning. José Harris (1977) shows, on the basis of Beveridge's contemporary correspondence, how his thinking about the five social evils shaped his thinking about employment policy. Social policy reform could address "Want" but went only part of the way to address "Idleness," which, to Beveridge's thinking, probably was the worst evil. The elimination of disincentives to work had been a primary objective in his design of social programs, but the elimination of unemployment was inherently more important. This was to be the topic of the sequel report, *Full Employment in a Free Society* (Beveridge 1945). Beveridge had hoped to produce the report for the government, but Churchill complained about Beveridge's constant interference and banned all civil servants from speaking to him (Addison 1982, 243).

The second report was written with a group of young Keynesian economists, including Joan Robinson, Barbara Wootton, and Nicholas Kaldor. By this time Beveridge had concluded that only the imposition of total government control over production and consumption made full employment possible (Harris 1977, 432). He espoused nationalization and direct control over industry and a range of labor policies, from obligatory training schemes for the unemployed and compulsory arbitration to constraints on collective bargaining during periods with inflation. In 1943 to 1944 Beveridge took the initiative to meet with the TUC General Council.[21] Worried that full employment would be jeopardized by wage inflation in the postwar economy, Beveridge asked the General Council to outline what its responses would be if wage inflation occurred. The response was disappointing. The General Council would say only that should inflation occur, it would give "suitable guarantees about wage settlements and reasonable assurances that such guarantees would be generally observed." Its response was attached as an addendum to the TUC's own statement of a reconstruction program, the 1944 *Interim Report*. This was an early warning of subsequent disagreement over wage policy. (The TUC General Council's response apparently caused bad feelings in the joint Labour Party–TUC leadership and provoked Bevin to withdraw. See Minkin 1991, 59.)

Harris describes Beveridge's views of public–private relations in new detail based on private papers. Beveridge expected businesses and unions to work with the government "under the auspices of a 'Minister-Guardian of Voluntary Action.'" According to Harris (1990, 90), Beveridge said in discussions with the Ministry of Reconstruction that ownership of the means of production was not "one of the essential British liberties." Similar sentiments can be found in Beveridge's writings, albeit more tactfully expressed. In the *Full Employment* report, Beveridge (1945, 207) wrote that Liberty requires responsibility. If the people of Britain "are not sufficiently civilized" to be disciplined, they would also be "unworthy of freedom."

Beveridge's relentless self-promotion caused both major parties to shun him. He failed in his bid to get elected to Parliament in 1945 as a member of the Liberal Party. Yet he became the principal architect of the postwar social policies, and in practice his ideas were not that different from those of the chief architect of the welfare state's economic policies, Stafford Cripps. Cripps articulated strikingly similar sentiments about the proper relationship among industry, unions, and government in, for example, his introductory remarks to the *1947 Economic Survey,* which Cripps authored. According to Cripps, in a democracy planning has to rest on cooperation between "Government, industry and the people"; he then defined cooperation in this way: "the Government must lay down the economic tasks for the nation; it must say which things are the most important and what the objectives of policy should be" (Great Britain 1947a, 9).[22] Both men were prominent spokesmen for a distinctly *dirigiste* version of economic planning. One difference was that Beveridge was more inclined to apply the same measures to the unions that he would apply to industry. But he was not a member of the Labour Party.

The 1944 White Paper on Employment Policy

The 1944 White Paper was produced jointly by the Treasury and the Economic Section under the War Cabinet.[23] It presented government economists' views regarding what postwar economic policy should look like. The knowledge that Beveridge was working on a report about employment policy caused justified concern that he might eclipse public debate (Tomlinson 1987, 64). This White Paper presented the first public statement of proto-Keynesian principles by linking the attainment of full employment to aggregate demand and government spending policies. The final Paper was a compromise. Not surprisingly, it did not present a coherent statement of theory or policy. The Treasury's opposition to deficit spending and a permanent rise in government debt occasioned some conflict, but Hugh Dalton and other influential actors within the Labour Party were similarly skeptical about the benefits of running protracted deficits because of what they might do to interest rates and the "cheap money" objective (Tomlinson 1987, 54). Even as the Paper signaled a radical shift in official economic policy by committing the government to maintain "a high and stable level of employment," it was the more conservative of the various outlines of postwar policy perspectives. The Paper avoided defining exactly what was meant by "full" employment, a topic that Beveridge had spent much energy on. On one hand, it explained the principles of stabilization policy and the use of the budget as a means for economic planning. On the other, it also supported the continuance of economic controls after the war.

The reactions of unions and industry groups were mixed. A series of business reports in response to the Paper indicates that business attributed some importance to it at the time, but on balance the reactions also show that much of British industry and business were more interested in other aspects of economic policy, particularly the preservation of sterling and the imperial trading system. The reactions did not indicate much understanding of new economic theory. Full employment was seen as a good idea because it would keep up domestic demand and benefit domestic trade. The National Union of Manufacturers (NUM) complained that the Paper at times had "the air of a lecture by a kindly and able headmaster to his pupils" and did not treat business as a partner in a cooperative relationship (NUM ca. 1944). Still, NUM supported many of the Paper's proposals, particularly those that tied in with continuing controls: plans to maintain controls on supplies and raw materials after the war, central planning, and a British-backed scheme for the creation of an international authority referred to as the "International Council" to regulate international trade. Like the Chamber of Commerce, the NUM was particularly worried that "the Americans" would not "play along" with British ideas about the organization of money and trade after the war. As it turned out, they did not. The National (London) Chambers of Commerce (1944) took pains to emphasize the importance of trying to solve British imbalance problems by boosting exports rather than by reducing imports, only to call for agricultural protectionism next. The report opposed currency convertibility and worried that, if openness had to be at the cost of expansionary policies, the chamber wanted the latter and not the former.

The Labour Party's National Executive Committee (NEC) issued a report, *Full Employment and Financial Policy,* which was preoccupied with the necessity to keep wartime controls during peacetime in order to protect the national economy against "bad trade," whatever it meant by that. It acknowledged that "[f]ull employment and a full standard of life require full trade" and implied that exports would play some role. After declaring support for "progressive and mutual reduction of tariffs," the report went on to state in a direct criticism of the White Paper that:

> This emphatically does not mean that there should be any return to *laissez-faire* or "free trade" in the capitalist sense. Socialists believe in the planning of imports and exports and the present apparatus of control—foreign exchange control, import programmes, allocation of scarce materials for the export trade—should remain in existence. Wartime arrangements for bulk purchase, through State agencies, of foodstuffs and of raw materials, should continue. State trading, as the war has proved, brings great benefits to the

peoples. We must not let this Socialist advance be halted or turned back. (Labour Party 1944, 7)

The NEC report was strikingly naive on the question of the dynamics of foreign trade and British needs. On one hand, it castigated those who "exaggerate the importance of our export trade." On the other hand, it also (accurately) estimated that postwar exports would have to increase by 50 percent in order for the country to pay for essential imports. The British historian Keith Middlemas has argued that by linking economic outcomes to political collaboration, the Paper implied a social contract, even if it did not actually outline one. Stable wages, rising productivity, and competitiveness were needed to make possible the desired rise in living standards and social benefits. All required the collaboration of unions and employers, the political parties, and the financial community. Middlemas argues further that a consensus which excluded both the criticism from the Marxist left and the Hayekian right emerged that this was the way to go. Consensus died ten years later, in his view, due to "external threat and internal decay" (Middlemas 1991, 447; 1986, 101).

The problem with Middlemas' argument is that not only was the Paper feeble with respect to the question of means, it also expressed a consensus that was confined to economists and intellectuals, and an already "state-broken" industrial elite. The official responses to the Paper show that both industry and unions had other means and objectives in mind, even as they supported a continued role for the state in regulating economic activity. Despite the success of wartime corporatism, there existed no ideological appreciation of the "social partnership" aspects of Keynes' thinking among interest groups or among government leaders, from Bevin and Attlee to Churchill. The control economy was considered a success, but policymakers noted mostly the expansion of the state's powers and paid less attention to the concomitant expansion of societal organization and the exceptional origins of the new deference to the state.

The TUC's Interim Report

The White Paper fell short of what the unions wanted. Their vision of peacetime economic policy looked a lot like war without the military side. "The choice before us," stated the TUC in its 1944 *Interim Report on Post-War Reconstruction,* "is not between control or no control, but, in principle, between control by public authority responsible to the community, or control by private groups. . . ." (par. 28). The report proceeded to demand the immediate nationalization of certain industries, starting with coal, gas, and electricity, and transportation. The list of industries to be nationalized included cotton and the woolen industries, chemicals, cement, rayon, soap and margarine, metals, rubber, grain mills, and tobacco. Another list, presumably of wishes to be put forward after the first list had been completed, began with the auto industry and ended with shipbuilding. Yet despite this preference for state regulation, the unions went to great lengths to stress the importance of "freedom" on one issue: Any restraints on trade union behavior would violate the principles of a "free society" and would cause the unions to "cease to be Trade Unions." Everything was to by fixed by government except wages.

The TUC supported comprehensive nationalization but threw obstacles in the way of trade union representation in economic planning by rejecting anything more than an advisory role for the unions in planning decisions. The unions refused to be bound by management concerns. The 1944 report addressed the matter of trade union representation outside collective bargaining in some detail and outlined clearly what the unions' role should be. Any attempts to negotiate or determine wages outside the established collective bargaining framework were unacceptable. Still, the unions were eager to get representation on all boards of nationalized industries and on government committees, and the report even stressed that "every worker should be afforded the opportunity to achieve managerial position" (par. 95). The working class had a democratic right to have a voice in the determination of its destiny, and in any case workers possessed special knowledge that would benefit the way industry was run. The quality of management required that the working class be represented. The unions should control the selection of "nominees," but, once placed on boards, they could speak only for themselves. As members of managerial boards, they would be committed to the joint decisions made by the boards, and despite their trade union roots they henceforth belonged to management. The report spoke of the undesirability of creating "double-duty" for the representatives, but the formalistic language could not obscure the fact that the real issue was trade union freedom to pursue maximum wage claims (par. 99–100).

The equivocations about the nature of industrial democracy reflected the unions' deep reluctance to assume any responsibility for the economic well-being of nationalized industries and national economic performance at the cost of their ability to press for maximum wages. The perceived conflict between managerial interests in nationalized industries and trade union interests revealed the unions' continuing distrust of the state and the contradictions of socialist reform in capitalist society. These were real issues; in Sweden they had caused the Social Democrats' chief architect of economic policy, Ernst Wigforss, to conclude that nationalization inevitably would put a breach between unions and left governments, once

those governments had to assume responsibility for the performance of nationalized industries. The Social Democrats resolved the conflict by revising their nationalization platform (see chapter 4); Labour did so by failing
to reconcile trade unionism in nationalized industries with responsible
management policies.

Labour's Postwar Program

In its 1945 electoral manifesto, the Labour Party referred to itself as a socialist party and called for the creation of "a Socialist Commonwealth of
Great Britain." It blamed the war on capitalism and gave Labour credit for
preventing the profiteers from making a profit on war this time. It
promised that the Labour Party's program was a "practical expression" of
the spirit of Dunkirk and the Blitz "to winning the war of peace." The
party embraced Beveridge's "plan" with reluctance; fearing that social reform would attenuate efforts to create a socialized economy. Where Beveridge spoke about "freedom from want," Labour spoke in its election
manifesto more moderately about protection on "a rainy day," a national
health service, and promised children's allowances and maternity benefits
"to prevent Britain from dwindling." The last promise reflected the same
pronatalist, quasi-eugenicist ideas that at the time had attracted the atten-
tions of reformers from Sweden to the United States (Wolfe and Klausen
1997). The manifesto also promised full employment; since everybody else
also was promising full employment, Labour distinguished its view of what
this implied by pointing out that it would do more than simply boost public spending during slumps. This was a dig at the Keynesians and the 1944
White Paper. The manifesto promised to maintain price controls, relocate
factories to fit social needs, and nationalize parts of industry. One section
was dedicated to agriculture and the promising prospects of a "Red-
Green" alliance based on bulk purchases and subsidies by the government,
food cartels, and appropriation of the land of absentee landowners. It also
promised housing development, urban planning, and the creation of a land
trust for the acquisition of land for public purposes. It reminded voters
that, if Labour and the trade unions could be trusted to help win the war,
peace could be trusted to them too.

The manifesto and the TUC's report articulated two highly contestable
principles of reform. The first was the principle of trade union civil liberties. The second was the firm belief that social objectives were best served
by retaining bureaucratic controls on economic activity. Looking through
the lens of today's thinking about what it takes to bring about a planned
approach to national economic development (see, for example, Wade

1990), it was a curious blend of social libertarianism and economic ortho-doxy. In reality, however, the Labour Party and the unions were less firmly committed to either of these beliefs than the manifesto and the TUC's re-port let on. Even as both were being written, programmatic discord was brewing.

Conclusion

The means by which British political leaders chose to mobilize resources to fight in World War II left to the postwar order a legacy of cross-class constitutionalism and new capacities for economic planning. The link be-tween military mobilization and social protection was spelled out clearly in promises of a New Jerusalem. Bevin (1941, 63) recognized the achieve-ments of "war socialism" and what it had done: "for the first time in the history of England, every penny, every inch of land, every item of wealth, factory and workshop is now at the disposal of the nation. Private indi-viduals can be compelled to subordinate any private interest or gain to the common weal."

The war experience brought about a ubiquitous shift to the left and in favor of social reform across class and across party allegiances. The shift helped Labour in the 1945 election, but as subsequent elections showed, it was hardly the mandate for socialism that Labour took it for at first. Key decisions regarding the path of reconstruction had been made prior to the election. Had a Conservative government been elected in 1945, it is fair to expect that it too would have engaged in social reform and state activism. The emerging consensus around the full employment objective is a major example. A minor example is the 1945 Family Allowance Act, the last joint social legislation produced by the coalition government. The act provided families with a weekly allowance per child. Embodying the new univer-salist principles, it included no means test. (The TUC originally had op-posed family allowances because it worried that generosity of this kind would undermine trade union bargaining power. See remarks by Arthur Deakin, TUC Report 1941, 301–302.)

War mobilization brought an unparalleled expansion of the reach of the state. Corporatist controls and collaboration between unions and employ-ers under the auspices of Bevin's Ministry produced a kind of corporatist arrangements that facilitate economic planning and "inclusive unionism," which is generally understood an institutionalized recognition on the part of organized labor that union strategies must be mindful of the interests of weakly or unorganized workers (Visser 1990). The war economy also pro-duced a state of cordial relations between government and industry that planners had aspired to without success during the Great Depression (Tomlinson 1994a, 134). The Labour Party recovered from the devastating setback it experienced in the 1931 election. The recruitment of a new elite of civil servants who were economists and statisticians was another change, which signaled broad changes in the language and instruments of policy and administration.

THREE

Great Britain:
The Socialist Economy
in the Free Society

The 1945 Election and Political Adjustment

W hen the Labour government presented its program in August 1945, it called upon the British people to apply to peacetime "efforts comparable in intensity and public spirit to those which have brought us victory in war" (H. C. Debates, August 10, 1945, cols. 55–56). But the coalition government had given way to a divisive electoral campaign and partisanship. The Conservative Party had supported most of Beveridge's recommendations when the coalition government assumed joint responsibility for social reform with the publication of the two social insurance White Papers (Great Britain 1944d-e; Brooke 1992, 183). Land-use planning was another area where near-consensus existed. The 1944 Employment White Paper likewise had expressed consensual support for full employment and for the government's responsibility for maintaining a high level of economic activity, but no agreement existed, even among economists, with respect to what this meant in practice. A Conservative minister of education, R. A. Butler, had been responsible for educational reform, although part of his party had been unhappy about the legislation. Lord Woolton, who was elected chairman of the Conservative Party in July 1946, wrote upon taking office in 1943 as minister of reconstruction, "I can see no political profit to be made out of condemning these thoughts and ideals [the Beveridge report] as uninstructed and unattainable . . ."(Woolton 1959, 269). The Conservatives' election manifesto, titled "Mr. Churchill's Declaration of Policy to the Electors," presumably was written by Churchill himself. It reiterated the coalition government's agreed-to plans for postwar reform along the broad outlines defined by

William Beveridge; social security, national health service, and full employment. Despite the manifesto's concessions to the "New Jerusalem" consensus, the Conservatives approached the election striking adversarial tones.[1]

One group within the party, the Tory Reform Committee, proposed that the 1945 Conservative election should stress the need for continued austerity and "ask consumers to postpone a return to peace-time standards of consumption in order that continued savings can be used for increasing productive equipment" (par. 16). On June 4 Churchill held an election radio broadcast in which he warned darkly that a Labour government would bring along "some form of Gestapo." Attlee went on the radio the next day and spoke in measured and reassuring tones about freedom and social justice, and he, not Churchill, captured the sympathy of middle-class voters (Attlee 1954, 198–201). John Charmley (1993, 641) argues in his political study of Churchill that Churchill's aversion to partisanship during the war had left the Conservative Party without an electoral strategy. The election may have reflected the voters' condemnation of Conservative prewar policies and a decade of deflation and stagnation, as political scientist Patrick Cosgrave (1992, 24) has argued, but more than that coalition government had left the Conservative Party divided and without a program.

In retrospect, the 1945 election ushered in a realignment for both parties. In the Labour Party generational change was postponed until after 1951, as the "old guard" plugged their way through 12 years of government office despite poor health and exhaustion.[2] The election of Hugh Gaitskell to party leader in 1955 and the 1956 publication of Anthony Crosland's *Future of Socialism* portended the conversion of the party elite to a "new socialism" emphasizing expansion of the economy and generous social legislation as the core of Labour reform program in place of nationalization and physical controls.[3] On the Conservative side, the opposition years brought forth a new generation. (Churchill formed the first postwar Conservative government in 1951, but Anthony Eden soon replaced him.) The Conservative Party changed between 1945 and 1951. One of the vehicles of change was the adaptation of the 1947 "Industrial Charter," a statement written largely by the party's Research Department and its head, R. A. Butler, whose status increased along with the new platform (Beer 1965, 302–317). The charter accepted most of the nationalization measures and supported a role for the state in economic management and the welfare state. (Butler became responsible for financial policy in 1951.) The next generation of Conservative leaders, including Butler, Eden, and Harold Macmillan, were all moderate Conservatives committed to social legislation and full employment.

Consensus or Socialist Revolution?

Labour's 1945 Election Manifesto placed the nationalization program at the center of its reform policy, but nationalization was only the first step. In 1942's *Old World and the New Society,* the party called for the "retention of War-Time Controls" that had "put in the hands of the community the essential instruments of successful planning" (par. 21.) At that year's party conference, a resolution was passed declaring that "the measures of government control needed for mobilizing the national resources in war are no less necessary for securing their best use in peace" and demanding that "the whole economy be put, progressively on a socialist basis, with workers sharing control" (League for Industrial Democracy 1943, 17). The party's programmatic outlook had changed little from the days of the Labour and Socialist International (LSI) and the 1918 party constitution.[4] Outside the nationalized sector, Labour proposed the creation of a National Investment Board with the power to "direct investment."

The legislative program put forward by the new government in 1945 was loyal to the electoral manifesto and to promises made during the reconstruction debate. Between August 1945 and August 1948, nationalizations were carried out of the Bank of England, coal, electricity, gas, communications, railroads, waterways, aviation, and parts of road transportation. Only steel nationalization, which was not carried out until 1951, aroused sustained controversy and opposition (Morgan 1984, 98–110). The absence of controversy in the other areas is not surprising, considering that most industries involved had been put under public control in one way or another earlier. Another reason was that nationalization promised to produce a reorganization of inefficient industries that were a burden on other industries. Labour's claims that the nationalization program would move Britain along to a Socialist economy did not resonate with the actual consequences of nationalization policy.[5]

Industry Views

Industry and business organizations objected to the ideological aspects of Labour's program but also could find things to applaud. In 1942 a group of 129 industrialists produced their own platform, *A National Policy for Industry,* which went further than the Federation of British Industries had in support of planning. It called for the creation of an "Industrial Tribunal" to weed out inefficient firms and "rationalize" industries.[6] Samuel Courtauld, a large industrialist with many public interests, was an exponent of Christian commercialism, which in many respects mirrored Stafford Cripps' Christian socialism. Courtauld wanted to nationalize certain industries including transport, communications, and land (agricultural land excluded), and to take over troubled industries for the purpose of "fixing" them. He favored restricting competition, through cartels, and argued in general against "gambling" in industry. He also wanted a "social partnership" with the unions and reminded industry that trade unions were the best machinery that existed for regulating industrial relations (Courtauld 1949). Paying no attention to contemporary pieties about "essential freedoms," Courtauld demanded legislation that would give collective bargaining legal status, as there was too much competition in the labor market. It was unfair to both workers and to industry that different wage rates could be paid for the same work, he argued. He thought it possible perhaps even to equalize wages across industries.

In response to a request from Stafford Cripps, who had just been made president of the Board of Trade, the Federation of British Industries produced a report in 1942 in which it outlined its views on postwar policy. The organization's primary concern was the prospects for sterling and the preservation of British export markets after the war. The industrialists feared that the United States would require large shipments of goods for free as payback for wartime loans but hoped—almost against reason—that all debts would be canceled instead. The FBI anticipated that wartime controls on foreign trade would be stayed for "some considerable period" (FBI 1942, par. 20) and envisioned that postwar international trade would take the form of bilateralism, even "barter," which it considered acceptable. The FBI strongly supported the continuation of interimperial preferences. The Americans had to be convinced of the need to preserve "the empire" as a trading system, it argued. Protectionism was also popular with the FBI, which wanted subsidies and protectionism for British agriculture (1942, 21), tariffs that would keep the home market safe for British industries (8), and a tax system that would help business "build up reserves for post-war purposes" (18). As for planning, government controls on industry should be removed judiciously only as industry self-organization was ready to substitute for direct state controls.

There are no indications that the FBI changed its mind before the end of the war. The fact that United States was not playing along had by then become clear, but that fact merely reinforced the FBI's desires for help from the British state. Its outlook on controls changed somewhat, as worries increased that the state might usurp policy decisions that industry preferred remain with the associations. The distinction between corporatist self-government and dirigiste planning began to move into focus. A 1944 FBI report on industry organization reflected a more acute sense of the threat to business posed by the shift in public policy and public sentiments. It included a stark warning that "unless industry itself takes steps [to organize,] the Government may find itself compelled by the pressure of circumstances to devise channels of administration of its own" (1944a, 5). It held up the successful incorporation into trade associations during the war as prima facie evidence that the associations must be the future form of organization for industry. It also spoke repeatedly of the "duty" of business to organize and of its social role. Making trade association membership compulsory was briefly discussed but rejected as unnecessary. The view was that as long as the government designated trade associations as the official channel of communication between industry and government, problems of insufficient support for the associations could overcome. After the 1945 election, the FBI struck a conciliatory note to work with the government and promised to judge policies on "merit," not on "program" (FBI 1945).

What one study called "a marked change in climate of opinion" took place between 1945 and 1950 (PEP 1957, 42). The British Employers' Confederation (BEC), never as open to the benefits of corporatism as the FBI, used language that resonated with Hayek's *Road to Serfdom* in a doomsday response to the government's 1947 Economic Survey, a document that aspired to initiate economic planning in Britain: "Our conduct will now decide whether our place in the world, our hard-won rights to live as free men, and our steady gains in social standard, are to be maintained, or whether we sink into unemployment, poverty or distress" (quoted in Middlemas 1986, 144). Nevertheless, significant divisions existed all along within industry circles.

State Power and Programmatic Adjustment

The postwar Labour government suffered some ill luck but also benefited from the good fortune of power. It retained—on paper at least—many of the extraordinary powers held by the wartime coalition government. Continuing shortages perpetuated the need for control boards and rationing, and the profusion of cartels, purchasing pools, licensing requirements, and administrative orders that had kept the war economy going were extended. Of particular importance was the antistrike provisions of Order 1305, which was not rescinded until 1951, when it caused full-scale conflict between the government and the unions. Harold Wilson's much-noted "bonfire of controls," while he was president of the Board of Trade in 1948 left many controls untouched. The "bonfire" eliminated the need for a wide range of permits and licenses, but was in no way intended as a policy reversal. It took place in the context of Wilson's asking for new legislation to impose "good" controls that would help full employment (H. C. Debates, Nov. 4, 1949, col. 2499). The statutory basis for the controls, the 1940 Emergency (Defense) Powers Act, was extended throughout the government's tenure. Some thought was given to replacement legislation, which would allow the state in peacetime to "regulate production, distribution and consumption and to control prices" (Rollings 1992, 15). The legislation went through several drafts, first as an "Economic Powers Bill," until it was renamed to the "Full Employment Bill" (reprinted in Rollings 1992, 30–32).[7] Obvious similarities existed between the failed Economic Powers Bill and the "Full Employment Act," which was introduced in the U.S. Congress in 1945 and in 1946 was enacted as the much weaker Employment Act (Stein 1969, 197–206).

Labour continued to be confounded about the problem of the state. Neil Rollings (1992) concludes that electoral politics was the cause of the bill's demise. Labour had become too identified in the public's mind with unpopular consumer controls to make discussion of new controls wise. The party's declining popularity also forced the planners within it to confront an issue that the unions had been sensitive to all along. Any permanent expansion of state powers amassed during a Labour government also would benefit a Conservative government. Faced with this "democratic dilemma," the unions chose to reject the strong state. The unions' squeamishness did not prevent Labour's left-wing from embracing the one-sided application of state power, as long as it was against business. The remarks Tony Benn (1990, 148), a long-term stalwart of the party left, entered into his diary in 1974 illustrate how strong the allure of perpetuated state power was: "This concept of a working-class power structure, democratic and organised in parallel with the government's structure—in effect joint government of the country by the Labour Party and the trade unions—makes an awful lot of sense. . . . We could govern in conjuncture with the trade unions, just as the Tories have always governed in conjuncture with the City and big business" (Benn 1990, 148).[8]

Benn's assumption that trade union domination via the state was a democratically acceptable substitution for liberal democracy strikes contemporary readers as philosophically naive. A worse problem was that it was also politically naive. Montesquieu's observation in De l'Esprit de Lois that power can be used against power, "le pouvoir arrête le pouvoir" illustrates the dilemma facing the unions: whatever means you apply against your political opponents may at some point become available to them. The unions were keenly aware of this problem and considered the state an unreliable ally. The majority of the unions preferred instead to use the state to carve out an area of legal protection for the unions, a principle known as "voluntarism." (For a comparative discussion, see Chapter 5.) There was another option that was never discussed, namely the creation of a cooperative framework that had something to offer for both unions and industry. The obvious reason that this option was not debated was that it was not necessary. The unions saw a way to get what they wanted without compromise, and so did industry once Labour's political fortunes began to change.

The New World Order and Postwar Adjustment

Postwar planners soon were forced to modify their designs in response to unanticipated circumstances, such as international events that intersected with domestic interests and the political doctrine that shaped Labour's economic policies. On his way to the Potsdam Conference in August 1945, President Harry S. Truman canceled the Lend-Lease program through which the United States had provided financial and material assistance to the United Kingdom for the war effort. J. M. Keynes was dispatched immediately to Washington to negotiate a new loan agreement; he succeeded in doing so only after protracted and difficult negotiations. (Keynes died shortly after, on April 21, 1946.) Recipients of American aid agreed under Article 7 of the Lend-Lease Agreement to participate in constructing a multilateral world trading system after the war. The 1944 Bretton Woods agreement included similar stipulations (Gardner 1980; Kindleberger 1993). The length to which the United States intended to press for the new order was brought home to British policymakers when sterling's convertibility with dollars was made an unconditional stipulation of the loan agreement negotiated by Keynes and an immediate currency crisis ensued.[9] The 1947 convertibility crisis and a subsequent devaluation in 1949 were significant events with almost cathartic consequences. On September 18, 1949, sterling was devalued from $4.03 to the pound to $2.80. Aside from a readjustment in 1967, when sterling was pegged at $2.40, a fixed rate was maintained from 1949 to 1972 (Tew 1978). Discussions were held in the 1950s of "Robot," a floating rates scheme, but they went nowhere. The conflict between planners in favor of a "National Plan" and public control of industry and the budgetary planner who aimed to use stabilization policy to maintain steady growth, in practice, was resolved to the latter's favor.

The triumph of short-term adjustment policy over long-term policy was somewhat incongruous considering that the "crises" themselves were expressions of severe structural problems. The persistent "shortages" of dollars had many causes, but high on the list were an overvalued sterling and the dependence on the sterling bloc (which largely coincided with the remnants of the British Commonwealth). Alec Cairncross (1985, 169) estimated that, had the 1949 devaluation not occurred, it would have been necessary to raise exports 75 percent above their prewar levels while at the same time holding imports constant. In addition, British export trades would have to be shifted from the colonies and the sterling area to the dollar area. Balance-of-payment crises were an inevitable symptom of structural imbalances. Inflexible support for sterling compelled successive governments to emphasize borrowing, exchange controls, and stop-go cycles of alternating contractive and expansive fiscal policies (Strange 1971). The drain also was felt on the personal level, as commonwealth concerns took Bevin away from the area of domestic industrial relations that he had managed with great skill during the war (Bullock 1960).[10]

Agricultural Controls and Postwar Policy

British farmers do not conform readily to standard European sociological and political paradigms. Early industrialization and a unique political history robbed the class of the historic role as coalition partner with the industrial working class in late-developing continental Europe. Curiously, the divergent paths of the past mattered very little by 1945, when British agricultural policy began to provide us with an example very much in mainstream European policymaking of successful corporatism and generous government subsidies. Agricultural policy presents us with a theoretically interesting problem. With the absence of a significant farm vote and British agriculture's past tradition of free trade, we would expect wartime protectionist policies to have been dismantled and corporatist solutions to the industry's problems to have had little chance of surviving. Instead agriculture offers us an instance of lasting public-private cooperation.

Wartime food shortages initially were caused by a lack of shipping space that occurred because freighters were redirected to military transport. After the May 1940 Nazi invasion of Denmark, the food situation deteriorated as Denmark had been a primary source of British food imports. Rationing books were sent out on September 29, 1939. The last restrictions on consumer goods were removed only 20 years later.[11] Agricultural control policy was caught on the horns of the same dilemma that afflicted wage policy. Inflation control was a primary objective, but low farm prices deterred increased output. In August 1940 the War Cabinet agreed to a system of agricultural subsidies based on high producer prices and low consumer prices, with government subsidies bridging the gap. The government negotiated minimum prices with the National Farmers' Union (NFU), which was awarded exclusive rights to represent farm interests. The system, which is far from unique, continued throughout the war and subsequently was reaffirmed by postwar farm legislation. Similar principles today guide European farm policies in general and continue to inform the European Union's common agricultural program (CAP).

The historic importance of the 1940 decision was that it put an end to free trade principles that had dominated in Great Britain since the repeal of the Corn Laws in 1846. In 1906 the Liberal Party won on a platform that called for "no taxes on food" after Joseph Chamberlain had led the Conservative Party in an abortive campaign to impose protective tariffs on agricultural imports. Britain entered World War I expecting that the Royal Navy would keep food imports coming, but the efficiency of German submarines caused problems. In February 1917 Parliament voted to guarantee prices on grains and potatoes. The Agricultural Act of 1920 promised to keep price guarantees forever, but it was reversed nevertheless in 1921 when agricultural policy reverted to the free trade mold. In the 1920s the Conservative Party committed itself to agricultural protectionism with the argument that agriculture should not be regarded principally as an industry but valued for "the stability, solid morality, and wisdom of the countryside" (cited in Cooper 1989, 1). The Great Depression caused new support for agricultural protectionism (Astor and Rowntree 1938; Hammond 1954).[12]

A 1931 Agricultural Marketing Bill (apparently modeled on the American 1929 Agricultural Marketing Bill) permitted farmers to create agricultural cartels for the purpose of fixing minimum prices, but the NFU was against agricultural cooperatives and opposed the bill. It was instead the 1940 war controls that shaped the way agricultural regulation would be carried out. The wartime Ministry of Food was set up in conjunction with a network of local control committees with farm representatives. The NFU and the two responsible ministries calculated farm incomes and expenditures, developed schedules of prices, and published annual price reviews.[13] The price control and review network became the backbone for the NFU, a framework that continued unchanged after the war.

In 1940 the government became the sole purchaser and distributor of agricultural supplies and output. It distributed fertilizer, seeds, and feed to farmers at fixed prices through local businesses operating in "pools," and sold food to consumers at controlled prices and in rationed allotments. Producer prices were set high to stimulate farm production. Farm subsidies came in four broad categories: (1) direct assistance such as land grants for the plowing up of grassland, (2) indirect grants to improve livestock and drainage, (3) grants to increase marginal (that is, economically inefficient) production, and (4) guaranteed prices. Net agricultural incomes more than tripled between 1938–1939 and 1944–1945 (Murray 1955, 379).

Farm Organizations and the Parties

The structure of farm interest organization predated the war controls but was greatly expanded in response to them. In 1865 large landowners had formed a national Chamber of Agriculture; independent farmers formed the NFU in 1908. Both organizations sponsored members of Parliament just as trade unions and employer and business groups did.[14] The NFU worked with all parties, Liberal, Conservative, and Labour. The 1945 Labour Party's espousal of farmer-friendly policies requires explanation, considering its previous history of support for farm collectivization and other staples of Marxist farm policies. At the party's 1942 Annual Conference, a resolution called for "national ownership of agricultural land to enable its full utilization by the development of a planned system of agricultural production" (League for Industrial Democracy 1943, 38). Working-class consumption patterns based on preferences for imported food, such as Argentinean beef and Danish bacon, and the small size of the farm vote would, in theory, indicate little need for a domestic "worker-farmer" alliance based on agricultural protectionism.[15] Yet Labour's agricultural policies became increasingly farmer-friendly. The need to alleviate food scarcity readily explains the willingness to subsidize the farm sector during the war but the question is, why did Labour continue to embrace expensive agricultural policies after the war?

Agricultural subsidies became a staple of both Labour and Conservative policies after 1945. Britain's inability to produce enough exports to pay for imports worked to the advantage of agricultural interests by providing a rationale for supportive pricing policies aimed at boosting domestic output, even in the face of obvious inefficiencies. The NFU stayed neutral in the elections of 1950, coining the slogan "Keep agriculture out of politics." The meaning was clear enough: Keep farm subsidies out of party competition, thus guaranteeing that both parties would support the system.

Postwar Farm Policies

In 1944 the War Cabinet had agreed to maintain wartime schemes for guaranteed minimum prices until 1947, at which time a new act was passed that ratified previous policies. The redistributive and conspicuously expansionary aspects of agricultural policy, with the government providing both low prices to consumers and high prices to producers, make it a paradigmic example of Keynesian growth-oriented demand management.[16] That it also was economically inefficient mattered less compared to the low currency reserves. After 1945, "dollar-shortage" and the perceived need to ration foreign currency effectively substituted for economic autarky as a reason for policies aimed at encouraging agricultural self-sufficiency and boosting output. The real issue was not if farmers had a moral claim on government support or, for that matter, the political need to meet farm interest; it was that alternative policies were less palatable.

The Labour Party's defense of the "Agricultural Expansion Program," set in motion by the Agricultural Act of 1947, used rhetoric that evoked the Soviet New Economic Program: "Nothing less than the maximum production of which the industry is capable will suffice" (Labour Party 1948, 33).[17] A numerical target of a 50 percent expansion compared to prewar output was set as the goal. The farm program came with all the embellishments of "economic planning," including targets that never were met. Home production accounted for 31 percent of total calorie consumption prior to the war; in 1948–1949 it accounted for 38 percent (Great Britain 1949, 13).

Labour was committed to food controls for reasons other than the need to boost production. Keeping prices low was also an important social objective (Self and Storing 1963, 67). The 1947 act required the Ministry of Agriculture to conduct annual reviews of the economic condition of agriculture and to provide economic guarantees for a specified list of commodities encompassing 80 percent of total agricultural output (23). The right of the NFU to be represented in the policy process, through the annual price review, was written into the act. It also was stipulated that the purpose was to serve the "national interest" in getting food on the table, a goal that could have been better served by the import of cheaper foodstuffs if sufficient foreign exchange was available. The act had strong social policy components, requiring that the government be responsible for "proper renumeration and living quarters for farmers and workers in agriculture." It epitomized the Labour government's social and economic agenda. It also helped the NFU become a prototypical corporatist interest organization based on near-universal individual farm memberships in local branches supporting a national hierarchy based on indirect representation (Self and Storing 1963, chap. 2; Wilson 1977, 36).[18]

Between 1954 and 1956, price guarantees amounted to roughly 251 pounds sterling per head of the active agricultural population, or 24 percent of total agricultural output. In the postwar years, British farmers received the highest subsidies of any in Europe (McCrone 1962, 51). After the 1955 election, the Conservative government tried to curb the growth in farm subsidies, but the basic system of representation and redistribution was left unchanged. Over the years the Conservative Party modified its stance from 1921, when it was forthrightly protectionist, to being reluctantly protectionist. Yet policy changed only at the margins. The Ministry of Food and the Ministry of Agriculture were merged in 1956, and a year later the Agricultural Act was amended to restrict the scope of the price guarantees. (In 1973 the system was supplanted by the European common agricultural program when Britain joined what was then the European Economic Community [EEC].)

The main reasons listed by both Conservative and Labour governments for continuing farm subsidies inevitably referred to the "public interest," which alternatively was defined as a matter of international security—protecting the British people from becoming wholly dependent on food imports—to references to the importance of the farming community for the "British way of life." Social values commonly have played a role in justifications for postwar agricultural policy in a number of countries. Identical reasons were given, for example, by Swedish Social Democratic governments for continuing a similarly expensive system of agricultural subsidies. (See chapter 5.) In Sweden, the electoral importance of the farm vote—also for the election of Social Democrats—helps explain the left's embrace of farmers as a partner in a Red-Green alliance, but a political explanation obviously does not apply in the British case, where the farm vote constituted only a small share of the electorate. An alternative explanation focuses on the affinity between subsidizing farm incomes and Keynesian planning. Expansionary farm policies were an integral part of the postwar economy, in tune with the functional requirements of an emphasis on stabilization policy and demand management. The rhetoric of "fairness" also identified farmers as party to the postwar social compact. In addition, and perhaps ultimately more important, the primacy of balance-of-payments concerns pushed import-dependent countries to boost domestic agricultural production even at great costs. But the corporatist nature of British farm policies also raises another set of questions. If governments and British agriculture could come to agreement on a consensual corporatist approach to the industry's problems, albeit an expensive one, why not government and industry?

Nationalization: Between Power and Consent

Labour's thinking was deeply influenced by a "cult of efficiency" tied to Fabians like G. D. H. Cole and Sidney and Beatrice Webb (Durbin 1985; Francis 1997) and the "municipal socialism" chiefly represented within the party by Herbert Morrison. Cole's planning manual, *Economic Planning* (1935), made many references to "superior" and "parallel planning authorities" with the authority to hire and dismiss managers and power to regulate the "output of all goods and services" (315). He called for the creation of a "Department of Economic Inspection" to manage the National Plan, a National Planning Authority to make it, a National Planning Commission to set priorities, and a National Investment Board to find the money (326–328). Cole also envisioned the creation of a National Income Planning Authority with union representation and representation from professional associations and other income groups, in effect, an "economic parliament." The scope of the structure envisioned was expanded to make room for matching regional and sectional authorities. The war economy very nearly realized Cole's planning fancy.

Planners attributed to states a capacity for "fairness" that markets lacked. The presumption was that "wasteful" competition would be replaced with "rational" bureaucratic decision making and through economies of scale an efficiency gain could be realized that would pay for social reform. It also was assumed that with more than 50 percent of the national economy controlled by the government, the scourge of recession would be eliminated. These assumptions partly explain some of the lacunae in Labour's economic program, for example, the scant attention given to fiscal policies.

Coal

The central problem with coal was that the industry's difficulties, in particular its fragmented nature, impeded the supply of coal needed by the rest of industry. In 1919 a commission of inquiry reported some 1,500 mines owned by 1,400 colliery companies. By 1947 the number of companies had been reduced by approximately half. Voluntary cartelization had been attempted in the interwar years but failed. One reason for instability was that the Mining Association was not empowered to negotiate wages, which were set by individual owners. In 1939 the owners agreed to a national council to set wages during the war (Clegg 1994, 30, 171). The minister of fuel and power took operating control of coal mining in 1942. Representatives from owners and the Miners' Federation were appointed to the coal board, which began to negotiate wages, and a commission was created to recommend to creation of a joint (unions and owners) national negotiating machinery.[19] The minister (a Conservative) proposed in 1943 to nationalize the industry for the duration of the war, but Churchill ruled it out as likely to cause controversy (Morgan 1984, 104). Manpower shortage was a major issue. In 1942, 36,000 workers were conscripted to the industry from other jobs. Bonus schemes were introduced to attract labor, but higher wages turned out to produce lower output as workers needed to work less to make the same pay (Parker 1957, 231). Generally, pay bonuses were not very effective in boosting productivity because consumer shortages meant that there was little to spend the extra pay on.

After the war's end, the Labour government continued to rely on wartime regulations to keep supplies flowing; one such regulation was the Essential Works Order, which prevented mineworkers from seeking employment elsewhere (Hancock and Gowing 1949, 506). In 1945, when the new Labour minister, Emanuel Shinwell, undertook to nationalize the industry, the public corporation model prevailed. A National Coal Board was established composed of an "independent" chair, a former owner, and representatives from both "sides of industry." The unions were represented by "nominees" from the TUC and the NUM, the newly created unified National Union of Mineworkers (Morgan 1984, 105). About 1,000 mines were put under public ownership. A regional organization was carved out with regional control boards replicating the national board. In February 1947, one month after nationalization went into effect, however, fuel shortages occurred that disrupted the supply of electricity and caused weeks of industry shutdowns. The crisis obviously contradicted Labour's claims with respect to the economic benefits of nationalization and was a source of some political embarrassment.

The principle aim of nationalization was to rationalize and reequip the industry, but the balance between subsidization and restructuring was elusive. More than perhaps any other industry, coal mining illustrates that public ownership is no panacea. The unions had gone to great lengths to avoid taking responsibility for nationalized industries, worried about the "double bind" that their representatives could find themselves in. The more serious "double bind" created by nationalization turned out to be the one imposed on governments when attempts to rationalize the industry gave rise to spectacular labor conflicts. Possibly the last major such conflict took place in 1984–1985, when NUM, under the leadership of the inexhaustible Arthur Scargill, went on strike against pit closures and the government's rationalization program (Reed et al. 1985; Adeney and Lloyd 1986; Howell 1989). The widely perceived failure of the nationalized industries helped the Conservative Party and Margaret Thatcher make the case in 1979 for privatization and retrenchment of the state.

Steel

The impetus for steel nationalization was hindered by the industry's respectable performance after the war. Labour's 1945 electoral manifesto and the TUC's 1944 *Interim Report on Post-War Reconstruction* had included steel on the list for immediate nationalization. The decision to move forward was made only after a narrow vote in the Parliamentary Labour Party, with 81 to 77 in favor of nationalization.[20] A bill was introduced in 1947, but it moved on to a third reading only in May 1949.[21] Opposition from the House of Lords forced a compromise, which stipulated that the transfer of properties could take place until after January 1, 1951, with the expectation that a change in government was likely in the upcoming election. Labour narrowly won the 1950 election and nationalization proceeded. The board created by the 1950 nationalization act had the authority to plan industry capacity by setting numerical targets (a "plan"), to fix maximum prices, and to approve development plans. But in 1953, after the Conservatives returned to government power, the steel industry was partly sold back to the owners. In 1967 parts of the industry were renationalized by a Labour government.

In the case of steel, continuity militated against action. The administrators sitting on the wartime Iron and Steel Control had been recruited from the British Iron and Steel Federation. After the war, the control was replaced by a consultative Iron and Steel Board, which basically replicated the previous control and included representatives from trade unions, manufacturers, and independent members. The industry was happy with existing arrangements and opposed nationalization because it broke up what the Iron and Steel Federation considered to be 15 years of "successful industrial statecraft" (quoted in Rogow 1955, 159).

It is difficult to explain why, in the end, Labour forged ahead with a nationalization initiative that already had caused much dissent. According to the British historian Kenneth Morgan's account (1984, 115), minutes of cabinet meetings showed that the government found it difficult to backtrack on steel nationalization at home while it was pressing ahead with nationalization of the German Ruhr industries, against the objections of the U.S. occupation authorities. (See chapter 5.) Political pressure from the party's left and the National Executive Committee also informed the decision to go ahead.

Industry reaction to the steel nationalization program illustrates perfectly why business and industry were both supportive and hostile to the nationalization program. The industry wanted some of the package but not the part that had "planners" civil servants, involved in running industry. Industry and business organizations want to see government sustain and enhance their capacity to plan, not usurp it. In the administration of wartime controls, business had worked for the government and the government generally relied on industry representatives acting on loan from large companies or through trade associations to do the job. The warfare state was critically dependent on private support, and the private sector depended on the state for its defense; thus it was a "mutualist" relationship. The welfare state had much to offer industry, not the least the prospect of an expanding economy, but the prospects of continued administrative put business and industry organization at a disadvantage in the decision-making process. (The president of the FBI, Frederick Bain, outlined industry's strategy at the federation's annual meeting in 1948. The best business could do, he said, was to shift the government's focus on controls to "internal industrial administration" (Rogow 1955, 90).[22] Planning was fine, it seems, as long as industry and business would be doing most of it.

Industrial Planning: The Development Councils

No wonder that planning-by-cartellization looked good to much of business and industry in 1945. Price-fixing worked to keep prices up, not just down. State-purchasing cartels and licensing rules protected profit margins (which had increased nicely in the last years of the war) by keeping out competitors and sustaining the market power of existing businesses. In the postwar years, the trade associations continued to do what they had done during the war: They processed applications for licenses to import and permits to build, coordinated bulk purchases of supplies, took care of statistical requirements, and fixed prices and quotas for delivery between suppliers and retailers. These were the things that trade associations did well. In practice, government officials were helpless without the assistance of trade associations because they lacked both the knowledge and the administrative capacity to carry things out on their own. Conflict arose when the government began to assert its authority by shifting the power to make planning decisions from consultative boards and joint councils to civil servants endowed with the capacity to "plan." At the same time, trade associations and industry groups acted to protect their organizations against permanent government encroachment.

"Working Parties" were set up in 1945 to prepare plans for how to create more permanent planning structures in 17 industries. Most industries were dominated by medium-size firms, and the Working Parties replicated wartime cartels and control boards. At first business support was considerable. In the interwar years, the FBI had repeatedly encouraged industry rationalization and self-regulation. The organization even had outlined an enabling act that would permit the creation of national "Advisory Councils" for different industries. The idea was apparently inspired by the Code Authorities created in the United States in 1933–1934. Also, a 1944 report by the FBI's Organization of Industry Committee had argued for closer collaboration between government and industry, aiming to fulfill the dual goals of maintaining full employment and fixing the trade imbalance. The general design called for a range of approaches to the planned economy. While the Working Parties aimed to determine how to approach planning in industry broadly defined, nationalization and direct controls were intended to bring prioritized industries under immediate government management.

Stafford Cripps, now president of the Board of Trade, defined the purpose of group representation in his brief for the Working Parties in unproblematic terms: They were to discuss the aims of industry, good points and bad points, present and future, and make suggestions for improvements (H. C. Debates, Oct. 15, 1945, cols. 692–694). At the time, Working Parties were created for cotton, pottery, furniture, hosiery, and footwear. A civil servant from the Board of Trade acted as chairman and supplied a permanent secretary. Employers, unions, and so-called independents were appointed to the Working Parties. Employers were represented by 3 to 4 nominees on each board. The unions had a similar number of nominees on the boards, except no nominees had been found for the hosiery and footwear industries. (Cripps publicly complained of the lack of good union representatives, enraging the unions.) No shortages existed of "independents"—majors, engineers, economists, and scientists—who were amply represented (see table, H. C. Debates, Oct. 15, 1945, col. 695).

When the initial phase of the nationalization program proceeded with relatively little objection, Cripps moved to set up planning agencies—called Development Councils—to replace the Working Parties. The subsequent 1947 Industrial Organization and Development Act gave the president of the Board of Trade—at the time still Cripps—the power to set up permanent councils in particular industries by administrative order. The councils would allow for "consultation" between the government and owners in industries that were not—yet—slated for nationalization. The 1947 act listed a number of functions for the councils: standardization, collection of statistics, recruitment and training, design and certification of products. One sticking point was that the act authorized the councils to collect a levy from the industry to support their work. Industry did not like that, and the trade associations were opposed because they thought that the councils would supplant them. It was not so much that the planning was controversial but *who* was going to do the planning. Industry wanted the government to provide the money and the needed enabling legislation, and then allow self-administration. The planners wanted to "consult" business and industry groups but, having done so, they would make policy. Industry wanted the councils to be advisory only. The cotton industry provided an example of consensual planning. A critical variable here was that the creation of a cotton board was accompanied by a promise of a government grant, estimated to amount to 25 percent of the cost of reequipment, on the condition that the money be spent to consolidate small manufacturers (H. C. Debates, June 24, 1947, col. 34; Rogow 1955, 75).

Numerous reasons have been given for the failure of the 1947 act. The Labour Party later blamed the FBI and decried industry's political motives. (See the speech by Harold Wilson in the House of Commons on the occasion of a Conservative proposal to dissolve the Clothing Industry Development Council, one of Cripps' 1947 initiatives, H. C. Debates, December 16, 1952, cols. 1331–1337.[23]) Cripps' official biographer argued that Cripps himself no longer had time to cajole industry into submitting to his plans (Cooke 1957, 339). Cripps did seem to lose interest in the councils after he replaced Dalton as chancellor of the Exchequer. The organizational restructuring also implied an important shift in the nature and means of economic policy and in the Labour government's concept of economic planning. That reorganization in turn reflected broader changes in the aims and means of the government's economic policies. The Treasury supplanted the service ministries as the central actor in economic policy, and staff and functions that in the war years had moved to the Economic Section under the War Cabinet now returned to the Treasury. The Board of Trade lost out in the process. The shift also had large-scale implications for societal actors. The trade associations were not well equipped to represent business interests there, nor did the Treasury have much reason to deal with them.

The councils have been portrayed as an early attempt to pursue what we today call "structural" industrial policy. Structural industrial policy generally aims to "pick winners" among and within particular industries and to train public and private efforts on the enhancement of competitiveness by improving productivity, concentrating investment to competitive sectors, and nurturing long-term planning for research and innovation. Advocates have pointed to French, German, and Japanese economic achievements as evidence that the Anglo-American model does not work. Arguably the Development Councils represented an early and forward-looking example of structural industrial policy. Shonfield (1965, 98) identified them as the model for subsequent French planning efforts, the *commissions du modernisation*. Opponents have portrayed the councils as a paternalistic move by hubristic Labour intellectuals who arrogantly thought they knew better than private industry (Barnett 1986, 1995). Quite possibly, both scenarios apply. The councils were conceived in arrogance (or naivete) about the ability of civil servants to prevail over private interests but, had they succeeded, they would have enabled a very different postwar trajectory for British economic development and economic policymaking.

A General Planning Staff

The Ministry of Production had been created in February 1942 as vehicle for a "Production General Staff" that would coordinate between the production and supply ministries and fill a "gap" between strategic-military planning and industrial planning (Postan 1952, 250). The industrialist Lord Beaverbrook was put in charge first but lasted only three weeks in office, when the ministry was given to a civil servant, Oliver Lyttleton. The ministry inspired later ideas about a general economic staff, what in France became a *Commissariat Général du Plan,* to be put in charge of economic planning. A Central Economic Planning Staff (CEPS) was created in 1947, partly in response to the fuel crisis that followed in the wake of coal nationalization. The crisis, which was entirely domestic in origins and consequences, coincided with the decision to make sterling convertible in connection with the Anglo-American loan agreement and the first severe balance-of-payments crisis. It was a disappointment to the planners that CEPS was put in the Treasury and subordinated to the balance-of-payments concerns that dominated there. A larger Economic Planning Board was set up at the same time with inclusive interest group representation and modeled on the experience of the wartime National Production Advisory Council on Industry (Hall 1986, 73). The new board lacked both a supportive structure comparable to that of the plant-level Joint Production Councils (see chapter 2) and the special attention from a minister that Bevin had given to wartime corporatist organizations. Instead of the top-to-bottom line organization of planning agencies that planners had hoped for the Economic Planning Board became an oversized assembly for interest-group representatives without mandates to bind the organizations that they represented.

"Where Shall All the Money Come From?"[24]

Hugh Dalton, the chancellor of the Exchequer, concluded from the resistance to his dispatchment of Keynes to Washington to ask for a loan immediately after the cancellation of the Lend-Lease agreement that "some people" in the party preferred Keynes to fail because in that case Britain would be forced into autarky and allowed to chart its own course. "It seemed almost impossible," he later wrote, "to convey any real sense of urgency" to the fellow members of the government and their advisors (Dalton 1962, 70).[25] The opposition came from the two "incorrigible rebels" in the Labour Party (Morgan 1984, 148), Shinwell and Bevan, and a group of left-wingers who opposed the conditions of the loan. On December 13, 1945, 70 Conservative and 13 Labour members voted against the loan agreement. Conservative imperialists joined left-wing planners to oppose the agreement's proscription of protective exchange controls. In the end Bevan voted for the loan, having concluded that it would help pay for social programs.[26]

The economic situation deteriorated quickly from the fuel crisis caused by coal shortage in February 1947, to the introduction of currency convertibility on July 15, 1947, and its subsequent suspension on August 20. A second currency crisis in 1949 caused sterling to be devalued. It was not made convertible again until December 29, 1958, in connection with U.K. membership of the European Payments Union.

Stabilization Policy

The beginning of the European Recovery Program (the Marshall Plan) brought relief, and with the reimposition of banking and import controls, the economy improved in 1948. One estimate held that in 1949, after Wilson's 1948 "bonfire," over 90 percent of imports and 49 percent of consumer goods were still controlled with additional indirect controls exercised by "pools" and restrictive price-setting (Dow 1970, 174–176). The currency crisis and trade imbalance provided a new rationale for the controls. A shift took place in economic policy as the government embarked on an offensive to promote growth and productivity planning in connection with Stafford Cripps' "productivity campaign" inspired in part by the Marshall Plan (Hogan 1987; Maier 1978, 1987). Productivity improvement moved to the forefront of Labour's economic policy thinking (Tomlinson 1992).

From February 1948 onward, the government repeatedly appealed to the trade unions to restrain wages. Labour's leaders had arrived at a new understanding of the role of foreign trade in shaping domestic economic conditions, more in line with the objectives and means suggested in the 1944 Employment White Paper than the espousal of wartime "socialism" found in the 1945 Manifesto. The conversion was reflected in a White Paper, *Statement on Personal Incomes, Costs, and Prices* (Great Britain 1948b), from February 1948 that laid out three principles that would assume great importance for subsequent policymaking.[27] The first was a parity principle that prices, dividends, wages, and salaries should be treated as analog incomes and move upward only in concert. The second was that wage increases be contingent on increases in productivity, except for special cases where equity concerns indicated the need to bring up the wages of disadvantaged groups. Third, it was also respectful of the principle of "free wages," stating that it was "not desirable for the government to interfere directly with the incomes of individuals otherwise than by taxation." This latter principle obviously was at cross-purposes with the first two.

In 1947 the government began publishing the annual *Economic Survey*. That year's version read more like a textbook on planning policy than like an actual statement of policy, but over the years the survey became increasingly more sophisticated in applying statistical tools for economic forecasting. The 1949 *Economic Survey,* a highly technical document, pronounced budgetary planning the essence of all planning. In the four years that passed from 1945 to 1949, the government had moved from a planned economy to a mixed economy and the weight of economic policy had shifted from direct physical controls and nationalization to income stabilization and budgetary planning.

This did not mean that the control economy had been forsaken; it had merely become a means for policy stabilization rather than for long-term economic reform. General price controls still applied. For example, the local "Price Regulation Committees" were not closed down until May 1953. Despite Conservative promises to set the consumers "free" in the 1950 and 1951 elections, Conservative governments relied as much on the controls as did Labour. In 1956–1957 a Conservative government, hoping to stabilize the balance of payments, reimposed a panoply of control measures that was similar to wartime stabilization policy (Blackaby 1964, 118).

Fiscal and Monetary Policy

Labour's 1945 electoral manifesto said little about paying for reform, in part because nationalization was expected to pay for itself. It contained an attack on inherited wealth, but raising taxes presented a conundrum for Labour. The party wanted to repeal wartime taxes on company profits, preferring instead to encourage companies to invest. The government was also keen to reduce the income tax affecting wage-earners. It was generally assumed, even by Dalton, the Exchequer, that a combination of extra taxes on inheritances, low interest rates, and "cheap money" policies would raise enough revenue to pay for social reform. Since "cheap money" policies also indicated a preference for a balanced budget, the difficulties associated with matching the expenditure side of the government's program with revenue-raising policies were considerable. Dalton's decision in October 1945 to lower interest rates on Treasury bills to 0.5 percent reflected the government's commitment to "cheap money."[28] On the income side, another critical mistake was that nationalization was expected to pay for itself, as planning produced an efficiency gain and additional growth. Low interests rates consequently assumed immense importance, in view of a government debt overhang from the war years of more than double the national income and the need for additional borrowing to compensate owners affected by the nationalization program. Very low interest rates were abandoned only when it became clear that inflation, not deflation, was to be the obstacle to macroeconomic balance, but low interest rates were not forsaken altogether. The raising of interest rates as an anti-inflationary measure was not added to the stabilization policy toolbox until March 1952, when the Conservative government raised interest rates to 4 percent (see Howson 1994, 237).

Wage Policy and Economic Decline

The 1950s had a sheen of stability and prosperity that concealed relative economic decline. The British economy grew by an average of 2.4 percent per year from 1949 to 1959. In the same 20 year span, Swedish growth rates averaged 3.4 percent; the French 4.5 percent; and German 7.4 percent (average annual compounded rates of growth of gross domestic product, see U.N. Economic Commission for Europe 1964, 12). The comparison of growth rates is admittedly complicated by the low starting points of countries such as France and the Federal Republic, and in the case of Sweden by the country's escape from significant physical destruction during the war. Yet there can be no doubt of Britain's relative economic decline. Econometric studies routinely point to a shortfall in productivity improvements caused by restrictive labor practices, investment and management quality, and slowness to restructure (Crafts 1995). British workers, like farmers, were better off than they had ever been, but after 20 years they were still less well off than workers elsewhere. One estimate of real wage growth in the main European countries pegs it at 5 percent to 5.5 percent per year averaged over 1950 to 1975 to control for the dip immediately after the war. British wages grew by 2.6 percent per year in those years (Scholliers 1989, 232). Considering that 13 of those years were spent under Conservative governments, the burden of responsibility for low wage growth has to be shared.

Planned Wages or "Free" Wages?

Four different positions can be distinguished within the unions and the Labour Party on the merits of wage policy for the year 1947. The "traditionalist" position was articulated by an old guard including Clement Attlee, Ernest Bevin, and Walter Citrine, who held to the precept of "voluntarism" that stressed principles of responsible self-government. A second position had support from the trade union hierarchy anchored in the stronger unions of skilled workers who agreed with "voluntarism" but took a different view of what "responsible" trade unionism meant. A third group from what was called the "weaker trades," organizing in fragmented industries or in occupations where skills posed few obstacles to labor substitutionality, argued for what was called "a national wage policy." They wanted the Trades Union Congress to exercise a role in collective bargaining, for example, by functioning as a clearinghouse for wage claims. They also wanted to maintain many of the wartime rules, including compulsory arbitration, because of the benefits weaker unions derived from the compulsory system (which applied to labor as well as employers). This group railed against "irresponsible" unionism.

A fourth group consisted of academic planners and included, among others, Barbara Wootton, Harold Laski, and Nicholas Kaldor. They advocated wage "planning" and emphasized the need to tie wage determination to questions of overall macroeconomic stability and economic planning. Many were committed to the ideas articulated in the 1944 employment paper. (See chapter 2.) Wootton and Kaldor had worked with Beveridge on this second report (Beveridge 1945). Room existed for compromise between the different positions, but in practice none emerged. One possible compromise, which would have put British wage policy on a trajectory not unlike that later taken by Swedish wage policy, would have brought the "weaker trades" together with the wage planners' camp. One reason that this was an unlikely axis in the British case was that neither the left Keynesians nor the "weaker trades" dominated the thinking within their group. Wootton (1955, 120) concluded a study of government and union attitudes to wage policy by saying that a picture emerges "of a community determined . . . to fix standards of renumeration that are fair and no less determined to abdicate from all responsibility for the definition of general policy or for the actual decisions made." Wootton argued against the unions' emphasis on maintenance of wage differentials as the primary objective for wage negations and for an egalitarian wage policy, which would help halt inflation and have the added benefit of forcing employers in poorly performing industries to better their performance (179). Similar arguments were put forward at the time in Sweden.

"Free" Unions in the "Controlled" Economy

In the discussions of the 1945 electoral manifesto, the TUC made the restoration of "free" trade unionism through the repeal of the 1927 Trades Disputes and Trade Unions Act an unconditional demand. The TUC approached the coalition government during the war in the hope that a compromise could be made and parts of the 1927 act repealed (Clegg 1994, 264). The unions were apparently willing to keep the antistriking provisions (against general strikes) in exchange for removing political restrictions on the unions.

The 1945 repeal camouflaged a complicated and tenuous compromise between the party leaders and the TUC. Party leaders opposed a commitment to an outright repeal in the 1945 electoral manifesto, arguing that it would provide the Conservative Party with an opportunity to accuse Labour of supporting political strikes during the campaign. In the end, they promised to repeal the act and the TUC agreed to ask officially only for an amendment to allow civil service unions to join the TUC (Allen 1960, 261–264; TUC Report 1945, 244). Disagreements over what to do with the 1927 act went far back. During the war, a bipartisan compromise had looked possible, and the TUC asked the coalition government for a partial repeal that would leave the ban on political striking and secondary labor conflict intact. The government strung the TUC out for two years, until March 1945, when Churchill wrote to the unions to say that the issue had to await the "upcoming" election (Clegg 1994, 264).

The unions had good reasons to want changes to the old legislation. The 1927 act prohibited political strikes, by which was understood strikes that, as the act put it vaguely, harmed the community. The prohibition included sympathy strikes, also known as secondary strikes. Notably, lockouts were prohibited too, a provision that struck against employers. The act had been passed in a fit of Conservative outrage after the 1926 General Strike, a nine-day strike called by the TUC in support of striking miners. Provisions that prevented civil service unions from joining the TUC and forbade union collection of money for the Labour Party, the so-called political levy, were costly to Labour. They eliminated the common practice that union members had to "contract out" if they wanted to avoid the "political levy," whereby workers had to sign a form expressly refusing to pay the levy in order to prevent the union from making an automatic deduction from union membership fees for the Labour Party.[29] The 1945 repeal restored this practice, with the result that the share of fees-paying members nearly doubled (Harrison 1960, 32).

In terms of the legal position of trade unions, the 1945 repeal took British industrial relations back to a legal state created by the 1906 Trades Disputes Act, which had exempted unions from antitrust legislation. The main aim of the act was to protect unions against hostile courts, but it was written in a way that, in effect, granted unions a protected status above the law, super legem. It stated simply that a trade union could not be sued for "any tortious act alleged to have been committed by or on behalf of the trade union." At the time, the act had been intended to encourage self-regulation and responsible unionism. It reflected an agreement between the unions and a reform-minded government that trade unions had a legitimate role in the regulation of industry; it was not intended to imply the blanket theory of trade union liberties that "the voluntarist principle" was made into after 1945 (Brown 1986, chaps. 2 and 3).

After the 1945 repeal, the concept of trade union "immunity" was stretched to cover numerous aspects of trade unionism that were not foreseen in 1906. Some of the trade union practices that in the 1970s became the most controversial and, by 1979, caused Conservative attacks on the unions, were post–1945 inventions, and yet were allowed to develop under the protection of the legal umbrella created by the immunity doctrine. The development of a large public sector with a unionized workforce was unanticipated entirely at the time. For that reason alone, the applicability of the immunity doctrine to the public sector should be an open question. Another issue was the violence-prone tactics of so-called flying pickets, one of the first objects of anti-union legislation during the Thatcher governments. These are bused-in activists that unions can use to shut down nonstriking suppliers to companies involved in industrial strife. The immunity doctrine also was used to delegitimize industrial reform legislation that fixed timetables for collective bargaining and to deny the TUC authority over any aspect of affiliated trade unions' activities.

In the postwar years, the doctrine not only lost its original association with trade union self-government, but also became a tool in the hands of militant unions against union centralization and self-discipline. The corollary of trade union liberties was an extreme decentralization of authority within the unions that made it impossible to distinguish between "authorized" and "unauthorized" industrial action. Serendipity does not explain the problematic aspects of trade union voluntarism, because there is plenty evidence that the 1945–1951 Labour government was aware of the problems and wanted to act. The government's effort to maintain compulsory arbitration on a temporary basis after officially agreeing to terminate Order 1305, and the TUC General Council's acquiescence to a compromise present us with the most striking evidence of awareness. We can conclude that both the General Council and Labour leaders were cognizant of the political and practical benefits of restricting the voluntarism doctrine. (For a discussion, see below and Clegg 1994, 328.) The 1945 repeal of the 1927 act was intended to prevent a Conservative government from using the regulatory machinery created by the act against the unions. That decision cannot be second-guessed. The 1927 act was punitive and fell short of providing an impetus for responsible trade unionism. The problem was that no permanent regulatory framework was put in place to replace and reform the wartime apparatus.

The Failed Efforts of the "Weaker Trades"

The development of a doctrine of trade union "freedoms" did not go uncontested. A minority of unions wanted to make parts of the wartime regulatory machinery permanent. They supported both a greater role for government and TUC oversight of collective bargaining procedures. They represented what was called "the weaker trades," that is, industries and occupations where the absence of industry organization or fragmented ownership structures made bargaining difficult, or simply trades where workers' lack of skills provided the unions with little leverage against employers. These unions benefited from state action and confederational centralization, which allowed them to compensate for their economic weakness. In the early discussions of reconstruction policies, the arguments of the "lesser trades" had found resonance with the stronger unions. A common fear of postwar deflation on the heels of a short inflationary boom, as in 1920, had caused more unions to be inclined to keep controls on wages. But as fears of deflation abated, support for the wage regulation machinery became limited to low-skill unions and those organizing in fragmented and poorly organized industries.

At the 1944 TUC annual congress, the Furnishing Trades Association and the General and Municipal Workers Union, both were unions that controlled less than half of their potential labor markets, staked out what later became the minority position. The two unions cosponsored a resolution calling for an extension of wartime wage-setting machinery after the war and of the trade boards that had been set up in various industries to set wages and facilitate industrywide planning. The unions also proposed that two wartime orders—the Essential Works Order and the Registration for Employment Order—be kept. The benefits to unskilled workers of the regulations were substantial. The first order, which covered nearly 6 million workers, provided them with job protection by guaranteeing that no one could be laid off from a job, except if a National Service officer granted permission. Even tardiness and or absenteeism as insufficient grounds for dismissal. Employers also had to guarantee workers' wages when production was halted temporarily. The second order provided workers with cash support in cases of relocation and could well have formed the basis for a comprehensive structural labor market policy providing workers with training and relocation services in peacetime.

The Furnishing Trades also proposed a resolution obliging the TUC leadership to take steps toward proposing "a national wage policy." It was carried by a majority vote, but the spokesman for the council, Sir Joseph Hallsworth, made it clear that the General Council would not consider itself bound by it. He took pains to point out that the TUC did not want to infringe on the principle of unfettered collective bargaining. If the unions could do it on their own, there should be no room for "State interference," he argued (TUC Report 1944, 237–239). Full-blown conflict erupted in 1946 between proponents and opponents of wage regulation machinery in connection with a proposal calling for a statutory minimum wage policy and for a national wage policy aimed at reducing of pay differentials. The proposal was defeated but deserves attention because it represented yet another attempt to formulate an approach to collective bargaining that would have put British wage determination on a path similar to that of Swedish wage policy. It proposed a uniform minimum wage standard (applying to both sexes) and obliged the General Council to prepare a report on "the means whereby a more satisfactory lasting and equitable wage standard can be achieved" (TUC Report 1946, 418). In support of the proposal, one speaker invoked a moral economy argument, calling the existing wage system "out of date" and daring the delegates "to tell me that the labourer's child eats less food than the skilled man's child." It implied that intraclass equity was a necessary supplement to the language of class justice. Some supporters argued in favor of linking wage setting to productivity improvements, anticipating an argument that the government began to lay out in 1947–1948 as part of its conversion to a Keynesian perspective stressing growth and macroeconomic stability.

The TUC leadership and the stronger unions emphatically opposed the proposals. Arthur Deakin from the TGWU (Bevin's old union) argued that they would drag down the wages of the better-paid workers, because the pay of the lowest and poorest industries would set the standard, and accused the proposal of being "water on the Tories' mill." Speaking on behalf of the TUC General Council, Hallsworth called it "naive." Despite the opposition of key trade union leaders, the resolution was only narrowly defeated on a card vote, with 57 percent opposed (TUC Report 1946, 422–424). This was perhaps the closest the TUC ever got to endorsing a road different from the one taken with regard to wage planning.

Similar issues were at stake in connection with the compulsory arbitration system created during the war. Some unions liked it, because it compelled employers to the bargaining table in response to any official trade union request for negotiations (TUC Report 1946, 369). Others did not like it, because it also compelled both unions and employers to abide by arbitration and thus raised the possibility that the stronger unions might see results obtained at the bargaining tables reduced by means of arbitration. More important, the order prohibited unofficial striking. Once again, a split occurred between the "weaker trades," which favored a system of compulsory arbitration, and the large unions.[30] But in this case, the government also wanted to keep the order. Apprehension about the influence of renegade groups, which Ernest Bevin referred to as "Trotskyist," was one reason given. Until 1951 the TUC General Council and the cabinet agreed to repeated extensions of the order. The agreement put the TUC in an awkward position. At successive annual congress meetings, the TUC General Council was forced to defended the order at the same time as it also reiterated the commitment to voluntarism. In 1951 the compromise broke down when two industrial conflicts—in which Communists allegedly played a role—caused the government to use the order to prosecute union activists.[31] Pressured from below, the TUC General Council demanded that the government rescind the order immediately. On August 1, 1951, the temporary extension of Order 1305 was replaced by a new order eliminating the penal provisions of the old one. It created a new Industrial Disputes Tribunal that made arbitration voluntary. The tribunal was subsequently rescinded by a Conservative government in 1958. The majority at the 1951 congress followed the lead of the TUC General Council in defending voluntarism and attacking the Labour government (TUC Report 1951, 232 and 512). When it was clear that the "weaker trades" had failed to translate beneficial wartime regulations to peacetime, the minority spoke bitterly about the "soap-box oratory" of the large trade unions and denounced their constant demands for "freedom of action" (TUC Report 1951, 508).

Disunity and the Collapse of the Reform Government

In practice the compromise between the TUC and Labour leaders allowed the retention of wartime restrictions on trade union activities and helped shield the government from full exposure to the implications of the voluntarist principle in the years between 1945 and 1950. Wage policy became a matter of great concern first in 1947 in connection with the debt crisis and then again in 1949 with the currency crisis that resulted in devaluation. Once government policies shifted toward the emphasis on fiscal policy and stabilization policy, which inevitably brought wages within the orbit of government policy, relations were increasingly strained.

The government secured the TUC's consent to two and half years of voluntary wage restraint, running from February-March 1948 to the end of 1950. When the first appeal was made the unions consented, but beginning in April 1949, with Cripps' presentation of the 1949 budget, disagreement smoldered between the unions and the Labour government as union opposition to austerity policies grew. A second appeal for wage restraint made in September 1949 in connection with the devaluation of sterling was met with the TUC's reluctant consent, and, in January 1950, the TUC General Council once more accepted strict limits on wage increases. This time consent was linked to an agreement that wage increases were permitted in step with increases in the cost-of-living index, a decision that recalled wartime parity policies with respect to incomes. Since the TUC had no direct role in wage determination, its consent reflected an agreement by trade union leaders to assume responsibility for persuading affiliated unions to stay within the specified guidelines. Union compliance was based principally on union self-discipline and the strength of deference to Labour's leaders. The continuance of the controversial wartime arbitration rules provided some additional guarantees of discipline, albeit increasingly ineffective ones as unions began to challenge the agreement.

Discontent resulted in a rebuke of the government's economic policies in the form of a resolution at the 1950 TUC annual congress demanding that steps be taken to control profits instead of wages and that all wage restraint policies be abandoned. The TUC General Council managed to defeat the resolution narrowly, but the opposition had the last say anyway when the General Council's report was voted down because of its support for the Labour government's economic policies. This meant that the TUC in effect went into opposition against its own government (TUC Report 1950, 467–473). The conflict ebbed as the government backtracked and on January 10, 1950, the date for the next election was announced. The election reduced Labour's parliamentary majority to eight seats. In October 1951 a Conservative government was formed, and for the next 13 years the Conservatives held power.

The rise in unauthorized strikes created an apparent dilemma for the TUC. The General Council's official report to its 1951 annual congress condemned "unofficial" striking; a difficult term to use since no rules existed distinguishing "unofficial" from "official" wage bargaining. The General Council meant to condemn industrial action taken against contracts negotiated by established union channels. The problem was that the General Council also opposed any disciplinary means for upholding those contracts. Striking pious tones, the General Council reported that "It came as a shock to many to be reminded of [the penal provisions against striking] last autumn in the unofficial strike of some gas maintenance workers. Strikes by a minority within a union against a settlement negotiated by the union undermine both union democracy and negotiating machinery it has taken years to build. But this reminder that strikers could be punished by law caused grave misgivings" (TUC Report 1951, 233). The contradictions of the General Council's position are clear when we consider that it repeatedly had agreed with Labour's leaders to extend the wartime order and yet had refused to consider rule changes that would have sustained trade union discipline. But at the same time, the trade unions embarked on a transformation that put control in the hands of local union leaders and undermined the TUC's authority as anything more than a political lobby for the trade unions and the trade unions' instrument for controlling the party. The entrenchment of the voluntarist principle opened the gate for a process of devolution within the trade unions that returned the TUC to its original state earlier in the century as "a mailbox" or a lobby organization for the unions (Batstone 1984).

Retrospectively, the accord that prevailed between the TUC General Council and the Labour government from 1945 to 1950 on wage policy was an aberration and was uncharacteristic of later relations, which inevitably deteriorated into acrimony. It also rested on unique foundations that soon proved nontransferable. A replay of the events at the 1950 TUC congress occurred at the 1969 TUC congress, this time with the TUC General Council cast as the instigator of the opposition to a Labour government's stabilization policies. The offending issue was a proposal to initiate

statutory regulation of industrial relations, which principally aimed to reduce strikes. The TUC General Council denounced the proposal as "a campaign against the trade unions" (Martin 1980, 308; TUC Report 1969, 72.)
By this time the trade unions had moved into a position of more or less
generalized opposition to the state and to whatever government was elected
to manage policy. Two years later the TUC recommended "civil disobedience" against a Conservative government, again because of proposed legislation that aimed to curb union autonomy.

Trials and Tribulations:
Postwar Industrial Relations Reform

Great Britain's postwar political history is littered with failed proposals to
broker a "social contract" among unions, employers, and governments
about the determination of incomes, investment, and growth. The collapse
of wartime corporatism implied that a new machinery had to be created
from scratch, this time in the face of strong union opposition to allow the
TUC a coordinating role and without the War Cabinet's special powers to
coerce results that failed to materialize from voluntary coordination.

A Conservative 1957 White Paper, *The Economic Implications of Full Employment,* restated the conclusions of Labour's 1948 White Paper on productivity and consumption, with added warnings of dire consequences if
wage restraint was not exercised. That year a Council on Prices, Productivity, and Incomes was established to review profits, wages, and salaries and
make pronouncements on the proper balance. Another currency crisis in
1961 caused the declaration of a "pay pause," a euphemism for a wage stop.
Without the means for enforcing it in the private sector, the "pay pause"
applied chiefly to the civil service and to industries under public ownership. A 1962 White Paper, *Incomes Policy: The Next Step,* proposed setting
numerical targets for permissible wage increases. A new board of experts,
the National Incomes Commission (NIC), was created to administer the
targets, which were set as 2 to 2.25 percent. Both public and private wage
settlements fell under the commission's jurisdiction, but since it could review wage agreements only retroactively, it had little influence on actual
wage developments (Fels 1972).

With the election in 1964 of a Labour government, the unions had an
incentive to mind macroeconomic stability. Hoping to avoid a repeat of
the 1950 situation, the TUC and the government signed an agreement, the
Joint Statement of Intent on Productivity, Prices, and Incomes, affirming
the essential links between wages and productivity increases. It aimed to
mimic continental "social partners" agreements and also to revive the economic reform agenda in place from 1947 to 1950. The institutional

cornerstone for the agreement was the creation of a corporatist planning commission, the National Economic Development Council (NEDC). It was a belated response to Labour's 1945 electoral manifesto's demand for a National Investment Board. The Conservative incomes commission from 1962 was replaced with another corporatist organization, the National Board for Prices and Incomes (NBPI). Like its predecessor, the board lacked enforcement power and was constrained to retroactive review of wage settlements because it observed the "voluntarist" principle and avoided direct interference with trade union control over wage determination. In 1966 another currency crisis once again led to another pay and price freeze; this one was different from previous control policies only in that wages and prices were treated as functionally equivalent types of incomes. After an extension, two years later the "freeze" was replaced by less restrictive targets for permissible wage increases to be supervised by NBPI, whose supervisionary capacities were marginally enhanced.

Labour made another attempt at a "social contract" with the publication in January 1969 of a White Paper, *In Place of Strife,* which the unions quickly decided was abhorrent. The paper recommended the creation of a new compulsory arbitration framework, an industrial relations court system (tribunals) with statutory powers to order workers back to work for a mandatory waiting, or "cooling-off," period. The result of the deliberations of the 1965 Donovan Commission, the paper reflected an emerging bipartisan consensus (Metcalf 1988, 246–274). In 1967 dock strikes exacerbated an unfolding currency crisis that caused another devaluation of sterling. Strikes had undermined the wage "freeze." The sense was that the unions were transgressing beyond legitimate boundaries, and a new willingness emerged on the part of Labour's leaders to modify the protected status of the unions.

Nothing came of the proposal. Faced with protests and threats from the TUC to initiate civil disobedience—a choice of action that owed much to contemporary American antiwar protests—the bill was withdrawn. The attempt to impose legal curbs on the unions was badly timed, it turned out, because it coincided with a generational change within the unions. Two union leaders, Hugh Scanlon from the engineers' and Jack Jones from the transport workers' union, had recently risen to national prominence and were determined to make their mark (Jones 1986). It was a turning point in the relationship between the Labour Party and the trade unions. Ominously, it coincided with an international wave of trade union militancy and a neo-Marxist revival on the left (Crouch and Pizzorno 1978). Opposition to the proposal became a stepping-stone for the reassertion of militant trade unionism and trade union control over the party, and hence precipitated rather than halted the Labour Party's problems with voters (Coates and Topham 1986).

In the 1970 election, many Labour voters stayed home and a Conservative government, headed by Edward Heath, assumed power. The Heath government passed legislation very similar to that opposed by the unions under the previous Labour government, the Industrial Relations Act (1971), which made collective wage agreements legally enforceable. The act implied a new legal theory of industrial relations, which favored some degree of trade union centralization and a clear demarcation between "authorized" and "unauthorized" wage bargaining. But when the government responded to threatening hyperinflation by initiating statutory incomes policy, the TUC decided on a policy of "noncompliance" and called for a one-day general strike, the first since 1926. Not surprisingly, the Conservative offensive produced reconciliation between the Labour Party leadership and the unions (Crouch 1977; Cronin 1979). Labour promised to repeal the 1971 act immediately upon return to government in exchange for the trade unions' support in the next election.

An election in February 1974 resulted in parliamentary deadlock with the Conservative Party controlling 297 seats and Labour, 301 seats. A second election, in October, produced a majority for Labour. The new Labour government, headed first by Harold Wilson (1974–1976) and then by James Callaghan (1976–1979), repealed the 1971 act, gave up on industrial relations legislation and negotiated a voluntary "social contract" along the lines of the 1964 joint statement, with the unions aiming to keep wages down in exchange for specific workplace reforms. In ten years, from 1964 to 1974, the attempts to discipline the unions had gone from a voluntary agreement to self-regulate to criminalization of certain types of industrial action and back again to a voluntary approach.

Had those trade union leaders party to the agreement been able to do as they intended, it might have worked. Instead, more strikes took place during the 1974 to 1979 Callaghan government than during the 1970 to 1974 Conservative government or, for that matter, during any time since the war (Durcan et al. 1983). Record high inflation signaled that voluntary wage restraint was not sufficient, and, prompted by a worsening economic crisis, in 1976 the International Monetary Fund demanded stricter austerity measures in exchange for a loan agreement. When the Callaghan government cut public expenditures and restricted the money supply in order to curtail inflation, the unions responded by accusing the government of breaking the 1974 compact. In 1978–1979 cutbacks in the public sector caused a strike wave among public sector workers that resulted in the infamous "Winter of Discontent," during which fuel shortages and strikes among hospital workers led to generalized public outrage (Coates and Topham 1986).

At 1978 annual Labour Party Conference, the unions rejected the government's incomes policy. The events presented a replay of 1950, with the unions once again going into opposition against a Labour government. In the June 1979 election for the European Parliament, the National Executive Committee—on which the unions held a majority—rejected the recommendations of the parliamentary groups and passed an electoral platform that made the Labour Party run on an isolationist platform in the upcoming election (Kogan and Kogan 1982). After the 1979 election, Margaret Thatcher became prime minister and embarked on a series of reforms that aimed to curb the unions, arguably with the support of a large share of working-class voters (Crewe and Särlvik 1983). In 1981 the Labour party split when a group of Labour members of Parliament created a new Social Democratic Party.[32] The arduous climb back from extremism ended in 1997 with the election of a Labour government under the leadership of Tony Blair, after 18 years of Conservative control of the government (Coates 1989; Whiteley 1983).

Conclusion: Institutional Structures and Reform

Many interesting observations can be—and have been—made about postwar stabilization policy. It was largely ineffectual because, in the absence of the direct involvement of unions and employer organizations, it relied on administrative retroactive controls. For that reason, very little difference existed between Conservative and Labour policies on the matter. Labour generally could count on cooperation from the unions a little longer than Conservative governments, but then Conservative governments were more inclined to rely on numerical targets for permissible increases. Wage policy was based on an irreconcilable mix of administrative controls with few penalties and industrial decentralization. In the absence of mechanisms for self-government and the direct involvement of the national confederations of employers, industry, and trade unions, policies for determining and administering wage and growth policies remained feeble. The third alternative, a dirigiste format in which the state sets targets for wages, investments, and growth, died with Cripps' failed efforts to transform the Board of Trade to a planning commission; an effort that failed before it even was tried and probably for a good reason. As the subsequent case studies show, the dirigiste option has succeeded only in France or in the context of weak industrial organization and extreme economic scarcity, where the state present the dominant element in a difficult reconstruction process.

The source of British "exceptionalism," if we take that to mean the failure of state-lead postwar economic development, is not that the British people have no capacity for corporatist, dirigiste, or societal approaches to planning. All have been tried and have worked under certain circumstances. Nor do we have cause to regard the failure of planning as a defining aspect of "exceptionalism"; planning failed elsewhere too. The real puzzle is that the elements of a cross-class compromise were present—the commitment to full employment, the welfare state—but no accord excited with respect to the necessity to preserve the central state capacities needed for executing state-centered economic management policies. Keith Middlemas (1991) points to "state failure" as the ultimate cause of the collapse of planning. By that he apparently means something close to the kind of "democratic failures" predicted by Alexis de Tocqueville, the occasions when reason fails in the face of public desires.

The "democratic failure" thesis accounts for the fact that Conservative governments did no better than Labour's. Yet it fails to take into account what in a comparative view emerges as Labour's unique failure to reconcile the unions' expectations with respect to wage gains with the party's political responsibility to accommodate long-term economic reform with day-to-day gains. Compared to the Swedish Social Democrats' willingness to confront trade union resistance to national wage policy for the sake of political power, the organizational and constitutional framework for postwar reform seems to have put the Labour elite at a disadvantage. The comparison points to a dysfunctional construction of party-union relations and to the weaknesses of majoritarian government with respect to consensual policymaking as important obstacles to lasting reform policies.

The Labour Party began in 1900 as the Labour Representation Committee, created by the unions primarily to sponsor trade unionists for election to Parliament. The party formally adopted a Socialist program in 1918 and began permitting individual party affiliation through local constituency parties. But it continued to be dominated by collective trade union affiliation. The unions controlled the majority of the votes on the Labour Party annual conference—the party's highest authority—by means of a complicated voting system based on block votes. The party constitution required the party leadership to cooperate with the unions represented by the national confederation, the Trades Union Congress. The stipulation caused some friction during the 1945 to 1950 Labour government's tenure with the unions complaining that they were not sufficiently involved.

The functioning of the union-party exchange hinged on the confederation's position in relation to the affiliated unions and the balance of power between the union-dominated National Executive Committee and the parliamentary party leaders. During the war years, the tight relationship among Bevin, Morrison, and to a lesser extent Attlee[33] worked to bridge conflict between the unions and the party. Likewise, the enhanced authority of the TUC General Council worked to provide trade union unity.

The systemic properties of the construction of power within the majoritarian system impinged also on the opportunities provided to Labour for programmatic adjustment. The 1951 election unfairly deprived Labour of a chance to return to office and correct mistakes made earlier, an adjustment process that the experience of the Swedish Social Democrats suggests was a ubiquitous aspect of the postwar reform process. The Labour Party entered the reconstruction process with the experience of government responsibility and a victory in war behind it, but without an evolved theory about how to reconcile political power and reform with trade unionism. Institutionally and practically, both the party and the trade unions had been transformed by the war-time experience. Programmatically, however, neither had yet embraced a pragmatic vision of how working-class interests could be made compatible with those of capitalism and industry, except in the context of a socialized economy.

Two observations can be made by way of a summary. First, Labour's capacity to reconcile program with policy was compromised by the party organization's institutional dependency on the unions, particularly on the issue of trade union restraints. And second, the unions' capacity to influence policy over the long haul was compromised by their dependence on Labour. In the absence of a national agreement on the mutual rights and responsibilities of employers and unions, government policy was limited to the pursuit of short-term stabilization objectives.

Alternative Trajectories and Comparative Conjectures

The logical hazards of counterfactual reasoning notwithstanding, thinking about alternative paths can help elucidate the contingencies of actual policy. Once central planning had failed, what could a national recovery program have looked like? Speculations about alternative paths are conjecture, but a possible path was the one staked out by the policies of Cripps and Beveridge. It was an unfeasible alternative because it was critically flawed in its assumptions about the dynamics of group-based mass democracy and exaggerated the capacities of the state in peacetime (Gamble 1997). A second alternative has already been touched upon, an "axis" between economists favoring wage planning and the "weaker trades." If the previous alternative can be called the "French" alternative, this one can be called the "Swedish" alternative. (For this line of argument, see Fulcher 1991.) The reason that it was doomed to fail was that neither group was in a position to dictate the policies of its side.

A third alternative, which makes larger allowances for trade union sentiments against state involvement in wage determination, would have taken British industrial relations along a West German or American path based on a sectionalist "productivity bargain" between high-wage industries and unions, entering into "pattern-setting" agreements between employers and unions. This solution may well have been mixed with some form of statutory wage setting, by regional wage boards, in the "weaker trades." Scholars have been inclined to compare Swedish and British industrial relations and to focus on the lost opportunity to plan industry standards by means of confederational centralization. In actuality, the German and U.S. pattern bargaining provided a closer "fit" to British patterns of unionization, and for that matter also to the divisions on the employers' side.

Causal explanations of British liberalism generally rest on one of two grounds: insurmountable class antagonisms or psychological reasons, be they naïveté, deceit, or national character. In my view none of these are acceptable. Between 1939 and 1945, class conflict gave way to collaboration and to a new "one-nation" rhetoric of citizenship, nurturing high hopes about class reconciliation after the war. The immediate impetus for deregulation of the control economy came from the trade unions and on the question of wage policy, where a deep split existed regarding the state's proper role in the regulation of industrial affairs. The economic planning strategy that emerged after 1947 differed significantly from what planners had envisioned a few years earlier. Strategy was adjusted to the realities of a conflict between domestic and international goals, and had to make do with means for planning that were under the government's control: the budget and forward planning of the economic activity level by means of fiscal and budgetary policies. The shift did not eliminate the vestiges of the control economy created to administer scarcity and economic autarky so much as it supplemented them. Successful stabilization policy presupposed the capacity to utilize the controls to douse excessive demand and fix the balance between domestic and international economic cycles. None of this would have been possible in the absence of the institutional innovations of the war economy.

FOUR

Sweden:
War and Economic Thinking

War and Economic Policy

Sweden's direct exposure to the European crisis began with the Finno-Russian Winter War in 1939. In December 1939 the Social Democratic Party, Socialdemokratiska Arbetareparti (or SAP), asked the Conservatives, the Liberals, and the Agrarians to join in a National Unity Government, which lasted until the summer of 1945. With the German occupation of Norway and Denmark in April 1940, Sweden became cut off from trade with most of the world. The international halt to world trade put the country in a state of near-autarky and caused shortages and rationing. Like Great Britain, Sweden has never been able to feed itself, and without imports, core industrial products such as gasoline, rubber, and petroleum products disappeared. Steel exports to Germany continued despite the risk, but they too were halted in 1944 when the government interceded in response to U.S. and British threats to blacklist Swedish companies after the war.

The Finnish War with the Soviet Union and the German occupation of Norway and Denmark had severe economic as well as psychological consequences for domestic politics and policy. Swedish opinion was naturally inclined to side with Finland against the Soviet Union, causing many Swedes to welcome Adolf Hitler's invasion of the latter country. The government steered a difficult course of neutrality. In 1941 it felt compelled to permit transit transport of soldiers between Germany and Norway, a decision that continued to cause hard feelings in many places long afterward.[1] The stream of refugees—Jews and members of the Danish and Norwegian resistance—helped turn public opinion toward the Allied forces. When the Allies pressed for an open declaration of support toward the end of the war, such a pronouncement was made. Ernst Wigforss, the

Social Democratic finance minister and chief architect of Sweden's path-breaking economic policies in the 1930s in response to the depression, bluntly admitted in later years that Sweden had to hurry to get on the right side in time (Wigforss 1954, 245).

At first glance, Sweden looks like a case that challenges the thesis that the warfare state was the progenitor of the welfare state. As a neutral country during the war, Sweden would not be expected to have developed a control economy comparable to that of belligerent countries. Second, Social Democratic control of government prior to the war and again after 1945 presents us with an alternative explanation of the origins of economic planning and equitable economic policies. This chapter argues otherwise. The Social Democrats were keenly aware of the need for expanded state capacities, if their social and economic objectives were to be realized, and many of the ideas that guided the construction of the postwar welfare state predated the war. Nevertheless, wartime state expansion produced the administrative and technological means for economic coordination. This was not a case of the state becoming adapted to social democratic ideas about planning, as much as it was the ideas that were adapted to the new opportunities presented by a recast state. This chapter describes wartime policies and institutions that became a mainstay of the post-1945 welfare state. Aspects of the adjustment process are described in chapter 5. The account is tailored to provide a comparative backdrop to the British case, with particular attention to the response of interest groups to the control economy and its reconciliation with forward national economic planning.

War Preparations

Emergency legislation, *Allmänna förfogandelagen,* was passed on June 21, 1939, which gave the government authority to promulgate administrative laws and call upon the private sector to assist the state in serving national interests.[2] A national planning department, *folkhushållningsdepartementet,* was set up together with regulatory boards for food, industry, fuels, trade, transportation, and price controls. A war reparations board was created that primarily benefited the exposed Swedish shipping industry. Military conscription was initiated and redirection of labor power to defense industries begun. As in the United Kingdom, national registration of labor market "reserves" (principally women, youth, and the unemployed) also was begun to facilitate manpower planning and recruitment to essential occupations. Labor shortage problems were particularly acute in agriculture and in the production of substitute fuels and heating materials, mostly sod. A planned economy grew up around the management of shortage, trade and price controls, and allocation of labor.

Compared to the United Kingdom, Sweden entered the war with less preparation; it lacked both a history of a comprehensive administrative machinery in a national emergency and any equivalent to the "Imperial Defense Commission" with ready-made plans for resource mobilization. At the start of the century, Sweden was still an exporter of raw materials caught in a predominantly low-growth agrarian economy. Early deliverance from the Great Depression and extraordinarily high growth rates from 1934 to 1938 had pulled the country out of economic slumber, a development process that the war halted only temporarily.

Sweden was neutral in World War I and had benefited from vigorous trade with the belligerent countries until 1917, when submarine warfare made the surrounding waters impassable. When the domestic harvest failed that same year, scarcities quickly reverberated throughout the economy. Animal feed shortages cut down animal and dairy production, resulting in acute food shortages. The experience of near famine left an indelible mark on agricultural policy, which for decades thereafter was guided by a blend of national apprehension with "preparedness" and a well-organized producer interest in maximum protection and government subsidy (Hedlund and Lundahl 1985). In 1940, Sweden was once again cut off from products the country depended on, such as bread flour, fuels, and potatoes.

The Controls

The list of wartime agencies ranged from a fuel office to specialized licensing offices and new health services. The regulatory commissions were organized on the principle of comprehensive involvement of interest groups and consultation between the regulated and the regulators. Each commission was headed by a group, drawn from the civil service, that formally made all decisions but did so in consultation with appointed representatives of sectional and social interest groups. Labor and business representatives were invariably present. In addition, many agency heads and office administrators were recruited from the ranks of experts and interest groups in industry. Where administrative structures already existed—as in the case of agriculture—they were enlarged and fortified with new authority commensurate to the tasks at hand.

Agricultural controls involved everything from dairy associations to meat processors and farm organizations. Fuel controls were administrated by the association of coal importers and the shipping committee, both of which had been created in 1939 for that purpose. Import controls were administered by roughly 50 importers' associations. In addition, a number of public companies were created to ensure supply of products, particularly fuels and oils (Åmark 1952, 101). The emergency powers act allowed the government to compel involuntary cartelization in industries that did not voluntarily set up "pools" for supply and distribution.

Foreign Trade

Foreign trade was tightly controlled and subject to licensing and currency regulations. In 1941 the government introduced a general prohibition against exports without license. Import regulation had been initiated two years earlier, motivated by the inflationary effect of rising world market prices on the domestic economy. The same year a complete price stop was put into effect. Price controls included not only goods—both suppliers' prices and retail prices—but also all kinds of services, rents, and fees. A general ban on usury pricing was imposed to empower the government to control black marketeering. Foreign currency shortages and the control economy in general necessitated strict control of foreign currency transactions. Clearing boards, which first had been set up in 1934 in the wake of the depression and the collapse of the gold standard, administrated currency controls. They matched payments between Sweden and the other countries with which it traded strictly on a parity basis. The controls had a lasting legacy.

Between 1947 and 1949, Swedish foreign trade policy relied on bilateral agreements and strict controls, including quotas on specific goods that aimed to secure "fair" trade. It aimed principally to protect the home market against the importation of inflation and to protect currency reserves. How much the emphasis on reciprocal agreements retarded foreign trade is unclear. The standard argument against mutual trade agreements is that the overall effect is to deter trade. Since most Swedish exports were concentrated in categories of raw materials that were in high demand in international markets, bilateralism may well have hurt only other categories of exports. It seems clear that, on balance, trade policy worked to steer domestic consumer demand away from imports and, hence, to protect domestic light industries against foreign competition without penalizing the traditional export industries. International agreements and the creation of the European Payments Union (EPU) in the summer of 1950 began to free Swedish trade from the rigid system of bilateral agreements, although controls on U.S. trade were not eased until 1954.

Manpower Planning

A new advisory Labor Market Commission, arbetsmarknadskommissionen (AMK), had been created in 1939 as a consultative board overseeing local labor exchanges. In 1934 the Social Democrats had wanted to eliminate or change the system that predated this commission in connection with an unemployment insurance reform, but the compromise with the Agrarian Party failed to do the desired reform.[3] The changes were made belatedly in 1939. A year later the system was expanded and a network of local and regional offices was put directly under the board, which was put in charge of the administration of a national service act that allowed civilian conscription to prioritized industries. The commission also was made responsible for the planning and administration of a manpower budget, registration of industries and workers, training programs, and the reallocation of labor power to industries with labor shortages. During the course of the war, the AMK grew from 100 to over 500 employees.[4]

In a history of the board, the Swedish political scientist Bo Rothstein observes that the 1940 reorganization of the national unemployment and relief work administration provided the Social Democrats with a new agency that they could trust, in contrast to the old one, which was regarded as hostile to labor's interests. But, curiously, Rothstein dismisses the idea that the war played a role in the reorganization. Instead he attributes the Social Democrats' success in getting the reform of the contested system and overcoming employers' and the center-right parties' entrenched resistance to reform of the administrative system to the assiduous preparations of a small group of influential policymakers. Rothstein aims to show the importance of policy elites in shaping state expansion over competing explanations and cites the opposition of the national trade union confederation, Landsorganisationen (LO), to the national service legislation as evidence that the crisis created by the war played no role (Rothstein 1996, 91). But union opposition to national service did not prevent it from happening, nor for that matter did it prevent wage stabilization. The more interesting aspect is that the center-right's assertion of liberal principles was equally ineffective in preventing policy changes.

The board's activities included the registration of essential manpower and manpower "reserves" among youth, women, and retirees. Essential occupations included agriculture and the production of charcoal made from sod, a fuel substitute for oil and gasoline. Unemployment had been eliminated in the first years of the war in response to military conscription, which took part of the workforce away from industry—a reduction of approximately 15 percent—and to increased war production, which added to the demand for labor. AMK activities became increasingly focused on redirecting and retooling workers to priority industries, including the training of women for skilled jobs in the manufacturing industry. The wartime expansion of the board's activities was made permanent by new enabling legislation passed in 1947, which set up a successor agency, the statens arbetsmarknadsstyrelse (AMS).

Wage Stabilization

Wages were set by contracts negotiated by employers and unions but backed up by regulation that stipulated that all workers were to be paid contractual wages. Technically, the government did not interfere with wage setting, but from 1941 onward it persuaded employers and unions to extend existing contracts and tie wage increases to the government's price indices measuring inflation. The national confederations of employers, Svenska Arbetsgivareföreningen (SAF), and the LO negotiated annual contracts called "indexation agreements," which listed adjusted wage rates. Notably, both the government and the national confederations avoided a formal commitment to statutory wage fixing, allowing instead the interest organizations the authority to announce pay rates.

In Britain, the Treasury's preference for statutory wage stabilization policy by means of tying wages to the cost-of-living index had come up against the production ministries' wish to use performance pay schemes to boost productivity and attract labor to armament industries and coal. No comparable conflict existed in Sweden, and national wage stabilization policy prevailed. Wartime wage policy nevertheless still affected the relative balance between various occupations and industries. Agricultural wages were exempted from the stabilization requirement and permitted to increase ahead of the price index. The argument was that better pay would prevent agricultural workers from taking advantage of tight labor markets and shift into better-paid occupations. Even if the confederations formally were responsible for setting wages, their capacity to set priorities was suspended by the automatic adjustments provided for by means of indexation. Statutory regulation of working hours was another breech of trade union prerogatives.

Wartime wage-control policies were sorely tested by a six-month strike that began before the war was over, from February to July 1945. (The strike is discussed in greater detail in chapter 5.) It involved 125,000 machine-industry workers, most from the engineering union, Metall, and was the largest strike to take place since a 1909 general strike. In the war's tight labor market and with agricultural and forestry workers allowed higher raises than other groups, a realignment of relative wage differentials took place to the disadvantage of some groups, particularly skilled industrial workers, and the advantage of low-paid groups, including women. The 1945 strike worked to underline the political difficulties associated with wage planning, if it was applied to the disadvantage of the more resourceful groups.

The strike was in violation of antistriking rules and was concluded only after the LO intervened, pressed by the Social Democratic party, and forced the union to accept an arbitration settlement that a majority of the strikers voted down. The strike caused the LO to pass a resolution that officially condemned state interference in wage determination, and in 1945 both unions and employers agreed that free bargaining had to be reestablished as quickly as possible. The unions saw immediate economic advantages to decontrol, whereas SAF regarded a breakout from the restraints of the war economy to be important mostly for strategic reasons (De Geer 1986, 108). As a consequence, any extension of wartime wage policy after the end of the war was made politically impossible.

Industry

Industry's needs and interests were assigned to a national commission for industry, chiefly concerned with the planning and direction of industry's need for raw materials and other resources. A staff of technical experts and appointees was recruited from industry and organized into functionally defined and industry-specific sections, including, for example, a statistical section. The head of the Industrial Control Commission was Gustaf Söderlund, who was also director of the employers' association. Through Söderlund's involvement, business came to sponsor wartime economic planning. In 1942 he presented a memorandum on economic policy that staked out a consensual approach to wartime regulation. It reinforced that inflation control was the chief policy objective and stressed the need to prevent subversion of the Swedish krona. It also supported the government's choice of methods, listing tight price controls, wage controls, and tight monetary policies as the main measures for stabilization.

A planning section was added to the Commission in 1945. In 1946, it was reorganized again when the War Productions Section and other sections related to specific wartime issues were closed down. In 1950 the remaining sections were combined with the remains of the wartime trade board into a unified industry and trade commission.

Agriculture

Wartime agricultural policy built on depression-era policies, employing the principle of more of the same: fixed prices designed to encourage agricultural production, rationing, subsidies, and higher wages for agricultural workers to keep them on the land. Food controls were administrated by a newly created agency, Statens livsmedelskommission (LK), which also was in charge of subsidies and import/export licenses for agricultural products in general (fertilizers, seeds). Separate agencies were created for particularly sensitive products, including potatoes and coffee. Some 1,751 local control agencies were created to monitor compliance (Åmark 1952, 72). In 1946 some of the controls were lifted and the agencies reduced in size.

Economic Forecasting and Keynesian Budgeting

The Institute for Economic Research—Konjunkturinstitutet—which had been set up in 1937, was another depression-era agency that moved to center stage in the course of the war. The institute began publishing regular economic surveys and analyses in the last years of the war and continued doing so after 1945 under the direction of Erik Lundberg, a Keynesian economist. It provided the government and the confederations of labor and employers with seasonal economic forecasts of aggregate demand and market conditions, forecasts that formed the basis for stabilization policy.

A debate has sprung up regarding the sources of Social Democratic economic theories (Hall 1989; Weir and Skocpol 1985). Did they or did they not reach their conclusion independently of the ideas of J. M. Keynes? Keynes' *General Theory* was published in 1936, but ideas challenging liberal orthodoxy had inspired circles of new economic thinking in Cambridge, Stockholm, and Vienna since the 1920s. Bertil Ohlin (1972, 166), an internationally known economist who in 1944 became chairman of the Liberal party, has claimed that he was inspired by the thinking of other Swedes rather than by Keynes, and cited the early publication dates of key articles by Swedes, including work by Knut Wicksell and the young Gunnar Myrdal as proof.

While Social Democratic economic policy theory has some affinities with Keynes' work, it also has some important differences. The emphasis on social coordination as a way to compensate for the weaknesses of the market economy is an important parallel, as is the dislike of public ownership. The Social Democrats did not believe that deficit spending constituted responsible government policy. Ohlin (1972, 219) goes as far as to claim that Keynes' ideas regarding deficit spending as a countercyclical tool played no role in Swedish policy. Ernst Wigforss had believed since 1924 that underconsumption and low wages were the roots of the depression. He also believed that government spending could make up for the lack of private consumption and help bring about a return to growth. Although inspired by Marxist economic theories, his conclusions were similar to those of a diverse group of Swedish economists belonging to what became known as the Stockholm School. Despite the protestations of Swedish economists, they were part of an international discussion in which Keynes' influence was immense.

War Controls and State Expansion: The Swedish Case

This discussion has pointed to striking similarities between the administrative structures of British war controls and those created in Sweden. The Swedish machinery differed in that it was smaller and more oriented toward inflation control and rationing and less oriented toward industrial development and the reconciliation of military and industrial needs. Yet it is clear that the crisis itself, with the combination of a security threat and an international halt to foreign trade, brought on both state expansion and an enhancement of the state's capacities. Certain aspects of the machinery even assumed comparable forms in both countries, particularly the coupling of national interest organizations to activities of the central state and the state's penetration of local government and administration.

Civil service employment growth matched the precipitous growth of government agencies. General government personnel doubled between 1930 and 1945, expanding by some 100,000 new employees. It is noteworthy also that no overall reduction in government personnel took place after the war, from 1945 to 1950. General government personnel continued to expand in absolute numbers, although the number remained stable when measured as a share of the workforce. The numbers—close to 4 percent of the workforce—were still small in an international comparative perspective (Flora, Kraus, and Pfenning 1987, 230). The expansive and generous welfare state for which Sweden would later be renowned did not exist yet.

Interest Organizations

In 1914, at the outbreak of World War I, national interest organizations were few and mostly weak. Three-fourths of the population still lived in localities with fewer than 2,000 inhabitants; the majority was still engaged in agriculture or related occupations. Modern political institutions developed comparatively late. The incorporation of farm interests as a cohesive national interest organization got under way during the Great Depression. The primary farm organization, Riksförbundet Landsbygdens Folk (RLF), was created in 1929–1930. National organizations of meat processors and dairies were created in 1932–1933. Industry lagged behind farmers with respect to national organization. Cartelization and firm mergers burgeoned between 1914 and 1920, but associational activity was largely confined to workers (Heckscher 1946, 136).

The first organization of employers was the engineering employers' association, Verkstadsföreningen (VF), created in 1896 in response to the challenge of unionization. A number of crafts-oriented machine tool industry unions had merged in 1888 to create an industrywide iron and metal workers union, a precursor to Metall. The Swedish national employers' federation, SAF, was created in 1902 and negotiated the first national agreement with the Swedish trade unions in 1906. Despite an early beginning, the employers' association remained weak and unable to compel employers to coordinated action. The large companies, the "families," that controlled the key Swedish export industries—paper and paper pulp, iron and metal—were reluctant to tether themselves to organizations encompassing a large number of smaller employers. They worked through their own special interest organization, Direktörsklubben, or "the Big Five," which was active from 1933 to 1953.[5]

James Fulcher (1991, 74) contends in his comparative study of British and Swedish industrial relations that SAF was highly centralized "from its earliest years." This is an accurate characterization, if one looks at organizational charts, but it does not consider SAF's weak membership basis, nor the fact that at the time the organization routinely was criticized by its members for being powerless (De Geer 1986, 23). In 1935 more than 1 million workers belonged to unions affiliated with the LO. In contrast, the employers' association had only about 2,500 members representing 300,000 organized workers, less than one-third of the LO's membership, and the organization competed with other organizations for license to represent business interests. Until 1930 SAF employed roughly 40 people in its national headquarters, including drivers, secretaries, and other staff.

The organization was headed in the 1920s by Hjalmar von Sydow, a lawyer and since 1916 the leader of the Conservative Party in the upper house of Riksdagen. In 1931 he was replaced by Gustaf Söderlund, who oversaw the organization's modernization and increasing collaboration with both government and the trade unions. (Until 1939 the SAF chairman was also its executive director.) In 1935 Söderlund put distance between SAF and the Conservative Party's effort to criminalize striking by opposing legislation and inviting the unions to negotiate a private framework for industrial regulation. He also refused a position in the Conservative Party; thereafter SAF strove to maintain partisan independence, albeit not to stay out of politics. The political interests of the Conservative Party in exploiting the ideological aspects of the conflict clashed with the interests of SAF in getting a resolution that preserved organizational capacities.

Organization was based on principles of indirect representation. Firms took out membership in either an industry or a regional organization, which in turn affiliated with the national confederation. Firms that did not naturally belong in either of these two types belonged to a general group affiliated with the national association similar to the industry associations. Numerically more important, the national confederation tended to be dominated by small and medium-size businesses. Rule changes in 1928 and 1948 were intended to strike a compromise between large and small employers; they produced a complicated internal structure, based on weighted voting blocs that corrected for industry differences.[6] The political and organization cleavages within businesses mirrored the fault lines that also split British business organizations: Small versus large industries disagreed on how to deal with labor; export-oriented and home-market–oriented businesses disagreed on the focus of economic policy.

From 1935 onward the confederation of employers emerged as the more important business organization. In part, this reflected the greater weight of small and medium-size businesses within the business community and their interest in forming a common front against labor and in avoiding wage competition. In part, it was also a reflection of government policies that encouraged the organization of employers. Still, by 1945 the organizational makeup of industry and business interest representation was fluid and the reforms needed to shape a coherent "social partner" were far from complete.

Until it became involved in the determination and administration of wartime wage indexation agreements, SAF's primary activity was the administration of a strike fund, which for years was financed by a flat-rate levy on all members. Since the number of days lost to industrial conflict (strikes or lockouts) varied greatly from industry to industry, peaceful industries subsidized the conflict-ridden ones. This was a source of great friction. The textile industry, for example, complained that it lost some 5 million krona between 1911 and 1927 to strike-prone industries. The paper pulp industry, which was strike-prone, complained that it had been left to fend for itself in its 1932 strike and had not received enough support from the confederation. This became an issue again in 1945, when the large engineering employers' association, VF, accused other employers of leaving the association alone to stem "the Communist threat" in connection with an engineering workers' strike.

The Origins of Corporatism: A Controversy

No agreement exists on the origins of corporatism or its essential characteristics. Bo Rothstein (1992b) dates its origins to late-nineteenth-century political mobilization prior to the breakthrough of popular democracy. In 1966 another Swedish political scientist Nils Elvander undertook a survey of 19 major national organizations and pinned corporatism on the development of postwar stabilization policy. In his view, the development of a corporatist infrastructure was "above all a question of creating a broad consensus around the idea of the pre-eminence of macro-economic balance" (1990, 2), and corporatist organizations were "campaign institutions" used by governments to persuade social groups to mind national interests.

The pioneer study of corporatism was Gunnar Heckscher's *The State and the Organizations* (1946). Heckscher stressed the recent nature of what he called "organized society." He noted the superficial similarity between the role organizations play in modern industrial democracies and in fascist or nineteenth-century societies, but argued that mid-twentieth century Sweden had the better claim to the corporatist label. Here, self-governing associations collaborated voluntarily with the state. In fascist Italy, in contrasts, the associations were subsumed by the state. Heckscher also argued that between the Great Depression and the end of the war in 1945, both the state and the associations expanded their activities (1946, 220–221). In other words, rather than a zero-sum game between state and associations, the new corporatism presents both states and associations with an opportunity to expand. Collectivism worked to insert class and/or sectional organizations between the state and the individual, strengthening both state and organizations at the cost of the individuals role in politics. Heckscher explicitly rejected the thesis—recently revived by Rothstein—that nineteenth-century associations were forerunners of twentieth-century corporatism. The former were the result of the independent decision of the groups to pursue a common interest in "fixing" problems of mutual interest, while the latter was motivated by self-defense against legal regulation. In his view, the 1938 agreement between unions and employers on self-regulation marked the beginning of modern corporatism.

The admittedly arcane controversy speaks to an important question: Do we look to states or to society for the causal impulse for corporatist organization and collaboration? Elvander's thesis about corporatism as "campaign institutions" tied corporatism to a stabilization policy and, hence, implies that organization is a response to state-action. Heckscher also pointed to the state; Rothstein to society and tradition. No intrinsic reason exists to reserve the term for twentieth-century interest group coordination, except that this is the narrower and more traditional understanding of the term (Schmitter 1974). The ubiquitous role of the war controls and postwar stabilization policy in stimulating growth and consolidation of national interest organizations in both the Swedish and the British cases suggests that state capacity—the state's will and ability to exercise power—is a central aspect of corporatism. Likewise, the resistance on the part of organized interests in both countries to dirigiste policies—policies where the civil servant makes the decisions to be executed by societal organizations—suggests that the boundary between private and public power is both malleable and variable. Where the line is drawn is not a trivial question. Corporatism has eluded systematic theorizing in part because it is variable. At stake is the autonomy of societal groups from the organization of state power. While this may be a matter of great principle, it is also a matter of practical importance. What hangs in the balance is not only the capacity to plan wages and pricing policies, for example, but also large questions about industrial development.

Decontrol, Recontrol, and Postwar Reconstruction

The emergency powers act from June 21, 1939, was extended annually until 1949. That year the act was revised and extended until 1952. The revised legislation permitted the government to impose controls on economic activity, including appropriation, as justified by "national need." Not surprisingly, opponents charged that the government was less motivated by national concerns than by a desire to use the legislation to further the creation of a planned economy. Nevertheless, the wartime planning department was closed down in 1950. For the duration of the controls, the government published a comprehensive annual list of all rationing measures and controls. The list increased each year until it reached its maximum length in 1944. This suggests that in contrast to the United Kingdom, where controls were added even as the war drew to a close, Sweden initiated some decontrol at an earlier stage (Sweden 1944a). Yet the difficulties associated with the reestablishment of world trade after 1945 prolonged the life of many wartime controls on foreign currency and on trade. The general price "freeze" was stayed from 1945 to 1947; in cases where decontrol took place in 1945, controls sometimes were brought back in response to the 1947 currency crisis. The general prohibition on unlicensed imports was reinstated, for example, as part of a control package designed to reestablish stability.

The 1939 price control policy lived on in shape of the price control board, statens priskontrollnämnd (PKN), set up in 1947. Henceforth price "freezes" were renewed for six months at a time. Joined with wage control measures, price freezes entered the standard repertoire for postwar inflation control, making the price control agency one of the most important administrative postwar legacies. In 1950 part of the board's authority was transferred to the national bank, which became the clearinghouse for currency transactions, but many of the controls on banking and capital movement lasted in modified form until deregulation gained speed in the 1980s. As was the case with the British war controls, the first postwar extension of the controls boards and technologies was decided even before the war's end and justified by the prediction of continued consumer shortages, shortages of foreign currency, and fears of deflation. Within 18 months, inflation moved into focus as the main problem for stabilization policy, and the physical controls of foreign trade, currency trade, and the price controls merged gradually into postwar stabilization policy. (Wage stabilization is discussed in chapter 5.)

Gunnar Myrdal and Postwar Planning

In 1944 the Commission for Postwar Economic Planning was established under the chairmanship of Gunnar Myrdal, perhaps Sweden's most internationally famous economist. The commission formally ceased its work in 1954, but its main importance rested on the predictions about postwar economic development that Myrdal put forward in its name. The commission became controversial, in no small part because of Myrdal's role. Created by the coalition government, it was supposed to express the views of all parties. Myrdal did build on bipartisan support for demand-side management and the need to help businesses in order to bring about economic expansion, but, in practice, the commission reflected above all his own ideas.

The 1944 commission continued work begun by an earlier commission, known as the Unemployment Inquiry, Arbetslöshetsutredning, which produced an exceptional number of empirical studies and theoretical expositions on a "New Economics" between 1928 and 1935. Many of the authors were identified with the Stockholm School, as the "New Economics" was also called; among them were both Gunnar Myrdal and Bertil Ohlin. Swedish postwar planners had reason to be optimistic about the reconstruction process and postwar prospects for the country's economic development. Many of its traditional export industries could be expected to supply sorely needed materials to rebuild Europe. But even so, consensus among the economists held that "the chief matter for concern was the risk that demand would not be adequate to maintain a high level of economic activity and employment" (Lundberg 1957, 57).

The Great Depression and a "New Economics"

The intellectual lineage of the emphasis on demand management went back to the Unemployment Inquiry. Begun in 1928, the Inquiry predated the Great Depression, but its work was shaped entirely by that economic crisis and by the 1933 Crisis Agreement between a Social Democratic minority government and the Agrarian Party.[7] On April 7, 1933, the so-called cow trade was formed between the two parties. (The pact originated the so-called Red–Green alliance between the working class and farmers, or rather between their elected representatives.) In his published notes Ernst Wigforss (1954, 37) lists the core elements of the agreement. Reflation was to be achieved by raising wages and agricultural prices in concert. For the sake of parity across the classes, business was promised help too. In addition, the national economy was to be stimulated by means of cheap credit, currency depreciation, and protectionist measures ranging from tariffs to subsidies. In the absence of the means for directly raising wages, policy focused on alleviating unemployment. Public works projects, ranging from construction to increased logging, and improved unemployment assistance were proposed. Cartelization was to be encouraged in order to sustain prices. State credits to the Soviet Union and Finland aimed to help agricultural exports. The formation of government monopolies for the purchase and sale of certain consumer goods—gasoline, spirits, and coffee—also was discussed. The chief aim of these monopolies—aside from satisfying the political aspirations of a strong temperance movement—was to raise government revenues.

The agreement portended the postwar welfare state in many aspects and has been presented widely as an instance of "Keynesianism before Keynes" (Gourevitch 1986; Weir and Skocpol 1985). The accuracy of this characterization is placed in doubt by the obvious influence J. M. Keynes had on contemporary Swedish economists. The latter were not acquainted with Keynes' not-yet-published *General Theory,* but they were well informed about his other writings. More importantly, it also can be questioned how "Keynesian" Swedish policy actually was. Swedish economist Erik Lundberg has argued that the government's chief accomplishment was to maintain moderation in economic policy.[8] In a similar vein, another well-known Swedish economist Assar Lindbeck (1974, 23) points out that fiscal policies were as expansionary in 1930 to 1932 as they were in 1932 to 1934; in other words, fiscal expansion was not a significant factor. Lindbeck concludes that Sweden's quick recovery from the depression was a matter of fortuitous external circumstances or, simply, luck.

Still, the general belief that Swedish policies presented an alternative to both British monetarist orthodoxy—exemplified by the 1931 split in the Labour Party—and the protectionist and cartelistic policies of German economist Hjalmar Schact, who took control of creating a planned economy after the National Socialists took over power in 1933, is obviously valid (Gourevitch 1986; Luebbert 1991). The main achievements of the Swedish government in 1932 to 1936 may well have been political rather than economic. In December 1931 unemployment among trade union members had reached 26.5 percent. The depression had greatly diminished foreign demand for Swedish exports, and a series of drawn-out strikes had made industrial relations an explosive issue.

The Unemployment Inquiry published a total of 150 reports, memoranda, and supplements.[9] The economic program that emerged from its work went far beyond temporary stabilization measures. It delineated what was, in effect, a program for rapid industrialization and modernization of the economy. Some of the committee's ideas were not yet possible, principally for political reasons. On the issue of fiscal expansion, for example, the committee presented a comprehensive theory of countercyclical government action written by Gunnar Myrdal (Sweden 1934a). He laid out a cautious program stressing "good" housekeeping principles and the importance of a sound approach to government finances but also recommended that the national budget be used to adjust the economy on a regular basis. In fact, prewar economic policy did not utilize these ideas. The public works programs that were part of the crisis agreement were financed by loan-taking and special budgets. Good housekeeping principles also were used to argue for government crisis programs. The government would save money in the long run, it was argued, because it would get to do necessary construction during the slump when costs were lower.

The Unemployment Inquiry was prescient in many respect but had its feeble moments too. Its concept of the business cycle bordered on the mystical. A symmetrical relationship was presumed to exist between the cycle's peaks and the valleys; the higher the peaks, the lower the valleys. Hence, policy should aim not only to fill in the valleys but also to iron out the peaks. Myrdal, in particular, had very high expectations of economists' ability to time policy interventions precisely. He rejected outright the idea that government action would have inflationary consequences. The contraction that would take place when the government began to pay back loans was considered not only necessary for prudent reasons but also desirable fiscally because it would help "straighten out" the business cycle (Sweden 1934a, 272). Myrdal later changed his mind about this particular aspect of business-cycle theory. (See Sweden 1944c, 93.)

A frugal streak ran through many reports and policy recommendations. One report, from 1933, produced by the Agricultural Ministry, suggested that the government send the unemployed—who in any case were already being paid by public money—out in the woods to collect firewood and bark, which were of no use to the lumber industry (Sweden 1933a). That, it was argued, would encourage the substitution of expensive imported fuels, primarily coke and coals, with cheap domestic products and at the same time help the country save foreign currency and reduce unemployment.

Sweden was, at the time, still an economically backward country, dependent in large measure on expensive imports of consumer goods and other goods for which it paid by exporting raw materials. It was this state of economic backwardness, as much as the depression itself, that the Inquiry aimed to address. The Inquiry's primary achievement was the formation of a sophisticated new view of the relationship between wages and economic development that paved the way for the eventual development of a national wage policy that aimed to enhance productivity and further national economic growth. It nevertheless was wartime scarcities that gave birth to the innovations in government technologies and the concentration of state power required to realize the economic development program laid out by the economists in the 1930s.

Wages and National Economic Development

The Unemployment Inquiry's work departed from contemporary liberal orthodoxy by concluding that short-term wage reductions were not desirable (Sweden 1935a, 69).[10] The summary report was written by Dag Hammerskjöld, the Inquiry's secretary, who after the war became secretary general of the United Nations. It stated that short-term wage reductions were undesirable but was sensitive to the problem of inflation by recommending that wages be restrained at the peak of the business cycle, once a recovery took place. Alf Johansson, an economist, who wrote the key report on wages and unemployment, explained underconsumptionist theory at great length. He showed how wage reductions were accompanied by even greater contractions in demand and therefore accelerated rather than alleviated the crisis. He accepted that (high) wages played a role in cyclical unemployment and thus that wage reductions would be more harmful than helpful during cyclical downturns (Sweden 1934b, 100). Bertil Ohlin, also an internationally known economist, had no more patience with orthodoxy and the view that high wages were the cause of recession. Claiming that wages were "too high" was, in his opinion, as meaningless as stating that management was "too bad," investments "too scant," or pricing policies "too monopolistic" (Sweden 1934c, 156). In this case, economic theory helped pave the way for bipartisan consensus on economic policy.

The Inquiry helped shift Social Democratic economic policy toward an embrace of a "politics of productivity," which held out the promise of shared economic growth as an alternative to the traditional Socialist demand for shared ownership and socialization of the means of production (Maier 1987). In a report on economic rationalization and unemployment, the economist Gustaf Åkerman developed his argument for structural change as a source of increased wealth for workers and for employers (Sweden 1931c). In place of the Marxist explanation of the crisis, Åkerman's theory linked rationalization and productivity increases to positive gains for both employers and workers; if employers and unions could agree to work together, lower unit prices and higher wages would present rewards for both.

Henceforth, the official Social Democratic position changed. It was a small step intellectually—albeit a difficult one practically—to move on to the view that wage increases had a positive effect on economic efficiency and long-term growth. This view was later elaborated in a 1951 trade union report that became known as the Rehn-Meidner doctrine. (The English title was *Trade Unions and Full Employment*.) In the 1930s it was still only a theory suggesting policies that aimed to change the character of Swedish economic relations with foreign markets. At the time, the government had neither the means for influencing national wage policy nor collaboration from employers.

The emphasis on growth helped bring about a reformulation of union views on capitalist "rationalization," or what British unions called "the Machine Question," by which was understood the release of labor caused by enhanced productivity (Johansson 1989, 103–116). Union resistance to "the machine" reappeared during the war in connection with the question of "dilution," which in part was a question of allowing new production technologies mastered by semiskilled workers to replace skilled craftsmen. The Swedish unions' early espousal of productivity improvement as a source of growth and higher incomes for workers set them apart from British unions that remained stuck on the "machine-question."

Foreign Trade and Economic Development

It is notable that foreign trade attracted relatively little of the committee's attention. Exports were determined to be entirely dependent on foreign markets and consequently outside the reach of Swedish policymaking. The export industries therefore entered policy theory only as an independent variable. The final report reiterated the Inquiry's general conclusion that Sweden was a price-taker in international markets and that domestic wages played a minimal role in determining the level of exports. Swedish imports typically contained a high content of labor while exports did not, exchanging low-value added for high-value added goods. If wage costs were lowered relative to other costs of production—through investment and improved productivity—unit prices would fall and presumably Sweden would be able to reduce imports by means of import substitution.

In a historical perspective, the work of the Inquiry continues to attract attention because it provided the outlines of a high-wage and high-value-added development that stressed state capacities and the deliberate insulation of the domestic economy from the disruptive effects of international market fluctuations. A key phrase called for the creation of an "economic space" for independent countercyclical policy. (The Swedish expression was "det ekonomiske utrymmet för en självständig konjunkturgestaltning"; see Sweden 1935a, 35). The Unemployment Inquiry's greatest achievement was to present a new public philosophy of proto-Keynesian hue that was tailored uniquely to Swedish needs and circumstances.

During the last part of 1933 economic activity picked up again, and by 1936 Sweden had come out of the recession. By the end of the 1930s, unemployment had reached the lowest levels ever, roughly 8 to 9 percent. A comparative analysis of government spending in the 1930s puts the crisis program in perspective. In 1930 general government spending accounted for only 14 percent of the Swedish gross domestic product (GDP); defense accounted for 11 percent and social services for 46 percent of general government spending. At the time, the "big government" label could be better used to describe the spending patterns of the British and German states than that of Swedish state. General government spending amounted to close to 25 percent of GDP, in both Britain and Germany. While the British spent 16.4 percent of that on defense and only 36 percent on social services, the Germans—who were prevented by the stipulations of the World War I peace agreement from military buildup and spent only 3.7 percent on defense—spent 51.0 percent on social services. (Figures are based on Flora, Krauss, and Pfenning, 1987, chap. 8.) During the depression years, Swedish public spending increased at a moderate rate. Meanwhile, liberal orthodoxy informed British cutbacks and a course of steady deflation.

Exchange Rate Policy

The British economic historian, Donald Winch (1989, 119), has pointed out that a big difference between Britain and Sweden was that the Swedish Social Democrats assumed power after the breakdown of the gold standard while the British Labour government was still compelled to defend the value of sterling against gold and hemmed in by an immutable commitment to a fixed exchange rate system. Winch's point is supported by Erik Lundberg (1957, 97), who concluded that the key turning point took place on September 27, 1931, when "the abandonment of the gold standard . . . made it possible for Sweden to pursue an independent domestic economic policy."

On balance, the key contribution of the New Economics and of the 1933 crisis agreement may well have been to chart out a coherent approach to domestic economic development, one that combined import substitution with a careful policy of selective affiliation with the world market. The experts had recommended a flexible exchange rate policy. By neutralizing the effects of international market fluctuations in the Swedish economy, such a policy also would facilitate domestic stabilization and reflation, it was felt. In actuality, the krona was made to follow the fluctuations of primarily sterling and a number of other currencies until July 1933, when the national bank, Riksbanken, settled on a fixed rate policy that officially pegged the krona to British sterling. This resulted in an undervalued krona, which made exports cheaper and imports more expensive.

For most of the 1930s, Sweden experienced a surplus on its balance of payments. When prices picked up in important export markets during 1933, the exchange policy provided a boost to exports and discouraged imports. From 1947 to 1971 Sweden subscribed unvaryingly to a fixed exchange rate policy.[11]

Postwar Planning

As in the United Kingdom, preparations for the return of peace raised many questions about how the state and the new policies could be used to further peacetime goals. Myrdal's ideas about postwar planning went beyond the prewar economic reform program. It included, for example, a new emphasis on nationalization and a custodial role for the government in industrial "rationalization" that previously had been absent from policy and mainstream economic theory. A number of highly fragmented industries, including the insurance industry, gasoline and fuel, quarry industries, shoe manufacturing, and even textbook publishers, were targeted for nationalization initiatives. Most of these industries were already subjected to intensive war controls, and some had been subjected to involuntary cartelization measures. The commission stirred up controversy by introducing a series of parliamentary resolutions, the first step to legislation, in the 1945 parliament that in effect amounted to a nationalization plan. (For a list, see Lewin 1967, 256.) Myrdal's commission was formally expressing government policy. Since the coalition government still was in power, this meant that the center-right parties had been put in a position of formally espousing policies that they opposed. The tone of the commission's announcements was technical, arguing for wide-ranging economic policy purely on efficiency grounds. They made no mention of ownership rights, for example, nor of the political and practical problems associated with a nationalization program.

The stimulation of a high level of aggregate demand took center stage. Myrdal predicted a recession would follow after a short initial boom at the end of the war, as had been the case in 1921. He chose to ignore evidence of pent-up demand and economic overheating and, despite studies that considered large-scale postwar unemployment an unlikely event and some that even predicted labor shortages, he insisted on the need for both a public works program and an expansive program of economic stimulation (Myrdal 1944; Sweden 1944d). Myrdal believed, based on a theorem known as the Davidson norm, that an inverse relationship existed between prices and productivity and that "easy" money would help lower prices. (See Lundberg 1957, 127–129.) Quantitative monetary theory likewise caused him to predict that improvements in real wages would come as prices declined. If price controls were removed to allow prices to fall as productivity increased, real wages would improve.

Acting on theory, Myrdal ordered the national bank to encourage price reductions. In July 1946 the bank undertook to raise the exchange rate on the krona by 17 percent against the dollar, thereby making American imports cheaper and stimulating a round of price reductions (Lundberg 1957, 56; Sweden 1944c, 8). The wartime value-added taxation (VAT) on consumer goods also was eliminated ahead of schedule in January 1947 as part of the program. The program of lowering prices fueled an already inflationary economy and aggravated a trade deficit. (For discussion, see Lindbeck 1974, 27–28 and 72–73; Lundberg 1957, 133–143). Policy was reversed when Sweden devalued to match the British exchange rate adjustment in 1947 and with the concurrent reintroduction of controls. In 1950 the national bank was given a greater say in the determination of interest rates. The principle of fixed low interest rates was abandoned in 1955, when the bank raised the basic bank lending rate (the disconto rate) in order to curtail lending and inhibit inflation.

As in the 1930s, exports played little role in the commission's deliberations. The experts concluded that the demand for Swedish exports could not be influenced by Swedish economic policy. General agreement also existed that failing exports almost exclusively caused Swedish economic troubles, but this view merely reinforced the conviction that postwar economic expansion could be achieved only by means of a high level of domestic demand. Consequently, postwar policy should above all aim to maintain that demand. The downside of growing exports was that higher prices for key Swedish exports, such as paper, paper pulp, and lumber products—the pricing of which was determined entirely by international markets—affected domestic pricing and then migrated into the Swedish economy (Sweden 1944e, 3). Based on their analysis of the prewar economy, the planners believed that increased investment, particularly in the construction industry, which had the attractive property of having a high multiplicator effect within the national economy, could compensate for declining international demand for Swedish products (Sweden 1944d, 20). Although expansion in the construction industry also brought along increased demand for certain imports, the planners expected that import restrictions or exchange rate adjustments could be used to encourage import substitution.

Myrdal became minister of trade in 1945, but his greatest influence on postwar policy stemmed from his role as chairman of the Committee on Postwar Economic Planning. His alarmist prediction of postwar deflation was in part in tune with the underconsumptionist theories that dominated left-wing economic theory at the time, but it was perhaps also in part a self-serving construction to justify a large role for the government and, at its helm, for Myrdal himself. Dire predictions undergirded the authority of the committee and Myrdal—until they were proven wrong, that is. Wigforss devotes a whole chapter in his memoirs to Myrdal and observes with seemingly little regret that "It might be said that there is no room in practical politics, as it is practiced in [Sweden], for exceptional, discerning brains like Gunnar Myrdal's" (Wigforss 1954, 362). Myrdal lasted two years in the postwar government, then he went on to save India. By then most of his committee's recommendations had proved inapplicable.

The Labor Movement's Postwar Program

A special party congress, held on May 18, 1944, was dedicated to discussion of a new joint program between SAP and the LO, the Labor Movement's Postwar Program. The new program was produced by a committee headed by Finance Minister Ernst Wigforss and included, among others, Gösta Rehn, a young economist with union ties. The revisions concerned particularly the "Basic Principles" section of the old program from 1920, which was dominated by remnants of Marxian theory traceable to the Gotha and the Erfurter programs of the German Social Democratic Party. The new program is notable for its relative moderation.

The Social Democrats' ideological purity has been attacked and defended many times with no consensus in sight (Esping-Anderson 1985; Korpi 1978, 1983; Lewin 1988; Pontusson 1988).[12] An observer of Swedish political development, Tim Tilton, has argued that the party remained committed to its old tenets even as it revised its program and that ideology remained as important as ever; only the means had changed. He points to the Postwar Program from 1944 and the wage-earners' funds legislation from 1982 as evidence of purity and continuity, because they reaffirmed a commitment to "substantial nationalization of private industry" (Tilton 1992, 419). Yet the 1944 program did not include proposals to nationalize industry, except the insurance industry, and was quite ambiguous on the matter of socialization. In his speech presenting the new program to the congress, Wigforss stressed that planning was possible irrespective of ownership forms and that public ownership was no guarantee of economic planning. It was the concentration of economic power, not ownership per se, that the party intended to attack (SAP Protokoll 1944, 62–63). It was a radical departure from prewar—and in other countries also contemporary—views of what could be accomplished by means of nationalization. Wigforss went further and pointed to agricultural policy and the war controls as examples of coordinating policies that had shown that organization and pricefixing were powerful means for economic planning and stabilization.[13]

This line of argument was developed subsequently in a party publication explaining the program. Social Democratic policy was experimental and aimed to "test" industry. If private ownership proved compatible with the planned economy, there was no reason to socialize industry; if it proved incompatible, the party would move take "appropriate" measures (SAP Protokoll 1947, 29).[14] It is difficult not to conclude that the 1944 program was deliberately hazy on the matter of socialization. There was little disagreement on the matter at the congress, however. Instead, much time was spent discussing the revision committee's decision to eliminate the 1920 program's demand that the state church be socialized. This particular point aroused more controversy—measured by the number of pages in the protocol taken up by debate on the issue—than the revisions of theory contained in the "Basic Principles" and economic policy combined.

We can speculate that one reason for the lack of controversy over nationalization policy was that it was conspicuously clear to everyone that Sweden's primary problem was its generally backward economy. In 1941 the LO had published a discussion paper on private business, *Fackföreningsrörelsen och Näringslivet*. The paper included discussions of Swedish economic development and the rise of trade unionism that suggest that it was intended more for education and study in union circles than as position paper explaining policy to policymakers. The intended message was nevertheless clear: The growth of trade unionism had changed the workings of capitalism and overtaken orthodox Marxist theory regarding the means and goals of economic reform. The paper reflected a "developmentalist" sentiment that emphasized the paramount importance of economic growth.

The appended action program gave the national confederation (LO) a central role in representing workers on matters related to the distribution of economic power in addition to traditional wage issues. The paper contained many of the key elements of a "politics of productivity" to the point of prioritizing shared economic growth over shared property rights. Nevertheless, there was plenty in the paper to upset the center-right parties and employers. It challenged employer prerogatives, particularly the infamous Paragraph 23 in the employers' association statutes (reproduced in the 1938 "Basic Agreement") that asserted employers' right to management decisions, including hiring and firing (LO 1941, 176).

The 1944 program revisions were true to the emphasis of the 1941 paper in its attack on dogma. References to the class struggle, in particular the question of exploitation, were deleted from the old program. The proposed changes were opposed by some Social Democrats, who argued that 1944 was not the right moment to revise the program, an argument that barely hid ideological disagreement. Gustav Möller, the chief architect of the party's social policy, argued that since the conclusion of the war likely would result in a sweep of revolutions across Europe, the "objective conditions" for social change would be such that the Social Democrats might be able to proceed straight to reforms that now were being postponed to the distant future (SAP 1944, 89–92 and 96–97). Möller was not alone in expecting revolutions to sweep over Europe after the war and to make old Marxist prophecies about the inevitable decay of capitalism and its replacement with socialism come true.

It was on this point of dogma that the sharpest conflict arose at the 1944 congress. Wigforss responded that, even if Socialist revolutions were going to take place in central Europe, it would not (nor should it) change the views of the Swedish Social Democrats. It was, after all, not external "objective" conditions but Swedes themselves—he used the curious expression "the internal personal conditions," in Swedish: inra personliga förhållandena—that would decide when a majority of the Swedish people (folksmajoritet) would be ready for socialism (SAP Protokoll 1944, 68). In any case, he continued, what would people say if it became known that the Social Democrats were waiting for a revolution in central Europe to take place before they decided on their own program? Möller retorted that it was peculiar to give up on Marxist prognostications just when they looked ready to come true. He nevertheless failed to sway the congress, and the changes passed.

Paragraph 14 of the old program demanded that a planned economy should be created and that all natural resources—industry, banking, transportation, and communication—should be transferred to public ownership. This was replaced with a new paragraph that simply demanded the creation of a planned economy, planhushållningen, and if necessary also public ownership of parts of the previously listed sectors. Thus the new paragraph both expanded the reach of government and qualified it, compared with the old program (SAP 1944, 265–266). The new program also added the demand for full employment and for equal pay. The latter was subject to some negotiation with the women's association, which objected that the formulation made possible the continuation of discrimination against women and the exclusion of women from certain jobs (SAP Protokoll 1944, 237 and 263).

Other noteworthy changes included a new demand for progressive taxation and for government control of foreign trade. The latter revision did not attract much discussion but reflected an important revision of the party's trade policy. Likely it reflected positive feelings about the results of government controls on foreign trade in the wake of the depression and during the war. None of these issues invited nearly as much debate as the one that followed, party support for temperance. Of all the economic policy issues, only agricultural policy invited extended debate with many members speaking for protecting the smallholder (SAP Protokoll 1944, 318–347).

Constitutional Constraints and Political Reform

The striking dissimilarities in economic outlooks of British Labour and Swedish social democracy in 1945 have several explanations. The importance of the 1936 Crisis Government in shaping a proto-Keynesian policy consensus among economists and policymakers has already been touched upon. Sweden's global position as a backward and dependent country imposed a set of functional requirements for economic policy that diverged sharply from those confronting any British government. Sweden had no empire trading zone within which industry could seek refuge from U.S. competition. The krona was no sterling. None of these factors explains by itself why the Swedish Social Democrats were more amendable to proto-Keynesian policies than British Labour. They suggest only that the Social Democrats had good reasons not to stick to orthodoxy, not why programmatic adjustment took place. A similar (but different) set of "good reasons" could be—poor growth rates, for example—cataloged for why Labour should have embraced national economic development strategy.

The character of the Social Democratic Party and the parameters for strategic action set by political institutions are central to the explanation of the Social Democrats' capacity—will and ability combined—to reconcile government and program. The Social Democrats had been given a unique opportunity to lead a popular growth coalition. Development theory has Sweden pegged as a characteristic example of an economically backward, elitist regime that was transformed by an alliance between a nascent proletariat and an independent peasantry early in the twentieth century (Rueschemeyer, Stephens, and Stephens 1992). The revised party system that emerged in 1918 to 1920 upon the introduction of universal suffrage and proportional representation reflected in an almost ideal-typical fashion a four-corner sectionalist party system elaborated by Seymour Martin Lipset and Stein Rokkan (Lipset and Rokkan 1967, 1–64). It pitted land against industry and owners against workers. The party system of the 1920 was virtually identical to that of the 1960s, conforming to the Lipset-Rokkan thesis about the "frozen" party system. Having said that, it is also necessary to point out that at several points reasons existed not to take the system's stability for granted.

Sweden's modern party system descended from a voting rights reform in 1907, which set off a chain of subsequent reforms. A modified proportional method for distributing seats between the parties was first used in 1911; it retained special protection for the old elite. Subsequent reforms ended the last inequalities. The 1919 election took place with full and equal suffrage making Sweden an early convert to the rights of women. The party system remained virtually unchanged between 1917 and the 1980s. The Social Democratic Workers' Party, Socialdemokratiska Arbetareparti, was created in 1889. In addition to its ties to the unions, the Social Democratic Party also was shaped by ties to evangelical groups and the temperance movement, which played a large role in early popular mobilization for democracy in Sweden. By one estimate, in 1949 41 percent of the Social Democratic members of the lower house (Andra Kammaren) belonged to the temperance movement, the International Order of Good Templars (IOGT) (Therborn 1992, 12). The Conservative party was first know simply as the Right (Högern). With the dawn of mass-membership parties, it was incorporated as the National Association of Voters.[15] The Liberal party emerged as the largest party in 1911, attracting 40 percent of the vote. In 1923 the party split in two but reunited in 1936 as the People's Party (Folkspartiet).[16] The Agrarian Party, Bondeförbundet (or literally "the Peasant Alliance"), participated first in the 1917 election.[17] The party has had close ties to National Farmers' Union but, because rural depopulation eroded its social bases, it changed its name in 1957 to become the Center Party.

Social Revolution through Power Sharing

With proportional representation and a divided center-right, the prospects for Socialist domination were good as long as the working class' share of the national vote continued to increase. The political backdrop for the discussions of postwar policy of the 1944 congress encouraged confidence but also caution. The Social Democrats had received more than 50 percent of the popular vote in the 1938 election to the upper house, in the 1940 election to the lower house, and again in the 1942 municipal and local government elections. Nevertheless, in his 1944 welcoming speech party leader and Prime Minister Per Albin Hansson argued that the party should continue to consent to coalition government, even after the war ended. He reasoned that power sharing was the more "democratic" way (SAP 1944, 10). Cooperation was desirable, he argued, because it works to level societal conflict and facilitates agreement. This was a curious speech for the leader of a majority party. It harked back to a theme first developed by Social Democratic party leaders in the late 1920s, when the party's only hope of gaining into power rested on collaboration (Hansson 1935, 107–113).

This was a far cry from Hartley-Shawcross' boast in the British Parliament that Labour was the new master "for time to come." (See chapter 2.) Why did appeals to collaboration reemerge in Sweden at a time when it looked as if the Social Democrats could count on a one-party absolute majority? The emphasis on collaboration and democratic procedure had in the past served to distance the Social Democrats from the Communists and to reassure voters that the party would stick to democratic procedures. Hansson went beyond merely assuring respect for procedure to argue on principle that majority power was in any case unacceptable and incompatible with democratic government.

Appeals to collaboration have played a curious, and somewhat contradictory, role in Social Democratic strategy and theory of political action. It was important to the leaders that voters see the party as bent on accord and that the party keep all doors open for cooperation with different groups. As it turned out, the 1944 election was a disappointment for the Social Democrats—in part because a large share of the left vote went to the Communists—and they would have to wait until 1968 for another one-party majority.

The rhetoric of cooperation can be interpreted as a precautionary strategy informed by an apprehension of the capacity of a proportional electoral system to make even small shifts in voter attitudes felt at the level of government: Alternatively, it can be seen, more simply, as the functional equivalent of a hard fist in a soft glove. An exchange between Hansson and Wigforss at the first party executive meeting on September 25, after the 1936 election, suggests that the constant invitations to accord were more a matter of practical than principled politics. Hansson reportedly said, "Personally I am of course interested in having a government with the broadest possible base, but without significant concessions on our part"; Wigforss retorted, "None at all!" (quoted in Therborn 1992, 18).

In retrospect, the Social Democratic Party's dominant political position was established in 1932. The party would govern without interruption until 1976, 44 years later, but most of the time it was dependent on some kind of power sharing.[18] The precariousness of government formation in a proportional system is illustrated the Social Democrats' first experience of government power: six months in 1920 and 1921, two years from 1921 to 1923, and some 18 months from 1924 to 1926. Between 1917 and 1932 Sweden had 12 governments, all except the first minority governments. In 1932 the Social Democrats were determined to wrest political control away from the center-right parties; to do so, they were forced once again to seek support from another party. Only this time they chose the Agrarian party.

The war years represented a period of exceptional governmental stability, partisan collaboration, and also the pinnacle of Social Democratic electoral popularity. From 1940 to 1944, the party enjoyed a majority of 38 seats in the lower house and 14 seats in the upper house. The 1944 election cut the Social Democrats back to exactly half the seats (115 of 230) in the lower house.[19] The first postwar government was formed in July 1945 upon the dissolution of the wartime four-party coalition government. Since the Social Democrats held a majority in the upper house, no workable majority existed against them; yet they lacked the votes needed for a clear majority. The party was caught between cooperating with the small Communist Party in a "Red" majority or returning to collaboration with the Agrarians. While an immediate decision could be postponed, by the next election, in 1948, the tensions of the Cold War and a decline in votes for the Social Democrats had eliminated the Red majority. The Social Democrats returned to a coalition government with the Agrarian party from 1951 to 1957 and to the 1930s' formula of a "Red-Green" alliance.

In hindsight, the Social Democratic legacy of one-party dominance and 44 years in power looks formidable, but except for the years between 1945 and 1951, and again between 1968 and 1970, the lack of a political majority checked the party's exercise of power. The postwar Social Democratic hegemony was challenged periodically and often fragile. Swedish politics has been characterized by collaboration and conflict, often at the same time. From a systemic viewpoint, this apparently paradoxical phenomenon is a natural consequence of an electoral system that is keenly sensitive to marginal shifts in voters between parties. The uncertainty of government composition spawns heightened partisan competition, which in turn lends itself to making particular, but often somewhat unpredictable, issues subject to eruptions of political zest that owe more to opportunity than to the real interests at stake.

The opportunistic aspects of partisan competition imply that occasionally there can be smoke without a fire. Tage Erlander, Per Albin Hansson's successor to the position of party leader and prime minister in 1946, advanced this interpretation years later with respect to the so-called PHM campaign of opponents to economic planning. PHM is an acronym for *planhushållningmodstanderar,* which can be translated directly as "planned economy opponents." In Erlander's view, business mobilized fears of socialization in the hope of getting the Social Democrats to retreat on taxes (interview cited in Svenning 1972, 34–35.)

A Comparative Perspective:
Economic and Political Development

The disparate dynamic of government formation in a political system based on proportional representation to one based on plurality elections help explain some of the differences between the two reform governments. In 1945 the Labour Party could claim a landslide election, whereas the Social Democrats had to make concessions to other parties in order to hold on to power.[20] Constitutional variables interacted with sociology to produce different bases for the construction of power in the two cases. We need only imagine proportional representation superimposed on Great Britain in the year of 1945 to realize that a Red-Green alliance of "small peoples" did not have much to offer the British working class. Then there is the role of the British empire's vestiges in tying British policymakers to policies defending sterling. The point is made that Sweden was not Britain, and vice versa; it illustrates the difficulties associated with attributing causal importance to constitutional variables.

Social structure mirrors a country's level of economic development, and Sweden's social structure at the end of the war still reflected the importance of agrarian livelihoods and rural living. This would change quickly. In 1950 figures, manufacturing and mining accounted for 31.9 percent of the labor force in Sweden and farmers for 20.3 percent. In 1920 over 40 percent of the Swedish working population was engaged in agriculture. In 1960 that proportion was down to 14 percent. (All figures are based on Flora, Kraus, and Pfenning, 1987, chap. 7.) The comparable agricultural figures for England and Wales were 10 percent in 1921, 6 percent in 1931, and 3.4 percent in 1961. The numerical strength of farmers in Sweden and the central strategic position of the Agrarian party made agricultural reform impossible, whether Socialist or attuned to commercial gains. Family farming dominated, although a small agricultural proletariat existed (roughly 30 percent of the agricultural labor force). In contrast, the British agricultural labor force amounted to only 4.8 percent of the population in 1951 (for England and Wales).

Economic backwardness was, sociologically speaking, a fortuitous component in the formation of a Red-Green alliance between the Social Democrats and the Agrarian party from 1932 to 1939 and again from 1951 to 1957. Sociology compensated for the constraints of the political system by awarding the working class a partner to pursue a national development program. The cross-class alliance was not just external, a coalition between two parties, but also internal to social democracy. Economic policymakers in both countries used agricultural policy to argue for the benefits of economic planning. Economic forecasting, the use of the national budget as a planning instrument, and enhanced statistical capacities were important gains that nourished the ambitions of planners.

By 1945 the Swedish Social Democrats had gone further in revising their program and adjusting expectations to the constraints of democratic government than had the British Labour Party. The war years had provided the Social Democrats with a baggage of pent-up working-class ambition and a broad indictment of capitalism, together with a new set of tools for political mastery of economic activity. It was the divergent experiences and conclusions made by leaders of the two parties on the basis of the depression years that set them apart and explained the Social Democrats' greater willingness to modify their views on key issues related to Socialist theory; ownership and socialization was one issue that mattered, views of the possible benefits of productivity improvement and economic development was another.

Sweden and the World

In the postwar years the gap between neutrality and isolation soon proved uncomfortably narrow. In 1945 the Social Democratic government put much effort into attempts to reestablish trade relations with the Soviet Union. These efforts were well in line with the "crisis" government's inclusion of a similar state trade agreement with the Soviet Union in its antirecessionary package in 1932 to 1936 and in the recommendations of Myrdal's 1944 planning commission. In 1947 the Social Democrats championed a renewal of a trade program with the Soviets, consisting mostly of a large credit program amounting to 1 billion krona. This was three to four times the size of the loan Sweden received from the United States under the European Recovery Program. The agreement permitted the Soviet Union to purchase a carefully negotiated list of machine tools, technical equipment, and agricultural products with a loan from the Swedish state; the purchase would account for 10 to 15 percent of Sweden's export trade. The agreement was presented as a paragon of what "planned" foreign trade would look like. As it turned out, "planned" foreign trade of this kind soon proved unattractive, the agreement gives us a hint of what the "road not traveled" might have looked like. The unions and the left were enthusiastic sponsors. An LO publication heralded it as an example of how Sweden could participate in foreign trade without risking the contamination of capitalist business cycles and praised it as "a link in our fight against a future postwar depression" (Aktualla Frågor [9] 1947, 7).

Enthusiasm for a "Socialist" foreign policy cooled with the Prague coup in February 1948. Persistent rumors that the Soviet Union was preparing a Scandinavian invasion made maintaining "friendly socialist" relations with that country increasingly difficult.[21] Nordic collaboration was an alternative that for years has been regarded as the "almost was" that never happened. Many posited Nordic economic and military collaboration as an alternative to involvement with the superpowers. It failed conclusively, in 1949, when Denmark and Norway joined the North Atlantic Treaty Organization (NATO). After the Nordic alternative failed, Sweden became a charter member of the "nonaligned" group. Sweden was represented at the Paris Convention, in July to September 1948, but the country received no direct assistance (gifts) under the European Recovery Program between 1950 and 1954. It did receive some benefits from the program, in the form of loans, trade credits, and a bilateral trade agreement with the United States. Sweden participated in the European Payments Union and the General Agreement of Trade and Tariffs (GATT), and henceforth multilateralism took the place of a "planned trade" policy.

The official postwar trade policy was committed to foreign trade. In practice, the Swedish embrace of liberal trade principles was complicated. In a 1946 speech, Myrdal outlined the official position. The Swedish tradition of free trade was due to the country's position as "a small seafaring nation undergoing rapid industrial development." The country was dependent on the import of key raw materials for economic development, and the Swedish export industries were dependent on free access to all markets for "the best results." Myrdal nevertheless also pointed out that there were good reasons why some people harbored protectionist sentiments. Employment had been irregular and wages low in the export industries, he pointed out. But, he continued, "the realization that the sheltered home-market industries have profited at the expense of the competitive industries and that the general level of real income would have been lower if our foreign trade had been smaller" had tempered desires for economic nationalism (Myrdal 1946, 16–17). In other words, exports were important to the extent that they facilitated domestic industries and trade. What he did not mention was that agricultural policy was unequivocally protectionist.

The protectionist impulse extended beyond agriculture to small industries. A 1944 study by three other economists tied to the employers' association, Ingvar Svennilson, Axel Iveroth, and Erik Dahmén, looked at the prospects for postwar employment and economic development. The three warned against the risk that domestic economic activity monopolized policymakers' attention and that their willingness to dismiss discussion of foreign trade policy by referring to the prospects it might offer "at a later stage" meant that foreign trade was in fact neglected (Industriens Utredningsinstitut 1944, 18). The insulation of Swedish small and medium-size industries was illustrated by a 1960 survey of businesses engaged in export trade, which showed that most did not primarily orient themselves toward foreign markets but simply aimed to export the "surplus" production that could not be absorbed by domestic demand. It was common practice to let foreign partners go short, if unexpected domestic demand materialized.[22]

Program reflected reality. The Social Democrats had become increasingly leery of foreign trade liberalism in the 1930s. In the 1944 revision of the party program, one of the changes concerned foreign economic policy. A new paragraph calling for "government control of foreign trade" replaced one that instead simply called for "free trade" (SAP Protokoll 1944, 268).[23] Years later, in a 1958 speech at Yale University, Myrdal linked the "domestic trade first, exports second" sentiment to the development of the welfare state. The postwar welfare state and economic internationalization were antinomies, he argued, and it was the welfare state that was the way of the future. "It cannot be helped," Myrdal (1960, 131) said, "that everywhere national integration [in the welfare state] is now bought at the cost of international disintegration." The welfare state is both nationalistic and protectionist. The "internationalizers" and "free traders" who wanted to break down national barriers were dreamers, because no nation can reasonably be asked to compromise national economic development in order to sustain the realization of a world without boundaries and discrimination, he concluded with less-than-prescient precision.

In the postwar years, Sweden relied on what can be described as tempered economic nationalism. Subtle discrimination against foreign products played a large but often unacknowledged role. Meanwhile, economic policy encouraged the redirection of the export industries from low-wage, low-skill extraction industries to high-value-added, high-wage industries. This successful strategy led to rapid economic growth, economic change, and redistribution. But economic change takes time. As late as 1960, exports amounted to roughly one-fifth of GDP. Close to 60 percent of all exports were concentrated in the timber and iron ore industries and derivatives. Paper and paper pulp alone accounted for more than 25 percent of all exports, down from 50 percent before the war (Kärre 1954, 9; Strömbom 1964, 20). These were all regional industries dependent on unskilled or low-skilled labor drawn from rural areas and many seasonal workers. The high-pay, high-value-added manufacturing industries, including primarily the machine industry and car, train, and shipbuilding industries, accounted for close to 27 percent of exports in 1960. But with economic modernization, their share was rapidly expanding. That, in turn, gave rise to new conflicts over economic politics and policy.

By way of summary, Swedish Social Democratic postwar planning policies possessed certain similarities but also some important differences from those advocated by Labour. As in the case of Labour, the war years had given the Social Democrats an important opportunity to accumulate experience and trust in government. A critical difference was that the Social Democrats had come to accept some of the limits imposed by liberal democracy on social and economic reform, and in the "new economics" found an alternative program that emphasized a parity approach to economic development and pinpointed growth as the principal objective of economic policy. The rationing of scarcities had produced comprehensive changes in state-society relations, and a series of innovations in government institutions and policy technologies could be used for postwar planning. The country's protected position during the war had created both certain advantages and some disadvantages. The advantage was that physical destruction had been avoided; the disadvantage was that doubts had been cast on the country's commitment to Atlanticist cooperation and free trade.

FIVE

Sweden: From the Planned Economy to Societal Coordination

The Emergence of a Postwar Consensus

Between 1945 and 1949, a new international order was created. Sweden took very little part in the shaping that order, a "rule-taker" rather than a "rule-maker." The collapse of cooperation between the Allied occupation powers in the Occupation Council in Berlin between 1945 and 1947 put an end to Roosevelt's "Grand Design" for postwar world government based on U.S.-Soviet collaboration and also caused new tensions for Sweden. As American policymakers began to realize that a radical program for European economic revitalization was needed, Sweden was forced to chose between East and West. With the initiation of the Marshall Plan in 1947, European states were offered new opportunities but also obligations that impinged on the Social Democratic government's economic policies in unanticipated ways, much as they had impinged on the Labour government's choices.

The chapter begins with a discussion of the opposition to the planned economy and the concurrent shifts in postwar party programs as elites came to terms with the embellished postwar state. First, the recentering of the party system around a new proto-Keynesian consensus is discussed before the narrative turns to agricultural policy and wage planning. British and Swedish postwar policy adjustment presents an element of striking correspondence. In both countries, agricultural policy was protectionist and expansionist, and subsequently stressed income parity between the agrarian classes and other classes. Divergent trajectories often are allowed to obscure other similarities, for example, when the trade unions opposed the continuation of wartime control policies affecting the union, and in both countries, industry and business groups mostly favored continuing planning. The two countries' economic situations hardly could have been more dissimilar, however. Sweden was in what would be one of Europe's most rapid economic take-offs; Britain was facing the collapse of sterling and of the empire trading system. In contrast to Labour's declining electoral fortunes, the Social Democrats remained in power, uninterrupted, until 1976 and in 1968 obtained an unheard one-party absolute majority. In place of the cycles of accord and conflict between unions and governments that wrecked British economic policy, the Swedish trade unions consented to a national wage policy that stressed wage restraint and wage planning, or what perhaps more accurately should be called planning by wages. The discussion turns first to the recentering of the party system around a new proto-Keynesian consensus, and then to agricultural policy and wage planning.

The Center-Right Parties and the New State

Between 1944 and 1946, the main Swedish political parties revised their party programs, saw generational change in party leadership, and embraced a new public philosophy of government responsibility for economic growth and full employment. As we have seen, a similar change took place in Britain, only slightly later (in 1950–1951). The Social Democrats were not the only party to experience a setback in the 1944 election. The Conservative Party went from 18 percent to 15.9 percent of the vote, a result that was seen as a reaction against the party's strident defense of liberal principles and opposition to full employment policies and the emerging welfare state. A Conservative newspaper, *Svenska Dagbladet,* began a process of self-examination about the future of conservatism (Ljunggren 1992; Sandlund 1984, 125). Myrdal and his commission's deliberations on the creation of *folkhushållningen,* the "people's economy," had aroused the passion of a circle of business people and conservative intellectuals. Berthold Josephy, an Austrian economist who had lived in exile in Sweden since 1934, reiterated the general thesis of Hayek's *Road to Serfdom* for a Swedish audience (Josephy 1945). Conservative party leader and economist Gösta Bagge used *Svenska Dagbladet* to warn against corporatism in all its form and against the Keynesian "social liberalism" of Bertil Ohlin and the Liberal party.

But Conservatives could not agree among themselves.[1] In 1943 the party began publishing a series of booklets ("Blue Series") intended to stimulate debate on postwar reform and economic planning. In it the divisions among Conservative circles emerged clearly. Arguing against liberal orthodoxy, one writer, Harald Nordenson, suggested that cartels could be useful for industry, if not used for "unprofessional purposes." He supported allowing trade associations to assume responsibility for the administration of certain public policies. It might be bad in theory, he allowed, but the new way of doing things was good for business, as long as the right to "free association" was protected. Cartelistic planning was good if business did it, but bad if the government did it (Högerns Riksorganisation 1944).

Gustaf Söderlund, the chairman of the employers' association, contributed to the series with a speech held on May 24, 1945, shortly after the liberation of Denmark and Norway (Högerns Riksorganisation 1945). He addressed point for point some of the main components in the joint reconstruction program published by the Social Democrats and the trade unions in the Labour Movement's Postwar Program from 1944 and gave his views of business' obligations to society. Collectivism was a boon to democracy, he agreed. It provided a way for more people to be included planning the country's future, a provision that might benefit business when the Social Democrats were in power. He regarded the last election as an expression of popular majority support for socialization but questioned whether people knew what that implied. He warned that even though the Social Democrats presented themselves as pragmatic and wanting to proceed on a step-by-step basis, socialization and government coercion gradually might be introduced without anyone realizing how it happened. Many roads can lead to a particular goal, he argued, concluding that the Social Democrats were pretending, "like the Jesuits, that the ends justify the means" (Söderlund 1945, 5).

An acrimonious debate ensued. In July 1945 an exchange took place between the Social Democratic prime minister, P. A. Hansson, and Söderlund, in which the former accused the latter of being demented *(vanvittig),* when he claimed that the Social Democrats were less than forthright about their true goals. In print and speech, the Conservatives hammered away on the accusation that the Social Democrats were hiding their intention to sneak socialism in through the back door in order to make planning palatable to the Swedish people. The controversy obscured the fact that Söderlund's speech also revealed broad areas of common ground between industry and the Social Democrats on specific policy matters. Söderlund praised "the system of 1932," the policies that had help Sweden out of the recession in the 1930s, and the collaboration of the war years. "Why fix what works?" he asked. In other words, he was happy to go along with the New Economics of the 1930s, but not with the People's Economy laid out by Myrdal and his commission. Söderlund agreed that mass unemployment had to be avoided and that all measures had to be taken to create employment. He disagreed on the matter of means, not the goals. The problem was, he said, that Socialists mistrust private initiative but place limitless trust in the state (Söderlund 1945, 21).

The spat over the People's Economy soon gave way to controversy over tax reform. This was a fortunate shift for the Social Democrats, since public opinion did not favor the opposition on this issue the way it did on the matter of the planned economy. In 1938 the party had passed a tax reform introducing progressive taxation (Elvander 1972). During the war various emergency taxation measures were passed, including a value-added tax (VAT) on consumer goods. The new taxes were regressive—they aimed to depress consumption—and the 1944 postwar program made progressive taxation a matter of high priority. In fall 1945 the outline of a tax reform was made public, and a legislative commission was created to produce a bill. Because of upcoming local elections, the outline was disclosed prior to the formal introduction of a bill and the issue played a prominent role in the campaign. The proposal included a recommendation to tax personal wealth and inheritances, which brought out cries of protest from a normally secluded elite. The king, bishops, civil servants, and judges, the *éminences grises,* joined the outcry, claiming that estate taxes were unconstitutional and amounted to expropriation. Opposition to the new tax reform was soon seen as an elitist response, and the bill passed without obstacles.[2]

The tax reform issue had come up while the government was still engaged in Myrdal's cost reduction program, and the government was willing to consider lowering general taxes as part of the program. Wigforss, the Social Democratic finance minister, consequently was unusually (by his own admission) receptive to the Conservative party's pleas that tax relief should be extended well into the middle class (1954, 365–374). But when the Conservative party publicly boasted in *Svenska Dagbladet* that it had been responsible for reducing taxes the most, the Liberal party became enraged and said the reductions were irresponsible. The role reversal between the two parties, with the Liberals suddenly speaking for fiscal "responsibility," and the Conservatives for tax cuts, worked to end the old guard's control of the Conservative party, and in 1946 a new program was agreed upon that accepted the welfare state (Ljunggren 1992).

The Liberal party let go of orthodoxy first. The party program from 1944, "the Postwar Society," embraced social and economic reform and argued that "fashioned correctly," reform need not be a drag on the economy and could be made compatible with economic growth (Folkpartiet 1955, 7). The program spoke of "the age of collectivism," a boon to social inclusion and economic efficiency. It accepted the need for countercyclical policies and framed the full-employment goal as a matter of the individual's right to a job. The program also stressed educational reform and women's equality. The Liberals saw themselves as heirs to John Stuart Mill and a liberal tradition favoring the emancipation of women. For good measure, the party also supported temperance and the need for a "family wage" (försörjarlön).

The Agrarian party, the fourth main party, had been brought in as one of the pillars of the welfare state with the formation of the Red-Green alliance in 1933. Farmers are rarely thought of as a "state-building" class, but in practice few classes have more enthusiastically embraced state action than farmers and few policy areas have conformed to the neocorporatist mold as completely as agricultural policy, with agricultural interest organizations involved in both the negotiation and the implementation of policy. The party played a key role in the creation of the "social citizenship" state as a partner to the legislation establishing the 1948 universal flat-rate "people's pensions."[3]

Business and Industry Groups

Liberal principles had few defenders among business and industry organizations. Business elites generally divided their loyalties between the Conservative and the Liberal parties, with the more conservative groups less likely to accept proto-Keynesian policies. The official position of trade associations was quite positive. The national association of wholesalers, Sveriges Grossist Förbund, issued its own postwar program in 1944, *Sveriges Grossistförbund om Efterkrigsplaneringen*. The national association represented 41 branch associations of importers and wholesalers, which were in effect parastatal organizations responsible for the administration of suppliers' "pools." The organization accepted that planning was necessary but wanted to help in carrying it out. The fear was that the state would make the associations superfluous. The program refrained from any principled discussions of "liberty," and asked instead that the severity of the controls be eased and the national and branch associations' role be protected.

The employers' confederation, SAF, was represented in the debate by Söderlund, whose views have been discussed already. The role of self-interest in shaping the views of the trade associations—or rather of their staffs—regarding the need for coordinating policies cannot be ignored. As director of the wartime industry commission, Söderlund had overseen the rapprochement between state and industry. The process brought radical organizational changes in the confederation. Its activities included the publication of a paper, *Industria* (reorganized in 1946), and since 1948 a publication series, *Studieförbundet Näringsliv och Samhälle* (SNS), which in effect worked as a "think tank" for the confederation. As the main representative of employer interests to the state, SAF expanded its reach into areas normally reserved for political parties. The shift to centralized wage-contract negotiations in 1952 produced even greater changes, including rapid staff expansion. Postwar social reform legislation also compelled the organization to develop a voice on social issues, such as education and retirement plans. New responsibilities were added, and the administrative capacities of the organization increased also in the area of publications and public relations. In addition to political representation, training activities and legal assistance became part of the organization's activities, acting as what we may call selective incentives for firms to join. The statistical office was expanded. In the 1930s the confederation had employed a handful of people. By 1952, 100 were employed at the central office. By 1970 that figure had grown to 360 people. In addition, the organization acquired two regional offices and a mansion for retreats and conferences (De Geer 1986, 37 and 42). The more rules and regulations there were to negotiate, the larger the organization grew.

Agriculture: A Paragon of Planning

Already in 1942, a commission of inquiry recommended that the wartime price policies serve as a model for postwar policy. In 1947 Riksdagen, the Swedish parliament, approved the continuation of wartime price subsidies for agricultural products. The multiparty agreement was designated the Magna Carta of Swedish agricultural policy. Wartime control policies designed to increase production had led to a significant redistribution of income in favor of farmers and agricultural workers during the war years. The shift of resources benefited regions where agriculture was commercially less viable, particularly the vast and thinly populated Norrland, which gained at the cost of the urban and southern regions.

Efficiency or Equity

Agricultural reform occasioned prolonged discussion at the 1944 Social Democratic party conference. Some participants proposed radical agricultural reform that would "rationalize" Swedish agriculture and praised collectivization and the advantages of bigness, but the majority argued for the preservation of a lifestyle central to Swedish national character (SAP 1944, 318–347). In the end, the postwar program included a blanket commitment to raising living standard in the countryside, in part through social protection and in part through modernization. This policy conspicuously stressed equity over efficiency and was strongly criticized by planners. Gunnar Myrdal (1938) had cautioned against the perverse effects of price subsidies on agricultural productivity as early as 1938 but to no avail.

The investigative committee set up to prepare the 1947 act had not followed the lead of the 1942 committee. Its recommendation of a shift from the wartime system of guaranteed minimum prices—which the committee noted rewarded the least efficient farmers and encouraged overproduction—to direct payments to individual farmers was ignored. A system based on payments to individual farmers would allow for productivity rewards and could be attuned more easily to changing needs in case of overproduction. It also recommended the incorporation of vague goals for conversion of the most inefficient farms to woodland and a public loan program to support farm consolidation. The consolidation proposal stranded on an old land acquisition law that effectively prohibited consolidation and preserved small farms (Odhner 1992, 199). The compromise proved resistant to change, leaving economists to deplore inefficient policies and the protectionist measures that aimed to stem agricultural change for decades.

According to the 1947 agreement, the primary aim of agricultural policy was to fix income parity between farmers and other occupational groups. The embrace of social fairness and agricultural self-sufficiency as a matter of national security represented a major change in Social Democratic policy. The embrace of agricultural subsidies can be explained by the Social Democrats reliance on the Agrarian party for political support, but the appeal to equity indicate deeper reasons why the Social Democrats did not stick with socialist orthodoxies on agricultural policy, which generally called for collectivization and other policies that aimed to end private ownership in the agricultural sector. (See chapter 6 for a discussion of the German Social Democrats and their agricultural policies.) Many Social Democrats were elected by Agrarian votes (Micheletti 1990, 53). In addition, the party retained an emotional and ideological affinity with small farmers, and identified with a national romanticism about the values of rural life. The Red-Green alliance was an inter-party as well as an intra-party alliance.

Agricultural policy relied on a curious mechanism developed during the war called the "agricultural calculus" to estimate agricultural incomes and costs and to calculate subsidies. It treated all of Swedish agriculture as a single enterprise. Farmers, including agricultural laborers and adult family members, were in effect treated as state employees and provided with a salary supplement. The size of government subsidies were then calculated to provide farmers, and their dependents and employees, with an income comparable with that of other occupations (Sweden 1952a, 166–171). The 1947 reform retained this mechanism but made cost estimates negotiable with farm representatives appointed to an Agricultural Board. The inclusion of farm representatives into the determination of the "calculus" awarded farm organizations considerable power. Negotiations were often protracted and difficult. Once a round of negotiations ended, the outcome was almost completely resistant to change by ministers or parliament.

The agricultural budget utilized a concept of a model farm, or a typical unit, which in 1947 was set to be 25 to 50 acres. Subsidies henceforth were calculated to ensure that the "model farmer" had an income comparable to that of other occupational groups. The parity principle left little or no incentive for productivity enhancement. In 1959 the typical unit was changed to 50 to 75 acres after acrimonious debate. At the time, more than 85 percent of all Swedish farms were less than 50 acres, and 60 percent were less than 25 acres (Micheletti 1990, 89). The purpose of the new unit was to penalize the less-efficient farms to the point of forcing them out of business and to speed up modernization.

By increasing the "model farm" unit above the size of the average farm, the 1959 agreement deemphasized income parity objectives and aimed to encourage productivity improvements and cut overproduction. It was the beginning of a new competing "interest": the consumer. The protectionist principle finally lost out in 1967, when policy changed to stress the need for rationalization and lower agricultural prices by allowing a larger quota for food imports.

The 1956 Election and Political Realignment

Generous protective policies could not stem the migration from rural areas to urban ones. As the political importance of the rural vote declined, the Social Democrats began to give economic concerns greater weight in the determination of agricultural policy. In the 1966 local elections, the Social Democrats did poorly in agricultural areas. Despite anxieties within the party about the result, the shift in priorities stuck (Odhner 1992, 209). The impulse to protect rural culture waned in step with the inexorable dwindling of the rural population that even protectionist policies could not stop.

The 1956 election set in motion a process that would end the Red-Green coalition. The breakup illustrates the boundaries set by the Swedish constitutional system on the exercise of political power. It also illustrates the feedback between institutions and political strategy. Enough votes were moved from the left to the center-right that a center-right majority against the Social Democrats was possible, if the Agrarian party changed sides.[4] The Agrarian party faced a hard choice. On the basis of party documents and interviews, scholars have outlined the interests and concerns that informed the party's decision, which reflected pragmatic considerations of partisan advantage than political principle (see Jonasson 1981, on which this account builds).

The election forced the coalition partners, the Social Democrats and the Agrarians, to reevaluate their respective situations. The breakup of the coalition provides a picture of strategic action under the specific circumstances of a highly competitive multiparty system with parties tied down by close associations with particular interest groups. Both parties let strategic interests dominate their decisions. If the Agrarian party decided to work with the Liberal and Conservative parties, a "system change" to a center-right government was possible. The Social Democrats invited the Agrarians to continue in a coalition government provided they did not try to extract new concessions in exchange for continuing the coalition. If they did, the party leadership was prepared to identify issues to "explain" the breakup. Two issues were chosen: the Agrarians' wish to parcel out publicly owned forest to farmers and disagreements over pension reform for civil servants. If the Agrarian party decided to stay in the coalition, a compromise would be worked out.

The Agrarian party leaders were divided. It was widely agreed that rural depopulation and government participation were twin causes of the party's electoral losses. The Conservative party had successfully blamed the Agrarians for unpopular legislation and attracted agrarian voters. The Agrarian party was a small one, conforming in all major respects to Duverger's concept of a "mass party" with elaborate mechanisms for membership democracy. Roughly 100 people participated in the meeting of the Agrarian party executive committee that decided what to do, including representatives from youth and women's organizations, from the party-owned papers, from the parliamentary group, and from the party council.

Three choices were presented: (1) to stay in the coalition government unchanged (2) to demand new concessions from the Social Democrats in exchange for staying, or (3) to retreat into opposition. The party's youth organization argued that since voters had moved right, the party should do so too. At a minimum, it should create a brief government crisis to convince voters that the center-right alternative did not exist. The women's organization still preferred to stay in the coalition with the Social Democrats, and so did most of the party leaders. Surprisingly, the party chairman was against renegotiation of the government's platform. Doing so would raise the stakes, he argued, and make the party vulnerable to blame for the mistakes of a coalition government in the next election. In addition, the Conservative party would be able to claim credit for any new concessions that the Agrarian Party would make at that time.

When a vote was taken on the issue of continuing the coalition government or leaving, a majority voted for continued coalition (Ruin 1968). Yet this continuation of a coalition government concealed the beginning of the end. Both the Social Democrats and the Agrarians had in effect agreed to cooperate to breakup cooperation. The issue that was used to orchestrate a breach a year later was pension reform, the supplementary labor market (ATP) pensions. The Social Democrats wanted a new pension system benefiting wage-earners, while the Agrarians wanted instead to expand the existing universal pension system, the peoples' pensions (folkspension). The two parties agreed to put the issue to a consultative popular referendum and agreed to phrase the ballot in a way that would isolated the Conservative party.

The ballot gave voters three alternatives: a compulsory arrangement (preferred by the Social Democrats), a voluntary system (the Agrarian solution), and no pension reform (the Conservative position).[5] The LO, however, opposed a referendum and wanted the Social Democrats to do a horse trade with the Agrarians and get pension reform in exchange for parceling out public-owned forest land to farmers.[6] The result of the referendum was as hoped: the two choices supported by the Social Democrats and the Agrarians got the most votes, and, in a subsequent extraordinary general election, voters swung back to the Social Democrats and the Agrarians.

The Public-Private Welfare State

The Social Democrats ended up passing the ATP legislation with support from the Communist party and a one-vote majority in 1959. The reform was made "universal," which means that workers organized by the LO (and employers) had to participate. White-collar unions were given the option of negotiating their own pension plans, but the public system was made so attractive that they ended up joining. This helped bring the white-collar unions into the Social Democratic fold and heralded the beginning of a change in the party's public appeals from an emphasis on "little peoples" (workers and farmers) to that of "employees" or "wage-earners." In the end, a number of objectives had been accomplished. Pension reform was used to isolate the Conservative party and to end cooperation between the Agrarians and the Social Democrats in a way that allowed both parties to exit the coalition honorably. It also was used to redefine Social Democratic social policy, away from the flat-rate design of people's pensions that had never been the party's first choice, even though it was the one that Gustav Möller personally advocated and had used to put together a majority for the pension reform in 1946 (Olsson 1990, 90–100).

The core of the postwar Swedish welfare state was not based on the "citizenship" design exemplified by the 1946 people's pensions but the one embodied in the 1959 pension reform, the contributory principle embraced in the superannuation, or ATP, pensions. The postwar welfare state developed in two steps; the first was based on parity principles and the Red-Green coalition. In 1956 to 1959, a second phase developed based on the definition of a broadly defined class of wage-earners consisting of public and private sector employees, blue collar and white collar. The contributory system was expanded repeatedly and later came to play a large role in Social Democratic thinking about industrial policy and planning when the large pension funds provided investment capital for Swedish industries. In contrast to the flat-rate people's pensions, which were financed over the tax bill, financing of the contributory system was partly private and partly public. Since it was based on copayments by employers and employees, adjustments could be settled within the collective bargaining framework.

Even though public subsidy and public oversight are essential to the system, it was never regarded as part of the "state" but as a primarily private settlement. That protected the system against tax revolt. The connection to collective bargaining also allows the system to become a safety valve for wage restraint bargaining, because wage concessions could be leveraged with increased contributions to the pension system. The accumulation of large savings in the system under joint control by government and employers and unions compensated for low savings rates. Pension funds have played a ubiquitous role in residential and industrial construction. The template of the parapublic fund reemerged in 1983 as the model for a solution to a political "tar baby," the wage-earners' funds that originally had been presented as a radical measure for the socialization of investment capital.

Postwar Stabilization Policy and Planning

In 1947, Gunnar Myrdal gave notice of the Social Democrats' intention to proceed with socialization of a number of fragmented industries, affecting a large number of small and medium-size businesses. Nothing ever became of the proposal, but versions of it continued to crop up in the postwar years. In 1947 the LO suggested the creation of corporatist industry councils (branchråd) that were noticeably similar to Stafford Cripps' working parties and development councils. Business opposed the proposal (Lewin 1967, 327).

As in Britain, the emphasis of economic policy changed between 1945 and 1947 from attempts to capitalize on the war controls to establish direct planning in industry to macroeconomic stabilization and inflation

control. The 1945 metalworkers' strike already had shown that an austerity policy could drive a wedge between strong unions and a Social Democratic government. Accord between the unions and employers with
respect to the need to return to independent collective bargaining pre-
empted any discussion of proceeding with the wartime indexation agreements that provided only for automatic cost-of-living adjustments. In any
case, economic policymakers did not consider them a good idea. Myrdal
wanted to raise wages as part of his program to prevent the expected deflation from setting in, and both unions and employers were keen to
reestablish inter-occupational wage differential and particularly to raise the
wages of skilled workers. Consequently, the prospects of a return to "free"
collective wage bargaining initially bothered only the low-wage unions.

Government-Union Conflict

Between 1945 and 1948 wages were determined by means of independent
("free") annual contract negotiations between unions and employers. They
were conducted on basis of industry and crafts principles involving roughly
50 separate industries or trades. Almost as soon as collective bargaining had
been decontrolled, SAF began to ask for the LO's cooperation in con-
ducting centralized contract negotiations. In 1948 the problems caused by
wage inflation became apparent, and in response to pressure from the government, the LO agreed to recommend that the unions exercise "extreme
restraint" in the next round of wage bargaining. In 1949 a currency devaluation precipitated by the British exchange rate adjustment caused the LO
to fear a return of the kind of hyperinflation that took place in 1920–1921,
and the confederation recommended an extension of existing contracts,
which would leave room for adjustments only in "hardship" cases. The
principle of "wage solidarity" was invoked to justify the redistributive implications of minimal adjustments.

In order to decide which trades qualified for hardship adjustments, the
LO decided to exercise advisory authority and invited affiliates to submit
cases for evaluation. More than 20 unions submitted requests; a few even
submitted blanket requests for industrywide pay raises on hardship
grounds. A central dilemmas of the "solidaristic" principle had become
clear: Who should have the authority to decide which trades and occupations were disadvantaged? LO leaders feared that the national confederation would fall apart under the weight of the responsibility.

The stage was set for a difficult adjustment process that ultimately resulted in confederational responsibility for the formation of one integrated
national contract covering all industries and all trades, but not before years

of contention occurred and relations between the unions and the party leadership reached an absolute low point. Tage Erlander (1974, 33), who was prime minister and Social Democratic party leader from 1946 to 1969, later described the relationship between the government and the confederation's leaders in 1949 as, "in certain periods tense, yes, straight out bad." Wigforss' successor as finance minister from 1949 to 1955, Per Edvin Skjöld, found dealing with the unions difficult and did not hide it. The next finance minister, Gunnar Sträng, did even worse with the unions. As Erlander (1982, 262) put it delicately, "It is difficult to simultaneously be a trade union man and finance minister." Sköld argued for wage coordination on many occasions, and at the 1951 LO congress he lectured the delegates on the operation of international economics. Sköld had been a union man before becoming finance minister, but conflicts between finance ministers and the LO were unavoidable.

The Near Failure of the "Swedish Model"

The wage freeze of 1949–1950 had put the LO back in the position of negotiating directly with SAF, the employers' association, as it had done during the war. But as he left a meeting with LO leaders where he had impressed upon the unions the need to control wages, Sköld concluded that the LO was not capable of living up to the task. According to his own notes, he began thinking about measures that could be used to correct for overly generous wage contracts, including higher interest rates (Jonasson 1976, 192). At this moment there existed a real possibility that Swedish economic policy, like that of Britain, would be marred by the inability to control collective bargaining and Swedish governments would be put in a position of habitual conflict with the unions.

As anticipated by Sköld, the LO decided in December 1951 to return to uncoordinated contract negotiations, with each union bargaining individually (Meidner 1974, 31). The LO attached calls for strict price and rent controls to its recommendation, and in effect passed the responsibility for inflation control onto the government. The confederation also included a new demand for the development of a supplementary automatic indexation agreement with employers that would provide for built-in guarantees for wage adjustments in concert with price inflation. The wartime "indexation" agreements inspired the idea, but a critical difference was that the size of the adjustments would be negotiated ahead of time through collective bargaining. Henceforth the insertion of an automatic escalator clause into wage contracts became a primary LO objective.

Confederational Authority and Wage Coordination

The implications of the "free unionism" principle pronounced by the LO in the aftermath of the 1945 metalworkers' strike were far from clear. One interpretation held that the principle implied that the LO was to refrain from assuming any responsibility for collective bargaining; another, that it meant that the government should abstain from dictating wages. Swedish unions were as deeply divided on questions of "planned wages" and confederational authority as British unions were. In Sweden, however, the disagreement was resolved in favor of confederational responsibility for collective bargaining and in favor of a planned approach to wage determination that was formally respectful of the "free unionism" principle. Still, wage policy remained a contentious issue for two decades.

The debate unfolded in union papers and journals and at congress meetings. At the 1946 LO congress, August Lindberg, the head of the confederation, sharply attacked the idea that the LO should conduct a planned wage policy. Doing so would involve a transfer of authority from the affiliated union to the LO that lacked constitutional and practical foundation, he argued. As for the low-wage unions' desire for wage solidarity, the solidaristic principle was a matter of "moral support" from the LO to the weaker trades (LO 1946, 167 and 190). Anything more than that he considered a highfalutin principle that perhaps would be right for the future but was not right then.

Lindberg's position came as a surprise to the supporters of the solidaristic principle, who thought that rule changes to the LO's constitution in 1941 had aimed precisely at providing the LO with the authority to conduct a planned wage policy. A 186–185 hand vote subsequently forced Lindberg to take his words back and declare that the executive committee was not "negatively disposed" to the idea when the congress passed a resolution in favor of "a planned wage policy" and greater LO authority in wage determination (LO 1946, 192). No apparent change in policy followed.

Rudolf Meidner (1974), a trade union economist, argued years later that the 1946 vote was a victory for those who wanted planning and reflected solid support for the "solidaristic" principle. He blamed resistance in the LO top echelon, particularly Arne Geijer, the general secretary, for the failure actually to implement the solidaristic policy until years later. Nevertheless, a close reading of the congress protocol from 1946 suggests that the resolution did *not* present a clear mandate for a planned wage policy. The slim majority was produced by an alliance of groups that had in common only their opposition to the sitting LO elite. Some wanted to use the resolution to chastise the LO leaders for their support for wage restraint during the war years, while others wanted to compel the LO to seek "fair compensation for members affiliated." They could agree on criticizing the LO for passivity but could not say what the LO should be doing instead.

Late in 1949, the LO's magazine, *Fackföreningsrörelsen,* continued the debate over wage policy occasioned in part by the government's request for wage restraint and in part by occasionally fierce internal disagreement over policy. The debate revealed the problems involved in wage planning even as most agreed to the need to reconsider the role of the unions in economic policy in view of the Social Democrats' governmental responsibilities. The sentiment that the unions had *no* responsibility—which was a conspicuous element in contemporary British debates—was absent even as the different trades came out in favor or against central coordination of collective bargaining. With the exception of the engineering union, Metall, which subsequently changed sides, the cleavage lines articulated in 1949 held firm over the years. The debate consequently provides us with a view on the interests at stake and the motives involved in the conflict.

In a discussion of the pros and cons of confederational authority, the former had the most supporters but the latter held the controlling vote. Eight union leaders outlined their positions in the first round of discussion. The representative from the paper pulp industry union declared that centralization was essential in order to prevent wages and prices from chasing each other. The union represented low-pay workers in an industry where wages were determined mostly by fluctuations in international demand. Its members were particularly sensitive to domestic inflation. The representative argued that "the privileged" (by which he meant not capitalists but the high-pay unions) would have to give.[7] The railroad workers' union representative argued that if "we want free trade unionism, we will have to give up planning." His argument was unclear, but he appeared to prefer planning over union freedom. Arne Geijer from Metall, whose views are particularly interesting to us, since shortly afterward he was elected head of the LO, proclaimed that "centralization was not the answer." The unions, in his view, had to reject compulsion and defend free trade unionism. The authority to set pay had to rest with the individual union, and the solution to problems with inflation would have to depend on voluntary adjustment, which also was a decision the individual unions had to make. By conceding that solidaristic wage policy had been necessary in the past but saying it was not "the way of the future," Geijer managed to state his opposition to past policy without criticizing present leaders.

In their criticisms of the national confederation and the dominant unions, some of the trade unionists used phrases that were remarkably similar to those used by some British trade unionists (discussed earlier). The agricultural workers' general secretary attacked "selfish unionism" and submitted that centralization had to be forced upon the resisting unions. He favored "far-reaching intervention under democratic forms" in wage determination. The clerical workers, a poorly organized trade in an industry dominated by small employers, were less supportive of centralization. Their representative expressed fears that a centralized contract would give workers a reason not to join unions. British unionists often used this argument against statutory minimum wages, and it was a partial reason for the cumbersome system of wage councils that evolved instead. The general secretary probably was right to be worried. When the national contract was adopted, Swedish unions worked hard to provide workers with alternative reasons for joining, principally by means of the so-called Ghent system in which access to certain welfare benefits is contingent on trade union membership (Rothstein 1992c).

Knut Larsson from the woodworkers' union argued strongly for centralization and called for rule changes that would provide the LO with the authority to act on behalf of affiliates. Together with Albin Lind, editor (from 1937 to 1961) of the journal in which the debate took place, Larsson had been one of the strongest proponents of coordination and of the solidarity principle. The unskilled factory workers' union representative spoke in defense of free trade unionism but also for the need for LO affiliates to sacrifice their sovereignty; apparently he was unaware of the conflict between the two principles. He was clear that he and his union wanted the confederation to assume the authority needed to direct wage policy. The lumber industry workers' union representative also spoke in favor of centralized wage policy and went a step further by seeking a differentiated wage policy that would provide some occupations with increments ahead of others. Voluntarism was no longer possible, he concluded.

The centralizers held a majority over the advocates of "free" trade unionism, but no clear consensus existed on the purpose of centralization, or on what the solidaristic principle meant in practice. In a subsequent issue of the journal, LO general secretary Axel Strand outlined the confederation's position.[8] Despite what people thought, the existing constitution did not give the LO the authority to conduct centralized negotiations; in any case, he did not think that the "movement" was ready to accept centralized determination of questions of essential interests.[9] The latter sentiment expressed the fear that all organizers harbor of venturing too far ahead of the membership and suddenly finding themselves cut off from their base.

In subsequent contributions to the debate, union activists raised additional issues. One pointed out that when the government had asked the unions to restrain wages in 1948–1949, the lumber industry was at full capacity, yet the unions were prevented from taking advantage of this to improve their lot. Another trade unionist complained that the unions had put the national interest first for so long and asked how much longer they could be expected to sacrifice their self-interest. The complaints pointed to the problems associated with a blanket policy of restraint, which satisfied equity considerations by equalizing the burden of restraint but neglected to accommodate the unevenness of the business cycle across industries to the detriment of workers. They also pointed to an important difficulty with a national wage policy, namely that it might set workers back in comparison with the rest of society and penalize workers for their solidarity.

The debate revealed conflicts over wage policy stemming from union self-interest and some of the intractable practical problems associated with "planned" wages. Wage policy had to be flexible enough to address social concerns with pay inequities but also avoid distorting the allocation of labor across industries to the detriment of economic efficiency. It had to provide enough reasons for the stronger unions to stick with the national confederation while still satisfying the weaker unions. Wage restraint was needed in order to control inflation, but it was also important that the gains employers derived from bridled unions would be shared and used to produce higher economic growth, rather than simply line the employers' pockets.

Planning by Wage Contracts: The Rehn-Meidner Model

In 1951 a report written by the two LO economists, Gösta Rehn and Rudolf Meidner, *Fackföreningrörelsen och den fulla sysselsättningen,* presented a comprehensive economic theory for how to make full employment compatible with economic stabilization and real growth by means of a planned wage policy. The report built on the discussion at the 1946 congress and on earlier resolutions from the 1936 and 1941 congresses in favor of wage solidarity and a planned wage policy. Twenty-two resolutions regarding wage policy were put forward at the 1951 congress, most in favor of coordination and some element of wage solidarity. Delegates from Metall and a union of construction workers were opposed.[10] A majority of delegates favored centralization, but the LO's official position remained set against.

The Rehn-Meidner model bridged the efficiency-equality trade-off brilliantly by marrying a number of seemingly incongruous objectives. It has become equated with the "Swedish model" of wage determination even though reality never fully conformed to theory (Martin 1984). The ideas gave labor an opportunity to become involved in economic policy, protected trade union autonomy, and still addressed cost concerns. The central contract was essentially turned into a substitute for economic planning (Lewin 1977, 83). Wage solidarity started out as a commitment to "equal pay for equal work" but in its application went far beyond this somewhat opaque maxim. It meant, first, that national contract settlements should aim to remove local and regional wage differences in order to create standardized pay schedules for all trades. This in turn served to squeeze the profit margins of the least efficient producers and forced productivity improvements, what the authors referred to as the "rationalization" of industry. Second, low-paying work categories would receive a higher proportional raise than high-paying work categories did in the general contract negotiations. A long-term consequence was to eliminate certain industries that relied on low-paid and unskilled labor. This too was considered to be to the greater benefit of all workers, even if individual workers were forced into unemployment. At that point, the newly enhanced labor exchanges, the AMS system, would take over and retrain and relocate them.

The solidaristic principle was an unusual blend of utopian morality and practical economic policy. Rehn, Meidner, and the other early proponents of wage planning and the solidaristic principle wanted to have the unions (or rather the planners) determine wage premiums for industries and occupations where they wanted to attract labor, and some even began to advocate moral reasons for rewarding certain jobs. The general idea was that wage policy should be a tool for economic planning and making social priorities. Therefore the determination of wages could not be trusted to individual unions, nor could wages be allowed to become a tool for competitive union organizing.[11]

Ideas about occupational "valuations" that would reward particular deserving occupations—physically strenuous work, for example—were aired. The acceptable limits for social engineering were drawn short of where the proponents of the Rehn-Meidner model wanted to go. When Arne Geijer at the 1971 LO congress at long last gave the LO's official endorsement of solidaristic wage policy, he was careful to point out that by that he meant the narrowing of wage differences around the statistical mean, irrespective of occupational differences regarding the character of work.

Employers' Response

Employers had been asking for centralization since 1947 but were reluctant to trade it for the inclusion of automatic escalator clauses for fear that wage indexation would fuel the price index and hence precipitate spiraling wage increases. SAF had other reasons for wanting centralization. In April 1951 an editorial in *Industria,* the association's monthly paper, lamented the waste associated with having hundreds of organization representatives engage in months of negotiations. Contract negotiations had become increasingly protracted. The previous year's round had begun in earnest in November and ended in April, and one year's contract was barely finished before next year's round began. It was proposed that employers instead use the government's arbitration system to settle difficult negotiations, but Swedish employers disliked that system because it invited the unions to inflate demands due to the tendency of the neutral (or rather bipartisan) arbitrators to arrive at a solution by splitting the difference between employers and unions. SAF acknowledged that the principle of free trade unionism was worthy of respect but concluded that full employment made it impossible to isolate the economics of industry from national economic policy (April 1951, 3). The employers were ready to curb organizational freedom (and principle) for the sake of planning.[12]

The 1952 agreement combined a centrally negotiated frame agreement with local agreements determining industry-specific details. (In Swedish industrial relations, "local" bargaining refers to contracts settled by means of industrywide negotiations, and not to firm-level or shop-floor contracts, as it does in Great Britain.) It included provisions for higher raises for women and a wage guarantee that provided for automatic pay increases in response to increases in the price index but with a fixed maximum adjustment. The following year it was the employers' turn to oppose central negotiations. Lead by Verkstadsföreningen, or VF, Metall's counterpart, employers now favored industry-specific negotiations because they anticipated that the looming recession would cause the unions to modify their demands.

Employers were concerned about the international competitiveness of Swedish industries and concluded that labor costs were too high. Negotiations failed, however, and a contract agreement was reached only after both sides agreed to arbitration. Stranded negotiations in the textile industry threatened to produce a lockout, and a month-long conflict broke out in the food industry over complicated arrangements involving confectioneries and bakeries.[13] In the end, SAF declared victory; meanwhile, the opponents of coordinated wage bargaining within the LO began to reconsider. In 1954, contracts once again were concluded under the threat of a lockout and with employers on the offensive. In the late 1950s domestic growth exceeded growth in export markets, and Metall, the largest and most powerful union within the LO, reversed its position to support wage coordination. On the business side, the effect was to reinforce sectional conflict. In 1962 the export industries organized to make SAF more sensitive to their interests. The employer groups involved in the mutiny represented 50 to 60 percent of the workers employed by firms included in the association. They advocated that the exposed export industries should set the wage norm but were split on how it should be accomplished. Wage drift—wage increases above the calculated increases provided for by contract agreements—had emerged as a difficult issue for both sides.

A New Wage Policy Emerges

A critical shift took place in 1955–1956, when employers forced the LO to accept central negotiations. For the first time, separate but coordinated contract negotiations took place with the white-collar confederation, the TCO. Early in 1956 negotiations broke down and arbitration began. A compromise was reached but, at the last minute, the LO rejected the contract proposal because final changes awarded white-collar workers a percentage increase that it found unacceptable. In the end, to save the central contract, employers agreed to close the gap by awarding blue-collar workers an additional increase. But unhappy with the 1955–1956 round, the LO decided to revert to local negotiations in September 1956.

The entire fall was taken up by discussions over format. Arne Geijer repeated his view that the national confederation did not have the authority required to coordinate wage negotiations. Coordination with the white-collar unions was another point of contention. This time some employers decided to insist on a strict limit on wage growth and on a centrally negotiated contract. Verkstadsföreningen in particular was determined to obstruct industrywide and local negotiations. Negotiations were resumed between the LO and SAF in February 1957, and a contract agreement reached which produced a 4 percent frame agreement for all trades, in effect producing national wage coordination but without the differential elements favoring low-paying groups that some people had wished for.

Two factors stand out as critical for the shift to peak-level bargaining. The first is that a majority within the employers' association wanted a central contract and organized to compel one. The second was that the metalworkers' union switched from opposing to supporting a centrally negotiated agreement. In both cases, international economics loomed large as a motivating factor. At Metall's 1956 congress, Geijer pointed out that activity in the metal industries lagged behind the general economy and stressed the importance of the international situation. The LO's annual report similarly stressed the importance of recessionary trends in certain industries as well as the uncertain prospects brought on by international tensions, this time the Suez crisis (LO 1956, 4–5; Metall 1956).

A number of pathbreaking innovations were introduced through the Frame Agreement. In exchange for centralized bargaining, employers had been forced to accept wage indexation by means of an automatic escalator clause, which included an automatic wage guarantee. Nevertheless, inflation overtook the wage guarantee midway through the contract period, and the LO considered the experiment with the two-year contract a failure despite the inclusion of the much-wanted escalator clause.

National Planning by Wage Contracts

The 1959 contract round soon proved to be very difficult, complicated in no small measure for employers because of linkage to social legislation and the increased involvement of social policy issues in collective bargaining. The ATP pension reform included employer contributions. Working hours had been shortened by collective agreement. The LO demanded special improvements for women on top of regular standard improvements. Extension of paid vacation days was another issue. From 1960 onward, two- or three-year contracts with escalator clauses became common. The format was flexible, mixing confederational frame agreements with industrywide negotiations at various stages in the process.

The shift to national negotiations allowed collective bargaining to substitute for legislation on certain issues, and on some issues, it was considered the preferred way to obtain welfare improvements. The system had a built-in self-perpetuating dynamic. Contract negotiations had reached a level of complexity that presupposed central negotiations and the direct involvement of peak organizations. They had become so involved that complexity itself hindered defection from the system. For the next 25 years, the national framework held for negotiations of wage contracts and welfare issues.[14] Both parties were determined to make it work.

Wage planning through the national contract was nevertheless not unambiguously successful from the viewpoint of economic policy. From 1960 to 1980, when the wage equality norm officially informed wage policy, wage drift accounted for approximately 50 percent of the actual increase in total wages (Calmfors 1990). Contractually determined increases accounted for the other 50 percent. The implication is that the planned wage policy did not work, or at least did not work as well as was expected. Employers were unhappy with wage drift because it stimulated wage competition between firms in tight labor markets and made predicting wages difficult. Unions were unhappy because it primarily benefited high-pay groups and undermined official policy that stressed pay equality.[15]

In a recent study, Douglas Hibbs and Håkan Locking (1996, 109, emphasis in original) concluded that wage drift was the "dirty secret" of Swedish wage policy: "*Wage Drift* evidently was an important mechanism blunting some of the distributional goals of the central *Frame Wage* plans under solidarity bargaining." They also argue that both employers and union leaders were well aware of the importance of wage drift and included it in their projections when negotiating wages. This is an important conclusion because it sustains a more skeptical view of the real role of the "solidarity" principle in Swedish wage policy.

The "drift" problem has theoretical implications for the Swedish-British comparison. If Swedish wage planning was only half-way successful and the success of the national contract is only half the story, Swedish wage policy emerges as less "different" from British unionism than comparisons of formal wage policies indicate. In place of an overriding commitment to a solidarity norm that Meidner (1974) and Tilton (1988) applauded, we find a much more ambiguous mix of economic and political motives and means that made deliberate use of wage drift—and of flexible wage systems based on piece rates—to accommodate the dual goals of maintaining trade union control over wages while also making sure that wage policy was flexible enough to allow for the efficient allocation of labor and to satisfy workers with a great deal of market power.

A Politics of Productivity

If one-half of the Swedish model was about wage control, the other half was about productivity pay and local wage settlements. This second half has received much less attention than the first half. A critical difference between Swedish and British postwar economic policy was that the former found a way to reconciliate the redistributive consequences of economic growth and innovation with trade unionism while the latter did not. Central to the new politics of productivity was, in the historian Charles Maier's words, "a buoyant belief in the power of economic rationality" and the idea that economic growth could supersede class conflict (Maier 1987, 130 and 146). Swedish unions responded to the productivity mantra with an enthusiasm that bordered on naïveté. The Social Democrats saw both substantial and strategic reasons to emphasize growth as a primary objective. Economic development brought benefits to everyone. And while socialization was difficult to accomplish within the procedural limits of liberal democracy, redistribution was eminently compatible with competitive electoral politics.

Incomes policy—broadly conceived as wage determination, agricultural incomes, and even fiscal policy—was treated as a means for imposing a so-

cial dimension on economic activity. Only in the case of agriculture did social objectives trump productivity. Wage policy provided a substitute for
more onerous types of economic planning and acted as a bridge between
social and economic policy, once consensus had been built around national
contract settlements. It was a project that was not predestined to success, nor
had it been fully envisioned by any planners ahead of time. It was the result
of practical politics and some fortuitous circumstances.

Twentieth-century Swedish growth rates were impressive. In 1933 the
Swedish krona was pegged to sterling at 16.40 krona to 1 pound sterling.
Measured in the 1933 exchange rate, the average annual Swedish national
per capita income in the years from 1880 to 1889 was 18 pounds against
a per-capita income of 35 pounds sterling in the United Kingdom. From
1924 to 1933, Swedish national per-capita income was 90 pounds to 97
pounds in the United Kingdom, the difference had been reduced from 1:2
to almost 1:1. By the postwar period, 1946 to 1955, Swedish average incomes had jumped ahead of British incomes, 321 pounds to 280 pounds.[16]
The discrepancy in income growth between the two countries diminished
in later decades, as Swedish growth rates began to level off.

The leveling off illustrates that early high Swedish growth rates were in
part a product of the country's original position as an industrial latecomer.
The Social Democrats' stewardship from the Great Depression and
through the first three postwar decades was nevertheless associated with a
national economic expansion that in comparative terms was impressive.
British gross national product (constant prices) grew by 49 percent between 1951 and 1965 while Swedish GNP grew by 75 percent. In the following decade, 1965 to 1975, the last of the high-growth decades of the
"Golden Age" of capitalism, the British economy grew by 25 percent
while the Swedish grew by 36 percent (Mitchell 1980, 835–836).

Swedish unionists and Social Democrats hardly needed instruction
from their American counterparts in how to apply the principles of productivity politics, but delegations still went off to the United States in 1950
to 1951 under the auspices of the U.S. State Department and the Marshall
Plan to visit unions and factories. Returnees' reports extolled the miracles
of size and of Taylorist scientific management.[17] They also brought home
piece rate systems and scientific management.[18] The Swedish worship of
economic development and efficiency can seem like a quirk. Economic
backwardness and a national fondness for rational solutions made union
elites susceptible to what in retrospect seems like a naive admiration for
growth and efficiency. Asked about it in 1982, Tage Erlander agreed that
the party had placed high value on growth but that it had to be judged
from the vantage point of the time (1982, 11–25). The standard of living
was very low after the war, he noted, and in the absence of rapid growth,

later improvements, such as the 1959 pension reform and the promise from 1964 to built a million new housing units, would not have been possible.

Piece Rates and Industrial Conflict

Discussions of Swedish wage policy have centered on the solidarity element (Swenson 1989, 1991, 1992) while little attention has been paid to the other strand in postwar wage policy: the emphasis on productivity improvement. A study by the Swedish historian Anders L. Johansson (1989) is an exception. Once socialization gave way to shared growth as the primary objective for Social Democratic economic policies, beginning with the 1944 party program, the perceived gap between the interests of workers and those of employers on matters related to productivity improvement and the organization of work narrowed. Agreeing to boost output seemed easier, if unions and workers could feel reasonably assured that they would be allowed to share in the benefits of growth.

A new "politics of productivity" consensus informed a 1948 agreement between employers and the LO on the creation of a joint council for time-motion studies and piece rate work.[19] The unions accepted Taylorist techniques and time-motion studies because they thought it possible to bend the system to serve trade union objectives. The agreement tied certain trades and occupations to performance pay and piece rates for decades. On balance, the victory of Taylorist principles signaled a defeat for social unionism on a scale that easily matched the resistance to the solidaristic principle. Twenty years later, it was Taylorism and not pay equity (or the lack thereof) that produced Sweden's most intractable labor conflicts.

Important issues about the organization of work and social issues were at stake. In 1945, some Social Democratic union leaders started an offensive against piece rates and Taylorist time-motion studies. Arthur Sköldin, a metalworker who was a Social Democratic member of Riksdagen, argued that time-motion studies caused health problems and nervous breakdowns among workers and introduced a resolution that would begin to legislate the use of such studies and create a government board for regulating piece-rate systems.[20] When Riksdagen, after some discord, set up an inquiry on the matter, the divisions within the Social Democratic Party suggested the possibility of legislation disallowing Taylorism. Finding the prospect of statutory regulation disagreeable, SAF and the LO moved quickly to preempt legislation—as they had done in 1935—and initiated negotiations over a joint compact for collaboration in the determination of piece rates and time-motion studies. The result was the 1948 agreement.[21]

Despite the LO's enthusiasm for the 1948 agreement, it was a disappointment to the unions. They wanted a guarantee that time-motion studies could not be used to lower general wages and wanted to create shop-floor and firm-level time-motion study councils for codetermination. Union representation in shop-floor determination of piece rates subsequently became a lever for codetermination. In 1948 Pentaverket, a division of Volvo, made a model agreement with workers of a piece-rate wage system. The LO began educating trade union officials in the art of Taylorist techniques and the pseudoscientific foundations of Methods-Time-Measurement (MTM).[22]

The LO found it difficult to deal with conflicts over piece rates or flexible wage systems, as they were called. Conflicts cut across union boundaries and were often local in nature. Short of abolishing piece rates, there was little the confederation could do. Piece-rate agreements had become a tool for relieving the pressures of the uniform wage systems created by the national contract. Both unions and employers agreed that they were needed for economic reasons. Not only did they help companies such as car makers Saab and Volvo or the northern mine districts to attract labor by offering workers better pay, they also acted to improve productivity.

Second Wave Labor Militancy

Swedish and British postwar industrial relations were in one respect more similar than dissimilar. In both countries, the major conflicts of the high inflation years between 1968 and 1979 can be traced back to decisions made in the immediate postwar years. Conflict over piece rates set off industrial action on December 9, 1969, among 30 mechanics working in a garage in the publicly owned mining company LKAB. Within two days close to 5,000 workers were on strike in the northern mining district centered around Kiruna, a town north of the Arctic Circle. The government had taken over a majority shareholder position in the company in 1957—ignoring Wigforss' admonition that nationalized industries would drive a wedge between workers and government—and had invested heavily in increasing productivity. In the early 1960s productivity-enhancing wage systems were introduced. A contract concluded just prior to the onset of the strike had failed to address local friction around flexible wage systems, which workers thought sped up production without giving them adequate compensation. A change in piece rates could result in lower aggregate wages.

The strike lasted 57 days and became a symbol of a new kind of labor militancy directed against the trade unions and against authorized contracts, so-called wild strikes that tested the LO's authority and the Social

Democratic hold on the unions. Shortly after the Kiruna strike had ended, a new one broke out at Kockums, another publicly owned company. In the next five to six years, unauthorized strikes shattered Sweden's postwar record of industrial peace. In the course of two years, 1974 and 1975, when the activity peaked, more than 400 unauthorized strikes were reported, most involving only a limited number of workers and the majority directed against piece-rate contracts sanctioned by union leaders (LO 1977b).

The overwhelming majority of strikes affected members of Metall. The union had in 1972 concluded some 300 local piece-rate agreements, which some members regarded as a "blessing." A 1969 survey estimated that 63 percent of all working hours were based on flexible wage systems of some kind (LO 1973, 186–187). In the spring of 1970, the LO conducted a survey of members' views of flexible wage systems and received some 37,000 responses, most from the rank-and-file. Asked if there should be wage differences, 80 percent of respondents agreed that there should be. So much for the "solidarity" principle. Only 8 percent were in favor of piece rates, however. Asked what wage system they would prefer, 63 percent of the respondents answered that they wanted fixed monthly salaries. Only 15 percent wanted monthly pay with merit bonuses (LO 1973, 186–187).

The survey revealed that the overriding ambition of most blue-collar workers was to become more like white-collar workers. They wanted wages to be calibrated according to some occupational principle of "difference," but they did not want performance pay by "merit" or by measures of output. Workers wanted to be paid like functionaries.

A Turn to the Left

From a hotbed of industrial militancy in the interwar period, Sweden turned into a rose garden of labor peace in the postwar years. Between 1956 to 1965, on average only 1,500 workers were involved in industrial conflict per year. The sweep of industrial militancy and leftist radicalism that hit other countries in 1968 left Sweden largely untouched. The 1969 LKAB strike, however, set off a series of local strikes in circumvention of union rules that, characteristically, involved as little as ten workers to at most a few hundred. The resurgence of industrial militancy in the late 1960s posed a severe challenge to Social Democratic controls. It also suggested that Swedish unions were perhaps less different from their British counterparts than had been assumed (Panitch 1981).

In 1968 the Social Democrats got a one-party majority in Riksdagen but lost it again two years later. Olof Palme succeeded Erlander as party leader and prime minister in 1969. In 1971 the congresses of both the Swedish and the Danish labor federations passed resolutions calling for legislation leading to economic democracy.[23] The Swedish unions settled in 1976 on a plan proposed by Rudolf Meidner, who saw the creation of wage-earners' funds as a remedy for an unresolved aspect of centralized bargaining and the 1951 Rehn-Meidner doctrine for wage determination: They would allow the unions to socialize "excess" profits in high-productivity industries that benefited from the union's anti-inflationary wage policy. The Meidner plan also called for "collective capital accumulation" by means of a 20 percent tax on company profits (in English, LO 1976). Meidner had put forward proposals for the creation of industry funds at LO congresses in 1961 and 1966, proposals that sought to address problems created by wage concession agreements that allowed an "excessive" accumulation of private capital in firms with above-average productivity.

The argument for reform was phrased in universalistic, humanistic terms: "the right to be able to influence conditions for one's own life and work is self-evident. It does not need any justification other than that of human dignity" (LO 1977a, 7). Codetermination, which could be accomplished by means of industrial relations reform, soon proved much easier than socialization and the creation of "wage-earners' funds."[24] The rekindled ardor for socialization and planning hurt the Social Democrats with middle-class voters, and its absolute majority in 1968 diminished in the next elections. The 1976 election produced a center-right majority, and the Social Democrats lost control of the government for the first time since 1932. They returned six years later and held government power again from 1982 to 1991.[25]

Sectional Conflict and Programmatic Adjustment

When the Social Democrats returned to power, the question of how Swedish control over investments and the national economic fate could be enhanced pushed aside old appeals to social justice as the main reason for why wage-earners' funds should be created. The argument was that "wage-earner funds do not move to Liechtenstein" (Bergström 1973). Fund opponents were given a bleak picture of what might happen—inflation, unemployment, recession, and even Thatcherism—if the plan was not passed (SAP/LO 1983, 6). The failure of the funds would reverse the "Swedish Way" because the flood gates would be opened for privatization and deregulation. The funds represented a bulwark against liberalism and were presented as a new pro-growth alliance between business and labor that could replace the old "cow trade" with farmers (LO 1984, 7; *Veckans affärer*, June 16, 1983, 54–55). The choice was starkly put between "economic democracy" or a neoliberal agenda.

Skeptics opined that the funds were a vehicle for power grabbing on the part of unaccountable trade union leaders or, simply, a new tax on wage-earners.[26] Business was disinclined to accept the invitation to enter a new nationalist growth coalition based on "funds socialism."[27] In 1983 the funds issue was finally put to rest. The final legislation was much different from the original proposal, yet it still aroused controversy because of its implied expansion of public control of capital funds. Instead of the original industrywide national funds under union control, five regional funds under independent administration were created. They were scaled down in size and were made statutorily obligated to underwrite the national supplementary labor market pension plan system (ATP) instead of pursuing industrial policy objectives. Each fund received 400 million Swedish krona (approximately $37 million) every year until 1990. By then they amounted to roughly 15 to 20 billion Swedish krona or about 3 to 4 percent of the value of all shares traded on the Swedish stock exchange. The funds were financed by an extra 0.2 percent wage tax payable by employers and by a special tax on corporate profits.

Business still mobilized against the act in a fashion that recalled the 1944–1945 PHM campaign against Myrdal's "people's economy." On October 4, 1983, residents of Stockholm were treated to the spectacle of businessmen in suits marching through the streets in a demonstration sponsored by the employers' federation and "The Committee for Resistance Against Wage-Earner Funds." In the end, only the Social Democrats voted for the law; it passed with a narrow majority of two votes over the strong objections of the other parties and business groups (Från Riksdag & Department, 40 1983: 7).

Collapse of the Central Contract

The more significant change to the postwar system was not the breach of faith with owners presented by the wage-earner fund legislation but the collapse of the central contract. In 1983 the engineering union defected from the central contract negotiations and initiated separate negotiations with VF. The union subsequently returned to the central contract, but employers had lost interest in centralized bargaining, and, in 1990, SAF announced that it had decided to dismantle its negotiating department.[28]

Explanations of the collapse of the central contract have focused on the influence of economic liberalization and integration of product markets as a chief cause. A more immediate explanation may well be organizational changes in the employers' association caused by rising white-collar employment, in both the private and public sectors. Since the 1960s a decline in manufacturing industries began to erode the organization's traditional membership basis. Mergers with white-collar employers changed the organization, shifting the balance between blue-collar employers and employers of salaried and other white-collar workers. In 1950, 19 percent of the employees of member firms were white-collar and salaried employees. In 1970 their share had already increased to one-third.

In the 1970s and 1980s the confederation's orientation changed from one of almost exclusive focus on relations with the LO to become more inclusive of white-collar organizations and employers in the service sector. The shift fueled sectionalist conflict within the organization but, more important, made the central contract a less useful tool for macroeconomic planning and stabilization policy.

The Third Way, Revised Edition

In 1982 the Social Democrats proclaimed a new approach to the Swedish "Third Way," which was popularized by the finance minister, Kjell-Olof Feldt (1985).[29] A 16 percent devaluation was supported by tight fiscal policies. The decision to devalue reflected something of shift in policy, in that full employment was made secondary to competitiveness. It was also decided to deregulate banks and the historically insignificant and highly controlled stock market. An export and credit boom followed, but the combination of high inflation and high interest rates in 1989 and 1990 caused the government to seek to cool the economy with restrictive fiscal policies.

The "new" Third Way was an apparent failure. In February 1990 the Social Democrats proposed a crisis package that included a ban on strikes, a wage and price freeze, marginal tax reform intended to let people keep extra income from working harder, and cuts in social benefits. Palme was assassinated in 1986, and Ingvar Carlsson succeeded him. The "system change" that failed in 1976 finally took place in 1991. Social Democratic voters did not like what looked like an attempt to void the commitment to balance fairness and efficiency concerns (Huber and Stephens 1996). The election caused a realignment in Swedish politics for the first time since the 1920s by uprooting the old four-corner sectionalist party system. An antitax party rose to prominence, and both an environmentalist party and a Protestant Christian party expanded their representation. The Social Democratic party was as small as it had been in 1928.

The party has since recovered and returned to government on a revised program of European Union membership, decontrol, and "wage-earner" feminism (Jenson and Mahon 1993; Klausen 1998). In 1994 the Social Democrats recovered government power; after having successfully stressed gender issues in the electoral campaign, their cabinet consisted of 50 percent women. The party's unique ability to adjust and change after an electoral setback cautions against premature conclusions, although it is safe to conclude that the reborn party is very different from the one that emerged from World War II.

The Origins of Societal Planning

The failure of centralized planning, as envisioned by Myrdal, was caused first by the mistaken assumption that a postwar depression was imminent and second by sectionalist conflict and the trade unions' fixation on union autonomy. The central contract, the "Frame," formally respected associational autonomy (that of SAF as well as the LO) but in practice circumscribed wage determination to a degree that makes the commonly made claim that Sweden did not have "income policy" ring hollow. The national frame agreement on wages, and eventually benefits and a range of social issues, became a substitute for *folkhushållningen,* the people's economy. Wage determination continued to be marked by a dualism between productivity-enhancing wage systems and a "moral economy" of trade union solidarity (Swenson 1989).

Swedish unions were not inoculated against the sectionalism that created a vicious cycle of decentralization and fragmentation in British unions. The internal debates between low-wage and high-wage trades and industries strike similar notes, as illustrated by the 1949 airing of differences in LO publications described in this chapter. The important question that follows from the observation of convergence is why Swedish unions got centralization while British unions got decentralization. One answer centers on the contingencies involved. The precipitating variable was the engineering union's turn-around from opposing to supporting the central contract after concerns about loss of jobs in response to foreign competition became an issue in 1956–1957. But even more important was the fact that the government sided with the employers in their demand for centralization and that Social Democratic government leaders had the capacity to take a stand separate from the unions and prevail. This was not a certain outcome, in view of the 1951 conflict between the unions and the finance minister. The functionally equivalent moment—or moments—in Britain came during the Wilson and Callaghan governments, and their failure to compel the unions to a "social contract." The critical institutional variable that explains this difference is the constitutional relationship between party and unions in the two countries.

In 1945 Britain's Labour Party remained tied to orthodox Marxist precepts that did not hamper Sweden's Social Democrats. The latter's receptiveness to new economic thinking and willingness to experiment stands out. Yet ideas and elites alone cannot account for Britain's failure to reconcile government power with trade unionism and for Sweden's success. Both are in any case no more than relative terms; Labour did not always fail, nor did the Social Democrats always succeed. Innovative ideas about planning and an engaged policy elite were widely available in both cases. Consequently, neither can explain divergent outcomes.

Constitutional variables matter greatly. The national confederation, LO, was formed in 1898, a decade after the creation of the Social Democratic Party. (The first national union, of printers, was formed in 1886.) The affiliates opposed the creation of strong central authority, and the LO started out as a weak organization. The trade unions' relationship with the Social Democratic Party was a matter of contention. At first, the constitution required every local to join the party, but when the largest union, the metalworkers, refused the requirement was modified. The unions decided that collective party membership was a hindrance to union recruitment, and it was abolished in 1909. Constitutional variation goes further: In the 1920s and 1930s the influence of Agrarian interests worked to curb the position of unions in society.

The Red-Green alliance was predicated on Social Democratic acceptance of curbs on the unions, including statutory restrictions on strikes and compulsory arbitration. In Britain the unions dominated the Labour Party, partly for constitutional reasons through the infamous bloc vote and the National Executive Committee and partly for reasons of practical politics. There equivalent threat existed to that of the threat of loss of power—and perpetual exclusion from power—from recalcitrant coalition partners. The Labour Party was never put in a situation where a compromise with the Conservative Party represented a political advantage.

War and Economic Development

A convincing case can made that trade union centralization was a functional prerequisite for the Social Democrats' transformation into the "party of government." The argument implies the primary importance of institutions in shaping the prospects of economic reform. The problem is that in both Sweden and in Great Britain, wartime wage controls had made unions weary of too-close association with the state, and in both countries the unions exploited their powerful position in 1945 to evade wage controls. It has been common to regard the weakness of British business organizations (see the discussion in chapter 2) as the cause of the lack of central coordination in Britain. Conversely, the comparative strength of Swedish business organizations has been regarded as a reason for the success of central coordination in Sweden (Fulcher 1991).Yet it was not until 1938 and the war years that the Swedish employers' organization successfully assumed the mantle as the representative of business and industry.

One clear difference between postwar British and Swedish business organization goes back to the format of war controls. In both countries, business organizations of all sorts flourished during the war. The two employers' organizations, SAF in Sweden and BEC in Britain, had in the past been stumped by the reluctance of large employers to tether themselves to political organizations dominated by small or medium-size firms but were greatly strengthened by their participation in corporatist war controls. SAF may well have come out the war better equipped for a continued role in postwar policymaking than the BEC did. Swedish employers began asking for centralized negotiations in 1947; they continued to be foiled in this objective by trade union resistance until 1959–1960. Central contracts had been concluded in 1952, 1956, and 1957, but in each case it was in response to government intervention or because local negotiations had failed.

Centralization often has been seen as a "bottom-up" phenomenon, but in fact the war controls were essential in producing centralization of economic interests on both sides of industry. Once the war had ended, emergency legislation had to be lifted, and organizational freedoms were restored.The return to competitive elections also blunted state capacities.

The war helped bring Sweden from a backward economy dependent on the exportation of raw materials to highly cyclical world markets to a producer of sophisticated high-value-added goods by creating a protective cocoon of controls and a greatly enlarged state supported by national interest groups, capable of binding domestic economic actors to a national economic development strategy. There are similarities between Swedish economic development policies from the 1930s to the mid-1960s and those applied in later decades by the Newly Industrialized Countries (NICs) in Southeast Asia, as they have been analyzed by Robert Wade (1990).Wade lists six prescriptions for micro- and mesolevel economic interventions that were critical to the success of the NICs.

Like the NICs, Swedish economic policy aimed above all at stimulating domestic economic development (Wade 1990, 351).There was an emphasis on supply of cheap credit. Import substitution was pursued mostly by means of policies that encouraged conservative consumption patterns, preferring domestic designs and domestic products over imports; consider, for example, the influence of the Social Democratic cooperative retail system. Discriminatory pricing policies coexisted with tariffs and, in rare cases, because of fears of retaliation against Swedish products by foreign purchasers, import controls. The warfare state provided an approximation to the authoritarian development state, fixing state-society relations in a public-private exchange. It worked to reorganize domestic social relations and fix the means for stabilization policy and to slow and regulate the elimination of economic controls created to regulate economic autarky. The protective shields set up by the war economy afforded a backward economy a chance to develop nationally prior to engaging in direct international competition in home markets and abroad. Import substitution, cheap credit and bank controls, price and wage controls, comprehensive manpower planning, incomes policy, and agricultural subsidies—all of which were advanced during the war years as a matter of national emergency—facilitated national economic development.

After 1945, policy additionally aimed to encourage exports and productivity enhancement. The idea that prices were determined almost exclusively on the cost side—not the supply side, as current monetary theory holds—caused the government and the national bank to seek to lower the costs of investment as much as possible (Lundberg 1957, 132–154). Swedish policies were often supply side and based on incentives, a far cry from the command economy envisioned by advocates of "central planning." Public decisions—dirigism—were rarely allowed to replace private ones, and political mechanisms—the wage contract—were used to steer the competitive process in the direction of higher technology and higher-wage activities. Income equalization enhanced domestic demand for basic consumer goods—which until the 1970s were mostly produced at home—and added a Fordist consumerist dimension to growth policies that combined import substitution with export promotion in a sophisticated fashion.

The Social Democratic governments stayed away from nationalization, with the exception of LKAB, the troubled northern mining company, and have avoided giving assistance to specific industries, in order to eschew "picking winners" as well as subsidizing losers. Government industrial subsidies grew to significant proportions only between 1976 and 1982, during a center-right coalition government, which proceeded to subsidize the failing porcelain and timber industries and the LKAB. Upon their return to power, the Social Democrats promptly cut all subsidies. They have preferred balanced budgets to keep interest rates down and, until 1976, generally succeeded in keeping inflation low. Sweden has also—until reforms in the early 1980s—used a bank-based financial system under closed government supervision and historically had a small and insignificant stock exchange. As the Swedish economist Lars Jonung (1994, 346) puts it, "In short, Swedish monetary policy from 1939 to 1989 can be summarized as a process of financial regulation which prevented financial markets from functioning 'freely,' replacing them with centrally-given orders, followed eventually [in the 1980s] by a process of financial deregulation. . . ." Bank and credit policies, financial regulations, and tax rules ultimately aimed to alter managers' time horizons and to encourage employers to retain employees during slumps, to think of employment as a fixed investment, and to benefit long-term planning over short-term shareholder expectations and the stock market quote. All these policies are a stock in trade of successful state-centered development policy, in NICs and elsewhere (Wade 1990; Zysman 1983).

As for the importance of the constitutional framework, the political deadlock between left and right forced compromise building and in effect put a brake on political adversarialism. If reform was to proceed, it had to be accomplished by means of coalition building within the Social Democratic Party, first by attracting rural voters and the white-collar voters, or by working with other parties. That led to an emphasis on parity between the classes; an emphasis in effect that muted competitive pluralism. The parity approach that had helped build consensus for economic reform in the 1930s and sustained wartime economic policies trumped Myrdal's state-centered socialist approach to postwar economic policy, until, that is, the breakup of the coalition with Agrarian party in 1956 to 1959. The legacy of Myrdal's postwar economic planning commission was revived in 1968, when the Social Democrats' captured—for a second time—an absolute majority, which encouraged the revival of ideas about socialization and a new enthusiasm for economic planning. The longterm importance of the "wage-earner funds" controversy lies primarily in the way the reform played out in party competition and its irksome impact on the Social Democrats (Pontusson 1992).

In a general summary of the argument presented here, the broadly similar role of wartime economic controls in causing a radical expansion of state institutions and a new consensus, with respect to the role that the state could (and should) play in directing the economy, is notable. In both countries the constraint on spending policies and income formation, created by the external balance requirement was a very significant factor in forcing planners to change their purposes of planning views. Organization opposition was also a factor that worked in the same direction for both countries, creating a difficult dilemma for left governments that were forced to find the means for imposing discipline on collective bargaining. It is at this point that the two cases depart; in Sweden the unions eventually consented to wage coordination. Ideas and institutions played a critical role in producing this outcome. Without the New Economics' grand scheme for national economic development and the early conversion of the Swedish

Social Democrats to a "politics of productivity" perspective, it is difficult to imagine that the unions would have accepted wage control. (In this respect, the dual system for wage determination also was of critical importance, since it allowed a lawful dispensation from the rigors of the national Frame Agreement.) The second critical variable regarded the constitutional relationship between unions and the Social Democratic Party, which granted priority to the party and to electoral and political strategy. Having said that, it is important to note that significant trade union (and employer) opposition in various stages of wage planning derailed coordination. Likewise, it is also the case that planning only succeeded after a very difficult adjustment process that yielded the planner many disappointments. It was the Social Democrats' luck that the ideas that emerged in the 1930s about Swedish economic development proved to be highly compatible with the "embedded liberalism" of the postwar years (Ruggie 1983). It provided a fall-back strategy when the more socialist ideas, articulated in the People's Economy proposal, proved to be unworkable both at home and within the constraints of the international order.

SIX

Germany: Planning the Social Market Economy

War and Reform: The Theory

The experiences of Sweden and Great Britain recounted thus far provide some proximate conclusions as to the importance of wartime economic policies for the means and the direction of the postwar welfare state. Wartime expansion ushered in a long list of new institutions and new technologies for managing the economy: manpower planning, expansionist agricultural policy, stabilization of wages and prices, industry and banking control, revenue raising fiscal policies, new organizations attaching interest group representatives to public policy decision-making and implementation, new statistical offices and economists engaged in economic forecasting. Continuity derived in part from persistent shortages and economic bottlenecks after the war and in part from changes in the state itself and in state-society relations.

Postwar political mobilization and interest articulation took place in reaction to and in defense of wartime planning policies. Societal cooperation—voluntary or involuntary—with the state and heightened organization provided a new basis for collective action. Farmers, unions, industry, and business associations had become deeply involved with the state during the war years. Pleased about their elevated position in society and the benefits of access to the state, associations were keenly concerned with preserving their influence and found much to like in planning. But while anxious about the continued support of their members after years of hardship policies, they quickly moved nevertheless to protect their organizational autonomy and to assert independence in articulating and representing group interests from those of the state.

The resistance of societal interests—of civil society, to use a currently popular term—to the state's encroachment after 1945 confounds society-based explanations of twentieth century state expansion, at least those that see the state as an instrument for class power (Korpi 1978; Swenson 1997). Group interests play a powerful role in shaping electoral politics and policy, and no theory of the welfare state can be complete without recognizing the capacities of groups to influence policy (Schattsschneider 1960). Yet group interests are articulated in response to state action directed to the state. Group action is in that respect reflexive.

States are a special type of political organization, set apart from other organizations—society- or market-based—in part by their coercive and legitimizing authority (Tilly 1975). States are ensconced in bodies of rules, and possess resources and autonomous authority (Poggi 1990). They are, in Theda Skocpol's memorable phrase, "independent actors" (1985). States are also historically contingent institutions, and the warfare state of 1945 had more rules, more authority, and more autonomy than ever before. Liberal democracies went to war in 1940 based on a modern version of medieval constitutionalism, which awarded the state extraordinary emergency powers and temporarily voided constitutional protections. The presumption of just cause and a promise of protection in exchange for the citizenry's support provided legitimacy for the democratic welfare state. The preceding chapters have described in some detail aspects of the warfare state's control apparatuses in relation to resource mobilization: national service, conscription, manpower planning, wage and price fixing, cartelization, rationing, and licensing. All of these policies directly affected how workers, farmers, and industry went about their business. Priorities were established to support the war effort above all other concerns, including the lives of citizens.

There were rewards. Full employment, class harmony, and the economic redistribution of the war years proved that planning could work. British and Swedish Socialists readily recognized that "war socialism" was a gift to the left, providing a new practical and political opportunity to bridge the gap between long-term programs for social and economic change and the constraints of constitutional and electoral democracy. The warfare state and the reconstruction process provided a "window of opportunity" for reform government. The ability to transpose state power to serve new purposes hinged on electoral consent. The welfare state implied a permanent reconciliation between the state and society, which required group consent. Corporatism stepped into the breach.

Wartime corporatism curtailed competition in the name of the common good and abridged the public-private distinction. Organized interests agreed temporarily to accept a subservient role in the control economy, but the transition to peace made a significant difference for consent could be withdrawn. Interest organizations were in a position to use their new organizational resources to reassert self-interest without risking national interests. Peacetime planning soon proved to be more difficult than expected. From the postwar conflict between the state and organizations eventually arose a new public philosophy in the form of the welfare state, with its dual commitment to social and economic planning based on societal coordination. The construction of the international order imposed certain functional requirements on economic policy but left room for diversity in how states and organizations compromised about the institutional arrangements and the range of reciprocal commitments.

This chapter broadens the discussion to include the Federal Republic of Germany (FRG). It begins by placing the German case in relation to a comparative theory of the postwar transition process. The economic policies of the occupation governments are discussed next, as are the contingencies of the postwar party system and the role of economic planning in shaping the policies of both major parties, the *Sozialdemokratische Partei Deutschlands* (SPD) and the *Christlich Demokratische Union* (CDU). Finally, the chapter returns to the comparative argument and addresses the question of how the German case fits in the warfare-to-welfare state thesis.

The Comparative Perspective

The German case poses some distinct challenges to the theory just outlined.[1] The thesis that the warfare state shaped the postwar welfare state seems implausible in the face of state collapse. The Nazi state relied on corporatist war controls, centralized planning, price controls, cartelization, and military and industrial conscription, much as liberal democracies did, but with a difference: The fascist state abandoned public-private distinctions. In this case, the war effort, military defeat, death, and subsequently occupation and national partition combined to cause the collapse not only of the state but also of German society.

Critical parts of the reconstruction debate took in Washington, D.C., and to a lesser extent in London and Moscow. The postwar legacy of Christian Democratic government control and apparent neoliberal economic doctrine presents an obvious challenge to the warfare-to-welfare thesis. The new constitution, the 1949 Basic Law, expressly forbade some of the practices—compulsory memberships in any association, for example—that buttressed social partnership in other European countries.[2]

The comparative matrix undergirding the discussion of the German case rests on the identification of the Federal Republic as a "most different" case from the two previous cases and hence a strong test of the continuity thesis. Findings of continuity between the warfare and the welfare state, even under circumstances of state collapse, point to the primary importance of scarcity and autarky in producing preconditions for economic planning. The postwar hegemony of Christian Democracy and neoliberalism also sets off the German case from the other countries discussed. Postwar policy convergence across partisan variations suggests the irrelevance of politics. A number of possibilities arise. It is plausible to argue, for example, that the critical element is the geopolitical situation rather than specific national institutional variables. We have already touched on the functional requirements imposed by the international state system upon national governments with respect to external macroeconomic balance and stabilization policy, which worked to sustain economic planning. On the other hand, the case for convergence can be overstated. The constraints imposed by "embedded" liberalism were malleable and did not actually determine national policies. Political actors had latitude to chart out national development programs. The common denominator is the state, and the question of what to do with state power. The privileged position of the state was itself a product of the international crisis, war mobilization, and autarky.

Christian Democracy and the Sonderweg

In contrast to Sweden and the United Kingdom, the German left failed to take control of postwar government. Between 1949 and 1963, the Christian Democrats formed a government five times, each time with Konrad Adenauer as chancellor, the German equivalent to a prime minister.[3] The CDU at first depended on additional support from three small parties, the centrist liberal party, the Free Democrats (Freie Demokratische Partei, FDP), the German Party (Deutsche Partei, DP), and a party representing German refugees and expellees (Bund der Heimatvertriebenen und Entrechteten, BHE). From 1961 on the FDP became the sole partner. The German Party merged with the CDU in 1960. In 1966 the Social Democrats and the Christian Democrats entered into a "grand coalition" government, allowing the Social Democrats to assume government power for the first time since 1930. Three years later the Social Democrats entered an alliance with the FDP and the CDU went into opposition. Until 1974 Willy Brandt was chancellor. He was replaced by Helmut Schmidt. In 1982 the FDP switched sides again and the CDU returned to power, with Helmut Kohl as chancellor.

Standard historiography on postwar German economic policy describes it as neoliberal: in that respect Germany is exceptional in comparison to the emphasis in other European countries on economic planning and state control (Wallich 1955). The neoliberal label was proudly claimed by German politicians, particularly the chief architect of postwar West German economic policies, Ludwig Erhard, a Christian Democrat. Referring to discussions with British and American policymakers during the summer of 1948, Erhard (1958, 1) wrote later, "I outlined my attitude to the ideas which were then in the air about the distribution of incomes. I explained my refusal to allow them to take hold again, for I considered them false."

Germany's past was used to explain the hegemony of neoliberal ideas. Postwar planners could hardly point to the Nazi years as positive examples of the benefits of planning. Hjalmar Schacht, Hitler's first minister of economic affairs, had introduced a "plan" as early as 1934. The links between planning and military aggression were difficult to sever. Albert Speer's *Zentrale Plannung* was initiated in 1942, after the defeat on the Eastern Front. The argument that, by 1945, Germans had had enough of planning had intuitive appeal and has been widely accepted (Allen 1989; Willgerodt 1976).

Erhard's remark implied a construction of a new German self shaped in distinction to a forgettable German past and wrong-headed foreign opponents. By using the word "again," Erhard implied similitude between Nazi and Socialist planning efforts and the goals of the occupation governments. The statement blends antistatist rhetoric and economic philosophy with a subtle appeal to German hostility to occupation government. It reinforced a picture of a German identity different from the past, yet it also assuaged the occupiers' fears of a rebirth of a strong German state. It was a myth.

It was partly true that wartime planning institutions were discredited by their Nationalist Socialist origins, but Germans continued widely to regard the period from 1933 to 1938 as the "best years," and Schacht's economic policies as successful even after 1945. The "discredited legacy" argument also fails to take the Austrian experience into account. If Nazi abuses soured the Germans on planning, why not the Austrians? Austria shared the discredited past since the Anschluss (1938), but still embraced corporatism, nationalized control of industry, cartelization, public ownership, and wage and price fixing after 1945.

In 1965, when Andrew Shonfield published his famous book *Modern Capitalism,* he found German policies to be out of the European mainstream and shaped by liberal sentiments more like those found in the United States. Still, he also saw a "powerful undertow" of centralizing power (Shonfield 1965, 239). Another study conducted in the mid-1960s concluded that postwar German economic policies amounted to "a policy of positive, coordinated State intervention carefully molded to achieve specific and limited objectives" (PEP 1968, 77). Indeed, in recent years theories espousing "stake-holder capitalism" or the "Rheinish" economic model based on collaboration between state and industry have held German capitalism up as a model of state direction worth emulating (Albert 1993, Kelly, Kelly, and Gamble 1997). In practice, the Federal Republic did not repudiate planning, only certain means for planning. The CDU endorsed informal public-private collaboration, but resisted a direct role for the national state in economic development, at least publicly. In practice, policy was more complicated. Simon Reich (1990), for example, attributes the superior performance of Volkswagen over other European automakers to the German government's stake in the company after 1945.

This chapter argues that postwar Christian Democratic governments were reform governments like the others discussed in this book. The CDU espoused state direction of the economy and made use of the enhanced state capacities produced by economic autarky and military government. The proposition to be argued here is that the Federal Republic was not a discordant case with respect to the critical importance of the state in shaping postwar policies, nor with respect to the presence of postwar "reform government" (formed not in 1945 as in Sweden and the United Kingdom, but in 1949), by which is understood a government ready to use the state to reconstruct the economy and society in its own image. The question to be discussed is not why planning failed in the Federal Republic—it did not—but how Christian Democracy molded the state to its purposes. A secondary question is why the SPD failed to appropriate the "window of opportunity" created by the crisis for Social Democratic domination of the reconstruction process.

Left Exceptionalism

The idea of German exceptionalism, or *Sonderweg*, has had much currency. Ludwig Erhard accused the occupation governments of wanting to impose illiberal and statist solutions "in fashion elsewhere" on a postwar Germany that had had enough of the state; the Social Democratic Party leader, Kurt Schumacher, similarly accused the Allies of preventing Germans from doing what came naturally, namely to turn to socialism. The left has continued since to blame U.S. policymakers for preventing deep reform, giving birth to a myth of capitalist restoration, in German: "verhinderte Neuordnung" (Schmidt 1970).

With the release of archival material from meetings between party leaders and representatives of the occupation governments, another interpretation emerges. It raises doubts about the political skills of the Social Democrats, and paints a picture of the party as a depleted and bankrupt organization that had survived Nazi suppression only in spirit. A party that was still enmeshed in the Weimar Republic and, like Rip van Winkle, clueless about the challenge ahead. This ought not surprise us. It was not the Allies that robbed the SPD of their opportunity to take hold of power, it was the Nazis. The party did not shake that legacy until the 1950s through a process that culminated in the adoption of a new program, the 1959 Bad Godesberg program.

On July 26, 1947 Schumacher issued a "telegram" stating his and the SPD's fundamental opposition to the policies of the occupation governments and of the plans being made for German reconstruction in the Western occupation zones. In his view, British and American policies were aimed at capitalist reconstruction and allowed the CDU to hoard political power. Allied policies and the CDU conspired to prevent change and renewal (Miller 1986, 160). The statement was meant as a declaration of fundamental opposition to the new state; a conviction that became a fact when Schumacher ruled out collaboration with the CDU in the temporary advisory control organs set up by the occupation powers. The SPD's declaration engendered a theory of power based on a narrative of blocked reform and rightist restoration, which has been picked up by left-wing scholars. Within the context of revisionist historiography evolved a New Left criticism of U.S. hegemony that blamed the failure of the German left on American intervention (Abendroth 1975; Markovits 1986; Schmidt 1970; Sohn-Rethel 1978. For a critical review, see Kocka 1979). The revisionist arguments to some extent mirrored their antagonists' appreciative accounts of the pivotal role of the United States in saving West Germany from totalitarianism (Ball 1982). In both cases American actions rather than German actions were held accountable for German domestic political development; both were accounts of German victimization and exceptionalism.

The Problem of "Native Narratives"

Comparative analysis is inherently skeptical of claims to exceptionalism, in part because there are so many. How many "exceptionalisms" can there be? (Zolberg 1986) Comparative theory approaches "native narratives," that is, an account that affixes general causal importance to special national circumstances or events with obvious difficulties. I have already discussed Swedo-centric explanations of the welfare state, which have tended to overestimate class solidarity and underestimate sectionalist conflict. Leo Panitch's (1976) fashioning of the Labour left's self-serving story of a treacherous party elite selling out to capitalism into a theory of the failure of "real" economic planning also exemplifies a "native narrative." Arguments about special national circumstances, or "exceptionalism," confound comparative theory that looks to integrate national developmental paths with a common perspective on political development in general.

Working broadly in the tradition of Stein Rokkan, comparativists have begun to stake out an approach based on path dependency—the preposition the sequence matters—and arrived at a series of testable hypotheses about democratic development; for example, the presence of an elite of large landowners as a barrier to democracy (Rueschemyer, Stephens, and Stephens 1992). Conversely, they also have concluded that an alliance of agrarian smallholders and the working class was a powerful force for popular democracy. The late Gregory Luebbert (1991) exemplifies an integrative, comparative perspective that sees Swedish Social Democracy and German National Socialism as path-dependent responses to the Great Depression and the accommodation of popular democratic mobilization.

If we want to avoid the Scylla and Charybdis of native narratives and totalizing comparisons of "systems," Luebbert's method represents an attractive—and ambitious—alternative. The heinous crimes of National Socialism were exceptional and left a delicate legacy that was uniquely German. Occupation government, German partition, and the psychological and political burden of guilt shaped German postwar politics in unique ways. An argument for "exceptionalism" implies that the case cannot be explained by variables applicable to other cases, and also that it does not speak to comparative theory. But do we not also recognize in German postwar political development the same elements that shaped trajectories elsewhere? Postwar West German parties had to respond to the past by constructing new political identities, but they also had to produce policies capable of bridging economic autarky and shortages, an embellished state, societal opposition to encroachment on organizational prerogatives and fears of loss of autonomy, group demands for parity sacrifices in the name of stabilization policy, and claims for representation and redress. The omnipresence of the state—in this case, a state shaped by the peculiar experiences of Nazism, national collapse, and occupation—was the beginning of all politics and politics in 1949.

Military Occupation and Its Consequences

The German surrender on May 7, 1945 was followed by the Potsdam conference, from July 17 to August 2, where the "Big Three"—the United Kingdom, the Soviet Union, and the United States—divided Germany into four occupation zones, one for each power and a fourth to be occupied by the French. In the east, previously German territory was given to Poland and the Soviet Union. Extended midlevel negotiations in London in preparation for occupation had not clarified occupation policies. One plan, associated with U.S. Treasury Secretary Henry Morgenthau, had called for the creation of a North and a South German state and international administration of key areas, including the Kieler canal and the Ruhr district. (Morgenthau's "plan" is contained in his book from 1945, *Germany is Our Problem*.) It also proposed that only the elimination of all German industrial capacity and the return of Germany to a state of perpetual economic underdevelopment would suffice to stem for the future German aggression.[4] This did not happen.

The Potsdam conference assented to a principle of German economic unity, and the four occupation powers were supposed to act together in an Allied Control Council with headquarters in Berlin. Lucius D. Clay was put in charge of the military government as U.S. deputy military commander, and Robert Murphy was appointed as political advisor to the military government, in effect President Roosevelt's representative in Berlin.[5] Clay (1950, 61) later observed that the organization of the occupation government was determined by military and strategic needs. This was undoubtedly true, and it also accounted for some of the problems that the United States faced later in meeting political objectives in German reconstruction.

The assumption that the United Kingdom and the United States would continue to work together in world government—Roosevelt's so-called Grand Design—guided American policy at this early stage. A publication by the New York-based Council on Foreign Relations from July 1944 stated what in retrospect would emerge as a key mistaken assumption behind the plans: "[W]e shall assume that Russia will collaborate with the United Kingdom and the United States in establishing and maintaining a system of international security, either within the framework of a United Nations organization or in the form of a tripartite understanding. Failing such a collaboration, a Russo-German rapprochement seems certain" (1944, 1).

U. S. policymakers did not predict the breach between the Soviet Union and the Western countries. The critical role of West Germany for the European recovery was not anticipated, nor how soon the country would move from being a vanquished enemy to an esteemed ally. Roosevelt's declining health and death on April 12, three weeks before German capitulation, and the necessary focus on the military aspects of the European operation retarded consideration of the political aspects of German reconstruction. The Morgenthau plan's punitive perspective influenced a Joint Chief of Staffs resolution, JCS 1067, that outlined U.S. occupation policies. The resolution called both for an affirmative program of political reconstruction and for punishment of a vanquished state. The evident conflict between punishment and state building seems not to have been recognized at the time. Nor was an assessment of the costs or manpower needs of occupation made, in part because it was decided early on that Germany was to pay for those costs. (Obviously Britain's Labour Party was not the only actor with unrealistic cost expectations at the time.)

The Council on Foreign Relations subsequently worked to modify the influence of the Morgenthau plan and to create understanding for the need to allow German economic recovery to take place (Council on Foreign Relations 1947; Wala 1993). The Council's publications still supported the idea that this should be done within a framework of cooperation with the Soviet Union and the so-called level of industry plans, one of the instruments originally conceived for the purpose of German deindustrialization (Galbraith 1946, 1948). A great deal of contention arose from American policymakers' different ideas about the need for economic planning.

The American Reconstruction Debate

The debate over the role of planning in German reconstruction tied in with larger discussions about U.S. strategy in Europe, plans for the creation of an international authority for the Ruhr industries, and subsequently the development of the Marshall Plan. Much has been written about this topic, and readers are referred to this literature. It is of interest here only to the extent that American emphasis on planning subsequently influenced German actors. The letters of Charles E. Kindleberger (1989) provide an interesting microscopic lens to the conflicts among American policymakers. Kindleberger had served as planner for the Strategic Bombing Command in London during the war and then became responsible for economic reconstruction as chief of the Division of German and Austrian Economic Affairs in 1946–1947 in the U.S. Department of State.

Broadly speaking, two camps—three, if we include the Morgenthau camp—emerged in the U.S. State Department, pitting the planners against the "Southerners," the latter being the two secretaries of state, James F. Byrnes and George C. Marshall, and the assistant secretary of state for economic affairs, Will Clayton, and in Germany Clay and Murphy. Clay and Murphy were averse to planning and preferred a federal model for German reconstruction. They were also anti-Communists, a sentiment that was reinforced by their daily difficulties with the Soviet representatives in the Control Council. (Their diaries provide ample evidence of growing personal frustration, Clay 1950; Murphy 1964.)

Kindleberger's letters make clear that the planners clashed with the military men (Murphy included) on all nearly all matters of economic policy. When Kindleberger called for the nationalization of foreign property, Clay declared U.S. policy "diametrically opposed." When Clay was angry about Soviet appropriations of German property that he thought in excess of the agreement, Kindleberger wanted to permit the Soviets to take more in the (futile) hope that collaboration could be salvaged. Clay was similarly opposed to allowing the Soviets to keep shares in West German industries, which Kindleberger would allow.[6] (Needless to say, the "southerners" prevailed.) Another well-known economist involved was John Kenneth Galbraith, who declared already in 1948 that "The distinctive feature of the popular discussion of the German economy since the end of the war has been its almost unrelieved incompetence" (Harris ed. 1948, 91). Like Kindleberger, Galbraith was against the rapid decontrol of the German economy and wanted to keep U.S.-Soviet collaboration alive. The divisions produced policy disagreements and exercised contradictory pulls on German political developments, but conflicts sometimes arose from the fact that one hand of the military government did not know what the other was doing.[7]

U.S. policy on planning was far from consistent. Clay was personally averse to socialization and centralized economic planning, and disparaged French and British plans for socialization in the Ruhr district. In the case of the Ruhr industries, international issues, Franco-German relations in particular, worked to check the antitrust sentiments of U.S. policymakers. In the end the United States and Clay's successor, John McCloy, endorsed the Schuman Plan for resolving the problems of European coal and steel, despite the fears in the United States of a cartelistic restoration (Gillingham 1993; Milward 1984, 144). Konrad Adenauer, leader of the CDU and after 1949 Chancellor of the Federal Republic, was an early and enthusiastic supporter of the plan, which saved the Ruhr industries from what he considered a worse fate, by which he presumable meant both American antitrust philosophies and British socialization.

Occupation Controls

Policy debates notwithstanding, the reality on the ground was that everything was done by means of government and bureacratic command. German surrender created a practical problem. With surrender, all preexisting state and local governments were automatically dissolved. As Nazi officials fled their posts, the occupation troops were left with the responsibility for restoring functional government on top of the many other political, military, and even economic tasks that fell to them. Lack of manpower almost immediately became grounds for a greater measure of German self-government than Resolution 1067 of the Joint Chiefs of Staff had allowed for. It was also grounds for continuing many Nazi-era economic regulations.

In the absence of civilian government, the military government was obliged to rely on preexisting rules and institutions to a greater extent than envisioned. U.S. denazification rules held that members of the National Socialist party, the NSDAP, and its affiliated organizations were banned from appointment or employment, except in menial jobs.[8] The rules soon proved a problem, for reasons made clear in the turgid language of an official State Department announcement: "The strict enforcement of the law would result in the elimination of many leaders of the former dominant classes from posts of influence and thus transfer power to groups unaccustomed to its exercise" (U.S. Department of State 1947, 19). Occupation government proved to be more akin to a social revolution than the U.S. military advisors felt comfortable with. A large number of wartime rules and regulations were kept. Among them were a 1936 *Preisstop*—a price stop—and a 1942 *Warenverkehrsordnung*—a comprehensive and detailed trading ordinance regulating consumer goods. Nazi rules on rationing of food, services, and consumer goods were kept largely intact.

In the U.S. zone, cartels were prohibited and free trade—*Gewerberfreiheit*—legally protected as a step toward the elimination of industrial cartels. In the British and French zones, policymakers were less clear on the malignancy of cartels. French rules even called for compulsory cartelization. In 1948 American views on cartelization prevailed against some opposition in the writing of the new constitutions. The issue subsequently became a major point of contention between industry groups and the government and within the government itself. The Allied Control Council proceeded laboriously to undertake legislation on a broad range of issues, ranging from the elimination of racist marriage laws, reestablishment of postal service, protection against police searches (which did not apply to military police, only German police), a law for control of scientific research, and legislation that provided for codetermination for workers in management and protected trade union rights. The industrial relations framework was another controversial bequest from occupation government.

The Control Economy and Economic Autarky

The Nazi military collapse produced autarkic conditions. From 1945 to 1946 the supply situation went from terrible to catastrophic. A landlocked country, Germany had benefited from trade with occupied and neutral countries during the war and did not experience the full effect of a collapsing war economy until 1943–1945. Alan Milward (1965, 106) writes in his study of the German war economy that "Even in 1944, the list of consumer goods still produced would have made interesting reading for the UK War Cabinet." Shortages resulted from the destruction wrought by Allied bombings and military retreat in the East.

Industrial production had been kept up with forced labor, Russian prisoners of war, or concentration camp inmates. With liberalization, an acute manpower shortage arose. In his study of the Ruhr industries, Roseman (1992, 24) cites sources to the effect that nearly 50 percent of the work force in the German coal mines consisted of foreigners. In 1945 the British government, acting through the Coal Control agency, was saddled with the problem of restoring Germany's coal production. Industrial conscription administered through labor exchanges was tried, but when the British did not post guards to keep workers on their jobs, most conscripted workers absconded. German prisoners of war were also sent to the mines. Bombing raids had destroyed workers' housing and disrupted transportation, and it fell to the occupation powers to restore what they previously had destroyed.

Official food rations dropped to an estimated 1,180 calories per person per day, roughly half of the needs of an adult woman and far too little to nourish anyone engaged in heavy physical work. By one estimate, the real ration was only 815 calories in the British zone (Gollancz 1946, 19). The arrival of German refugees from the eastern territories made the food situation worse. By January 1, 1947, an estimated 9 million German expellees and refugees from the eastern territories arrived in the West. No refugess were allowed entry into the French zone, and all were resettled in the American and British zones. Foraging for food became the main occupation. High absenteeism, with often one-third or half the workforce absent, was common. Industries and businesses, which in any case mostly paid their workers in kind, still hoarded labor. With food shortages still prevailing in Britain, the primary responsibility for avoiding mass deaths from starvation fell to the United States. With no exports, Germany in any case could not pay for food imports and had to pay for the shortfall between domestic production and food needs, which had to be covered by the occupation powers or international help agencies.

Industrial Planning

Allied economists and administrators were busy working up so-called levels of industry plans for the Control Council, an industrial census used to determine war reparations and industrial quotas. Core industries tied to the Nazi military apparatus—steel and the chemical industries—had been slated for demolition by the occupation governments. Industrial policy was approached differently in each zone. In the British zone, the occupation authorities set out to create a comprehensive new state organization, arguably an exercise in excessive state building in light of the Potsdam agreement's stipulation that German economic unity should be protected. The flagship institution was the Central Planning Directorate—*Zentralamt für Wirtschaft*—which had 7 main sections and 35 control agencies. (For an organizational chart, see Schriften des Bundesarchiv 1964, 104–105.) A Social Democrat, Viktor Agartz, was appointed director. In 1947 Agartz became the first director of the newly formed Economic Council for the British and American zones.[9] The British campaign to transplant the Labour Party's collectivist and centralizing vision to the new Germany had relatively little long-term importance, with the exception of industrial relations and codetermination legislation in particular. The *Zentralamt* subsequently was incorporated under the Economic Council.

The institutions that resulted from occupational government were a complicated mix of recycled German institutions and replicated British, French, and U.S. designs. French dirigism was allowed to dominate the reconstruction of the Ruhr industries, but British and American trade unionism was used as a model for trade union reform. Nazi institutions survived intact in a few areas; farm and business organizations are major examples.

Agriculture

Food scarcity imposed strict constraints on occupational policy, as did military concerns. As long as exports failed to provide enough revenue to pay for food imports, needs could be met only by domestic production or by gifts or purchases made by the military government. As long as that was the case, American taxpayers in effect were partially responsible for feeding Germans. Before the war, German agriculture had produced only enough to provide for about two-thirds to half of German food needs, and self-sufficiency was not a realistic goal. German partition had cut off the "breadbasket" in the east from the industrial areas in the west. Aside from aggrevating the food situation, the loss of the agricultural area also had important political, social, and economic implications for the Federal republic. Farmers were a numerically important social group, accounting for 23.3 percent of the total labor force in 1950. Employment in mining and manufacturing accounted for 33.7 percent. Small and inefficient family farms dominated. Farmers and their family members accounted for 77.9 percent of the agricultural labor force (Flora et al. 1987b, chapter 7). The German tradition of agricultural protectionism and subsidies was among the more important regime continuities allowed after 1945.

The central ideological and economic importance of the farmer to the NSDAP's program had caused farm organizations to become deeply involved with the Nazi system. In southern and western Germany, independent farmers and small holders dominated, while in eastern Germany vast land holdings sustained a class structure consisting of a hereditary elite (Junkers) and a mixed group of yeomen and dependent agricultural workers, albeit legally free. Partition worked to eliminate the large-scale differences in ownership structures and to create a homogenous agrarian class of predominantly independent farmers. The National Socialists pursued a policy of resettlement of the urban population and agricultural self-sufficiency. To that end a compulsory organization of all producers, manufacturers, and distributors of agricultural products was created, the *Reichnährstand,* or RN (Wunderlich 1961). All previous agricultural organizations, including chambers of agriculture, were incorporated into it. Formally a self-governing institution, it was controlled entirely by the state. Disrespectful of property rights, RN appropriated the land of "unreliable" persons and changed property laws to allow the transfer of property to Aryan men only.

The infrastructure of the RN, its local agricultural organizations, was recycled by the military governments. Cut up to fit zonal boundaries, the RN lived on as an agricultural cartel. The rule-making functions were transferred to the Ministry of Agriculture. In 1946 a precursor to what became the German Farmers Union, Deutsche Bauernverband (DBV), was formed as a national peak organization for the local and regional farm organizations. The DBV organized an estimated 90 percent of all farmers (Katzenstein 1987, 28), and it generally has been a loyal supporter of the CDU/CSU.

Agricultural shortages helped explain other aspects of postwar German economic policy. Industrial exports were urgently needed to pay for food imports. The early emphasis on stimulating export industries was a rational response, even though domestic needs for consumer goods and other industrial product were acute too. The position of the farm organizations and the farm lobby grew in part as a result of the very policies designed to ameliorate the weakness of German agriculture. Decades later German agriculture was contributing to the European agricultural problem with its over-production of animal products, chiefly milk and butter. Political desires to preserve a particular type of agricultural production, because of its social and political importance, largely account for this economically wasteful position situation (Kluge 1993).

The SPD regarded the German farm class as the backbone of Nazism and as a "reactionary force." At the 1947 party congress, agricultural policy was dicussed at some length. There was full agreement for land reform and the socialization of agriculture. It was agreed that land should be parceled out in lots of no more than 100 hectares per farmer (SPD 1947, 185–197). Land reform was also on the Allies' agenda, and four years later, at the 1952 Dortmund Party Congress, the SPD still called for land reform, but also spoke about building an alliance with the "little man." Compared to both Austria and Sweden, two other countries in which a large proportion of the electorate was composed of small farmers and was tied to village life, the SPD's dissociation from the farm population is striking. The history of farm support for the right had been a problem for the SPD in the interwar period. It was no less a problem—speaking purely in strategic electoral terms—in the postwar years.

Bizonal Government and German Partition

The road to partition started in 1945, with the Potsdam agreement dividing the occupied territories (and the city of Berlin) into separate zones. Worried about the costs and the implications of extended occupation, the United States invited, in July 1946, the other Allies to merge zones. The French refused; only the British accepted. After some haggling over the distribution of costs, negotiations began to integrate the economic management of the two zones. Actual merger was delayed for another 12 months, which were taken up with maneuvering in the Berlin Control Council over who should be blamed for the impending breakup, the United States or the Soviet Union. In 1947 a new bizonal administration based on partial German self-government and partial Allied control was set up with administrative headquarter located in Frankfurt am Main.

The Economic Council created under the bizonal government was in effect the first postwar German government. It was exceptionally important in deciding the makeup of the Federal Republic's new elite and in shaping postwar party alignments. The occupation authorities retained control over the council, even as it allowed for a measure of German self-government. As the Labour government became increasingly preoccupied with domestic problems and dependent on U.S. assistance, U.S. influences and interests came to predominate.

Ludwig Erhard was propelled from obscurity to the center of government by his rise to the helm of the bizonal economic administration through a process that makes his career seem almost accidental. The first appointee to the position was a Social Democrat, Viktor Agartz. Agartz believed in central planning and the primacy of the class struggle, and he had benefited from the support of the British occupational authorities. U.S. policymakers regarded him as anathema, and Clay was responsible for his dismissal in July 1947, after only six months in the post (Schriften des Bundesarchiv 1964, 121). After Agartz's removal, the CDU was allowed to fill the post with Johannes Semler. He was soon fired for making a speech that was openly critical of the occupation powers and their policies. His dismissal, in turn, paved the way for Erhard's rise to power.

The SPD and CDU each controlled 40 seats. The small Liberal party (FDP) controlled 8 seats and the Communist Party (KPD) 6 seats. The remaining seats were divided among three small parties (Eschenburg 1983, 560). When it was the small parties' turn to nominate a candidate, they nominated Erhard, who assumed the post in June 1948 as the FDP's candidate. At the time he did not belong to any party.[10] In hindsight, luck played a large role in pushing Erhard to the top, where he was now in a position to take credit for the success of the currency reform carried out under the auspices of the bizonal Economic Council on June 20–21, 1948.[11] The reform was practically identical to the so-called Colm-Dodge-Goldsmith plan that had been worked out two years earlier but was delayed by the haggling with the Soviet Union.

Partition and Constitutional Reform

Upset about the Soviet exercise of control in Poland, Winston Churchill predicted in May 1945 the advent of "Iron Curtain" between East and West Europe. On March 1, 1948, the curtain was drawn when the Soviet military halted all traffic between Berlin and the western occupation zones.[12] On June 25, 1948, the United States began the Berlin airlift, a massive air transportation program providing the western sectors with food, raw materials, and everything else needed to keep the city functioning.[13]

With the final breakdown of East-West relations established as a fact, the Western occupation powers proceeded to create the Federal Republic of Germany. In September 1948 a Parliamentary Council met to formulate a new Basic Law, defining a constitutional government for the Western occupation zone. It was agreed not to use the terms "constitution" and "constitutional assembly" to avoid acknowledging the existence of two German states. The Federal Republic was formally founded in 1949. National elections were held in August of that year. From then on represented by a High Commissioner rather than military governments, the three Western powers continued to reserve final say in a number of policy matters by means of an Occupation Statute, promulgated simultaneously with the Basic Law in 1949.

Allied responsibilities and the statute were finally terminated with the signing of the European Defense Community (EDC) agreement in May 1952. In less than seven years, the United States had moved from punitive plans for the emasculation of the German state to proposing rearmament.

The EDC was halted subsequently by a negative vote in the French National Assembly.

Constitutional Reform and U.S. Influence

The Basic Law provided a constitutional basis for economic and political liberalism. By creating an autonomous central bank, Bank Deutsche Länder, and dividing fiscal and budgetary authority between national and state governments, institutional impediments for reflationary policies were created at the outset. British desires to create centralized government in the image of Westminster and capable of centralized economic planning had come up against American preferences for federalism and a "states' rights" type of constitution. The U.S. guidelines for the drafting of the new constitution were contained in a memo—instructions really, referred to as an aide mémoire—from November 22, 1948 (Litchfield 1953, 40; Hahn 1993, 33). The new constitution represented a compromise by creating, in Peter Katzenstein's (1987) words, a semisovereign state. Institutional checks were introduced that provided for a liberal reconstruction, one that favored certain political tendencies while impairing others. Schumacher's opposition to federalism was instrumental in enhancing the capacities of the federal government.[14]

After 1949 the Western powers, principally the United States, retained control over certain issues. As spelled out in the Occupation Statute, the Allied High Commission, which replaced the military governments in 1949, controlled policymaking related to foreign trade and decartelization. When British sterling was devalued on September 19, 1949, the U.S. High Commissioner, John McCloy, made the decision to devalue the Deutschmark (DM). The decision to fix the mark at the pre-1933 exchange rate assumed symbolic significance but was nevertheless somewhat coincidental. The precise figure for the devaluation was set at 20.6 percent against the dollar, compared to a 30.5 percent devaluation in the case of sterling. The High Commissioner continued to influence policymaking with varying success. In the first quarter of the new framework, McCloy found cause to admonish the Federal Republic to do something about unemployment and to complain about German pricing practices (Office of the U.S. High Commissioner to Germany [hereafter: HICOG] 1949, 20).

In 1950 McCloy suggested that the creation of a "Grand Coalition" government might be a good idea; this idea was firmly rejected by Kurt Schumacher. McCloy also rebuked the Federal minister of justice for unseemly remarks regarding German responsibilities for Hitler's rise to power (HICOG 1950, 4, 8). Perhaps McCloy's most important interference related to the new government's attempt to eliminate military legislation that provided the unions with codetermination rights and cartel legislation.

The Basic Law was designed to eliminate what was seen as dangerous political pathologies caused by the Weimar constitution, and aimed to achieve a simplified party system. A change to plurality elections was proposed but stranded on German opposition. Allied occupation policies initially came dangerously close to repeating the patronizing and punitive schemes of Versailles, but cost concerns and security interests conspired to bring about a very different solution, one that relied on the procedural constraints of a liberal constitution and a massive economic stimulation program to bring about a new democratic culture and economic growth.

Political Reconstruction and the New Party System

The preceding chapters have described Swedish and British political realignment as one of the consequences of the social experience of war and the question of the state's role. In the Federal Republic, the recreation of a democratic party system was complicated by legal restraints and immense practical problems. The absence of transportation and communication between the zones impeded geographical integration of parties and interest groups, but transzonal organizational activity in any case was prohibited by the military governments. In the face of impending national partition and constitutional change, the strategic circumstances for postwar party formation were politically constrained yet also fluid, in that the old party organizations had ceased to exist. The last free election had been in 1933, and a re-formation of the party system from the Weimar period plainly was not desirable. Travel was permitted only with Allied permits in hand, and the new party leaders traveled only with the assistance of the military governments.

The ban on national political activity had unintended consequences, and the occupational governments (in the British and U.S. zones) soon found themselves in the business of encouraging the development of political organization. The breakup into zonal activities encouraged regional variation in early patterns of political and associational activities, which were further stimulated by variations in the policies of the occupational authorities. Warring factions within the parties occasionally exploited zonal authorities for their own purposes. In the first free elections to local and state governments in 1945–1946 in the British and American zones, the SPD and the CDU competed for control.[15] The first state (Länder) governments were mostly broad coalition governments. The military government allowed parties to organize only after licensing them. License was denied to the extreme left and right, to an anti-French party, and to the refugee-expellee party (BHE).

The merger of the British and American occupation zones in 1947 exerted a nationalizing pull on party development. An advisory "parliament" consisting of 52 members appointed on a proportional basis by state legislatures was attached to an executive committee, the "government" for the sprawling bizonal administration. The roles assumed by the main parties in the council anticipated those they assumed in the Bundestag from 1949 to 1966; the SPD was cast as the opposition and the CDU as the party of government.

The first national election in 1949 resulted in near balance between the two large parties. The SPD obtained 131 seats in the new national assembly, the Bundestag. The CDU got 139 seats. The remaining 132 seats were divided among small parties, the largest of which were the Free Democrats and the Communist Party. It was not until the subsequent election, in 1953, that the CDU pulled clearly ahead; then it got 45.2 percent of the national vote and the SPD, 28.8 percent. The Free Democrats received 9.5 percent.

The CDU: One Big Tent for Conservatives

The CDU was allowed to form first in the British zone. Its first economic program, the Ahlen program of 1947, had espoused Christian Socialism "Sozialismus aus Christlicher Verantwortung." It called for economic planning, power sharing, and a solidaristic economy, using alternatively the terms *Gemeinwirtschaft* (social economy) or *Gesamtwirtschaft* (collective economy).[16] The program has been subject of much scholarly bewilderment, because it seemed to contradict the neoliberal mantel that the CDU would assume in 1948, in conjunction with the currency reform and Erhard's economic decontrol effort (Heidenheimer 1960, 126–31). Technically, the program applied only to the CDU within the British zone. The Berlin party nevertheless passed a program that also spoke of socialization and socialism from a "Christian perspective." (The Berlin program was put out as a pamphlet, *Wege in die Neue Zeit,* in 1946.)

The Ahlen program's emphasis on planning was also confirmed in a critical interchange between the CDU and the SPD in connection with Schumacher's 1947 declaration of the SPO's fundamental opposition to the reconstruction process under way. Konrad Adenauer responded by referring to the existence of a basic convergence of opinion between the two parties with respect to economic policy, an accord agreed to earlier by both parties. The CDU too, Adenauer continued, favored socialization of certain industries and economic planning—the term used was *"planvoller*

Wirtschaftslenkung" (planned economic association). He also pointed out that the party represented socialism from a Christian perspective (Scholz and Oschilewski 1954, 131–132).

The CDU's conversion from collective economy to social market economy between 1947 and 1949 illustrates the contingencies of party development at the time. The conversion arose in part from a process of party development, which reached back to Weimar period but ended in a new West German party system. It was tied, in part, also to the difficulties associated with developing a new party under the watchful (and meddling) oversight of occupation governments.

Adenauer is widely held to have had no personal interest in program or theory, a view that of course also precludes him from having held any particular allegiance to neoliberal principles. Hence the possibility exists that Adenauer would have been inclined to support planning and "social partnership," had he found that the more opportune path to power. A number of possible interpretations exist for his support for the 1947 program and its espousal of Christian socialism. It could have been a tactical decision, informed by the need to please the British and to keep the party together. At the time, there was also, as Adenauer pointed out, broad consensus between the official positions of the parties. Everyone was speaking of planning in one way or another. The distinction between the CDU's *Gemeinwirtschaft*, Erhard's *Soziale Marktwirtschaft*, and the SPD's *Volkswirtschaft* was not at all clear.

Recently released sources seem to indicate that Adenauer supported the Ahlen program more enthusiastically than scholars had assumed. As late as October 1951, he would use the program in internal CDU discussions to justify his opposition to generalized codetermination outside the iron and steel industries, hanging on to ideas about catholic unionism. Not until 1952 did Adenauer officially declare the Ahlen program outdated (Forschung und Quellen 1986, 34 and 167). On the basis of a comprehensive review of internal CDU documents and meetings, the German historian Horstweiler Heitzer argues that Adenauer accepted the Ahlen program as a synthesis of different branches in the party and saw it as a unifying platform that was not Christian Socialist, as most observers have read it, but social Christian (Forschung und Quellen zur Zeitgeschichte 1988, 750).

There was little reason why Adenauer should have been predisposed to economic liberalism. Erhard's neoliberal ideas did not move beyond the confines of a small elite of liberal economists until 1948–1949. They centered around what was called the Freiburg school, which included Walter Eucken, who died in 1950, and two younger economists, Franz Böhm and Alfred Arnack-Müller, who both became advisors to Erhard.[17] Although politically liberal and opposed to the kind of cartelistic forces within German industry that had collaborated with Hitler, and earlier had worked to undermine the fragile democracy of the Weimar period, this group did not conform to Hayekian neoliberalism. The economists wanted to use state power to shape the economy—for example, by restricting monopolies and safeguarding ordered (and orderly) competition. It was the "competitive order," not laissez-faire that they wanted. The group was not comprised primarily of Christian Democrats; in fact, it was the FDP that was the most receptive to the neoliberal ideas. Ludwig Erhard's rise to power and the CDU's espousal of his economic ideas were intimately related to internal struggles over control of policy and party integration.

Without any official repudiation of the 1947 program, Erhard's neoliberal ideas were accepted as economic policy guidelines at the CDU's 1949 congress. In the 1949 election, Erhard stood as a candidate for the CDU, not for the FDP, which originally had promoted him to the post (Eschenburg 1983, 438). As minister of trade from 1949 to 1963, Erhard became the principal architect of postwar German economic policies. If his rise to power seems accidental, in other respects the overall picture that emerges from the highly contingent circumstances that led to the incorporation of the three Western occupation zones into the Federal Republic and 17 years of CDU-controlled government comes across as nearly inevitable.

The SPD: Happiest in Opposition?

The Social Democratic Party was allowed to re-form in 1945, as the first postwar German Party. Banned since 1933, the party barely survived Nazi persecution and the exile or imprisonment of its leaders. In 1945 the party reasserted tradition by republishing the party's program from 1891, the Erfurt Program. This was more than a symbolic act, however. They meant to reassert the past, and with that socialist orthodoxy.[18] A small group of survivors—people who had lived through the Nazi period in Germany—dominated the re-formed party, in part because the Allies did not allow the exiles to return until after the party had been reconstituted (Miller 1986). The SPD more so than the CDU reemerged in 1949 as a party of the past, impaired by interrupted development. The SPD's predicament comes into focus if we imagine what would have happened to Britain's Labour Party and the Swedish Social Democrats if they had approach government in 1945 on the basis of principles and ideas from the 1920s. No free discussion and no experience, except that of suppression, had been allowed to affect the party between 1933 and 1945.

The SPD party leader, Kurt Schumacher, was a veteran of World War I and a concentration camp survivor of extraordinary resolve. With his health destroyed, he firmly expected that his day had come and a breakthrough to power was at hand in 1945. In his political biography, the political scientist Lewis Edinger (1965) describes Schumacher as man of sharp intelligence but whose intellectual development had been arrested by suppression and isolation. In contrast to the SPD's émigrée leaders, who had absorbed the reformist ideas of the labor parties in their host countries—Scandinavia in the case of Willy Brandt and Britain in the case of many others—Schumacher still held fast to the worldview of the Weimar party. His Marxian conceptions of social change told him that a proletarian revolution in Germany was imminent, stalled only by the presence of the Allies.

Schumacher defended Germany's right to self-determination, but he nevertheless also distrusted the political instincts of Germans. These contradictory and dogmatic precepts combined to produce a strong sense of entitlement. Not only did Schumacher and his deputy, Erich Ollenhauer, expect that the SPD would now become the party of government, they also thought it was the only way to save Germany. A reading of early statements by the two men leaves one with the impression that the party leaders expected the Allies to compensate for any lack of electoral support, if that proved to be the case, and to hand power to the Social Democrats. In their view, the SPD was "die Deutsche Regierungspartei" (the German party of government), and represented the Allies' only untainted German partner.[19] The SPD had earned its right to become the next party of government because of the injustices it and its members had suffered under Nazi tyranny. Schumacher was angrily disappointed when election results gave the CDU an edge.

Coalition Government: The Path Not Taken

With reason, the Allies found Schumacher difficult. At a series of unofficial meetings from September to November 1945, at which Schumacher was not present, "a gentleman's agreement" (Adenauer's term) was made between representatives for the SPD and the CDU to cooperate in the government of Germany and to exclude the Communists. (At that time the Communists were included in some Länder governments). After the official founding of the British zone CDU in January 1946, a meeting was scheduled between Adenauer and Schumacher. At the meeting, which took place March 6, the two leaders both spoke and began by noting agreements between the two parties regarding industrial policy (Ernärungsfrage) and the ongoing demontage of German industry, which they both opposed. A convergence of opinion was confirmed.

Schumacher then declared the SPD ready to collaborate with the CDU, on the condition that the CDU first recognize the SPD's leadership: "You and your young party, Mr. Adenauer, must recognize the SPD's claim to leadership" (Forschung und Quellen zur Zeitgeschichte 1988, 655).[20] He continued by saying that this was not an unreasonable demand—"kein unbilliges Verlangen"—since the SPD was the largest party and the one with the greatest potential, both now and in the future. Predictably Adenauer rejected this and suggested that they should wait for elections to decide the matter.

The dialogue was important because Schumacher contradicted previous negotiations conducted by other SPD party leaders and thereby established his autocratic leadership of the party. His actions undermined party leaders who supported collaboration with the CDU, and also attempted to put Adenauer in his place. The exchange nevertheless also illustrates the extraordinary contingencies of early postwar politics. Adenauer was of course the one to have the last say, and may at the time well have been delighted to give Schumacher and the SPD an opportunity to commit political suicide by means of overreach (Edinger 1965, 215–224). Without placing too much emphasis on what is obviously a counterfactual argument, it is intriguing to speculate about the trajectory of postwar economic policy, if the SPD had accepted inclusion in a government based on power sharing and the existence of a bipartisan consensus regarding the need for socialization and economic policies with a social dimension. The argument can be made that subsequent developments showed that a coalition between SPD and the CDU had no chance in any case. With Schumacher at the helm of the SPD, that is obviously true.

Regardless of how we interpret the sequence of events that failed to produce two-party collaboration and the importance of the March 6 meeting, important differences in the political instincts and styles of the two party leaders are evident. Schumacher was stuck in an early nineteenth-century mind-set of "correct" politics overdetermined by historical theory and derivative "laws." Adenauer, in contrast, was a twentieth-century politician who accepted that political history was made at the polls and at election time. Schumacher's expectation that power would be handed willy-nilly to the SPD was an important miscalculation. When subsequent opportunities and invitations to Grand Coalition government arose, they came from either the Western occupation powers or from a minority within the CDU that continued to have doubts about the neoliberal agenda and collaboration with the FDP (Schwarz 1981, 29). Then Adenauer would reject them out of hand.

The Road to Bad Godesberg

At the 1952 party congress in Dortmund, Schumacher's last, modernization began. Much as the CDU had dismissed the Ahlen program and

Christian socialism (or was it social Christianism?), the SPD severed its ties with the Weimar era. It was the liberal Karl Schiller and not Viktor Agartz that led the debate on economic principles. The congress also passed a new "Action Program" designed to give the party a new look in place of the old refrains from the Erfurt program (SPD 1952). The good thing about the program was that there was little in it that could arouse controversy. That was also the bad thing, for there was also little in it to set the SPD off from the CDU.

After Schumacher's death, Ollenhauer became party leader, and the reform effort proceeded slowly. In 1954 the party congress passed a new constitution and preparations were made for a new program, the 1959 Bad Godesberg Program. With the new program, the SPD joined the reformist mainstream charted out by the other European labor and Socialist or Social Democratic Parties, although it differed in one respect by being ahead of the times. The Bad Godesberg Program represented significant change. It did not embrace the communitarian perspectives so important to postwar British and Swedish Social Democrats. Claims to social rights based on national fellowship implied a degree of Germanness and national integration that was too difficult to embrace and was considered unacceptable given German history. (For a discussion of the difficult history of German citizenship norms, see Lemke 1997.) Appeals to national fellowship could not provide a comfortable formula for the adaptation of class to nation. The SPD instead espoused a thoroughly liberal understanding of social and political justice that stressed individual responsibility and freedom. The purpose of social security was to enable citizens to be responsible for their own life. One sentence from the program illustrates that the SPD went far in the affirmation of liberal individualism. It read: "Man's life, his dignity and his conscience take precedence over the group." No other labor or Socialist party of the time was ready to affirm liberalism in quite so strong terms.

The Reconstruction of Industrial Relations

As the Nazi Reich collapsed, the trade unions were the first to organize. At its founding in 1949, the German trade union confederation—*Deutscher Gewerkschaftsbund* (DGB)—had about 5 million members. It was an entirely remade organization. The unions had been banned in 1933 and all union property seized by the Nazi labor organization, Deutsche Arbeiterfront (DAF). Albeit scarcely a union, there was one aspect of the Nazi organization that postwar union leaders aspired to emulate: It had organized white-collar with blue-collar workers and erased confessional confederations. They succeeded in averting a re-formation of the old confessional system but not in preventing a separate white-collar organization from forming. The Allies supported the formation of a unitary organization but forbade union affiliation with any party, including the SPD. In actuality, the Catholic union organization could do little against social democratic influence.

Since the military governments continued statutory wage controls, known as *Tarifordnung,* at first the unions were prevented from engaging in collective bargaining. Allied policies aimed to encourage self-regulation and orderly industrial relations, but often various control policies got in the way. Wage regulation made meaningful collective bargaining impossible. A ban on employer and industry organizations complicated attempts to set up a system of joint regulation and consultation for the resolution of industrial conflict.

Various control acts passed by the military government laid the groundwork for an industrial conciliation and arbitration system, and although the ban on national employer and industry associations was not lifted formally until 1949, Allied policies encouraged the informal consolidation of such associations. The development of a statutory system for conflict resolution stands out as a significant Allied contribution to the development of postwar German industrial relations, particularly against the backdrop of British and Swedish conflicts over industrial governance. Still, conflicts occurred. The difference was that the wrath of unions and employers was directed against the occupation government. A study published by the Manpower Division of the U.S. Office of Military Government (hereafter: OMGUS) in October 1948 painted a picture of Allied failure and inability to convert German union leaders and employers to Anglo-American ideas about conciliation and self-regulation. It concluded that "both workers and employers hate Control Council Law no. 35 [compulsory conciliation machinery]. They do not understand it" (OMGUS 1948, 12).

Allied Labor Policy

The Basic Law's prohibition of compulsory membership also disallowed partisan unionism, and certain familiar trade union practices that, in the past, had sustained the close relationship the SPD and social democratic unions, and continued to be allowed in other European countries—for example, British "closed-shop" arrangements and collective trade union membership in a political party. In 1920 the social democratic unions represented about 75 percent of all trade union members, the Christian confederation, only 10 percent (Visser 1990, 147). The 1949 ban did not have the anticipated effect of leading to union pluralism. The DGB, although formally politically independent, in practice was controlled by Social Democrats. Article 9, section 3 of the new constitution also prohibited political striking or general strikes. In some respects, the Basic Law also sustained trade union power—for example, by guaranteeing the right to organize and by prohibiting statutory wage policy. The autonomy of collective bargaining—*Tariffautonomie*—was protected by the 1949 Collective Agreements Act, which also included a crucial provision making it possible to extend collective agreements to unorganized employers and employees by means of a declaration of "general binding."[21]

Labor relations rose to the top of U.S. policy concerns in connection with the changes brought about in policy by the European Recovery Program, particularly after the American CIO and the British TUC founded the World Federation of Trade Unions and American unionists became involved in German reconstruction plans. In 1948 British domestic politics—Cripps' productivity drive and trade union anti-Communism—merged with American fixations on converting European trade unionists to a procapitalist perspective in the creation of the Anglo-American Council on Productivity and a separate program under the Marshall Plan for "technical assistance" (Carew 1987).

With the shift from demontage and the elimination of German industrial capacities to a new politics of growth and economic stimulation, the trade unions assumed an increasingly important place in American designs. At first the unions received protection from the Allies because they helped screen for Nazi members in management and otherwise were useful in the industrial reorganization. With the shift to a procedural rather than a punitive approach to reconstruction and denazification, the Allies wanted to buttress the unions to become a countervailing force to the lurking dangers of industrial political power.[22] But in order to play that role, the unions had to conform to the framework set up for procedural politics and the new "politics of productivity" based on collaborative industrial relations and peaceful bargaining over the benefits of economic growth. Within this context, codetermination legislation assumed importance to the Allies.

Codetermination

Control Council Law no. 22 would prove to be of exceptional importance for the subsequent development of German trade unionism. The act provided a statutory right to the organization and activities of work councils. These were to be democratically elected, to be allowed "to cooperate with the recognized trade unions, and to be accorded broad rights regarding all matters relative to the interests of workers in individual enterprises" (U.S. Department of State 1947, 209–211). The law notably did not provide for union influence on management decisions (which planners did not like because it interfered with planning goals), nor did it allow linking work councils into a network of socializing power, as envisioned by Social Democratic planners. Nevertheless, this legislation was the first step toward the creation of a legal foundation for codetermination.

Allied policy on labor issues probably was more confused than any other aspect of occupation policy. In September 1948 Clay suspended state work council legislation passed by SPD-controlled Länder governments, with the argument that future unity would be jeopardized if the rights of states to pass such legislation were recognized. Obvious discrepancies existed between U.S. preferences for political decentralization on one hand and for economic unity on the other (Cole 1953).

Clay's decision passed the problem on to the first postwar government, but the CDU resisted action. Konrad Adenauer was deeply resentful about the Allies' role in eliminating Catholic unions and was disinclined to take action that would benefit the SPD-controlled unions. In 1950 the unions voted to strike if codetermination legislation was not passed. On March 30 and 31, 1950, Viktor Agartz made an official presentation of the union view, characterizing codetermination as a constitutional issue and as a matter of restitution. The union position was that they were asking for protections they had in the Weimar period. In what could be considered a threat, he added that it also was a matter of forestalling widespread social conflict and mass struggle, "Massenkämpfe" (Quellen zur Geschichte 1984, 33).

Adenauer was not willing to yield, and the prospects for conflict were considerable.[23] The U.S. High Commissioner entered the fray between the unions and the government on the side of the unions, with McCloy reversing Clay's earlier decision to stop Länder codetermination legislation. McCloy put pressure on the government to work with the unions and made it clear that the United States was not willing to allow hostility between the unions and the government to escalate (U.S. Dept. of State, HICOG, 1950b, 35–38). In 1951 a bill was passed that protected the codetermination arrangements that Allied control legislation had provided for in the steel, coal, and iron industries, but subsequent legislation failed to satisfy the unions.

The DGB condemned the 1952 Works Constitution Act when it finally passed. The Act required any industry with at least five employees to form a works council, but provided for independent elections to the councils. In the view of the unions, this created a dual system of labor representation. By specifying that the councils should be loyal to company interests, the act also prevented them from becoming the instrument of socialization and planning that the unions hoped for. Changes to the legislation had to await the SPD's rise to government power. In 1972 the act was revised, then in 1976 it was replaced with the new Codetermination Act that equalized the system across industries. But by then, it appears, as Kathleen Thelen (1991, ch. 4) has argued that neither the SPD nor the unions considered works councils to be essential to a new framework for industrial planning, and the legislation was used to divert a new wave of trade union militancy away from organizational reform and from wage demands.

Wage Policy

One effect of postwar rigidities and the influx of refugees from the east was to postpone the moment at which full employment nourished wage militancy and the need for inflation control arose. In 1951–1952, inflation took place in the context of unemployment. Predictably, union wage policy began to change once full employment was attained. In 1954 Agartz launched a new wage theory, which argued that the unions had a social obligation to pursue an "expansive wage policy" that would help keep up demand and push productivity increases and economic renewal (*Die Quelle*, Feb. 1954, 49–51). Agartz, who at the time was director for the trade unions' economic research institute, used left-Keynesian arguments to argue for a structural wage policy—*Strukturpolitik*—that at the same time would increase wage shares and by imposing a "profit squeeze" on industry force modernization.

The DGB's new wage theory had obvious parallels to the ideas discussed in chapter 5 that were being launched at the same time in Sweden by Rudolf Meidner (a German emigrée, who never returned) and his collaborator, Gösta Rehn. German inflation rates did not approximate those of Sweden, much less Britain, until the late 1950s, and in the early 1960s government attempts to curtail wages were restricted to the publishing of guidelines for expected productivity increases and the linking of wage improvements to such forecasts. Agartz's arrest in 1957 at a border control for currency smuggling (from the GDR) ended his political career, but the DGB did not substantially change its wage policy, which continued to stress productivity-enhancing wage determination—that is, high wages. In an issue of the DGB's theoretical journal, *Die Quelle* (Sept. 1957, 380), it was argued that wages and not competition should be the primary lever for economic development.

In 1966 the SPD gained government power just as the economy began to turn bad, even though the downturn was still mild compared to elsewhere. In 1966–1967 corporatist concepts such as *formierte Gesellschaft* and later *konzertierte Aktion* were tried; these aimed to coordinate private wage agreements with public policies. Meetings were held among the central

bank, employers, unions, and the government, but statutory incomes policies were avoided, as were any real changes in the format of contractual
agreements. In 1974 the Bundesbank introduced a new element by converting to fixed norms for monetary policy. By shifting the burden of adjustment to interest rates and currency appreciation, the Bank became the
central player in economic policy, as it has remained ever since. Kathleen
Thelen's excellent (1991) account picks up from here.

In sum, German wage policy evolved along a predictable trajectory.
Deference to the first leader of the DGB, Hans Böckler, until his death in
1951 combined with fears of inflation and unemployment to restrain wage
militancy. In a comparative perspective, codetermination stands out as a
substitution issue around which the unions could mobilize. When codetermination failed and with the attainment of full employment, wage militancy developed. When the economy improved, the centralized
framework for contractual negotiations enabled the unions to pursue both
social and economic improvement by means of private agreements. The
SPD reaped one benefit from its isolation from power from 1945 to 1966:
It did not have to confront the unions early on over destabilizing wage increases, but by the 1960s the economy was so strong that neither did the
Christian Democrats.

The Left and the Postwar State

The combined result of the SPD's retreat into opposition to the new state
and trade union reconstruction was to isolate the German left from the
state. Anglo-American efforts to shape labor relations were more successful than generally acknowledged. While they may have failed to shape the
kind of pluralist trade union culture they had hoped for (and for which the
British unions could hardly constitute a model), they were highly successful in making the unions restrict their ambitions to the industrial sphere
and focus on matters of "more," as Samuel Gompers had wanted American unions to do. A semiofficial history of SPD postwar economic policies
claimed that the shift in the mid-1950s to include social benefits in contractual negotiations with employers was a victory for social equality (Hesselbach 1984, 167). Perhaps; but it was also a move that eventually would
expose German workers and industries to the debilitating effects of international wage competition, much as American automobile workers and
industry were exposed in the mid-1970s. By emphasizing contractual benefits in place of an expansion of the welfare state, contractual negotiations
between unions and employers replaced electoral mobilization and legislation as the chief means for the left's social policy. It was instead the CDU
that could take credit for passing social legislation.

The Political and Economic
Reconstruction of Industry

Nazi policies to business have been the subject of much academic controversy. Where some have seen a monolithic and culpable business community, others have seen business responses to Hitler as divided and in part acting in self-defensive against Nazi controls (Abraham 1981; Turner 1985). In 1933 independent business organizations were banned. As Milward writes, "the task of mobilizing Germany's resources was a political one as well as economic," and it could not have succeeded without the support of business, just as the British war effort could not have succeeded without business and industry support (Milward 1965, 132). A few individuals associated with the old German business elite were opposed to Hitler—for example, individuals belonging to the Kreishaus Circle, a group responsible for planning several attacks on Hitler's life—but the Allies placed collective responsibility on German industry and industry organizations for Hitler's rise to power.

The decision to treat industry as collectively culpable and ban national organization as part of the denazification and decartelization process served, at least in theory, both prophylactic and punitive purposes. Nevertheless, the Western Allies quickly found themselves in the business of encouraging the incorporation of business interests. The old system of chambers of commerce, which encompassed not just retail but also crafts and trade associations, known as *Handels-* and *Handtwerkskammern,* was allowed to continue. The system was tailored to small businesses and in any case had played only a minor role in Nazi economic policies.

As part of the denazification process, tainted officials were prohibited from holding office. The prohibition required the military government to maintain lists of "vetted" persons who could be appointed to positions of responsibility. As a result, the military government was responsible for the recruitment and selection of a new German political elite. Doing this for business and industry organizations was much more complicated than it was for labor unions. The Allies soon found themselves in the awkward position of appointing representatives for organized interests that, strictly speaking, were not permitted to organize.

In 1949 the founding congress of the *Deutscher Industrie und Handelstag* (DIHT)—along with the peak organization of trade associations, the *Bundesvereinigung der Deutsche Arbeitsgeberverbände* (BDA) and the *Bundesverband der Deutschen Industrie* (BDI)—took place at the same time as the establishment of the Federal Republic. One big change compared to the Weimar years was that big industry became integrated under the umbrellas of national employer and industry associations, which meant that fragmentation along industrial and regional lines was avoided, as was a breach between small and big employers. Afterward, small employers began to grumble that their interests were overlooked in the organizational system, and the CDU/CSU and the organizations began to develop remedial middle-class policies—*Mittelstandspolitik*—to address some of their complaints. The prohibition on involuntary cartels in the 1949 Basic Law did not end the Kammer tradition and small business' propensities for cartelistic business practices (Bührer 1989). In 1956 small business received an exception from the cartel legislation with the passage of an act, *IHK-Gesetz,* that allowed the chambers of commerce and industries affiliated with DIHT to operate on the basis of compulsory membership, which gave them license to regulate and restrain competition in the retail sector and among small crafts industries (Simon 1976, 122).

By 1949 effective national industry organizations had been created in the Western occupation zones that made up the Federal Republic. At the BDI's founding meeting in Cologne on October 19, 1949, 92 percent of all industries were represented (Mann 1994, 219). In spite of 13 years of compulsory incorporation with the state and the Nazi planning apperatus, and a five-year ban on formal incorporation, industry and business organizations were reborn as fully fledged centralized national interest organizations.

The employers' confederation (BDA), assumed from the beginning a leading role in the representation and articulation of employer interests, and it moved quickly to centralize bargaining and avert local wage competition from becoming a principal source of trade union mobilization. Firms that belonged to the BDA were obligated to pay contractual wages. In addition, the confederation issued a list of welfare and wage issues that members were prohibited from negotiating with the unions; this effectively made industry associations responsibile for determining wages in collaboration with the unions (Thelen 1991, 41). Although the BDA generally has not been directly involved in contractual negotiations as Swedish confederations were in the late 1950s, the confederation provides help and advice to the industry associations responsible for those negotiations.

Continuity was perhaps most conspicuous in the case of the BDI, which was a successor to the *Reichsverband der Deutschen Industrie,* an association of 400 national associations and cartels that resulted from the 1919 merger of two rival industry associations. The association had been divided over support for Hitler; at first it was dominated by groups that wanted to disassociated from the Nazis. By 1932, however, many large industrialists in the organization—Krupp, Thyssen, and others—had begun to provide money for the NSDAP.

In April 1933 the Nazis assumed control of the organization, and in June 1933 the employers' confederation and the association were merged into a quasi-governmental organization, the *Reichsstand der Deutschen In-dustrie.* In 1934 the Führer principle was applied to the organization, which implied full incorporation with the Nazi state. It was subsequently reorganized as *Reichsgruppe Industrie,* to fit Nazi planning policies, and called for economic self-administration by means of large cohesive state cartels. Despite the appearances of convergence and integration, the vari-ous industries and industry associations maintained separate lives within the Reichgruppe Industrie, and "planning" often amounted to compre-hensive, disorganized sectional bargaining over production quotas and al-lotments of labor or raw materials (Milward 1965).

Business Politics

An official history published by the BDI after the war applauded the in-dustry leaders within the RI for their efforts and success in protecting "self-administration" during the years of National Socialist domination (BDI 1956, 309). It reserved the use of the word *"Katastophe"* to describe the events of 1945, the year of collapse, rather than the preceding years of mil-itary aggression and totalitarianism. This remarkable account also describes the association's road to re-formation in 1949 as one of difficulties—the British Labour government was singled out as the principal source—and yearning for oneness against divisionary influences, saying that "In spite of these pressures, the idea of unity and cooperation remained alive in the German employer class"(311).[24]

True, the military government did apply a one-sided ban on industry and business organizations, but the authorities nevertheless also allowed Fritz Berg, then a leader in the iron and metals trade association in the British zone and later president of BDI, to gather representatives from 23 industry associations in the so-called Wuppertal conference as early as Au-gust 1946 (BDI 1954, 39). The BDI soon emerged as the most powerful business organization in the Federal Republic.

Unity did not prevail against cartel legislation. Erhard wrote the leg-islation on behalf of the government, but the text owed more to U.S. diplomats than it did to the formally indicated authorship. The BDA (and the BDI) readily accepted collective wage determination in 1949 but op-posed most of the Allies' efforts regarding industrial relations and policy. The BDI particularly opposed U.S. applications of influence after 1949. The Occupation Statute gave the Allies (which in actuality meant the United States most of the time) supervisionary powers with respect to foreign trade and decartelization as well as to labor matters related to both those issues. Invoking those powers, the United States pressed for cartel legislation.

Ostensibly the legislation focused on the eradication of all vestiges of Nazi economic planning principles and of the *Reichsverbände*. Over time, decartelization policy evolved to include a number of different objectives and to serve different purposes for different people. The legislation evolved into a proxy debate about industry's political role, the relationship between competition and efficiency, and the nature of capitalist development. Notably, the SPD played very little role in this debate. U.S. objectives evolved from the simple desires to punish and to pay heed to the "never-again" sentiment expressed in the Morgenthau plan to a much different question of international trade policy and fair competition. (For an example of the former, see Borkin and Welsh 1943.)

The change is illustrated by the increasing and consistent weight that the U.S. State Department placed on the issue in later decades, when fears of Nazi resurrection were plainly not justified (U.S. Department of State 1964). American goods were cheaper and better than domestically produced goods, but even if import restriction could be overcome, price fixing and cartels often provided rearguard protections for domestic producers. The cartel issue was vexing to American diplomats for political, cultural, and economic reasons. From being an issue related to the particulars of German reconstruction, it had become a generalized trade issue.

The cartel legislation controversy commonly has been seen as evidence of the tenacity of German cartelistic inclinations. In a semiofficial study of U. S. reconstruction efforts, Henry C. Wallich (1955, 133) observed that, "The German tradition of legalized cartels is almost as old as the American antitrust legislation." Actually antitrust was not as embedded in the U.S. tradition as Wallich implies; cartels also have had much support in the United States. It took an angry chicken farmer from Brooklyn who wanted to sell his chickens in New Jersey, and a Supreme Court decision in his favor, to end the 1933 National Recovery Administration's Code Authorities, which otherwise might have continued to eliminate competition for any number of years.

The generalized ban on cartelization in the Basic Law lacked enforcement power in the absence of secondary legislation, which had been left to the new German government to do. There were early signs of intransigence to such legislation. German experts—one of them Franz Böhm, Erhard's advisor and a prominent member of the Freiburg School of neoliberal economics—produced the first outlines of an anticartel law in collaboration with Erhard from 1947 to 1949. It contained a ban on cartels similar to that included in occupational law. It also provided for a federal role in policing the ban by creating a custodial agency, not unlike the U. S. Federal Trade Commission, and for criminal prosecution in the case of noncompliance.

The BDI opposed the legislation, particularly the creation of an agency and criminal sanctions. It favored a bill that would restore 1923 cartel legislation, which allowed for business self-regulation by means of voluntary cartelization. This, of course, was exactly the kind of cartelization that we already have seen British and Swedish businessmen embrace as an acceptable form of self-regulation. But subtlety was not the BDI's style. The published proceedings (in French, English, and German) from a July 1951 conference on the issue concluded that "With the exception of one speaker at the discussion, everybody else supported the view held by a majority of the national economists and legal experts in Germany and the rest of Europe, namely in favor of a form of legislation for the prevention of abuse" (BDI 1951, 32–33).

The "concluding" minutes from the conference listed why the BDI was against the government's legislation. It would be in contradiction to other European legislation on cartels, against the Havana Charter, against the ECA agreement with the United States, against the principles of the Council of Europe, and against the resolution of the United Nations Economic and Social Council from September 13, 1951. If that was not enough, it also would endanger the structure of small- and medium-size enterprises, "which is characteristic of Germany and Europe." It would prohibit cooperation by contract, and hence further concentration, and render European integration extremely difficult. In addition to all that, it was also unfair (BDI 1951, 34).[25]

Some of the BDI's objections were valid. Neither Austrian nor Swedish business and industry would have accepted legislation of the sort the United States imposed on German industry and business. Cartelistic sentiments comparable to those that informed the international movement to self-regulation in the 1920s were very much in fashion again, and played an important role in shaping much of the postwar European response to multilateralism and negotiated free trade. (Free trade negotionas are an oxymoron, in place of "free" trade we ought to speak of "freer" trade.) The criticism of U.S. policy had merit. The Schuman Plan and the European Coal and Steel Community, which the United Stated had endorsed, were based on negotiated output and price schedules, as well as a rationing of production between different producers.

The anti-cartel legislation stalled. In 1950 McCloy put pressure on the German government, and by the end of the year he threatened to make use of the powers given him by the Occupation Statute to promulgate legislation. Erhard sent his experts back to draft new proposals numerous times. The BDI's position was clear: It wanted cartels to be legal and only the "misuse" of cartel powers to be regulated. U.S. policymakers tried to push the Sherman and Clayton acts as a model. The BDI repeatedly referred to "European" conditions that made the American tradition unworkable (BDI 1951).

Eventually Erhard allowed the BDI to meet with ministry representatives to draft a bill, and apparently a compromise was reached. Erhard nevertheless reintroduced an old bill in 1954, with the predictable result that the BDI wildly objected. BDI unity broke down, as some members departed from the official line and endorsed the bill. The CDU too split on the issue, when Böhm and 19 other party members introduced a version closer to the first draft and closer to a bill introduced by the SPD. With three bills, it was possible that the government would lose control over the process. Erhard's bill eventually passed the Bundesrat in 1954, on a one-vote majority provided by a CDU nominee from Hamburg. Still, final ratification of the legislation dragged on to 1957. In his study of the restructuring of West German industry from 1945 to 1973, Volker Berghahn (1986, 157) finds reason to believe that Erhard had changed his mind about the legislation in the meantime after realizing that industrial concentration was key to German competitiveness. Berghahn sees the conflict in part as a matter of sectionalist conflict. Hamburg represents a more liberal, less "Rheinisch" attitude toward competition.

The controversy was a test of the reach and limits of U.S. designs for postwar Germany. The BDI had been defeated, but the legislation was also unsatisfactory to U.S. policymakers. German practices were even farther off the mark that the U.S. had set. The cartel legislation episode illustrates the power that U.S. policymakers attributed to procedure. They assumed that with the right procedures, things could never go too badly. Procedural rules came up against entrenched business practices. The cartel legislation episode finally is indicative of the SPD's feebleness. The party had played next to no role in one of the major issues in postwar German economic policy. Unable to chose between hatred of industry and sympathy for the idea that cartels could be useful means for economic planning, the SPD only belatedly decided to treat the question as a matter of consumer interests.

Recovery and Adjustment

With German partition, the Federal Republic was permanently cut off from historically important trading partners in the East and lost part of what had been an integrated economy, including the "breadbasket" in the Soviet occupation zone, soon to be the German Democratic Republic. In addition, the Federal Republic had to resettle a stream of refugees from the east that did not halt until the construction of the Berlin Wall in 1961. Those were the long-term problems. The immediate problem was how to proceed from the conclusion reached in the U.S. Department of State in the fall of 1947 that "The revival of the German economy is indisputable not only to European economic recovery but also to the growth of democratic political institutions in Germany, which is the policy objective of American language" (U.S. Department of State 1947, 43).

Industrial planning was a ubiquitous component of reconstruction. Certain industries were subjected to military governance and later parceled out to international control. One of the results of the 1945 Potsdam agreement was the engagement of economists and planners in the disagreeable task of writing "Level of Industry" plans; in effect, these were industrial censuses that were used to determine war reparations. With rapprochement between German elites and the Western Allies, and the latter's increasing alienation from the Soviet Union—the prime benefactor of demontage—the level of industry plans were adjusted repeatedly. In this case planning drove out planning. Next, planners were involved in producing estimates for U.S. assistance to West German economic development. The Marshall Plan required participants to produce planning estimates used to calculate assistance, which were set forth in a required Long-Term Program submitted to the Economic Cooperation Administration in 1948 to 1949 (U.S. Economic Cooperation Administration n.d. [1948a], n.d. [1949b]). The planning requirements imposed upon Germany under the aegis of Western collaboration and economic reconstruction brought along, under pressures of first sticks and then carrots, a commitment to a particular type of economic management, which, in many of the countries, proved an incentive to the development of Keynesian economic policies and forecasting techniques.

The Petersberg Agreement of November 1949 put an end to demontage (even if, in practice, it did not stop until 1951) and protected the Ruhr industries by creating a trans-national oversight authority that became a pillar of postwar European cooperation. Within the coal industry discussions of industrial planning and socialization were shaped a priori by military and insternational interests. The British had initiated nationalization of the coal industry by creating the North German Coal Control, which absorbed the Ruhr Coal Controls that the invading U.S. forces had created. Coal production and labor issues related to the industry—recruitment, housing, wages, and the like—were similarly put under administrative control.

With the transfer of economic policy authority to the new German government in 1949, nationalization was foreclosed but control policies were continued. Controls kept prices down and industry rehabilitation turned into a matter of public-private negotiation, all very much within the European mainstream of corporatist industrial policy and not at all in conformity with Ludwig Erhard's neoliberal rhetoric (Abelshauser 1983).

The Allies liquidated the German film industry as well as I.G. Farben, a chemical industry, as punishment for their close ties with the Nazi war machine. Industries that were featured on the British Labour Party's nationalization platform, including railways and some of the automobile industry (Volkswagen), were already nationalized by the Allies or the National Socialists. When we add coal and steel, the list is substantial. Other industries from banking to insurance and utilities operated on license and were subjected to strict public oversight. Some Länder governments moved independently on socialization; Hessen passed a general socialization bill in October 1950, and Hamburg also had a socialization plan. The occupation government continued to exercise an iron grip on the economy in both small and big ways. Until the December 1946 Byrnes-Bevin Agreement, which provided for the creation of a Joint Foreign Exchange and Export-Import Control—the first step toward a merger of the British and American zones—all foreign exchange was carried out on the accounts of the occupation powers. Early economic policy measures sent contradictory signals regarding the foundation of postwar economic policy.

Erhard's celebrated 1948 decontrol measures notwithstanding, a large number of controls and licensing requirements were retained, including export-import quotas and licensing, currency controls, and bank controls. New ones were added in 1951–1952 in response to the inflationary Korea boom—so many controls were made that the BDI complained in 1952 that Erhard's decontrol offensive had died at birth in 1948 (BDI 1952, 19). And finally, new controls were added in order to mold economic behavior. A system of export credits was used, for example, to steer producers into foreign markets and away from home markets.[26] Taxes were relatively high. The combined federal, state, and local budget absorbed about 35 percent of Gross National Product in the 1950s. Of total taxes, nearly 40 percent went to transfer payments, 20 percent to investment purposes, and 15 percent to pay for occupation costs (Flora et al. 1987). The conclusion that the neoliberal espousal of economic freedom and decontrol obscured a very statist reality is close to the mark.

The SPD's Belated Reconciliation to the Federal Republic

At the beginning of the chapter, we asked why the CDU and not the SPD benefited from the reconstruction process and from Allied policies that, on balance, favored a central role for government in reconstruction and economic reform. The obvious answer is that the CDU seized the process by mobilizing German hostilities against occupation government and merging opposition to occupation policies with collaborative nationalism. In hindsight, we can conclude that the SPD squandered its moral advantage by refusing to participate in the occupation administration. The SDP's nonparticipation allowed the CDU to appropriate credit for the success of reform—for example, the 1948 currency reform. While the SPD declared itself in "opposition" to the state, the CDU, despite its avowed oppostion to "statism," developed an affirmative program to use the powers accumulated by the state for purposes of domestic economic and social reform. The CDU also appropriated the social protection issues by stressing again and again the social dimension to reconstituted capitalism. It seized control of the center ground by being the "new" party, something that Schumacher wrongly thought should work against the party.

From a comparative perspective, the reversal of fortune between the left and the right was as much a product of circumstances as the British Labour Party's unexpected but in retrospect predictable (or postdictable, based on what we now know about the effects of the war on public and elite sentiments) victory in 1945. Compared to the Swedish center-right parties and the British Conservative Party, the newness of the CDU stands out as a key factor explaining the party's ability to adapt policy and program to the state and the institutional legacies—for better and worse—bequeathed to postwar German governments by the Nazis and by the Western occupation powers.

From contemporary sources—meetings, speeches, and statements—and Edinger's brilliant biography (1965), Schumacher's abrasive personality and dogmatic style emerged as factors that damaged the SPD's relationship with the Allies, even if in other respects it might well have been a political advantage. No one doubted Schumacher's singular importance in protecting the SPD from Communist encroachment and against splintering in the wake of German partition. Comparatively speaking, what stands out is the SPD's near-total lack of a unifying social program capable of rousing voters who did not subscribe the party's core belief, a program along the lines of the British "New Jerusalem" or the Swedish "People's Home." Any possibility of a coalition with farmers—a "worker-peasant" alliance—which elsewhere was key to the creation of a reflationary "growth coalition" was ruled out because of the SPD's hard feelings about rural society's support for Nazism. In 1946, Schumacher called in a meeting of the Advisory Council to the military government for land reform and socialization of German agriculture (Quellen zur Geschicte 1985, 571). The SPD later changed its mind about agrarian property rights and reassured family farmers in the 1952 Action Program, but by then farmers had already gotten what they wanted from the CDU. The SPD's early economic program rested on hostility to the capitalist state and a deep class resentment. In this respect the SPD was more like than unlike the British Labour Party, which also only slowly woke up to the need for a functional (if not psychological) alliance with farm interests.

An Opportunity Missed: The Economic Parliament

Like the British Labour Party, the SPD's programmatic development moved from the 1920s to the 1950s in a mere span of five years. In 1950 the SPD put forward a new economic program—*Entwurf eines Gesetzes zur Neuordnung der Wirtschaft*—based on two principal components. One was codetermination, which we have already discussed. The other was a proposal to create a national Economic Council, a *Wirtschaftsrat*. The council's proposal eventually evolved into a Keynesian council of economic advisors (and was passed as such in 1966), but at its inception, it was more like a second legislative chamber based on functional representation. The idea would have revived, albeit in changed form, an aspect of the old Ständestaat and its tradition of coordination and industrial regulation by "chambers," or *Wirtschaftskammern,* something that actually happened in Austria.

Surprisingly, the BDI took kindly to the idea, although the organization thought it best that the council remain advisory only. Citing the Swiss constitution as a model, the BDI declared it "a practical and fruitful path"—"in einfacher und fruchtbarer Weg" (BDI 1954, 22).[27] A joint BDI and BDA committee was created that also concluded that the council was a good idea. The BDI continued to support the idea for some years and began to specify the forms that the council might take. Council members should be nominated by the organizations. The council should consist of representatives from the "social partners," appointed by the BDA/BDI and the DGB, and by a third party.

The council's purpose should be to broker social compromise, even to preempt political conflict. Adenauer was apparently in favor of creating the council; Erhard against (Braunthal 1965, 186–191). Like Schumacher's rejection in 1946 of cooperation with the CDU in a Grand Coalition partnership, the council presents us with new evidence of a possibility of an alternative trajectory.

Would a council have changed things, by creating a corporatist foundation for cross-class negotiations on general economic policy? Would a decision in March 1946 to use a "Grand Coalition" have allowed the SPD to benefit from power and reconcile program with action at an earlier time? Or what if a Grand Coalition had materialized a few years later, when the Allies pressed for the creation of one between the SPD and the CDU? We cannot answer those questions, and only point to the alternative paths considered at the time. In retrospect, the SPD lost its "window of opportunity" to appropriate the powers of the reconstruction process for its own purposes very early, as early as in 1946–1947, when Schumacher rejected coalition government. At that time, the CDU was not yet a unified organization and the party's electoral support was uncertain. CDU leaders themselves were unsure that the party would stick together and what its program would be. Party identification was still weak and participation was low. Political legitimacy did not flow from voters to parties; it was derived from the state itself and from the reconstruction process. Once the opportunity was squandered, the SPD was confined to the unenviable position of the opposition party, looking to a slow "march through the institutions," to mobilize support through elections and from being out of office.

Conclusion: Ideas and Institutions as Sources of Political Power

The origins of German Christian Democratic dominance of the postwar welfare state highlight the critical importance of policy as a source of political power. The CDU's capacity to control policy hinged critically on the party elite's ability to reconcile strong state capacities with group interests. Part of that process involved a public rhetoric of hostility to the state, the ambiguities of which permitted the state to shape a new social order based on group autonomy and self-government within a framework of a statist strategy for national economic development.

Even if the worldview of the SPD stood out as a critical obstacle to the party's ascent to power in the days of occupational government, dogma ultimately played a role; less in the sense that it precluded the party from mobilizing support for its ideas, than because it caused Schumacher to miscalculate the consequences of an oppositional stance. Again the comparative perspective helps fine-tune our understanding of the causal mechanisms. The British Labour Party also subscribed to ideas that were rooted in the triumphs of the predepression years, and even the Swedish Social Democrats were critically mistaken in their understanding of the problems and constraints of reconstruction and the extension of wartime planning to peacetime conditions. Yet once in power, these parties and their ideas changed radically and quickly (although not always quickly enough). The British Labour Party's greatest advantage was that it approached postwar reconstruction from a position of preexisting inclusion in government and with the ability to both appropriate and benefit from the enhanced state capacities of the warfare state. The SPD had none of the advantages of power and lacked the experience and the knowledge to make sense of the changes taking place. As the "new" party, the CDU had clear competitive advantage on both scores, which allowed it to use the state to develop a new base for itself.

At the cost of stepping into institutional determinism, the advantage of power-sharing arrangements—illustrated by the Swedish Red-Green alliance and the National Government in Britain—is that it provides the opportunity for a party to redeem itself with skeptical voters and to steel voters away from the center. In Sweden and Britain (and Austria, see chapter 8), coalition government provided a focal point for otherwise diffused class interests and allowed a link between government and societal organizations; a social pact for the mobilization of all available national resources in the national interest. The sustaining power of compromise and collaboration rests in part on the exponential growth of the costs of conflict as collaboration becomes extended, but also on the centralizing consequences of organized coordination. The SPD's rejection of collaborative government implied a conflict prespective on German society that worked to isolate the party from the center of politics. The long-standing connections between German small-scale farmers and political Catholicism—and the absence of an independent Agrarian party—proved in this respect a disadvantage for the SPD, isolating the party from an important voting bloc.

One can object that the SPD, as the party of industrial workers, had few natural ties to the agrarian economy (which it regarded disdainfully in any case). One can also argue that differences over the re-creation of a centralizing nation-state were more important than the class struggle in fixing the SPD as the minority party. Comparative evidence suggests that the animosities between urban and rural voters could be overcome in a "small people's" alliance, based on generous spending policies providing farmers and workers with parity entitlement. The preferences of Bavarian Social Democrats for federalism and their opposition to Schumacher's centralizing designs for the Basic Law suggest that the conflict was as much a sectional conflict mirroring a north-south cleavage line, shaped by religion and by ties (or nonties) to a dominant north German state, as it was a matter of class conflict.

Comparative Theory and the German Case

The thesis advanced from different quarters of political science by, among others, Robert Goodin (1996) and Arend Lijphart (1975, 1977)—that certain constitutional frameworks promote virtuous cycles of compromise and generalized convergence of ideas about interests and policy does not stand up well in the face of postwar German adversarialism. Until the creation of a brief Grand Coalition between 1966 and 1969, conflict prevailed (more or less) in the post-1945 Federal Republic. Like Sweden and Austria, the Federal Republic utilized proportional representation—albeit with modifications that prevented party fragmentation—but "consociational" or collaborative policymaking failed.

West German policymaking has instead resembled British "majoritarian" patterns, in which an area of informal consensus tends to emerge from government to government. Continuity in postwar economic policy derived above all from the character of the postwar state and the capacity of political actors to appropriate the state for the purpose of policies that sustained *their* image of society and a social and political construction of power that favored core constituencies.

Ideas mattered in a number of ways. The transition process from war mobilization and, in the German case, occupation to peacetime invited "grand designs" about the nature of state-society relations. The very presence of the enhanced state capacities privileged an elitist competition for control of the state. Hence, reform governments prevailed due to their political and organizational capacities to amend programs to the new means. Ideas mattered, but only if they were flexible enough to bridge the schism between reform and constraint.

We can list the ways in which the SPD fell short in comparison to the British, the Swedish, and the Austrian labor parties. Lacking an alliance with farmers that could have sustained a Red-Green coalition, the SPD had to look elsewhere for partners. In the first postwar years, variable coalitions sustained Länder governments, but, at the national level, Schumacher's strategy left the party isolated in opposition. The SPD's nationalism was an embittered one, framed in opposition to communism and the Western occupation powers, in stark contrast to the promise of a "New Jerusalem" or a "People's Home" that attracted middle-class voters to the Labour Party and to the Scandinavian Social Democrats. In Sweden and Britain—and even in the United States—the war provided an opportunity for reconciliation between the left and the state; no such reconciliation took place in Germany. There, occupational government instead produced a reconstructed and "modernized" secular Christian Democratic Party. The CDU was the postwar German reform party of government. It used state power to coalesce interest groups around its program of the affirmative use of the state to reconstruct a new German social order and a planned restoration of private power.

SEVEN

War, Citizenship, and American Exceptionalism

The State and Social Cohesion

The United States presents us with a different test of the warfare-to-welfare state continuity thesis. Like the Federal Republic, the United States varies from Sweden and the United Kingdom by the absence of a postwar reform offensive guided by a left-wing reform government (the Truman administration hardly fits that bill.) Like the United Kingdom and unlike the Federal Republic, the United States participated in the war as a liberal democracy, and the wartime government raised the resources needed for the war effort on constitutionalist principles by allowing unions and industry direct representation in the control economy. Unlike Sweden and the United Kingdom, the United States did not experience extreme shortages. Protected by geographical distance from the theater of war and by size against economic autarky, the American home front was protected against analogous hardships.

Yet comprehensive economic controls and wartime resource mobilization affected the United States in ways not dissimilar to those discussed in the preceding chapters (Milward 1979). This chapter turns first to the control economy and then to the reconstruction debate. Domestic sources of support for a liberal revival and the decline of planning are discussed next. The chapter concludes with a discussion of wartime cross-class constitutionalism and postwar citizenship policies.

Convergence or Exceptionalism: The United States

From Werner Sombart (1976) to Frederick Jackson Turner (1920), scholars have linked American "exceptionalism," by which is generally implied the absence of a socialist tradition in the United States, to the frontier and the immigrant experience, or to the fact that the country lacked native elites capable of arousing the wrath of dominated classes. But scholars have also seen sources of convergence between U.S. and European development paths in both the statism of the New Deal and the expansion of the central state in connection with mobilization for war in 1942 to 1945 (Lichtenstein 1989).

The history of wartime convergence is pertinent to the present argument less for what it says about the United States than for what it says about the European welfare state. At the end of the war, discussion was not of "reconstruction" but of "reconversion," the readjustment of production to peacetime purposes. Nevertheless, as in Europe, "plans" were being made and hopes were being raised. These hopes were partly disappointed.

Federalism and sectionalism usually play a large role in explanations of the weaknesses of the postwar U.S. welfare state (Bensel 1984). Without diminishing the importance of these variables, it is worth noticing that sectionalist and federalist impulses were not absent in the European context either. The weakness of the American labor movement or the materialist orientation of those unions is also sometimes pinpointed as the cause of the absence of a socialist or social democratic presence in U.S. policies. The split between the crafts unions in the American Federation of Labor (AFL) and the industrial unions in the CIO prevented labor from acting as a unitary action, and even occasionally pitted the two confederations on opposite sides of the same issue. But then, sectionalism was also a strong force also in European trade unionism and was remedied only with the help of state action.[1]

The argument can be made that the narrowness of American trade unionism is the result of a blocked path, a dependent variable so to say, rather than an inherent attribute (Brown 1998). The actions and policies of Walter Reuther and the United Auto Worker's Union, which he led after 1945, suggest that American trade unionism was not averse generally to planning and to a more universalist—and inclusive—perspective on the unions' role in society. The standard interpretation of the war's consequences for U.S. capacities for planning policies generally has been negative. In a history of the National Resources Planning Board (NRPB), a New Deal agency that was terminated by Congress in 1943, Marion Clawson (1981, 271) concludes that the end of the NRPB also signalled the end of planning in the United States. Margaret Weir (1992) uses the Board to make an argument for the historical weakness of the U.S. state. Alan Brinkley (1995) similarly declares the war a road marker for liberal defeat. In this perspective, Walter Reuther's attempt to plan the economy by means of linking wages and prices and to use the unions as "coordinating central" appears to be little more than a dreamer's thinking.

Richard Polenberg (1972, 73) expressed this sentiment when he, after first acknowledging that the war had brought many gains in societal discipline and organization as well as a radical concentration of the state's powers, concludes that the war put social reform on the backburner and allowed industry interests to push out the remains of the New Deal. Much like other countries have produced "native narratives" explaining national exceptionalism—in Sweden it is the notion of the "democratic class struggle," in the Federal Republic the "verhinderte Neuordnung" thesis, which held the Allies responsible for the restoration of German business power, and in the United Kingdom, the failure of "parliamentary socialism"—the war has been held responsible for the reversal of the progressive achievements of the New Deal and the return of industry to the helm of the state in the United States.

In comparative perspective, the view that the war put an end to the New Deal and to hopes for an accommodation to a greater role for the state in economic regulation seems in part based on unrealistic expectations about what constitutes successful planning. The war ushered in many of the same institutional innovations in the United States that became the basis for postwar planning in Europe. One critical difference to countries like France, Sweden, and the United Kingdom, was that in none of these countries did the wartime state-expansion build upon a previous wave of state-expansion approximating that of the first New Deal, the National Recovery Administration (NRA), which lasted from 1933 to 1935. It stands for many U.S. scholars as the epitome of what a state, capable of planning, should look like. But the NRA, with is Code Authorities and comprehensive machinery for fixing prices and incomes (Lyon 1935), far exceeded anything that postwar planners in Europe achieved, even if they dreamed of it. Cripps' Development Councils, Myrdal's Industrial Commissions, and Monnet's *commissions du modernisation,* all resembled the Code Authorities that probably represented the common source of inspiration, but only the French commissions ever succeeded. There is another problem inherent in making the short-lived NRA the model for what a reform state might look like; it was declared unconstitutional. Moreover, one lessons from postwar European planning is that industry support was critical to the success of planning. The inclusion of industry in wartime control boards, for example, the War Production Board, hardly suffices to explain why planning failed in the United States.

In a comparative view, the more fundamental differences to the European counterparts were a constitutional system that posed hurdles to ambitious reform government and the nation's economic strength, which made the dollar the "hegemonic" currency and allowed the United States to dictate the main terms of the reconstruction of the post–1945 trade

order. As for the first point, the division of executive and legislative powers, with the courts as a third branch of government, posed significant institutional and political checks on policymaking (Skowronek 1982).
During the war the Constitution continued to function, competitive
elections were held, and the state's emergency powers reined in. Yet, by
the passage of the Second War Powers Act in March 1942, the United
States also had moved far in the direction of centralized state power
(Pohlenberg 1972). On the economic side, the United States, like the European countries, also subordinated its entire economy and population to
the task of war mobilization, but without creating the degradation and
dependency that afflicted the United Kingdom. Like Sweden, the United
States was poised to take advantage of favorable demand conditions after
1945. Unlike Sweden—and any other European country—the United
States was not hampered by the need to curtail domestic demand in order
to stabilize a weak currency and maintain a somewhat artificial peg
against the dollar.

The "dollar gap" that worked as a brake on the postwar European
economies worked as an accelerator on the U.S. economy.[2] The complaints
of the British Chamber of Commerce (1947, 4), occasioned by sterling's
1947 convertibility crisis, illustrate all too well the difference: "So long as
the United States maintained its large 'favorable' balance with the world,
the other nations could not provide us with the dollars we should need,
even though we sent excess exports to them; nor have they been so un-
wise as to accept an obligation to convert their currencies into dollars."

The comparison to the European countries illustrates the importance
of both the constitutional framework and the absence of an external constraint for domestic economic policies. What if we as a thought experiment
imagine that the planners' flagship legislation, the 1945 Full Employment
Act, had been put forward by a majority party controlling both the executive branch and the legislature? In that case, the bill may well have sailed
through without amendment, and instead of succumbing to instant death
it would have achieved permanence through the creation (or continuation) of a presidential economic planning agency. This is admittedly a
counterfactual comparison, but it helps us put American exceptionalism in
perspective. Imagine further that, from 1947 to 1949, the United States had
experienced wage inflation and trade deficits while obligated to sustain a
currency peg in the face of dwindling currency reserves. Is it not likely that
the War Labor Board with its capacities to fix wages and prohibit rogue industrial action in that case might have been brought back? Neither happened, of course, because the United States instead benefited from its
privileged position as the banker of the world and the producer of goods
much needed for European reconstruction. However, three decades later,

by 1968, when the United States began to lose these advantages, a second moment of transatlantic convergence took place, as incomes policy and protectionism gained popularity as means for protecting exposed domestic economic and social relationships. This time American consumers preferred foreign imports to expensive and undesirable domestic goods. The dollar was weak, and the government was obligated to try to sustain it. Both Republican and Democratic administrations sought accord with the trade unions, and "social contracts" were suddenly (albeit briefly) in vogue.

The Civilian War Controls

Transatlantic convergence picked up speed in 1942, with the invasion of Pearl Harbor. Early war mobilization plans called for the creation of an economic control agency directly under the president, which was to be headed by a civilian who was to work in collaboration with the chief of staff, the War and Navy secretaries, and the secretary of state. The military controlled the early planning process, which resulted in the creation on August 9, 1939, of the War Resources Board. In May 1940 the Advisory Commission to the Council of National Defense was created to include representatives of labor, farm organizations, and industry in the planning of resource mobilization.[3]

In 1941 the early machinery was replaced by the Office of Production Management (OPM) with power to "formulate plans for the mobilization for defense of the production facilities of the Nation, and to take all lawful action necessary to carry out such plans" (Industrial Mobilization for War 1969, 95). The determination of requirements and the ability to enter into contracts with producers and suppliers still rested with the army, navy, and other military agencies. The OPM could only "survey, analyze, and summarize" for "purposes of coordination." Successive expansions of the War Powers Acts gave the president the power to assign preference to deliveries of materials purchased at home or abroad for military purposes.

On October 16, 1941, the president was given powers to seize property needed for the national defense. This new power was not made operational until January 16, 1942, when a War Production Board (WPB) was created, headed by Donald M. Nelson as "czar"; he was given the power to assign "responsibility for all parts of the big job to particular agencies and individuals" (Industrial Mobilization for War 1969, 208; Nelson 1946). The creation of a "czar" was different from the central planning agencies created by European states for civilian war planning; it stressed coordination and a vertical division of labor between private and public actors in place of the corporate merger of public and private organizations. Yet the new organization also mirrored the "social partners" approach used elsewhere.

Union leader Sidney Hillman was made head of the WPB Labor Division and assigned a role within the administration that mirrored that given to Bevin in the United Kingdom. After successive reorganizations, labor issues were concentrated in the semi-independent National War Labor Board (NWLB).

In the first six months of 1942, the WPB expanded from 6,600 to 18,000 employees (Industrial Mobilization for War 1969, 248), and a number of functions were spun off, including food regulation, the rubber industry, and dealing with small business, which was given its own division, the Smaller War Plants Division (Catton 1948).

State capacities to plan for the war were strengthened once again with the establishment of the Office of War Mobilization (OWM) by Executive Order 9347 on May 27, 1943. The order gave the OWM the capacity to "develop unified programs and to establish policies for the maximum use of the national natural and industrial resources for military and civilian needs, for the effective use of manpower not in the Armed Forces, for the maintenance and stabilization of the civilian economy, and for the adjustment of such economy to war needs and conditions."

Central Planning in the Absence of Unity Government

This was the closest the United States got to *Zentrale Plannung*. A number of critical differences existed that set the U.S. warfare state off from the European counterparts. First, the Office of War Mobilization was created at a much later stage in the war; in fact, only one year later the agency already would be engaged in planning for decontrol and reconversion. A second difference was that Congress retained an active political role throughout the war. There exists no functional equivalent to the national unity governments, the *Burgfried* agreements produced by party collaboration within a parliamentary framework, in the U.S. constitutional framework.

In parliamentary systems, elections are called when the sitting government steps down or otherwise by a constitutionally determined expiration date. Emergency legislation suspended the expiration dates and collaboration eliminated opposition, with the result that partisan competition was suspended for the duration of the war. In the United States, however, presidential and congressional elections proceeded according to the normal calendar. This meant that, throughout the war, the president had to contend with congressional investigative committees and criticisms of excessive expansions of presidential power.

A third difference was that the core planning agency, the War Production Board, was set up as a dependent agency, a service agency for the military. The military had little interest in assuming a permanent role in national planning, and upon the surrender of Japan, it proceeded immediately to cancel contracts. Acting in concert, the War Production Board quickly revoked a large number of controls and quota systems—"schedules"—establishing priority for various industries, suppliers, and producers. On August 30, 1945, for example, automobile production was relieved of all quota restrictions (Industrial Mobilization for War 1969, 951).

In the European context, the functionally equivalent agencies were populated and controlled mostly by interest group representatives who owed their newfound power to the expansion of the administrative state or by academic economists who were attracted to the prospects of peacetime planning. The direct administrative coupling of wartime civilian planning to military requirements proved an immediate obstacle to ideas about using the existing machinery for peacetime production planning. There were institutional and practical reasons for this construction, but the fact that most controls were issued to boost production output rather than to redistribute scarcities—which could in any case not be eliminated simply by removing the controls—was an important difference from the European situation.

Fiscal Expansion and Redistribution

War expenditures produced a boom of unparalleled magnitude. Between 1940 and 1944, the last calendar year of the war, GDP more than doubled, from $97 billion to nearly $200 billion. In 1943 to 1944, war production rose to 40 percent of total production, with much of the increase in mining, manufacturing, and construction industries. The consequence was a dramatic increase in employment, which not only sufficed to eradicate the last vestiges of unemployment from the depression years but also drew in large numbers of new workers, including many women.

In the United States, nearly 20 million more people were at work in 1944 than in 1939. Even if certain goods became scarce, overall consumer purchases actually expanded in the cause of the war, and the production of consumer goods and services grew by 50 percent (Dewhurst 1947, 5; Industrial Mobilization for War 1969, 964). Agriculture benefited too, with a 25 percent increase in farm output between 1939 and 1944. The redistributive effects of the economic expansion were extraordinary. Farm incomes rose significantly, but so did the income of employees, from 65 percent to 72 percent of the national income. Private savings also rose, from 21 percent of the national income to 34 percent. This increase provided a "nest egg" of pent-up demand that fueled the post-1945 domestic boom (Dewhurst 1947, 7, 9).

Reconversion and Citizenship

In the immediate postwar years, union membership reached 14 million and union density approached 30 percent. These numbers translated into much higher concentrations of trade unionism in the swath of industrial states stretching from Pennsylvania and New York, over parts of New England and the industrial heartland from Illinois and Michigan to Wisconsin, and to the West Coast. Philip Murray, the president of the industrial trade union confederation, the Congress on Industrial Organization (CIO), suggested an extension of the wartime industrial relations framework in exchange for a peace agreement from the unions. In 1940 Murray, a Catholic and influenced by the 1931 papal encyclical *Quadragesimo Anno* about "social partnership," had argued for the creation of an "industrial charter" between unions and management (Lichtenstein 1982, 85).

Walter Reuther from the United Automobile Workers, who was a socialist, wanted economic planning. He proposed that the National War Productions Board be turned into the Peace Production Board, and supported legislation to ensure full employment (Reuther 1976). Business leaders such as Eric Johnston from the U.S. Chamber of Commerce and Paul Hoffman from the Committee on Economic Development (CED), who was involved with the Council on Foreign Relations and chief administrator of the European Recovery Program (the Marshall Plan), also argued for the importance of government planning and for full employment. From the vantage point of 1945, there is much reason to conclude, as did the late political scientists J. David Greenstone (1977, vii), "that the European parallel is less misleading than the alternative thesis that labor has only incrementally extended Gompers' self-proclaimed nonpartisan voluntarism."

Parity Politics and Planning for Peace

Between 1942 and 1945, war mobilization produced in the United States a range of changes in state-society relations and radical state expansion that were similar to the European experiences. Wage and price controls were applied and administered through corporatist control boards. Sidney Hillman, president of the Amalgamated Clothing Workers, one of the founding unions of the CIO, was appointed codirector of the Office of Production Management. At the War Production Board, the agency embraced a "politics of productivity" formula similar to that of the British Joint Production Councils—essentially a codetermination structure based on the creation of joint management-labor production committees. The unions benefited greatly from agency policies.

The redirection of shipping tonnage to military purposes led to short-ages and to rationing of certain raw materials and foodstuffs. Despite rich farmland in the United States, rationing of certain foods was necessary—even if scarcities like those experienced by the Europeans did not occur—and agriculture benefited from higher prices. The Lend-Lease Agreement and Allied dependence on American agriculture made agricultural policy a matter of strategic planning. Farm interests benefited greatly from subsi-dized pricing.

Military mobilization and war productions produced full employment, and even with higher wartime taxes, a high level of general prosperity and redistribution took place. In his study entitled *The Fiscal Revolution in America* (1969), the American economist Herbert Stein wrote about the experience and its implications for postwar policy: "One important lesson of the war was that the benefits of full employment were not confined to those persons who had previously been unemployed. Aside from the direct effects of military service, everyone, or almost everyone, was much better off than he had ever been before" (172).

The National Resources Planning Board and Postwar Planning

The NRPB was created on July 1, 1939, as a successor agency to the Na-tional Planning Board, a New Deal agency set up in 1933 based on the National Industrial Recovery Act. (In 1935 it was re-created as the Na-tional Resources Committee on a different legal basis.) It was shut down on August 31, 1943, when Congress refused to reappropriate money for it. The agency has attracted attention because of what it did and what it did not get to do. Margaret Weir (1992, 45) notes that its demise was a har-binger of the future collapse of the Full Employment Act and that oppo-sition to the board's work came from the same congressional coalition that had opposed the presidential reorganization plans from 1938.

The NRPB was not central to the administration of the war effort, but at an early stage it was charged with "Planning for the Future." President Roosevelt's uncle, Frederic A. Delano, was chairman of the board. Charles E. Merriam, a political scientist from the University of Chicago, was a board member, as was George F. Yantis, a former state legislator from the state of Washington. Charles W. Eliot was the director.[4] The NRPB's prior engage-ment in state and local planning, promotion of science, and planning of pub-lic works continued, but in 1941 it began advocating for an expansion of the federal government's commitment to social welfare and full employment.

In late 1941 the board completed a report, *Security, Work, and Relief Poli-cies,* which in many respects closely resembled Beveridge's 1942 report on

social insurance (U.S. Congress 1943a). Publication of the report was delayed by the president, who did not release it until March 1943.[5] The report was written by Eveline M. Burns, an economics professor from
Columbia University, who had been a student at the London School of
Economics when Beveridge taught there. Burns and Merriam denied that
the report was inspired by Beveridge's work, but the similarities are too
striking to be overlooked.[6] Contemporary reactions often referred to the
report as "our own Beveridge." Directly echoing Beveridge, Burns used
the expression "freedom from Want" to characterize the aim of the report's
recommendations.

Unlike previous reports, the NRPB also made strenuous efforts to pop-
ularize its findings. In September 1942 it issued a short pamphlet, *Post-War
Planning—Full Employment, Security, Building America,* which included a
one-page statement of "Our Freedoms and Right." It listed nine "rights,"
including the right to work, to fair pay, and the right to adequate food,
clothing, shelter, and medical care. It also listed a right that was not found
in Beveridge's writing: the right to live in a system of free enterprise. This
nod to private enterprise was not unconditional, including as it did the
right to be free from "irresponsible private power" and "unregulated monopolies" (Clawson 1981).[7]

Like Beveridge, the NRPB also conceived of postwar reform as a dual
stroke. In January 1942 the board published a pamphlet by the economist
Alvin H. Hansen, *After the War—Full Employment,* which argued, in keeping with Hansen's Keynesian views, that it was the responsibility of government policy to sustain a high level of demand and argued for deficit
spending (U.S. Congress, 1943b.) Both Burns' "Security" report and
Hansen's "Full Employment" pamphlet were subjected to congressional
criticism in connection with the appropriation debate and were used as
evidence that the agency was out of control. Nevertheless, it is not clear
that opposition to the ideas advocated by the NRPB was the only or even
the real cause of the agency's demise. The NRPB was still linked with the
ill-fated 1938 reorganization effort and to congressional fears of presidential expansion. A more immediate issue was the upcoming presidential
campaign. The war effort put limits on the campaign, leaving only certain
issues "safe" for political mobilization. The NRPB's irrelevance to the war
effort exposed it to criticism.

The agency died but its narrative of reform reappeared in Roosevelt's
message to Congress of January 1944, which spoke of a "Second Bill of
Rights" (Ausubel 1945, 27). The agency's June 1943 report entitled *Demobilization and Adjustment* included language that reappeared in the G.I. Bill
(Merriam 1944, 1083). And Hansen's ideas had a second run in connection with the Full Employment Bill.

Bipartisan Promises

The "one-nation" rhetoric and promises of inclusive citizenship that accompanied appeals to the dominant classes for fellowship in the war effort were as much part of the changing public psychology in the United States as they were in the United Kingdom and in Sweden. The new accord was bipartisan, bringing the Republican Party into the New Deal consensus (even if the New Deal legacy itself was modified by the war). Thomas Dewey accepted the 1994 Republican Party's nomination for president by making this promise:

> It would be a tragedy after this war if Americans returned from our armed forces and failed to find the freedom and opportunity for which they fought. This must be a land where every man and woman has a fair chance to work and get ahead. . . . We Republicans are agreed that full employment shall be the first objective of national policy. And by full employment, I mean a real chance for every man and woman to earn a decent living. (Stein 1969, 173)

The promise of citizenship informed both the 1945 Employment Act, which started out as the Full Employment Act, and the 1946 Housing Act. William Beveridge, whose entrepreneurship on the part of social and economic planning was discussed in chapter 2, was invited to tour the United States by the Rockefeller Foundation to advocate for his new ideas about social welfare (Harris 1977, 427). The Carnegie Foundation commissioned Swedish economist, Gunnar Myrdal, to write a study of American racism, published as *An American Dilemma* (1944). New support for citizenship also informed an attack on racial segregation that even the New Deal, with all its dirigism, had been unable to accomplish. Administrative machinery for Fair Employment Practices to address racial discrimination in the workplace was also created (Kesselman 1948; Reed 1991).

The Federal State: The "New Deal" Preserved

The wartime agencies for economic management differed from the New Deal's dirigiste public works "authorities" and the cartelistic and collusive self-administration that shaped the work of the Code Authorities set up under the National Industrial Recovery Act (NIRA) from 1933 by adopting a "social partners" framework that involved national interest groups in direct collaboration with the national state.[8] The wartime boards rescued the New Deal from itself by providing a new template for private-public cooperation. Change had already begun before the war, but by 1938 a certain disorientation about how to proceed with economic reform and planning beset the New Dealers. After NIRA was declared unconstitutional by the Supreme Court in *Schechter Corp.* v. *United States* (295 U.S. 495 1935), the rights granted labor by the critical section 7(a) were reiterated in the 1935 National Labor Relations Act, better known as the Wagner Act. Protected by the Wagner Act and by the War Labor Board, American trade unions flourished between 1935 and 1945.

The wartime lessons of full employment and the benefits of expansionary government spending were not lost on business either, except there was no agreement on what the lessons were. Business and industry organizations took opposite sides. Acting through the Atlanticist Committee for Economic Development, which had been created in 1942, the U.S. Chamber of Commerce, and the National Association of Manufacturers, business and industry lent support to both sides in the fight over the Full Employment Act, for example.

The creation of a new administrative machinery to fight the war produced a large number of jobs for a new generation of economists, many of whom arrived in Washington fresh out of college. Whereas the New Deal machinery had drawn upon people like Harry Hopkins and Leon Henderson, Bernard Baruch and other businessmen from Wall Street or large companies, who were also mobilized during the war, the new machinery drew also in an intellectual elite. From the departments of State and of Commerce to the expanded Executive Office of the President and the National Resources Planning Board, young economists educated in Keynesian theory moved in. The list of Keynesians who went to Washington during the war is too long to specify but includes Kindleberger and Galbraith, who were mentioned in earlier chapters, but also Alvin Hansen, Leon Keyserling, Seymour Harris, Walter Salant, and Gerhard Colm.

From the War Labor Board to Taft-Hartley

With the creation of the National War Labor Board (NWLB) in January 1942, the president imposed a prohibition on both strikes and lockouts. The board included both experts and labor and industry representatives, in effect creating the infrastructure for the Wagner Act from 1935. The board worked to fix industrywide wage patterns and set a standardized jurisprudence for arbitration in industrial conflicts. In April 1942 Leon Henderson, head of the Office of Price Management, and other economists insisted on a wage freeze. Since it was widely feared that the unions would resist a freeze, President Roosevelt instead announced a new stabilization policy, which aimed to fix wages to a cost-of-living index. A price-wage formula was first applied in the "Little Steel" agreement of July 1942.

("Little Steel" consists of small and medium-size independent steel companies.) After the war, United Steelworkers would continue to differentiate between "Little" and "Big" Steel, including in the latter group the 10 to 12 largest steel makers, for example, the USX Corporation (U.S. Steel.) The combination of administratively fixed wages and a large influx of new workers created a difficult situation for the unions, to which the NWLB responded by agreeing to a maintenance-of-membership rule. The rule applied to all cooperative unions—unions, that is, that agreed to administer the no-strike pledge. Once employed under a maintenance-of-membership contract, new employees had 15 days to withdraw from the union. If they did not give notice of withdrawal (and few did), workers were obligated to pay their union dues, usually by means of automatic pay deductions, and to abide by union rules. Otherwise, they could be expelled from the union and fired (Lichtenstein 1982, 80). The arrangement was in many respects identical to the British "closed shop," except that U.S. unions assumed managerial responsibilities that British unions eschewed. It is not surprising that the membership of the industrial unions swelled.

Wage Planning and the UAW's Postwar Offensive

Notable similarities exist between U.S. wage policies and those of Sweden and the United Kingdom described in the previous chapters. Wage-price indexation, uniform industrywide wage determination, tripartism, new trade union protections in exchange for collaboration, and the formation of path-setting wage agreements that subsequently would continue to shape collective bargaining patterns after 1945 were familiar elements. Experiments with parity norms for income developments across the different classes in response to a demand for equitable sharing of the burdens of war were also a common part of the picture. In 1942 the United Auto Workers asked the government to impose a ceiling of $25,000 on all salaries and incomes, in exchange for the union's agreement to allow workers to work extra hours without a pay bonus.

Reuther's campaign for an equality-of-sacrifice policy produced a promise from President Roosevelt that the companies would not be allowed to reap the benefits of wage concessions and that the extra profits would be confiscated by means of taxation (Lictenstein 1982, 100). According to the historian Nelson Lichtenstein, the UAW created a lot of attention for its program and got accolades from prominent liberals, but was stymied by conservatives in Congress, who deleted the administration's price control program and salary ceiling from proposed legislation (1982, 102–108).

The UAW's support for incomes policy occasioned sharp sectional conflict with the AFL unions and within the CIO. When several unions managed to obtain Sunday-pay privileges and otherwise eroded the pay-restraint policy, the UAW and the CIO were in bind. In the end, the CIO leaders ended up petitioning the President for enforcement of the prohibition on overtime pay and what was in effect relief from union competition. Irrespective of official policy, throughout the war tight labor market conditions continued to make a mockery of the "equality" standard.

As in Sweden and the United Kingdom, wartime labor market policies favored unionization and provided the unions with a new opportunity to get involved in national economic policymaking. With tight labor markets and new protections against hostile employers, union organization improved. Fearful of union resistance, states eschewed statutory wage policies and attempted instead to incorporate the unions in the administration of the wartime machinery. The new accord between unions and the state benefited unions greatly, but it also sowed the seeds of internal trade union conflict after 1945, when sectionalist conflicts over the benefits of the wartime machinery broke out and tight labor markets encouraged workers and local unions to seek wage increases though militancy.

A Setback for Unions

In the United States, the presence of a southern veto against any extension of the central state presented an immediate roadblock to a statist reform program (Katznelson, Geiger, and Kryder 1993).[9] The passage of the Taft-Hartley Act in 1947 by a conservative Congress and over President Truman's veto represented a definitive setback for any hopes of extending the New Deal and the wartime policies to a permanent framework for national economic planning.

The Taft-Hartley Act modified many of the gains labor had won in the Wagner Act. It carved out a narrow area of legality for trade union activities by codifying a list of unfair labor practices. These "cut both ways," extending protections as well as restrictions on unions. While the act forbade employers from refusing to bargain, it also disallowed coercion of workers to organize or to refrain from organizing, or from engaging in secondary boycotts. The act made changes in the administrative procedures and the structure of the National Labor Relations Board, changes primarily intended to curb administrative discretion. It also required unions to register with the Department of Labor, to file annual financial reports, and to ensure that union officers were not Communists. It strengthened the compulsory arbitration system and greatly expanded the scope for litigation in industrial relations. (For a detailed description, see Tomlins 1986, chapter 8.)

The act has obvious comparative parallels. It aroused as much hostility from American trade union advocates as the 1927 Industrial Disputes Act did among British trade unionists. The ability of the British TUC to get the 1927 act revoked in 1945 and the American unions' inability to avoid the 1947 Taft-Hartley Act presents us with a direct comparative measure of the strength of unionism in the two countries. Curiously, here the appropriate comparison for the predicament of U.S. unions is that of the German unions or, and in other respects a farfetched comparison, to the curbs placed on Swedish unions. In a situation of divided government—either as in the case of the United States between the executive and legislative branches of government or as in the case of Sweden within a government based on power sharing—the more probable outcome would have been some compromise legislation carving out an area of legality for trade unions. The act prohibited many union practices, including secondary pickets and closed-shop arrangements; many of these are also disallowed by Scandinavian and German labor relations rules.[10] The act had uncontestable negative implications for American unions. Lichtenstein (1089, 134) concluded that " . . . if Taft-Hartley did not destroy the union movement, it did impose upon it a legal/administrative straitjacket that encouraged contractual parochialism and penalized any serious attempt to project a classwide political-economic strategy."

By devolving certain rule-making decisions in industrial relations to the states and carving out a large role for court enforcement, the act also posed large roadblocks for a national political strategy. The devolution of enforcement to the state level is different from German industrial relations enforcement. The emphasis on litigation and adjudication in place of bargaining set the U.S. framework off from the European "social partners" emphasis on private agreements and regulations worked out between employers' organizations and unions. The act effectively prevented the creation of a national private collaborative framework. Where the New Deal institutions and the War Labor Board allowed for an element of organizational incorporation and self-regulation, the Taft-Hartley Act encouraged devolution and procedural regulations under the supervision of outside legal and administrative experts.

The seed for the statutory circumscription of union-employer relations had been sown already by the New Deal. The National Labor Relations Act of 1935 created the federal regulatory framework for the enforcement of industrial relations and imposed the procedural regulations of certifying elections as a precondition for union representation in collective bargaining. The need to win plantwide certification elections in order to represent workers in direct bargaining with employers forced unions into a plant-by-plant strategy of wage militancy that has made organization drives an exhausting and adversarial legal battleground. What at first had been envisioned as a protection for unions turned out in later years also to be a straitjacket and an obstacle to the development of "in-clusive trade unionism" that could balance recruitment with general eco-nomic policy objectives.

The Full Employment Act that Never Was

As the war drew to a close, ideas about how to manage the transition to peace proliferated. Walter Reuther proposed converting the War Produc-tion Board to the Peace Production Board. Small businesses demanded the continuation of quotas—"ratings"—that would guarantee them pro-tection against big industry in the competition for resources after the war. Farmers wanted continued help. In contrast to the United Kingdom, where the debate took place in the context of "plans" put forward by or-ganizations such as the TUC or the FBI, or by government White Papers, the vehicle for debate in the United States was a set of competing or complementary congressional bills. One bill would create a new agency under the Office of War Mobilization and Reconversion charged with "full employment and full production planning," in effect a *Commissariat du Plan* in the Executive Office of the President. The Farmers' Union sponsored a bill that would create a statutory obligation for the govern-ment to make loans or commence direct spending sufficient to bring the total national level up to a specified point (Stein 1969, 198). A third pro-posal, the Full Employment Act (S. 380), in the end concentrated the de-bate. The proposed legislation would have created a statutory obligation for the government—represented by the president—to ensure full em-ployment by means of public spending. By locating the responsibility for maintaining an expansionary economy with the president, the proposal attempted to fix the wartime expansion of the presidency's economic management responsibilities for perpetuity.

The history of the Full Employment Act is described in Stephen K. Bailey's *Congress Makes a Law* (1950) and shall not be repeated here. The act had strong similarities with the British 1944 Employment paper. (See chapter 2.) It was supported by a Keynesian alliance of economists and in-dustrial trade unionists, personified by Walter Reuther from the United Auto Workers, of leaders from one side of industry such as Eric Johnston from the U.S. Chamber of Commerce and Paul Hoffman from Commit-tee on Economic Development, and by New Dealers such as Senator Robert Wagner. The National Association of Manufacturers opposed the act. The legislation was passed as the Employment Act of 1946, but the final act little resembled the original proposal. In place of a "right" to full employment, the act specified only an obligation—to be executed by the President—to establish a national policy of achieving "useful employment opportunities" for all persons "able, willing, and seeking to work" was not accompanied by statutory commitment to any concrete measures. The creation of the Council of Economic Advisors was its only institutional legacy.

Herbert Stein (1969, 204) argues that the discussion around the act "did not create a new American fiscal policy . . . [but] confirmed the policy which existed." A consensus emerged in favor of fiscal stimulation to maintain economic activity, even deficit spending if need be, and a practical program of presidential responsibility (to be shared with economic experts, the Treasury, and the Federal Reserve) for economic expansion and stabilization policy. There were advocates of structural policies, including government investment programs for failing industries or specific policies for selected industries. (One was Leon Keyserling, who was chair of the Council of Economic Advisors from 1949 to 1953.) Whatever momentum the planners had coming out of the war was soon lost in the happy flow of a postwar boom.

Expansionist Fiscal Policy and the Red-Green Alliance

Karen Orren has argued that, contrary to the narratives of labor's loss of political influence after the 1947 Taft-Hartley Act, organized labor remained a central actor in the creation of a Keynesian consensus in the postwar years. She argued that labor "[was] the dominant private interest in national policy making" (1986, 216). Once it became clear that statutory economic planning was not going to happen, labor shifted its focus to support for economic expansion. Agricultural spending programs—from price guarantees to food stamps—were an important element. Orren's version of the Red-Green alliance is a little curious, in that the alliance was one-sided: labor supported agriculture more than agriculture supported labor. Labor did so, she argues, not out of party loyalty or in order to participate in log-rolling arrangements, but rather out of an interest in expansionary public policies stimulating aggregate demand.

This is not the place to go into the details of Orren's argument, which can be criticized for understating the influence of the farm lobby in order to overstate the influence of labor.[11] Orren argues that labor's support for high agricultural price support programs was not an example of labor's attempt to maintain an increasingly strained political coalition with agrarian interests but an accurate, self-interested assessment of the importance of inflationary pricing to labor. The influence of expansionists in Congress, Orren argues, allowed expansionary monetary policies to continue long after internationally responsible behavior would have dictated the need to constrict the money supply (1986, 230–231). The formation of a reflationary alliance between labor and farm groups presents us with a familiar picture. With the exception of the Federal Republic, where the unions and the SPD took little interest in farm policies, some form or another of a Red–Green alliance appears to have been critical to postwar Keynesianism in general. But fears of inflation and the hollowing out of wages that accompanies it also worked to check the alliance. U.S. labor was not always unconcerned with the distributional consequences of inflation. Inflation played a large role in Walter Reuther's thinking about labor's postwar policies—his ideas about wage policy were in general much inspired by European trade unionism—but not only was Reuther in the minority, his ideas about "planned wages" also failed due to a lack of means.

Incomes Policy and High Inflation: The Europeanization of the United States

Forced to depend on his own union, Walter Reuther tried unsuccessfully in the 1946 UAW strike against General Motors to use collective bargaining as a lever for societal and economic change by insisting that the automakers grant wage increases without passing the costs on to consumers or, alternatively, open the books to the public and justify raising prices (Piore and Sabel 1984).[12] In the absence of a comprehensive and universal welfare state, unions could secure for their members and their families "cradle-to-grave" benefits, and in the process bind members to them. These were, despite Reuther's programmatic declarations to the contrary, ultimately strategies that built on and heightened union sectionalism. This vision of the UAW as the political and economic vanguard of the American working class worked remarkably well as long as the American auto industry was producing for an insulated domestic market.

The 1946 UAW strike became a milestone in postwar collective bargaining history, resulting in similar contracts with hourly raises in the steel, electrical, and rubber industries. The 1946 automobile worker contract, and a subsequent one in 1948, represented a breakthrough for labor by setting the foundation for what later became known as pattern-bargaining: the creation of industrywide wage rates that permitted wage setting to be more or less independent from the competitive situation of the individual company within the industry. In 1949 the UAW and the USW both signed the first pension agreements.

Free Unionism versus Incomes Policy

In the steel industry, bargaining on an industrywide basis became formalized in 1956 when 12 steel manufacturing firms organized the Coordinating Committee Steel Companies (CCSC), although the USW for years had bargained first with U.S. Steel and then made the U.S. Steel contract the pattern for contracts with other companies. In 1955 the UAW introduced the concept of guaranteed annual wages, which was intended to force automakers to eliminate seasonal work. In 1976 the USW went even further and demanded that employers guarantee steelworkers a "Lifetime Security Program" that would insure that "a steelworker will have a job and receive full pay irrespective of circumstances outside his or her control" (*Monthly Labor Review* [11] 1976, 44–46). Pattern bargaining helped create a Fordist economy of economic accumulation characterized by consumerism, increasing real wages, and relative economic stability (Bowles, Gordon, and Weisskopf 1983, 84).

The high wage for high-productivity exchange worked as long as American goods were largely protected against foreign competition and as long as domestic inflation did not seriously undermine the dollar's position. As long as Bretton Woods convertibility rules prevailed—which they did from roughly 1959 to 1971—the link between domestic economic policy and international trade policy was partially disabled. (Eichengreen 1996, 128, provides a short history of the collapse). After 1971–1973, the dollar's inability to sustain the functions ascribed to it by the Bretton Woods system from 1944 resulted in the collapse of the old system. American policies then once again converged with those generally pursued by European welfare states. The Nixon administration applied price and wage controls, which were continued by the Ford administration in the Council on Wage and Price Stability (COWPS). A strategy of negotiated wage restraint, mimicking European corporatism, was first tried during the Ford administration in August 1974, when Gerald Ford attempted to conduct economic policy in a consensual fashion that emulated New Deal crisis policy.[13] Despite at least formal labor cooperation with the administration's initiatives, wages and benefits increased by more than 15 percent during 1974.

In a shift designed to appease labor, President Jimmy Carter emphasized voluntary and negotiated compliance with guidelines issued by the Council on Wage and Price Stability, and agreed to by business and labor representatives. In 1978, after most collective bargaining had been concluded, the Carter administration announced a new anti-inflationary program calling for a 7 percent ceiling on wage increases. The program failed spectacularly as labor refused to cooperate. Despite a revision of the guidelines, softening the interpretation of the 7 percent ceiling less than two months after the program had been announced, a spectacle ensued in which unions proudly boasted of exceeding the guidelines in new contracts, while the government assured that the contract was, in fact, in compliance.[14] The AFL-CIO challenged in court the government's requirement that federal contractors comply with the guidelines and denounced the administration's anti-inflationary program in general, insisting on the right of unions to engage in "free, unfettered collective bargaining" (*Monthly Labor Review* [6] 1977, 62; [1] 1979, 59; [2] 1979, 67).

By 1980 relations between the Carter administration and the AFL-CIO were frosty, with the latter condemning the former. The deterioration has striking parallels in the mobilization of British unions against the incomes policies of the Callaghan government in 1978–1979. In the United Kingdom, the unions' opposition to the Labour government helped elect Margaret Thatcher. In the United States, trade union policies helped elect Ronald Reagan. (In both cases, the antiunion candidate was elected with a significant share of trade union votes as well.) The unwillingness of the AFL-CIO to comply with the accord it entered into with the Carter government represents a striking confirmation of the German political scientist Fritz Scharpf's (1991) thesis concerning the perverse incentives that cause unions to defect from incomes policy accords under pro-labor governments. In contrast, labor is more inclined to cooperate with unfriendly governments, as in the case of the Ford administration, because they need not be sensitive to labor interests in order to win the next election and hence they offer a more believable threat.

"Free" collective bargaining failed to protect workers against industrial decline. Pattern bargaining and industrywide union wage rates broke down in the auto and steel industries once these industries were exposed to significant competition from abroad. When American consumers shifted demand to fuel-efficient foreign cars after the 1973–1974 oil price hikes, the weaknesses of the system became painfully clear. Domestic car sales plummeted throughout 1975 and 1976 while foreign car sales rose to as much as 21 percent of the market in the first months of 1975. Large-scale unemployment among autoworkers notwithstanding, the UAW decided in September 1976 to engage in a strike against Ford Motor Company in an attempt to preserve aggressive pattern setting despite the recession. The UAW won, and similar contracts were made with Chrysler and General Motors.[15] The American Motor Company, however, pleaded hardship, and the union agreed to wage concessions in 1977 and 1978. In 1979 Chrysler negotiated a special loan guarantee with the Carter administration and received successive wage concessions from the UAW. By 1981–1982, the union was forced to accept comprehensive industrywide reductions in pay, employment, and benefits.

Troy and Sheflin (1985, table 3.34) estimate that the UAW lost 32 percent of its membership between 1978 and 1983. In comparison, the steelworkers' union lost as much as 43 percent. In 1980 the United Steel

Workers union agreed to negotiate separately with the independent minor steel producers, or "Little" Steel. Many of these companies were in serious financial difficulties and, by the end of 1981, the USW began to give them special concessions. In December 1981 McLouth Steel—the country's eleventh largest steel producer—filed for bankruptcy and subsequently obtained considerable wage concessions from the USW local. By January 1982 the steel industry plunged into recession, and the union was caught up in a dynamic of competitive "concession" bargaining.[16] By the mid-1980s it was clear that the unions had lost the capacity to determine wages. In 1980 the UAW started lobbying for protectionist measures for cars. In 1982 the House of Representatives passed the so-called Domestic Content Act, which required foreign-produced cars to include American-made parts. The act died in the Senate, but the automakers persuaded the president to impose "voluntary" quotas on Japanese automakers. Steel followed suit. In 1988 Congress passed the first major protectionist measure of the postwar years, the Omnibus Trade Act, which both protected specific products and granted the president general authority to help distressed industries by means of protectionist measures.

The act was supported by the AFL-CIO, but the unions were not instrumental in its passage. The rush to protectionism was occasioned by a rapidly growing trade deficit between 1981 and 1984, but industrial decline and excessive costs in the face of foreign competition were only part of the story (Eichengreen 1996, 147; Kreuger 1996). The combination of large budget deficits and a monetary policy that drove up interest rates caused a de facto revaluation of the dollar between 1981 and 1985 of more than 30 percent, cheapening foreign imports and exposing "rustbelt" consumer industries to intense competition from abroad. Few legislators attempted to promote a congressional effort to address the causes of the fluctuations of the dollar had little success.[17] The Reagan administration's economic policies worked like a flash flood to clean out the "Fordist"—and unionized—industries that had dominated the postwar growth cycle, shifting economic policies to benefit an entirely new set of industries, principally financial ones.

Deregulation and the End of the Postwar Accord

The Reagan White House broke with the postwar bipartisan accord on employment policy that had been exemplified by Thomas Dewey's 1944 promise to the working man and woman. Like Thatcher, the Reagan presidency never planned to involve organized labor in policymaking. There were no invitations to participate in corporatist-style negotiations. A steep decline in blue-collar union jobs, low wage gains, and

government-supported employer hostility to union representation eliminated pattern bargaining and what remained of the postwar accord. The
linkage established in the immediate postwar years between high union
wages and high growth in manufacturing industries producing primarily for a naturally protected domestic market was eliminated, effectively
limiting trade unionism to the public sector.

Conclusion: The United States in Comparative Perspective

A number of conclusions can be drawn from the two moments when
American and European wage policies converged, in 1945 to 1947 and
again in the high-inflationary 1970s. In a comparative perspective, it is
clear that the external restraint imposed on European economic policies
by the external-internal stability requirement worked to preserve state capacities in the area of economic management. In Europe, comprehensive
"social partners" arrangements were needed above all because of the necessity of balancing growth with costs. In the absence of any need to em-
bark on domestic stabilization policy, American union were "free" to
pursue sectionalist gains and a "voluntarist" trajectory. The straitjacket imposed on American unions by the 1947 legislation was informed by domestic conflicts—conflicts that also had their parallels in Europe, where
hostilities to unions were no less than they were in the American South—
but would have been unthinkable in the absence of a hegemonic dollar.

Once again a counter-factual thought experiment helps make the
point. In view of the strength of American unions in 1947, would the Truman administration have embraced hostile trade union legislation if policy
in the Truman years had been facing an acute currency crisis? Forced to
return to wartime price and wage controls, would the government not
have appealed for the unions' cooperation in a continuation of wartime
control policies? When the decline of the dollar and changes in the international monetary system imposed the need for stabilization policy on the
U. S. government after 1971, inflation control emerged as a critical issue in
the United States. Both Republican and Democratic governments resorted
to incomes policies based on a distinctly corporatist—and prototypical
European—mold. The turn to bilateral protectionist measures injected another element of convergence.

While this shows that American "exceptionalism" may be less pervasive
than often assumed, the account of the rise and the fall of sectionalist trade
unionism in the United States provides a cautionary tale for European pro-
union approaches to economic regulation. It illustrates how the ability of
unions to thrive depends on general economic policy. It also points to the

importance of a critical paradox: Trade unions derive political and economic power on incomes policies, even as they resist and oppose governments trying to coax union compliance. As long as wage determination is
matter of intense public concern, unions possess an important lever for
generalized influence on economic and social policy. If, however, governments are relieved (or relieve themselves) of the obligation to bring about
macroeconomic stability, unions lose influence. Macroeconomic stability,
in this case, includes management of the trade-off between employment
and income growth.

The general conclusion nevertheless is that America's privileged position in the postwar order was both a strategic advantage and an economic
benefit for American unions. While it relieved the unions of having to
share responsibility for austerity policies, it also relieved the government of
any serious obligation to incorporate the unions into a larger framework
of stabilization policy, and hence eliminated any need for generalized economic planning. Free to pursue sectionalist advantage, the unions not only
exposed themselves to the economic effects of unplanned economic restructuring but also relieved the government of the political restraint of
having to mind the unions' interests.

War Constitutionalism and Postwar Citizenship

This book has pointed to the converging influences of wartime mobilization and economic autarky for state-society relations and for state development. The U.S. case shows that the two elements are separate. National
service with military and varying degrees of industrial conscription produced broadly similar policies with respect to trade union inclusion in the
administration of wage controls and labor market policies in the liberal
democracies discussed. In the Federal Republic of Germany, the need of
occupational authorities for an alternative power structure produced supportive trade union policies, which nevertheless focused on codetermination as part of the denazification policy objective and settled pay policy
issues by not doing anything. (A general pay freeze was in effect until 1949.
Collective bargaining resumed only with the creation of the Federal Republic in that year.)

As for social policy issues and full employment, the promise of an inclusive economic policy responsive to social issues became a bipartisan
commitment in liberal democracies early in the war. In the Federal Republic, full employment was never a first objective, and social reform
moved to the top of the postwar government's agenda only as electoral
motives and fears of lagging behind in the "system" competition with the
German Democratic Republic moved the CDU to embrace social policy.

Economic autarky in turn produced industrial control policies based on degrees of self-government and state planning of industrial resources that the United States did not experience because the sharing of shortages was not the main problem. A somewhat similar difference was observed between the United Kingdom and Sweden in the case of wage policy. In the former case, productivity-enhancing pay policies deflected income stabilization and parity principles in wage determination. In Sweden, inflation control had primacy over productivity and parity principles were strictly observed.

It has been argued here that certain common features can be found across countries independent of peacetime constitutional frameworks and historical legacies. Upon the cessation of war and the immediate crisis, the "embellished" state provided state elites with a window of opportunity for reform by means of the application of wartime state capacities to social and economic reform for the purpose of "winning the war of peace." National interest groups, which had benefited and flourished by participating in war controls, were therefore faced with a difficult strategic choice: whether to accept these enhanced state capacities as permanent or not.

These findings pose some distinct challenges to comparative theory and our understanding of the historical contingencies of the postwar welfare state. Additionally, we are faced with some important questions about state legitimation and the variable character of state-society relations, seen both in a comparative and a historical perspective. In other words, national variation is wrapped up in historical contexts with apparent convergence. The question of national variation will be addressed at length in the final chapter, and the discussion here now will turn to the general question about war mobilization and legitimation of the state within nations generally committed to liberal and democratic principles.

War and Citizenship

The conduct of war is not possible in the absence of labor and soldiers—and of food. Hence the control of labor and agriculture inevitably becomes a matter the highest priority for the warfare state. The concept of a liberal society at war is nearly meaningless, as all societies impose restrictions on liberal freedoms—freedom of speech, movement, and property rights—even on to the most important possession of all, life. Yet the difference between authoritarian resource mobilization (as in Nazi Germany and in the Soviet Union) and in liberal democracies (as in the United Kingdom, Sweden, and the United States) rested on an extension of the principles of medieval constitutionalism and peasant armies to the organized societies of the twentieth century. The beneficiaries were trade unions and farmers' unions, whose reward in exchange for the quiescent transfer of men and food to the war machine was the benefit of protective rights, subsidies, and consultation. Money and newfound inclusion into the government accompanied collaboration.

The unity of the nation-state as a national community was forged in the war. The capacity of groups to translate organized power and the promise of reform into the creation of a comprehensive national welfare state varied across states. The unity forged by the emergency and by the coercive power of the warfare state dissolved with the return of the right to dissent and with the resurgence of sectional conflicts, both new and old. Already by 1947–1948, however, the emerging state system became a source of yet another converging influence on government policies. Trade deficits and currency crises brought back economic controls and austerity policies.

By 1945 the scope and the breadth of national interest organization had reached a high point. Farm organizations, trade unions, trade associations, and other business organizations had been encouraged (even to the point of involuntary cartelization) by government regulation of the civilian economy between 1939 and 1945. J. P. Nettl (1965) is one writer who has stressed the role of government in sponsoring the formation of interest groups, a view that obviously corresponds to the one advocated here. (See also Grant 1995.)

When we speak of "class" as a political entity, we often willfully disregard part of the diversity of interests within each class. Classes are made and unmade in the process of representation. They do not exist outside specific political, economic, and social institutions. They are also imagined because the members do not know each other but feel—or are made feel—that they do by solidaristic narratives. Classes may well be the original imagined political community. (See Anderson 1991, 6.)

It is clear from this account that war making had drastic consequences for the dynamic of class formation and for the institutional capacities of states. Charles Tilly has written about the relationship between war making and state expansion. He says: "European states built up their military apparatuses through sustained struggles with their subject populations and by means of selective extension of protection to different classes within those populations. The agreement on protection constrained the rulers themselves, making them vulnerable to courts, to assemblies, to withdrawal of credit, services, and expertise" (Tilly 1985, 185–186).

Tilly's description of links between war mobilization and protective rights resonates with Brian Downing's (1992) study of the roots of medieval constitutionalism, in which he links citizenship to the rise of peasant armies. It also resonates with Bevin's promise to British workers that the reward for their support for the war effort would be socialism itself. German workers of course were given no such promises, because in the German case war mobilization took place by totalitarian and coercive means, unaccompanied by promises of rewards.

In view of this difference, Kurt Schumacher appears to have been quite justified in his assumption that German workers would claim for themselves the reward that had not been promised them. His mistake, in retrospect, may have been the collateral assumption that this meant that the SPD would be the beneficiary.

Class and Interest Representation

Throughout this account class has been considered to be a collectivity of shared interests that follow from political organization and association (Dahrendorf 1959, 238). One reason for the convergence across the cases with respect to class response to the warfare state is that interests are variable within contexts and defined by elites acting strategically in opposition or alliance with other groups (Hobsbawm 1964; on farmers, see Rueschemeyer, Stephens, and Stephens 1992, 91–94). In postwar Europe class formation flowed mostly from state formation, which helps explain why the contention over the right to articulate the content of class interests often took proximate paths. The state-formation process provided an organizing impetus.

The international crisis changed the fundamental calculus of coercion and consent between the state and functional interests. The threat of involuntary cartelization and coercive control was an inducement to consent, as was fear itself. The continuation of wartime policies, however, was dependent on a reworking of the calculus of consent in which the balance between the state and the interests shifted back in the latter's favor. Without the external threat of annihilation, groups were motivated by self-interests rather than by fear. Refracted by electoral institutions, sociology influenced politics and policy.

Farmers

Electoral democracy is a "numbers game," and that made the farm vote an important ingredient to any winning strategy. In the European cases studied here—all examples of inefficient family farming—farmers were also the one class that consistently and enthusiastically supported state direction of income formation. A source in most countries of progressive political liberalism in the nineteenth century, farmers were in the twentieth century a source of economic antiliberalism. (In countries with efficient agriculture such as Denmark, farmers also have been a source of liberal sentiment and of antiprotectionist policies.)

In 1951, between one-fifth and one-third of the working population was tied to agricultural production in Austria, Sweden, and the Federal Republic, a share large enough to make the farm vote critical to government power. In terms of numerical importance, the farm vote could match that of the working class: 29.1 percent of the Austrian labor force was employed in mining and manufacturing, while in Sweden, the working class share was 31.9 percent. In interpreting the importance of the figures, we also have to make allowances for the closeness between working-class lives and rural life, which was still significant in both countries.

In the United Kingdom, in contrast, less than 5 percent of the working population was engaged in agriculture. (All figures come from national census data published in Flora et al. 1987, chap. 7.) The difference reflected dissimilar levels of industrial development; it abated as rural depopularization proceeded in the 1950s. Nazi policies of agrarianization and refugee movements also had caused the rural population to swell in Austria and Germany during and after the war. The importance of the farm vote diminished in step with the transfer of resources from agriculture to industry; nevertheless, buttressed by rural overrepresentation in national political institutions, it has remained an attractive prize for governments and parties.

Strategic factors also worked to sustain state interests in agricultural policies. During the war years, the halt to international trade lent urgency to agricultural policies. Landlocked Germany retained access to agricultural suppliers during the war, but the Western occupation zones faced urgent food problems after 1945. The consequences for Allied agricultural policies and for the subsequent agricultural policies of the Federal Republic have been described in chapter 6. The point here is to underscore that even as trade was restored, currency shortages continued to make enhanced domestic agricultural production an important policy objective and tempered political impulses to cut farm subsidies.

The symbiosis of economic-strategic and political-tactic interests combined to make farmers a class of "state builders." Although this observation holds in a general way for all four countries, critical national differences nevertheless also shortened or prolonged the influence of the farm vote. In Sweden, the Social Democrats ditched the Red-Green alliance in favor of a broad coalition of white-collar and blue-collar workers in connection with the 1959 pension reform, which departed from the egalitarianism of the earlier "people's pensions." In Germany, the Christian Democrats reaped credit for postwar pension reform with the 1957 Rentenreformgesetz. The trade unions had little incentive to give up on using collective bargaining to get earnings-related social benefits in favor of a "little people's" alliance (Baldwin 1990). In Britain, the convergence of opinion between Labour and the Conservatives worked to abrogate partisan competition for the farm vote, which was in any case of less importance than in the other countries.

Business and Industry

The bifurcation of business and industry interest representation into employers' associations and industry or trade associations makes it difficult to generalize about the character of business behavior as instances of "class" representation. Corporatist self-regulation had enjoyed near-universal support in the 1920s but reached its epitome in the war years. The American assault on German cartels notwithstanding, the less spectacular instances of associational activities continued to sustain (and be sustained) by postwar trade policies that required governments to regulate foreign trade. Price fixing, cartelization, and associational control upon market entry were not only tolerated by governments but became an indispensable part of supply-side policies aiming at controlling domestic demand for foreign goods and currency rationing.

In *The Rise and Decline of Nations,* Mancur Olson (1982, 79) concluded that "There cannot be much doubt that totalitarianism, instability, and war reduced special-interest organizations in Germany, Japan, and France." Olson based his conclusion on a count of the dates of origins of business associations drawn from an encyclopedia of such associations. A larger proportion of associations were found to predate 1939 in Britain than in any other country. From that Olson (and Peter Murrell, a colleague) concluded that Britain's long history of democratic associations worked against the country's capacity for flexible adjustment, which confirmed Olson's thesis that democratic decline stems from "growth-repressing" organizations and institutions. One problem with this conclusion is that it is fallacious to conclude that the number of associations is proportional to their influence. (Olson indirectly acknowledged the fallacy when he stated that encompassing associations could be beneficial to growth since they could not export the externalities of control to other groups; see Cameron 1988.) Likewise, the count also ignores the possibility that postwar reconstitution of associations can hide important continuities. It is more likely that age is a spurious variable.

It is difficult to reconcile the arteriosclerosis thesis with the present study's conclusion that the associational influence was amplified by the incorporation of representatives of national business and industry associations (along with farm representatives and labor) in the administration of the civilian war controls. In Sweden internal divisions in the employers' associations were overcome when the association became the primary representative of business and industry interests to the state during the war years. In Britain the dualism between industry and employer interests was abridged, and the national organizations assumed wider responsibilities. The publication in 1944 of an FBI report that held out self regulation and national discipline as the only way to avoid government regulation illustrated that war did not protect British associations from the centralizing effects of state expansion.

In West Germany the Allied ban on industry and business organization worked as a stimulant to centralization and discipline. When freedom of association was extended to business and industry in 1949, the leaders of the Federation of German Industries (BDI) made hostile Allied policies an important tool for organizational mobilization and concentration, and the federation emerged as an exceptionally important interest group. On balance, the defensive position of business and industry worked to encourage organization and incorporation. In Sweden SAF, the employers' federation, mobilized in response to Social Democratic economic policies and the bargaining strength of unions fortified by an inflationary economy and full employment. In Britain opposition to Labour's socialization program provided industry and business organizations with a new focal point for membership drives and political activity.

The finding of significant continuities in associational activities between the warfare and the welfare state suggests a somewhat different perspective on the origins of neocorporatism. In one view, articulated by Colin Crouch but present also in Philippe Schmitter's original formulation of the concept of neocorporatism, European corporatism has deep historical roots, and the basic patterns of functional representation were in place prior to World War I. Crouch argues that, as in the case of Great Britain, postwar concertation of interests between employers and unions were doomed to fail if it was not already in place prior to 1914 (Crouch 1993, 347).

In another view, associated principally with Peter Katzenstein, neocorporatism was a spontaneous response to the need for domestic adjustment to foreign competition. A third view, the "democratic class-struggle" perspective, saw corporatism as a reflection of working-class mobilization and regarded it as a functional compromise between the needs of capitalism and strong labor. The perspective taken here suggests a wholly different view of postwar neocorporatism. The inherited institutional frameworks available to postwar leaders included associational activities and self-regulation. When central planning failed, working through associations emerged as a second-best instrument for imposing public policy objectives on private actors. Many of the associational activities (and indeed the associations themselves) have shriveled in step with liberalization.

The prominent position of business groups in postwar policies confounded the traditional thinking on the right about the proper role of states and exposed parties that traditionally had espoused economic liberalism. Conservative and right-wing parties were forced to rethink their programs. The programmatic disarray on the right after 1945 easily matched that of the left. In this respect, the "newness" of the German Christian Democratic Party ironically stands out as a comparative advantage, not only compared against the difficulties that beset the British Conservatives or the divisions within the splintered Swedish center-right but also in comparison to the SPD's steadfast espousal of the Weimar years as the mainspring for postwar strategy and program. The appearance of a language of business "rights"—the "right" to manage, the "right" to exercise freedom of association—is a striking illustration of the infectious character of group narratives based on claims to citizenship associated with the creation of the nation-state as a redistributive community.

Labor

The first economic policy objective in 1945 for unionists and labor leaders was to prevent deflation and erosion of worker incomes. Planning was needed for that purpose. Since the main threat was considered to stem from deflation and unemployment, the objective of planning was to boost incomes by generous social policies and by public works programs. Country by country, the depression had left an imprint on politics and psychology that would play an important role in 1945 and would work to discredit capitalism. It had also left labor with different conclusions about the good that could come from working with industry and government.

Foreign trade was regarded with distrust and as a potential source of ruinous competition and only secondarily as a source of desirable consumer goods or of growth. The postwar programs of the Social Democratic and labor parties called for some or all of the following: (1) government intervention to keep wages high and unemployment high but also respect for trade union freedoms; (2) low interest rates in order to keep investment flowing; (3) socialization and nationalization to serve the dual purposes of allowing for union oversight of management and the realization of an efficiency gain from the rationalization of private business; and (4) the transfer of resources from agriculture to industry.[18]

These policies spoke to different aspects of what Jelle Visser (1990) has described as "inclusive trade unionism." They were also in key respects incompatible. Economic and political objectives clashed in the case of agricultural policy, where strategic concerns indicated support for farmers' demands for subsidies while economic preferences indicated policies sustaining cheap agricultural products. In this case, economic interests had to be sacrificed. The conflict between trade union control over wage determination and the quest for planning was the cause of even greater friction, as when the realization of efficiency gains from nationalized industries clashed or wage policy objectives conflicted with trade union autonomy.

Deference to the political elite that had brought labor to the cusp of power and long-range theories about the inevitability of labor's rise afforded labor leaders autonomy to chart a practical course of compromise. Still, the needs for programmatic flexibility often exceeded the capacity. Political parties and interest organizations are transmission belts between state and society, representing societal interests to the state. But they are not perfect machines. Cultural, historical, and institutional variables shape patterns of party alignments and voter-party identification. So do elite ideas and interpretations about the nature of social change.

Parochialism coexisted with involvement in the international political movements of the century. Nineteenth-century political ideologies continued to shape mid-twentieth-century politics in part because of the age of the men involved. Kurt Schumacher, the German SPD leader, was born in 1895 and died in 1952, after having shaped party organization and strategies in ways that it took decades to undo. Ernest Bevin was born in 1884 and died in 1951; Clement Attlee was born in 1883 and died in 1967. The Austrian Social Democrat Karl Renner was born in 1870 and died in 1950. Swedish prime minister Per Albin Hansson was born in 1885 and died in 1946.

All had risen with their parties from positions of obscurity and in some cases disadvantage to become not only national leaders but also the first spokesmen for an altered, class-inclusive concept of the national community. In Germany, Schumacher refused support for the first transnational attempt to plan economic activity, the European Coal and Steel Community, because transnational planning infringed on German sovereignty. In Sweden, Wigforss and Erlander defined the "Swedish way." In Britain, Benjamin Disraeli was put to rest by Labour leaders who spoke for One-Nation Britain. European socialist internationalism expired as labor embraced liberal nationalism.

One result of the twentieth-century wars was the interruption of any attempts at international coordination of political representation and coordination of protective policies, exemplified by the nineteenth-century internationales of labor unions or parties. Programmatic flexibility was contingent on personalities, on party organizations, and not least on the lessons that leaders had drawn from their parties' fates during the Great

Depression. The Swedish Social Democrats had the advantage of having held government power for sustained periods of time prior to World War II. They were also, not surprisingly, the most flexible and most willing to adjust their program to fit the needs of government.

A Watermark of Change: 1968

In comparison to nineteenth-century political order, the new order produced by two European wars was both national and more inclusive (Klausen and Tilly 1997). National unity nevertheless still stressed order over the individual and implied the conspicuous importance of elites and deference. The year 1968 stands out as a time when deference was rejected; it marked a point of no return. The student revolts and industrial militancy signaled the end of quiescent deference to political elites and a challenge to the all-encompassing but elitist national communities—which many now saw as less than inclusive—created after 1945.

Party fragmentation and programmatic reorientation in favor of a new politics of postmaterialism—which really was not so much nonmaterialist as it took materialism for granted—gave political expression to social change (Kitschelt 1994, 27). In the industrial area, increased unauthorized striking and industrial militancy often was directed against Social Democratic or labor governments. In Sweden, unauthorized striking was of concern to the Social Democratic government in 1974 and 1976. In Britain, discord with the unions thwarted Labour policies repeatedly, from the dockworkers' strike in 1966 and 1967 until the final collapse of Labour's postwar balancing act between union activism and responsible reform government in the "Winter of Discontent" of 1979. In the Federal Republic, the SPD's rise to government power in 1969 after a three-year trial period in Grand Coalition with the CDU/CSU coincided with a strike wave.

Industrial Militancy and the Decline of Elite Control

The generalized decline in industrial conflict levels after 1945 is an oft-discussed indicator of the shift to socially responsible capitalism and trade union acquiescence. The last decades of the nineteenth century also had been marked by high levels of industrial conflict, but they were not nearly as high as in the first decades of the twentieth century.[19] The 1950s and 1960s were placid in comparison. After 1945, only British workers defied the trend toward industrial peace, but they too embraced acquiescence during the tenure of the Labour Government from 1945 to 1951, when the annual number of days lost to industrial conflict averaged to close to 11 days. In France, the average number of days lost to striking between

1951 and 1968 reached 24 days per 100 workers. In contrast, only 4 days were lost on average in the same period in Germany and Sweden.

Aggregate measures for working days lost blend a variety of social, economic, and political conflicts. Proclivities to striking are contingent on economic trends and particular national institutional frameworks and are not immediately comparable in cross-national analysis. Despite such caveats, a secular rise in industrial militancy took place between 1968 and 1979 to 1982; in retrospect, it signaled the decline of postwar accords, even if it did not signal the second coming of a worker militancy that many on the left took it for. Except for France and Italy, 1968 was still a relatively peaceful year, even though a clear shift had taken place.

Militancy indicated a decline in both deference and organizational cohesion within the unions and a whittling away at the moral cement of cohesive class politics. The 1968–1969 rise in worker disaffection with economic policy coincided with—and in part caused—a sharp rise in inflation (Crouch and Pizzorno 1978; Hirsch and Goldthorpe 1978). The durability of warfare state institutions is illustrated by the fact that the remedies chosen to fix the situation were modeled chiefly on the "social contract" framework for tying wages to prices first used in Sweden and Britain during the war years.

When voluntary arrangements failed, states resorted to wage-price freezes; thus they reverted to patterns set by wartime stabilization policy. Although Swedish unions and Social Democratic policymakers prided themselves on never succumbing to the use of incomes policy, the unions accepted very moderate wage agreements in 1973 and 1974. In response to union leaders' concern about the consequences of unauthorized striking, the subsequent wage agreements in 1975 and 1976 were generous— in retrospect, overly so. Sweden's business cycles did not match those off the rest of Western Europe, nor was the left's electoral setback timed to the same beat.

The cycles of recession and political change varied from country to country, refracted by nationally contingent dynamics of party competition (Lewis-Beck 1988). In Britain, incomes policy remained respectful of the lessons learned from the unions' revolt against wage policies in 1950 throughout the 1960s; binding schemes were avoided. Hyperinflation and escalating industrial unrest put the accord to the test, and successive Conservative and Labour governments experimented alternately with statutory controls and corporatist "social contracts" that signaled the state's intent to impose restraints on "free" unionism. Four decades of deference to the unions came to an end in 1979, when the Thatcher government initiated a series of Employment Acts that curtailed the unions and switched to monetarist policies. In the Federal Republic, the SPD introduced the concept of "Concerted Action," which also was a belated attempt to introduce corporatist coordination between economic policymakers (represented by the Bundesbank) and labor and industry (Scharpf 1991).

The resurgence of wage and price controls—by direct or indirect means—in the 1970s took place after the group discipline, which was sustained by the original shift away from centralized planning to societal coordination from 1945 to 1955, had begun to disintegrate (Braun 1986). Two conclusions follow from this observation. First, it is clear that sociological change and institutional transformation do not go hand in hand even if they are related. Second, peacetime incomes policies did not have the disciplining effects that government controls had in the war years. This line of argument will not be pursued further here, but arguably the recurrence of price-wage controls and incomes policy had the opposite effect and accentuated class disintegration (Gourevitch et al. 1984; Lindberg and Maier 1985).

The politics of social cohesion was undermined by the long-term economic consequences of the 1973–1974 oil crisis, which obliterated smokestack industries and sped industrial change. The microchip revolution of the 1980s eliminated assembly-line productions not already eradicated by the oil crisis. The declining economic importance of native male workers, triggered first by tight labor markets that attracted immigrants and women and then by the expansion of public sector employment that drew more women into the labor force, is another highly significant change in the social composition of the working class (Klausen 1998). From comprising more than one-third of the electorate in the postwar years, the core constituency of social cohesion politics—the unionized industrial worker—comprised less than one-fifth of the electorate by the 1990s. The cultural and ideological prerequisites of the redistributive "citizenship" welfare state began to erode even before the removal of the last lingering institutional protections that had sustained the national welfare state as a functional totality of protectionist, state-centered screens shielding national cohesion policies.

EIGHT

The Postwar State and National Economic Development

Continuities: From the Warfare State to the Welfare State

In *Governing the Economy,* Peter Hall (1986, 231) pointed out that state-centered theories of the state are of little help in view of the variability in the ability of states to resist societal interest. The theories Hall referred to claimed that states are rational actors and act in the national interests when pursuing particular economic strategies. Hence, cross-national variations in economic policy can be constructed as expressions of differences in national interests (Katzenstein 1985; Krasner 1978, 1982). But Hall observed that the British state was considerably less resistant to capture by societal interests than the French and that the variability could not easily be linked to differences in national interests.

Leaving aside the weakness explored by Hall and the near-tautological implications of the state-as-rational-actor hypothesis, state-centered approaches had the advantage that they helped understand why foreign economic policy tended to be relatively constant over time and only marginally affected by partisan differences in government. In this respect, the state-centered theories pointed to a weakness in domestic actor models. The debate quickly hit a standstill between comparativists who prioritized domestic variables and international systems theorists who accentuated the constraints imposed on states by systemic variables.

Hall helped bring along the debate by pointing to the importance of the institutional frameworks of states and how national institutions mold the representation and the articulation of interests, introducing an irreducible bias in the translation of interests to policy. He questioned the state-centered approach's emphasis on systemic causality and argued that commonalities in French and British politics derived from similarities in the institutional structures of policy institutions (political regime) in the two countries rather than from any systemic attributes of the international state system (1986, 261). The historical-institutionalist perspective was developed further by Margaret Weir (1992), who stressed the importance of *sequence,* by which she meant a number of things associated with historical contingencies, from policy learning to ill or good luck. From the viewpoint of comparative theory, this raises another methodological question. Can we generalize about historically contingent trajectories? It is to this question that this chapter now turns.

Did Hall's defense of endogenous development go too far? Between 1939 and 1945 the international crisis worked to reshape the national state. Scarcity and near autarky likewise originated with the international system, as did the construction of the postwar trade order and the associated constraints, signified by the balance-of-payments current account constraint, on domestic economic policies. Even citizenship policies broadly conceived as the ties between states and subjects were shaped by the war. In the Federal Republic, for example, guarantees to returnees and refugees captured scarce resources in the postwar period and replaced full employment as the first social priority. We can allow room for international variables without upending the basic insights of the historical-institutionalist approach. Global events and the constraint associated with the restoration of international trade worked to shape state capacities, not a system-specific logic of action.

The centrality of the state to postwar economic policies was a common denominator for European economic polices. The early elimination of war controls and the collapse of planners' designs for statutory full employment policies set the United States off from the postwar mold of increasing uses of public power and as a liberal case. The focus of German policies on export stimulation ahead of national economic development represented a variation on the "European model" that combined with the conspicuous absence of guaranteed full employment put the Federal Republic closer to the United States paradigm than to that of other European countries. The Federal Republic's status as an aggressor country obviated citizenship policies and absolved the postwar government from a critical social constraint that impinged on British policymaking.

The United States was an exception from the rule of state responsibility for economic development only to the extent that its policies focused on molding the geopolitical order and making international trade safe for U.S. producers rather than on the insulating the national economy. Nevertheless, expansive economic policies—from agricultural policies that worked to keep consumer prices down and producer prices up (with the government bridging the gap) and stimulative fiscal policies—suggest that we should not rush to conclude that state direction was absent in U.S. domestic economic development.

The warfare state changed how policymakers thought about governments' role in a general fashion and provided the practical means for planning. National-variations-of-capitalism theories usually ascribe differences to state traditions (Crouch 1993). The centrality of the French state to postwar economic policy is generally explained by the statist legacy of the French revolution, or simply a statist or republican political culture. In *Modern Capitalism,* Andrew Shonfield (1965, 71) began his discussion of postwar French planning by referring to the "essential French view, which goes back to well before the Revolution of 1789." (See also Schmidt 1996.) We plainly want to allow room for cultural variations and history as a conditioning influence on attitudes to the state. Nevertheless, consistent patterns of continuity between wartime economic policies and postwar policies suggest that in a medium-term perspective, the postwar adjustment process was above all molded by institutional variables of more recent origin.

It is not really surprising to find that social inclusion mattered more in the immediate postwar years in liberal democracies where regime constancy prevailed (Sweden, the United Kingdom, the United States) than in countries that had been occupied during the war or after (France, the Federal Republic, Austria). One reason was that the reconstitution of electoral politics took longer in the latter and pressing questions about economic reconstruction came first. But it was also a question of the fulfillment of certain promises. After all, in liberal democracies resource mobilization was based on an assumed social compact among elites, states, and subjects. Social guarantees influenced postwar domestic politics in these countries. No parallel obligations bound the postwar governments in countries where occupation produced a change in the ruling elites. Still, the ubiquity of postwar planning, in one form or another, shows that it was not the case that planning was compelled by the need to satisfy social guarantees. Convergence with respect to state-centered economic development policies after the war derived principally from two sources: scarcity and the fact of preexisting comprehensive state control. We may add to that a reorientation of national elites toward the state and the radical expansion of functional interest representation associated with the administration of economic controls, but elite inclinations to some extent were ancillary ingredients to the shift between public and private power (Shonfield 1965).

Policy choice is unavoidably contingent on resources and historical context. Social reformers approached the reconstruction process empowered by new resources and new legitimacy, but policy was still functionally and instrumentally confined to the reuse and reinvention of existing institutional resources. Likewise, the economic and political contingencies of the transition process worked to mold reform. Scarcity was an important fact, as was the need to observe social guarantees made early on in the war.

The relative balance between scarcity and social guarantees in shaping postwar adjustment process is discussed further in what follows.

This chapter argues that postwar national growth strategies were defined by the state's position as arbitrator of scarcity and of citizenship in the immediate postwar years. As prosperity replaced scarcity and domestic growth required increased access to foreign markets, the balance between protectionists and liberalizers changed. Change was neither gradual nor coordinated across countries. Liberalization took place in fits and starts and around particular issues or events. A secular trend toward liberalization and increased economic openness exists, but it is mediated by contingent national histories and development strategies. The chapter speaks first to the question of patterned postwar continuities and how the legacy of the warfare state molded postwar economic policies. Next the variations in national growth strategies are analyzed.

Austria: Power Sharing and Parity Politics

Austria conforms to a mold of societal corporatism sustained by the "hidden hand" of the state. Yet postwar Austrian political institutions—like those of the Federal Republic—were shaped by the presence of occupation government and affected by the taint of Nazism and state failure. Why did Allied influence not produce a liberal outcome here? Civil war in 1933–1934 and Anschluss to the German Reich in 1938 began 12 years of authoritarianism on Austria. The Dollfuss regime prohibited trade unions in 1934, and, unlike Sweden, another small country that settled on societal corporatism as the chief means for economic coordination, no partial reconciliation took place between employers and unions prior to 1933.[1] Here, postwar policymakers had to reach back to early twentieth-century legislation for precedence for postwar corporatism. New legislation passed in 1947 recreating industry organizations and trade unions, the 1946 *Österreichische Verstatlichungsgesetz* and the 1947 *Kollektivverträgsgesetz,* reiterated in part older legislation that had been voided in 1933. Subjected to native fascism in 1933, incorporation into the Nazi Reich in 1938 and to Allied military occupation in 1945, the authenticity of a postwar "Austrian" state tradition would be unexpected. Nevertheless, Austria often is regarded as a case illustrating the strength of tradition. In reality, the reemergence of tradition was the result of deliberate state action and of reconstruction.

Luck and Hardship

It is tempting to speak of luck. Wanting to separate Austria from Germany, the Allied powers agreed already in 1943 to declare Austria a "victim" of

Nazi aggression. When the Soviet military arrived in the eastern parts of Austria ahead of the Western occupation troops, it allowed an Austrian government to be formed in April 1945, prior to German capitulation and to the Western allies' invasion. National elections took place in November of that year, four years before national elections took place in the Western-occupied zones in Germany. Austrians were permitted self-government much earlier than the Germans, and the government was able to exploit U.S.-Soviet conflict to create political space for itself. The presence of an Austrian government compelled the Allies to refrain from micromanaging the reconstruction process in that country.

Karl Renner had been the first Social Democratic chancellor of the Austrian Republic in 1918; in April 1945 he became head of a provisional government appointed by the Soviets and later grudgingly accepted by the Western allies. (Renner died in 1950.) The first government included the Communist Party, KPÖ, but subsequently the Communists were kept out. Soviet influence began to wane already in 1948–1949, even if the Soviet role was not ended officially until 1956. The country was divided into four occupation zones, with Vienna falling in the Soviet zone. Economic recovery was hampered by the separation of the "breadbasket" in the east from the industrial zone in the west. Zonal divisions encouraged sectional differences. Currency reform took place in December 1945 and again in November 1947. In late 1947 industrial output was estimated to approximate roughly 45 percent of 1938 output.

Austrian integration into the German war economy from 1938 to 1945 implied a near-total loss of economic autonomy. With the occupation of Germany, autonomy was restored. The Allies took over most of the preexisting price and wage controls. Nazi planners had sought to bring Austrian policies into conformity with Nazi planning policies. Consumer prices were frozen and producer prices fixed within the cartelistic pricing system. In 1945 official pricing structures continued to reflect the influence of the Reich's artificially low pricing of commodities and agricultural products. Low prices encouraged hoarding and rampant black marketeering, hence also shortages.

War destruction was in many respects worse in Austria than in Germany. Bombing raids had destroyed industrial plants and housing; in Wiener Neustadt, an industrial suburb of the capital, an estimated 90 percent of the buildings were destroyed. Food rations dropped to as few as 850 calories per person in 1945–1946. Gross economic activity was reduced to one-third of the prewar level. A large number of industries were nationalized in 1946, amounting to roughly 20 percent of Austrian employment. After the Austrian State Treaty and the withdrawal of Soviet forces in 1955, responsibility for a large number of industries that had been nationalized by the Soviet occupation government fell to the Austrian government. Concentrated in the mining and steel industries, the nationalized companies specialized in trade with the Soviet bloc countries (Katzenstein 1984, 201; Mathis 1995). No serious attempts were made to identify owners and restore property to them. Privatization of the publicly owned industries was not considered seriously until negotiations over European Union membership were initiated in the 1990s.

The Austrian Road to
National Economic Development

The Austrian social structure resembled that of Sweden, with a natural Red-Green alliance between a large agrarian class of inefficient farmers and a working class tied to small and medium-size plants. As in Sweden, many small farmers voted for the Social Democrats. In some parts of the country as many as 25 percent of farmers vote for the SPÖ, yet the national farm organization was tied to the ÖVP (Krammer 1991, 373). In 1951, 32.5 percent of the Austrian labor force was employed in agriculture, only 29.1 percent in mining and manufacturing (Flora 1987, chap. 7). Austrian farmers were overwhelmingly small family farmers dependent on themselves or family members for labor; agricultural workers comprised only 20 percent of the agricultural labor force. Two decades later roughly 40 percent of the workforce was engaged in industry.

The dynamic of party competition resembled that of Federal Republic with two dominant parties, a Socialist and a Christian Democratic party, and a small liberal party in the center. Early postwar party activities were regulated by the occupation authorities. The two main postwar parties derived directly from prewar parties, but both underwent name and organizational changes. The old Social Democratic party became the Austrian Socialist Party, the SPÖ, and the Austrian People's Party, the ÖVP, replaced the old Christian Democratic party and other center-right parties.[2] A new centrist liberal party with no direct prewar ancestry was added in 1955, the FPÖ.[3]

From 1946 to 1966 Austrian governments were Grand Coalitions between the SPÖ and the ÖVP. Austrian Social Democratic theory had more in common with Swedish Social Democratic ideas about the state as an anchor for class collaboration than with the visions of unbridgeable class divisions and demands for socialization and a planned economy that dominated the programs of both British and German parties (Renner 1978).

The absence of a lively reconstruction debate set Austria apart from the "victorious" countries. The debates in Washington and London about German reconstruction touched upon Austria, but the country was not central to the planners' design for a new trade order. (Austria joined the Marshall Plan and the European Payments Union but was not included in any of the grand plans for European integration leading to the Treaties of Rome.)

The two major political parties re-formed in 1945 in an atmosphere of closure and with little overt discussion or dissent over program and principles. After 1945, Allied occupation and control of public debates deterred controversy and compelled unity. A present-day reader will be struck by the sterile nature of contemporary party and union protocols, no debates and no votes emerge from documents, only sterile consensual statements policy that frustrate a researcher looking for insight into conflicts and choices. When votes are listed they are inevitably unanimous. Adolf Sturmthal (1989, 169–180), an Austrian émigrée and an official in the Socialist International and later professor of economics at Bard College, described in his memoirs the party leaders' opposition to the return of émigrées, apparently based on the feeling that they would "rock the boat" too much and did not "fit." When the occupational forces were finally gone the coalition government sterilized party competition and cast party organizations as systems of patronage, providing members with jobs in local governments and connected interest organizations. Until the early 1980s, the system worked remarkably well to dampen political and social conflict.[4] The fossilization extended not just to the labor side, but also to the ÖVP and industry associations (Tálos 1991, 402).

Class Organizations

On the surface, post-1945 organizational patterns harked back to nineteenth century patterns of representation. Upon the elimination of the old guild system, a national system of chambers of commerce—*Handelskammern*—was created in 1848. As a modern equivalent to the *Ständestaat,* parallel chambers also were created later for labor and for agriculture. The labor chamber, which was not set up until in 1920, was replaced during the Nazi period by the enrollment of Austrian workers into the Nazi labor organization. In 1945 the 1920 labor chamber was re-created as a political "house" for the trade unions. The postwar system retained compulsory membership and a quasi-public status. Membership and dues paying to the chambers were made compulsory for "all physical or legal persons" in industry, commerce, finance, credit or insurance, and all wage- or salary-earners (Traxler 1991, 340.)

The chambers were self-governing organizations based on a hierarchical and rigidly territorial structure, with members voting only for local officers who in turn elected officers at the next level of the organization. The reconstruction process yielded an exceptionally cohesive system of "pillared" representation based on the national incorporation of class interests for workers, farmers, and business (Traxler 1986). A principal function of the labor chambers was to incorporate workers in nonunionized firms under the umbrella of the national "social partners" system.

The first organization of independent farmers in Austria, a regional chamber of agriculture, was created in 1922. Prior to that agrarian interest had been represented by the elite. The Nazi organization of agriculture was extended to Austria in 1938. After 1945, pre-1933 laws were restored. The agricultural chamber combined in the same organization small and large landholders, agricultural employers and employees, as well as producers and processors. The organizational structure lent itself to the dominance of the numerically stronger groups, small and inefficient farmers. The organization of farm interests was unique, but the policy and politics of agricultural regulation conformed to the general European paradigm of subsidized family farming and protectionism. As in Sweden, the left's support for agricultural subsidies and the preservation of the family farm allowed a rapprochement between farmers and the left.

Employers were represented in collective bargaining through the industry-based national Chamber of Commerce, with the various sectors organized separately in affiliated associations. Employers are organized in the *Bundeswirtschaftkammer* (BWK), which consists of a fragmented network of sectoral, regional, and trade-specific interest organizations (Traxler 1991, 340). Over the years compulsory membership has eroded, but by means of a general trading ordinance, *Gewerbeordnung,* which allowed the trade associations to regulate the industry, and competition in the retail and service sectors has been restricted severely. In addition to the labor chamber, a new Austrian trade union confederation (ÖGB) was created to replace the factionalized prewar trade union system. In this respect, postwar Austrian policies followed the German model. The ÖGB was set up with 16 sector-based unions, with the one organizing public sector employees the largest.

The unions became responsible for collective bargaining, but the central confederation has exercised strong control over bargaining. The exact mechanism for wage control is described below. Austrian workers are also represented at the plant level by works councils, which include nonunionized workers. At the national political level, the chamber of labor acts as a representative of employees vis-à-vis the other chambers.

War Controls and Incomes Planning

In 1939, wage determination had been delegated to the Nazi labor organization, the labor trustees, or *Gau,* which with certain exceptions mostly simply froze wages. In 1945, the wartime wage scales were retained and the military governments once again issued wage freeze orders. In 1946, the Allied Commission for Austria approved the transfer of the *Gau* authority to set wages to the Austrian Ministry for Social Affairs, which in turn delegated that authority to a central Wage Commission. An Inter-Allied Control Board continued to review the commission's decisions. The pay structure reflected the social policies of the Reich, with low wages for women and young workers and special adjustments for men with family responsibilities (Kravis 1948, 25).

In June 1946 Allied oversight was ended, and the authority to fix wages was assigned to a Central Wage Commission under the Ministry of Social Affairs while price-fixing authority was delegated to the Ministry of the Interior. In August 1947 the fragmentation of the wage- and price-fixing machinery was considered an obstacle to currency reform, and a temporary stabilization program was adopted that included representatives from commerce, agriculture, and labor. The stabilization program linked prices and wages to a comprehensive indexation agreement which put everything in relationship to 1938 prices on the basis of a negotiated formula. Between July 1947 and May 1951, a series of wage-price agreements were worked out among farmers, employers, and the unions.[5] Austrian reconstruction policies included a heavy dose of government control, hardly surprising considering the desperate food situation and presence of foreign military forces. The coalition government agreed on economic policies that aimed at an adjustment process that would approximate foreign pricing structures by means of controlled reflation.

Wage and price policy aimed at permitting a concerted increase in wages and agricultural prices while still protecting employment and ensuring that inflation remained moderate and under control. The first and only challenge to coordination took place in October 1950, when insurgent unions declared a general strike and demanded wage increases beyond those permitted by the settlement. The strike became the largest in Austrian postwar history. The Communist Party—aided by Soviet-occupying forces in the Soviet zone—allegedly played an important role. As was the case in connection with 1945 metal workers' strike in Sweden, the strike soured the trade unions on wage restraint. The early wage-price agreements included provisions for family allowances (a "family wage"). The 1950 general strike revealed the potential for sectional conflict to fuel oppositional trade union mobilization and caused the Socialist-dominated unions to resist continuation of the central price-wage agreements (Edelman 1954, 50).

In 1951 persistent shortages and inflation occasioned the creation of an "Economic Directorate" and five controls bills allowing for food rationing, wage and price fixing, and controls on foreign trade. The directorate included representatives from the economic ministries—finance, agriculture, forestry, trade, and nationalized industries—and representatives from the three chambers. The power-sharing principles of the Grand Coalition were extended to the directorate through the representation of all interests and through procedural rules that allowed only for unanimous decisions.[6] But in 1952 the Austrian Supreme Court found that system unconstitutional because it represented an unacceptable delegation of government responsibilities to private parties. The decision appears to have reflected the anticartelistic efforts of American policymakers. The establishment of a principle of separation between public and private power was a high priority for the U.S. High Commissioner, who harshly and repeatedly attacked the pervasive "subversion of competition" that resulted from postwar Austrian policies (Johnstone 1951, 1). Since then coordination has taken place within a framework of nominally "private" agreements.

The Austrian stabilization policy approach that evolved between 1945 and 1952 is interesting (even though it did not last) because it represents an attempt to resolve the coordination problem associated with social and economic reconstruction. The chief vehicle for coordination was societal organization, which nevertheless did not measure conformed to the liberal or voluntarist principles of the autonomous society. We have in this system an example of the state re-creating society. It is also interesting because the Supreme Court decision had few practical implications for the system's longevity.

The Parity Commission and Planning-by-Wages

After some experimentation in the wake of the 1952 decision, a Parity Commission for Wages and Prices—*Paritätische Kommission*—replaced the temporary framework for income allocation among employers, unions, and farmers in 1956. The commission has had no legal standing but, strangely, its creation nevertheless was approved by a parliamentary vote, sustaining a resolution proclaiming its creation. The Parity Commission has survived to the present, even though discipline is fraying. Decisions have been made in two subcommittees, one on prices and the other on wages. Each subcommittee was set up with equal representation from employers and labor, the "social partners." All decisions had to be unanimous, which in effect granted each party veto power. Superficially, the system resembled the Swedish national Frame Agreement except that farm incomes were included directly in the negotiations. But there were important differences in both function and origins. In fact, the Austrian system was more respectful of local unions than the Swedish national contract was.

(But then, because of local productivity agreements the Swedish Frame Agreement was not as powerful has it sometimes has made out to be.)

Wage planning through the Parity Commission was possible because, although individual unions in principle negotiated all contracts and bargaining formally was decentralized, unions had to apply to the Subcommittee on Wages for permission to initiate negotiations. Similar rules applied to price determination, and businesses or industry representatives had to apply for permission to raise prices. Since all applications to initiate contract negotiations were routed through the ÖGB before being brought to the subcommittee, the system also supported the authority of the central confederation. On the industry side, the system strengthened the powers of the national interest organization over the membership through placing a penalty on "unauthorized" wage increases. With respect to price increases, the price commission allowed increases only upon the documentation of "legitimate" costs, including only those wage increases negotiated through the centralized system, with no allowances for local wage drift. Business support for the procedures was stimulated by the fact that the system protected business and industry against wage and price competition and against government attempts to impose additional controls.

The system represents a finely calibrated mix of decentralization and centralization. The unanimity rule imposed tremendous self-discipline on the "social partners" by encouraging reciprocity and cooperation and penalizing self-interested behavior. It also effectively deterred local activism. Wages were negotiated locally and through more than 200 individual contracts, with the national "clearinghouse" system in effect creating a model contract by setting national norms that prevailed in local contract negotiations. The weakness of the system has become apparent only in recent years when the one-sided withdrawal from the system by individual or groups of employers has posed a new threat (Guger and Polt 1994). Some employers have rejected obligatory membership of chambers and challenged the legality accorded to the peak organizations (Crepaz 1992; Gerlich 1992).

The links between the wage and price determination system and government worked to provide for a constant, in theory voluntary (but in practice inflexible), system for coordinating income formation with fiscal and monetary policy. By one estimate, the price commission of the Parity Commission controlled about 50 percent of producer prices and about 20 percent of consumer prices (Tálos 1991, 404). Austro-Keynesianism differed from stabilization policies elsewhere by extending them to the peaks as well as the troughs of the business cycles (Braun 1986, 255; Flanagan, Soskice, and Ulman 1983). When labor shortages became a problem, the solution was to import temporary foreign labor rather than to draw on domestic labor market "reserves," a term that mostly implies women (Guger 1992, 342). And in contrast to Swedish policy, Austrian wage co-ordination has not aimed to compress wage differentials.

Austrian economic policies were nevertheless also shaped by some of the same characteristics that influenced postwar Swedish policies. Exchange rate stability has been a high priority, and for most of the period it implied a fixed-rate currency policy. Additionally, the government has pursued low interest rate policies (allowing for temporary upward rate adjustments as part of contractive stabilization packages) and a tightly controlled banking system. The combination of state trading, with as much as one-third of all foreign trade going to the Eastern bloc countries, and direct controls on foreign trade, in both goods and capital, shielded the national economy and domestic social arrangements against the disruptive effects of international business cycles and direct competition.

Austria in Comparative Perspective

Scholars have lumped Austria together with Sweden either as "star" performers using centralized wage determination to adjust costs to international cycles and preserve employment (Calmfors and Driffill 1988) or as instances of politically "challenged" corporatism in need of adjustment to a new politics of ecology and feminism (Kitschelt 1994; Klausen 1998). One does not preclude the other, although the rigidity of the system is undeniable. Yet it is clear that some of the persistent differences in Swedish and Austrian policies—particularly the absence of an egalitarian component to the latter—were due to the differences in the institutional origins of coordinating policies. Austrian wage coordination dates back to postwar control policies and retained wartime wage differentials in part as protection against left-wing sectionalist mobilization. Swedish egalitarianism emerged as a concession to sectionalism.[7] However, in neither case was centralization ever as complete as it often has been made out to be.

Trade union sectionalism and unhappiness with wage controls stimulated union opposition to the continuation—and reimposition—of controls as it had elsewhere, but opposition also was tempered by the parity policies of the Grand Coalition government and the continued influence of Soviet and U.S. political representatives with domestic policymaking, which further animated national unity government.

In comparison to the Federal Republic, Allied influence on postwar Austrian political reconstruction was hampered severely by the early decision to designate Austria as a "victim" country. Contrary to U.S. intentions, Allied control policies worked to enhance cartelistic and restrictive economic practices. The international situation as well as the occupation powers interference with Austrian political activities also encouraged reconstruction on a program of national collaboration and restoration.

The continuation of wartime control policies—from the *Gau* to the chamber of labor—and in the Economic Directorate prior to 1952 requires more research. The discontinuity on the level of regime appears to have been counteracted by the perpetuation of control policies. The Austrian case also points to the critical importance of scarcity for state-centered planning policies. In Austria, the pervasion of the price system caused by the integration into the German Reich and acute shortages made state control of economic reconstruction a necessity. The contrast to Erhard's 1948 decontrol policies nevertheless requires some explanation. Austria's ambiguous position as a country of "victims" and the high degree of self-government allowed by inter-Allied competition for influence sustained group coordination (corporatism) under state direction. The elite-centered nature of postwar Austrian politics may well have deep cultural roots (Bischof and Pelinka 1996), but it was plainly bolstered by the absence of a reconstruction debate like those that unfolded in Sweden, Britain, and the United States. Austrians did not enter the post-1945 period buoyed by promises of a "new Jerusalem," a "People's Economy," or a "Second Bill of Rights."

France: Discontinuity and Self-Government

France is another country that entered the postwar transition without promises of a French equivalent of the "New Jerusalem." With the Nazi invasion the country was divided in two parts, one occupied and one ruled by the collaborationist Vichy regime. The extent to which continuity exists between the Vichy regime and the French Fourth Republic is a question that shall not be addressed here. Recent controversy on the subject has focused on postwar political leaders with a tainted past in Vichy, not on continuities in state structure. The mainsprings of French planning were not derived from Vichy, although elements of the control economy were extended into the postwar period. The progenitor of French postwar planning was located in Washington, D.C., where in late 1943 the French Supply Council was set up with Pierre Mèndes-France as chair of the finance committee and Jean Monnet in charge of the supply committee. The council's primary assignment was working with the U.S. government to coordinate supplies for the French troops, fighting on the side of the Allies.

The chronology of French reconstruction was such that the main aspects of postwar planning were in place before a new political structure had been created. The Constituent Assembly for the Fourth Republic was appointed on October 21, 1945. Jean Monnet presented the basic outlines for the first postwar plan on economic reconstruction to the U.S. State Department on November 23, 1944, nearly a year before political reconstruction was initiated (Duchêne 1994). The timetable and administrative organization of the first plan were worked out between October 1945 and May 1946.

French Reconstruction

Preparations for French reconstruction took place in Algiers, London, and Washington, D.C. Monnet was in regular contact with John McCloy, Henry Stimson, and Dean Acheson, all important figures for postwar U.S. policy in Europe. In October 1943 Monnet relocated from Algiers to Washington, where the United States put him in charge of the Commission for Supply and Reconstruction. A High Council of Supply was set up in 1943–1944; it soon had more than 500 employees in Washington (Duchêne 1994, 135).

In May 1944 the French resistance forces set up a provisional government of the French Republic. A committee in London began planning for the return of the French exile government already by the time of Pearl Harbor. Rivalries between exile groups based in London and those based in Washington complicated the transition. In September 1944 Charles de Gaulle appointed Mèndes-France, not Monnet, minister for the National Economy. Monnet returned to Paris in September 1944 but not as a member of the new government.

After liberation, the Supreme military command (Supreme Headquarters Allied Expeditionary Forces, or SHAEF) retained control over shipping, transportation, and imports. All foreign transactions went over military accounts until economic authority was transferred in April 1945 to a French Commission for Supply and Reconstruction, which acted on the basis of a (preapproved by Washington) six-month plan for imports and supply and for the reconstruction of railroads and shipping. In September the United States canceled the Lend-Lease program that had kept supplies flowing, and the supply of foreign credit became an immediate issue.

When de Gaulle left the government in January 1946, Monnet returned in an official capacity. He immediately went to Washington and negotiated a loan agreement on the basis of which the plan administration, *Commissariat Général du Plan* (CGP), was set up.[8] Monnet's owed his return to power in no small part to the Communist-controlled trade union (CGT) that vetoed Mèndes-France's reappointment.

In his memoirs Monnet (1978, 236) wrote about his guiding principle for the plan: "the underlying philosophy was clear in my mind . . . a method of concerted action whereby everyone could see where his own efforts fitted in with everybody else's." Nevertheless, he was determined that civil servants should dominate the planning administration, not interest groups. (See chapter 1.) In 1946, 18 industrywide modernizing committees were created with group representation. In 1947, another six were created. The first plan, *Plan de Modernisation et d'Equipement* (1946–1953), focused on the rationing of access to scarce materials and capital, and awarded priority to particular industries: steel, cement, transportation, fuel, and power (Shonfield 1965, 126).[9]

The conclusion that "In some ways, the development of French planning in the 1950s can be viewed as an act of voluntary collusion between senior civil servants and the senior managers of firms" (Shonfield 1965, 128) seems accurate. The fact that civil servants assumed an exalted position in the determination of planning objectives has attracted much attention. But do we need to reach back to 1789 to explain the relative insularity of the state elite against the pressures of interest group and electoral democracy? No definite answer can be provided in the present context, but there were many reasons aside from century-old French state traditions, why interest groups would be weak and the newly created planning administration would be relatively insulated against societal demands.

The grass-roots weakness of French unions is legendary, and as Peter Hall (1986, 231) put it, "it was the French planning process that generated business power in France rather than the other way around." The first plan's origins in the administrative organizations, including Monnet's planning commission, set up under Allied military control for the purpose of supplying Allied forces on French grounds is one reason. The timing of the main planning decisions well ahead of the re-creation of French political organizations is another important factor. The planning apparatus and the plan itself preceded the reconstruction of French society, much of it had even been assembled in Washington, D.C. From the viewpoint of comparative methodology, it is inconvenient that French state tradition and the feebleness of French political organizations in the transition period from 1944 to 1946 acted in concert. In either case, we would expect the state to be allowed an unusual degree of autonomy in shaping policy. Hence no real test has been made of which is the more important variable. It may be that the contingencies created by Nazi occupation and subsequent liberalization and regime shift combined with acute economic shortages and a depleted national economy only *reinforced* preexisting proclivities for statism that would have reasserted themselves even against a different historical context.

Nevertheless, the Austrian and French cases both suggest an unexplored wider adaptation of the explanatory framework used here to account for variations in the postwar development paths of the European welfare states.

Patterns of Transition from War to Peace and Postwar Planning

The symmetries between wartime policies and postwar approaches to social and economic planning among all the countries discussed are summarized in table 8.1. Scarcity and economic autarky were the mainspring of postwar planning. American prosperity worked against any hopes for a continuation of planning after 1945 beyond what was needed for maintaining high aggregate levels of domestic consumption and international access for American producers. Not so in Europe, where the balance-of-payments constraint implied government responsibility for matching much-needed imports with exports.

The way states involved their subjects in war mobilization mattered for societal inclusion in postwar planning. Wartime constitutionalism imposed a corresponding obligation to include groups in the administration of the postwar welfare state. In other words, states that fought the war by democratic means were exposed to societal pressures after the war to a greater degree than states where no analogous mobilization of citizens took place during the war. In contrast, regime discontinuity in contrast awarded the state a degree of insulation against societal pressures. The comparative matrix reveals also an element of indeterminacy, which confirms Hall's point about the irreducible bias of national constitutional and institutional frameworks. Citizenship policies were not alone in molding the postwar adjustment of state power to the constraints of electoral democracy and interest group liberalism. The country studies contained in this book show that party systems, electoral systems, and socioeconomic variables were clearly important too. Unique national histories of contention and popular political mobilization worked to shape distinctive adjustment trajectories. These are contingencies that militate against grand theorizing.

Economic Autarky and Growth Strategies

The remainder of this book is dedicated to further explore the autarky thesis' implication for postwar growth strategies. The discussion is confined to the suggestion of an interpretative framework that may help us understand the roots of postwar change in a new light. It is a perspective that can emerge only as the defining characteristics of the nation state's insertion into an integrated European economy moves into sharper focus; a discussion that only can be carried out from a the vantage point of "the long

Table 8.1 Wartime Involvement and Postwar Policy Outcomes

| | Independent Variable | | Dependent Variable | |
	War Status	Economic Shortages	Planning	Societal Inclusion
United Kingdom	Belligerent Victorious	Severe	Yes	Yes
Sweden	Neutral	Severe	Yes	Yes
Federal Republic of Germany	Belligerent Defeated Occupied	Severe	Yes	No
United States	Belligerent	Mild	No	No
Austria	Occupied Victim status	Severe	Yes	No/Yes[1]
France	Occupied Victorious	Severe	Yes	No

Note: [1]Change with 1952 Supreme Court decision voiding state-controlled wage and price determination.

view." By 1938 the share of inter-European trade of the large countries—Britain, France, and Germany—had declined to a level below that of 1913, from 2.8 to 2.2 billion dollars (Dewhurst 1961, 653). By 1945 it had come to a standstill. Autarky was a side product of the war but did not come to an end upon demobilization. Free trade had to be planned. Purposive control of foreign trade was considered by some as a hallmark of "real" planning, and after 1945 states continued to control foreign trade vigorously. The restoration of foreign trade began to pick up in September 1950 with the establishment of the European Payments Union. Britain's short experiment with currency convertibility in 1947 supported those who argued for a controlled approach. (Notably, the German mark was not made convertible until 1958.)

Policymakers made a principled if ambiguous commitment to trade liberalization. (Myrdal's reassurances in 1946, when he was minister of trade, that Sweden needed foreign trade, even if "some people" saw it as a source of low-wages pressures, illustrates the mixed feelings held by many.) As Alan Milward (1992, 127) writes, "to an economy suffering from balance of payments constraints, which were sometimes said to be the unavoidable consequence of the higher investment, higher employment and higher welfare of the postwar years, 'export-led growth' seemed to offer away forward." Milward implies that this was not an accurate construction of alternatives and that there was nothing "unavoidable" about the balance-of-payments constraint.

Milward is particularly critical of the British willingness to let the external balance constraint dominate domestic economic policymaking (1992, 355). Standard explanations of the British postwar decline have focused on the country's inability to sustain exports at a level that could have "paid for" domestic development. The implication, which Milward presumably shares, is that a greater emphasis on domestic "catch-up" could have paid off in the long run. As is always the case, any discussion of counterfactual strategies comes up short against the evidentiary weight of what did happen. In good years, the British economy did well but still not as well as those of the other countries, and in bad years it usually also did worse.

Growth and Redistribution

The postwar boom was ubiquitous, but not all countries benefited equally. It is commonplace that economic growth is the best social policy. By that score the postwar years were good social policy. Between 1951 and 1974, when rapidly rising oil prices brought growth to a halt, the German economy grew by 180 percent. Two other high-growth countries were Austria, where the economy expanded by close to 200 percent, and France, where growth came close to 140 percent. Like Germany, both also started from a low point; a detail that in part accounts for the rate of growth. The Swedish economy expanded by 105 percent over the same period, and the British by 65 percent. From 1957 to 1959, a recessionary cycle, average growth rates for the three countries highlight the British problem: the Federal Republic grew by 5.2 percent; Sweden by 2.9 percent; and Britain by 1.2 percent.

It appeared that economic expansion did not need to come at the cost of inequality (Lange 1984; Okun 1975). In Britain and Sweden, the redistribution of incomes was particularly noticeable compared to the prewar years. Prior to World War II, the top 10 percent of the employed population earned 44.5 and 40.5 percent of total income respectively.[10] In 1973 the same groups earned only 27 and 19 percent respectively. In Austria, redistribution was more moderate but still conspicuous, with the top 10 percent of the population earning 31 percent of total income in 1933 and 25 percent by 1973. In Germany, however, income distribution remained stable. The top 10 percent earned 34 percent of total income in 1934 and also in 1971.

The rate of foreign trade expansion was particularly high in Germany and Austria, again a reflection in part of the low starting point. Between

1953 and 1957, the rate of annual growth reached as high as 25 to 27 percent in these two countries. For Sweden, 1952 was not a good year, but in the following years exports increased by 5 to 10 percent annually.

Domestic Politics and Economic Strategy

The concept of comparative advantage predicts that countries will specialize to their advantage in areas in which they possess an abundance of factors; land-rich countries will specialize in agriculture and those rich in labor will specialize in labor-intensive products. Modern updates to the theory hold that countries possessing capital and advanced technology will import low value-added products and export high value-added products, permitting domestic labor a cut. The prescriptive part of the theory ignores the tricky problem that ideally all countries would prefer to be at the top of the industrial "food chain" but if all opt for the strategy it cannot work. (For an example, see Reich 1991.)

The national-variations-of-capitalism argument contends that there is a way out of this problem, because national institutions inevitably shape divergent strategies of economic development, even if a rough convergence exists with respect to economic policies within the framework of advanced industrial nations (Berger and Dore 1996). In the absence of any natural foundations for specialization, strategy itself becomes the foundation. A close fit existed between domestic politics and national economic strategy. Strategically speaking, countries had simple choices. They could do what the British Labour Party and the Swedish Social Democrats had proposed in their postwar programs and focus on domestic stabilization by means of socialization and reflationary policies, letting the export industries take care of themselves. This choice naturally involved curbs on imports and agricultural subsidies. Or they could target the domestic economy to further exports and suppress domestic income expansion until the added income from exports stimulated domestic growth. This was the strategy laid out by the German Christian Democrats.[11]

The relative share of the export sector, and of public and private domestic consumption, of the gross domestic product (GDP) over nearly five decades is shown in figures 8.1a through 8.1d. Totals exceeding 100 indicate deficits on foreign trade and payments balances and/or government budget deficits. By 1950 the export sector constituted roughly 20 percent of the national economy in all four countries. Thirty years later the sector had doubled in relative importance in the two smaller countries, Sweden and Austria, and nearly so also in the Federal Republic. (It is natural for small countries to have larger export sectors than big countries.)

Figure 8.1a: Austrian Consumption and Exports
As a percent of GDP

Percent of GDP

Year

Government Consumption/GDP Private Consumption/GDP Exports/GDP

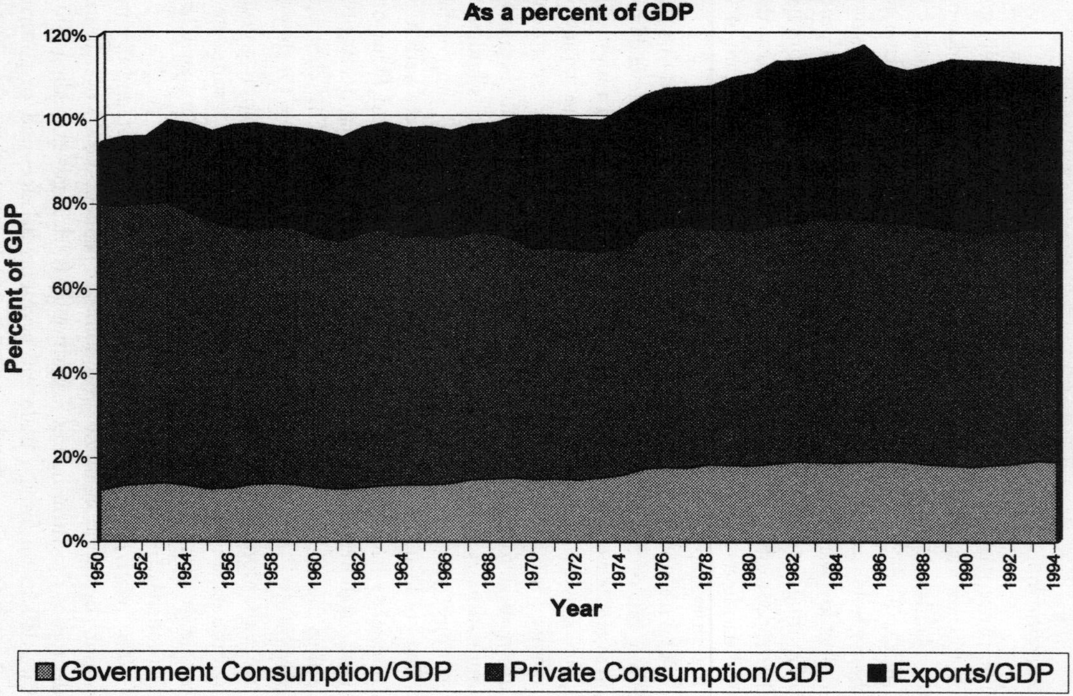

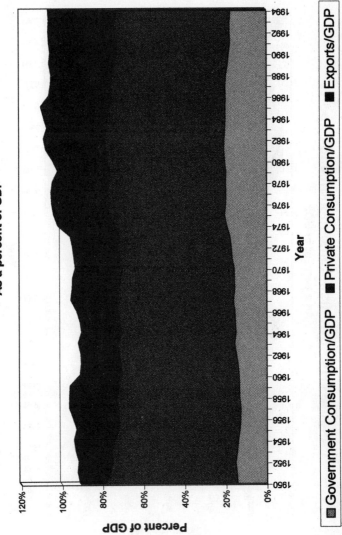

Figure 8.1b: German Consumption and Exports
As a percent of GDP

Percent of GDP

Year

■ Government Consumption/GDP ■ Private Consumption/GDP ■ Exports/GDP

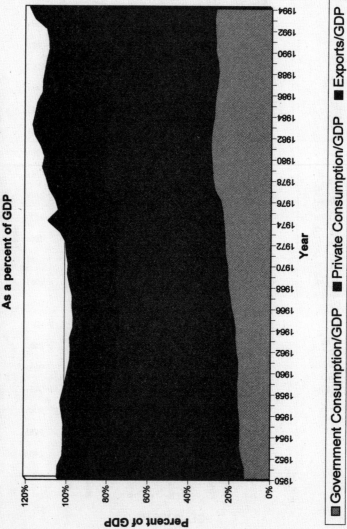

Figure 8.1c: Swedish Consumption and Exports
As a percent of GDP

Percent of GDP

Year

■ Government Consumption/GDP   ■ Private Consumption/GDP   ■ Exports/GDP

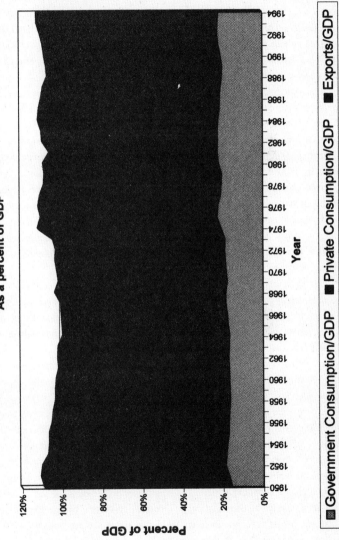

Figure 8.1d: British Consumption and Exports
As a percent of GDP

Percent of GDP

Year

■ Government Consumption/GDP   ■ Private Consumption/GDP   ■ Exports/GDP

In Britain, exports contributed close to 30 percent of GDP between 1975 and 1985 but have since declined somewhat in importance. The pervasive increase in the export sector is matched by an equally ubiquitous decline in the relative importance of private consumption. (We are talking about relative *shares* here, not absolute magnitudes, and the decrease in the relative share of private consumption does not indicate a decline in consumption but a shift in the balance between the difference sources of the national gross product.) The country graphs provide an intuitive illustration of the gradual change over time in the general orientation of national economic activity.

It is customary to use exports as a share of total economic activity as a proxy measure for economic openness. It is a convenient measure because it provides a consistent and quantifiable yardstick and is easily applied in comparative analysis. We presume that it is indicative of the significance of export markets for national politics and policy. The disadvantage is that this measure is blind to qualitative changes and invariably provides a picture of gradual change. Since a constant cannot explain a change, we are facing a problem with respect to the determination of limit values. It is easy to conclude that, somewhere along the way, foreign trade suddenly reaches a maturation point where national policy is "rushed" by exogenous variables outside the reach of national policymakers. The measure does not, in short, distinguish between magnitude and importance.

· For lack of a convenient indicator of the latter, we rely on the former as an approximation presuming that, everything else being equal, size matters. We may hypothesize that national policies will change to focus more on maintaining export industries as these become an increasingly important source of national income, but does is happen when exports are up to one-third of total economic activity, or at one-half? A number of possibilities exists, however. As more jobs depend on stable exports, more voters may be in favor of free trade (Frieden 1996). The opposite is also possible; those hurt by foreign competition may mobilize for protection. The particular intersection between foreign trade and domestic politics is highly contingent, but as the national economy becomes tethered to the world economy, changes in policy means and objectives are likely to take place. The important point however is that irrespective of voter response, policymakers are constrained by the makeup of the economy. The reality of the bloated state and the obliteration of foreign trade in 1945 did not prevent policymakers from declaring themselves free traders in 1945. Likewise, the reality of a large amount of domestic economic activity tied to foreign trade does not prevent policymakers from adapting a protectionist stance today; but the *meaning* of the two positions have changed.

Floodgate Theories and Their Critics

Comparativists vie to identify the starting points in causal chains of progressive market integration and the removal of national controls. Did international markets and bankers swamp states? Or did states decide to open the floodgates and then get flooded? Susan Strange (1996) and Paulette Kurzer (1993) have argued for the former view, adding worries about the depletion of democracy that follow from letting go of national controls. In his study of the emergence of global finance, Eric Helleiner (1994) pinpoints financial trade as the last one to succumb to trade liberalization and join the ranks of goods being freely traded across national boundaries. (This view ignores labor markets, which despite patchy liberalization between the member states of the European Union seem to become more tightly regulated as liberalization advances in other areas.)

Helleiner ascribes the difference between trade liberalization and financial liberalization to the fact that the benefits of financial liberalization are accrued by a small group and the cost dispersed. This is not a very satisfactory explanation. Policymakers did not proceed with banking liberalization in order to line the pockets of arbitrage brokers. The perception was that the benefits would be widely shared.

In a detailed analysis of the Norwegian government's decision to eliminate bank controls, Bent Sofus Tranyø (1996a and b) has shown that political views on controls changed well ahead of actual shifts in the magnitude of transborder financial transactions, a finding that makes sense considering that it is necessary to open the gates before you can be flooded. Lars Jonung (1994, 362) similarly has tied Swedish decisions to initiate bank deregulation to primarily domestic political considerations, particularly the need to finance (cheaply) a large current account deficit. Scandinavian policy changes may well be amendable to explanation by the adage that sometimes things have to change to stay the same. In this view liberalization happened not in response to pressures from global capitalism but because policymakers decided the national economy would benefit from it. The facts are the same; the interpretation differs.

National Institutions and Growth Strategies

Somewhat abstractly, we can say that postwar growth derived from growth in domestic private demand, increases in government demand, or exports. A multiple regression analysis comparing the contribution of private domestic demand, government demand, and exports to national economic growth between 1950 and 1994 leads to the conclusion that domestic private demand was the primary motor of national growth. This finding conformed to the basic assumptions of Keynesian theory. Domestic demand accounted for between one-quarter and three-quarters of the improvement in national growth. (Figures for GDP at market prices, government consumption, private consumption, and exports are from the International Monetary Fund, various years.)[12]

Exports added positively to growth, by an additional 2.3 percentage points in the United Kingdom to 12 percentage points in Austria. In all cases, growth in domestic private consumption (by firms or individuals) constituted by far the chief source of national income. However, the picture was not universal. In Sweden, where government consumption proved an important source of growth in national income, exports constituted the second most important source of growth. The results of the analysis are included in table 8.2.[13]

Differences in the relative importance of exports in stimulating domestic growth are striking, but we have to assume that country size matters for strategy. Exports played a larger role in the two small countries, Austria and Sweden. Econometric controls can be introduced to control for size, but there is little point to the exercise. Countries themselves cannot control for size.

The variation among the two large countries and the two small countries indicates nevertheless that more is at stake than size alone. If only size mattered, Austria and Sweden would do the same thing. Instead, size is one strategic variable among others affecting national economic strategies. The relative rise in exports is a secular trend within which other changes took place.

The expansion of the public sector is another ubiquitous aspect of postwar economic development. The figures do not accurately reflect public sector growth because they do not reflect the growth in transfer payments, only the institutional expansion of the welfare state.[14] The table does not reflect national variations with respect to transfer payments.

Postwar planners preferred domestic-led growth—by government consumption or private consumption—in place of export-led growth because they feared exposure to foreign markets as a source of loss of control. These fears were relaxed as foreign trade proved to be a more reliable source of domestic economic expansion than expected. The analysis contained in table 8.2. indicates that postwar planners were both right and wrong.

The protectionist school of thinking was wrong about the destabilizing implications of foreign trade in the postwar years but right about it in later years. The empirical analysis points to the somewhat paradoxical inference that, in the case of exports, less may be more.[15] As exports grew in volume and relative importance, they also ceased to contribute in a significantly positive fashion to national growth, although Austria is a notable exception.

Table 8.2   Relative Contribution of Exports, Private and Public Consumption, to National Growth, 1950–1994, Annual Change (Multiple Regression Coefficients)

	Private Consumption	Exports	Government Consumption
Federal Republic			
Entire Period:			
Adj. R^2	78.0%	81.5%	NS
beta	.80	.21	.04
Sig T	.00	.01	.65
1950–1972			
Adj. R^2	76.2%	80.5%	NS
beta	.80	.24	.09
Sig T	.00	.03	.35
1972–1994			
Adj. R^2	52.9%	NS	NS
beta	.74	.20	.07
Sig T	.00	.21	.66
United Kingdom			
Entire Period:			
Adj. R^2	69.8%	72.1%	NS
beta	.80	.18	.04
Sig T	.00	.04	.66
1950–1972			
Adj. R^2	53.2%		NS
beta	.74	.24	.16
Sig T	.00	.11	.27
1972–1994			
Adj. R^2	79.0%	NS	NS
beta	.89	.16	−.10
Sig T	.00	.12	.36
Sweden			
Entire Period:			
Adj. R^2	21.4%	36.8%	28.5%
beta	.31	.31	.35
Sig T	.02	.01	.01
1950–1972			
Adj. R^2	24.0%	31.8%	NS
beta	.46	.33	−.002
Sig T	.02	.08	.99
1972–1994			
Adj. R^2	13.2%	NS	NS

(continued)

Table 8.2 *(continued)*

	Private Consumption	Exports	Government Consumption
beta	.42	.25	.24
Sig T	.05	.24	.25
Austria			
Entire Period:			
Adj. R^2	59.9%	71.4%	NS
beta	.58	.58	.04
Sig T	.00	.00	.65
1950–1972			
Adj. R^2	56.4%	66.7%	NS
beta	.57	.39	.03
Sig T	.00	.01	.83
1972–1994			
Adj. R^2	43.4%	61.0%	NS
beta	.49	.47	−.09
Sig T	.00	.01	.55

Sources: International Monetary Fund's *International Financial Statistics Yearbook* 1979 and 1985. Missing years from Flora 1987, 340–399.
Note: NS: not significant at .005.

In a comparison of the growth potential of exports in 1950 to 1972 and in 1973 to 1994, the positive association between growing exports and growing national income disappeared from the first to the second period.

Plainly, a statistical association does not say anything about the causal mechanisms. The finding that exports had an overall positive effect on national economic growth based on average measures compounded over one period of time but not over another period becomes interesting only as a description of long-term expectations and constraints. We have to assume that policymakers above all want to do things that work. If export-led growth does not work, we would expect planners to think about alternatives.

Resuscitating Planning

A revival of protectionist and pro-planning sentiments took place in the 1970s. An ambitious collection of comparative and national studies of the postwar growth period published in 1981 concluded that "there was nothing inevitable about Europe's growth in the first two decades of the period" (Boltho 1982, 10). The implication that policy was all-important for a country's ability to maintain high levels of growth led to an intensification of controversy over the direction of economic policy.

One response to declining growth rates was a new emphasis on what was called "active" industrial policy, which argued for more direct government control over industrial investment. In Sweden, this implied a reversal of Wigforss' taboo against government ownership. There, as elsewhere, governments became increasingly involved in some of the "engines of growth": shipyards, car manufacturing, heavy engineering, and machine tool companies. Shipping and mining industries were particular targets of modernization plans. In Sweden, the Uddevalla shipyards and the northern mining company LKAB are examples of beneficiaries of increased government support. In the United Kingdom, Harland and Wolff and the Upper and Lower Clyde shipyards similarly benefited from an infusion of public support. Industrial policy should aim to "pick winners," it was agreed. In actuality, the subsidized industries were large blue-collar companies with "brand-name" significance for national economic self-esteem or of central importance to employment in depressed areas. Many of the same industries were subjected to privatization in the 1990s.

National planning efforts were rekindled. In 1963 the British National Economic Development Council published *The National Plan,* a more ambitious attempt at planning than anything done since Stafford Cripps. Six years later, another "planning document," *The Task Ahead,* was published by the Department of Economic Affairs (Meadows 1978, 412). In Sweden, the Social Democrats' efforts to revitalize industrial planning faltered between 1976 and 1982 during the center-right government. Government spending on industry subsidies increased more rapidly during those years than it had during the Social Democrats' tenure in government (Pontusson 1992, 138). (Upon their return, the Social Democrats cut subsidies.)

The revitalization of planning efforts in the mid- and late–1970s is often ascribed to the heightened presence of left-wing discourses in the wake of 1968. A more realistic interpretation is that interest in renewed planning stemmed from the difficulties that many large-scale national blue-collar industries were facing.

Remedial Strategies: Adjusting to a Liberal Order

A particularly interesting observation that can be made on the basis of the data analysis presented in table 8.2 is that cross-national differences increased over time and some new differences emerged after 1972. Foreign trade expansion continued to be associated with domestic growth in Austria but not in the other three countries.[16] The Swedish coefficients, although statistically somewhat ambiguous, indicated that public consumption became the more important source of growth there around that time too. One possible interpretation is that at this time, contraction of government spending reduced the growth potential of domestic consumption, and countries that continued to spend on government institutions made up for lagging worldwide growth. In the Federal Republic and the United Kingdom, as in Sweden, exports ceased to have a consistent and significant connection to improvement in national income.

Austria's ability to sustain exports as a consistently positive source of enhanced income is exceptional and merits further discussion. Sweden has taken a different road in the second period. There government consumption has accounted for close to 30 percent of the economy since 1980. In contrast, in Austria and Germany it has remained more or less fixed just below 20 percent since 1975. The increase in government consumption in Sweden (and in the rest of Scandinavia) reflects a second wave of welfare state expansion to accommodate working women, a wave that also was designed partly to boost economic activity at a time when the private sector went into recession. It was also part of a remedial strategy to take back control of domestic stabilization policy.

In small countries with open economies, private consumption of imports is high. The high import content of private demand posited a new problem for stabilization policy. If a government tries to counteract an impending recession by increasing social payments, part of the effect is leached abroad. To address this problem (and wage inflation concerns), Scandinavian Social Democrats tried demand-switch policies that attempted to boost public rather than private consumption (Mjøset 1996).[17] Demand-switch policies were tried only briefly, and a closer look at the graph for Swedish public sector consumption in figure 8.1 reveals a distinct abatement of public sector growth after 1983. A gradual but comparatively steep increase took place between 1960 and 1975 under Social Democratic governments. The "hump" in 1976 to 1982 coincided with a center-right coalition government.

How may we interpret these findings? And what do they say about the warfare-to-welfare thesis? One view is that "export-led" growth worked as long as the general economy was relatively insulated. States derived a privileged position from their insertion as regulators of domestic contacts with the world economy after 1945, but over time this position became less essential and the centralizing powers of the state weakened. In the relatively closed postwar economies, governments were in the position to shield domestic markets against the recessionary aspects of international trade and to reap the benefits of increased foreign trade while avoiding many of the disadvantages: increased exposure to downturns in the international business cycle or the instability associated with intense wage competition, for example. Over the long haul, exports have played a specific and distinctly positive role in national growth policies. In recent decades, however, they have increasingly failed to play this role, not because exports are less important to domestic growth strategies—they are more important—but because domestic exposure to international business cycles has increased as governments rolled back economic controls.

The Reconciliation of National Growth and Foreign Trade

Keynes too struggled with the question of how to reconcile the open economy with his ideas about the role of domestic stabilization policy in the stimulation of growth. He admitted that in an open economy, lower wages could stimulate investment and growth (Keynes 1973, 262) but listed various objections why it still was not a good idea to rely on (downward) wage flexibility. Most of his reasons were of a political, not an economic, nature. Downward wage flexibility redistributed incomes from wages to other factor incomes and from manufacturers to rentiers. The benefit was in any case likely to be short-lived, if workers reacted with the same optimism that informed investors and expect wage increases.

Attempts to negotiate wage reductions were likely to amplify social conflict, and Keynes noted that, for political reasons, the preferable way to reduce excessive wage gains was to increase prices by inflation. A general reduction of wages, as opposed to specific reductions, was in any case impossible in a democratic system, in his view. Moreover, general wage reductions might produce a temporary stimulus to growth but they would still be associated with a worsening of national terms of trade and of national real incomes in comparison with other countries. And even if a temporary stimulus to growth was to be derived from wage reductions, the future effect would be—everything else being equal—to diminish the incentives to efficiency improvement and postponement of both investment and consumption.

Yet in view of all his reasons why flexible wage policy would not work, it is noteworthy that Keynes still recommended that governments pursue stable wages, with allowances for a mildly inflationary economy with increased wages being hollowed out by increased prices, only on the basis of the presumption of a closed economy and, in an open economy model, on the basis of variable exchange rates (Keynes 1973, 264, 270). The postwar economy provided a practical approximation to Keynes' closed economy presumptions by allowing for some controls on capital, currencies, and trade patterns—even if fewer protections were allowed than he would have liked to see. However, what soon emerged was a very un-Keynesian economy: an open economy with fixed exchange rates. In a liberal international order, the rules of the game change (Carlin and Soskice 1990).

Over time the positive feedback between domestic expansion and foreign trade that characterized the first postwar decades turned into a difficult trade-off between domestic stabilization and engagement in a liberal international order. The conflict between government responsibility for social protection and national economic stability and a growth strategy relying on efficiency gains is apparent. The important point is that this did not happen so much in response to the gradual encroachment by international capitalism of domestic actors but in response to and refracted by deliberate and calculated changes in domestic politics and policies. The changing tradeoff reflects the shift from an "embedded order," which in retrospect really appears as a historically unique period of economic nationalism, to an international liberal order.

It is nevertheless significant that the analysis suggests that three distinct models of remedial action have emerged since 1972. One rests on boosting national incomes by means of boosting exports. It is associated with a contraction of domestic consumption in order to keep cost levels down. The Austrian case indicates that this is a strategy that a few countries can follow with success. Britain is another example of a low-cost growth strategy, in this case made possible by Thatcherite shock therapy and monetarist stabilization policy. It is fair to assume that small countries are more likely to be successful in this strategy than large countries, simply because they may have more luck at "beating the market." A second remedial growth strategy was the one followed by Sweden until about 1992. It relied on a "demand-switch" strategy, which substitutes increased government consumption for private consumption, but attempts to keep up standard-of-living improvements by increasing public services. Exports remained an important source of national income growth but not at the cost of domestic consumption. This particular option places high demand on national cohesion around a high-tax and large-state bargain, which suggests that political rather than economic variables may stand in the way.

The third model may be an option only for large countries. It is inward-looking in that domestic stimulation proceeds without regard for the resulting disequilibria, and foreign economic policy is used to export or ameliorate the problem by changing the behavior of trading partners. The United States has pursued this road; now the Federal Republic is trying it. A large political economy literature has attempted to deal with these issues, and does so better than I can here (Kreuger 1996).

In summary, distinct national models of economic development strategies emerged after 1945 and national variation increased over time. My research supports the national-variations-of-capitalism thesis that domestic political institutions become a source of economic diversification. A methodological problem arises. For this to be more than a default option, we have to assume that domestic political institutions are capable of planned action, a presumption that is not always fulfilled. Partisan preferences and national economic difficulties and opportunities merged to produce politically sustainable growth strategies. One implication is that room remains for national divergence and that adjustment to a new liberal order may take diverse forms. Another is that there is room for degrees of failure and success.

It is not given that a liberal, "open" order will result in low economic growth. The problem is the diffusion of power, which makes it more difficult for national groups to use political power to capture shares of the national income. The late nineteenth-century boom provides precedent for a high-growth, liberal order. The anomaly of the postwar boom stands in sharp contrast to the interwar years but fades when compared against the boom that preceded 1914. The German gross domestic product grew in real terms by roughly 46 percent between 1885 and 1910; Sweden's, by 67 percent. Britain, however, failed to produce comparable economic growth rates in that period. The diffusion of power in a liberal order—between states, international actors, markets, associations—shifts attention away from state power. The nation-state loses its concentrating power on national political life.

Conclusion: Historical Sociology and the Postwar Welfare State

Douglass North (1990, 4) has defined institutions as "any form of constraint that human beings devise to shape human interaction." Institutionalist perspectives at times can seem to emphasize the constraint part over the agency part of institutional development, but then North's definition of the institutionalist perspective errs on the other side. Institutions can be molded and changed to accomplish particular objectives, but the means are rarely neutral to the ends. The power of the warfare state to shape postwar policies was both insidious and inspirational. It was insidious in that it constrained policymakers to adapt existing resources and institutions to the purpose for "winning the war for peace," as they put it. Hence domestic stabilization policy was fitted to the available tools. It was inspirational in that radical new ideas about the state's role in the creation of a stable (and fairer) domestic order resulted from the experience of wartime mobilization. New political elites rose to power through their inclusion in the wartime machinery for regulating the civilian economy and in Austria and

West Germany through the Allied reconstruction effort and the demolition of the old state.

In Britain, the Labour Party faced near extinction after 1931, when the party leader, Ramsay MacDonald, formed a National Government with representatives from the Conservative and Liberal parties and a group of defectors from the Labour Party. (The Labour Party received 7.5 percent of the vote in the 1931 election; four years later, its share rose to 25 percent.) After 1945, it was the Liberal Party that faced the possibility of extinction. In Germany, the creation of the Federal Republic in 1949 altered electoral rules aiming to reduce party fragmentation. Partition also eliminated the Junker class and changed the political identity of German agrarian interests. Between 1920 and 1932, 13 parties received at least 2 percent of the national vote. In the 1960s, only 4 did. The main postwar party, the Christian Democratic Union (CDU), did not exist in the 1920s. In Austria, the two main postwar parties derived directly from prewar parties but underwent both name and organizational changes. There the key difference was the elimination of several small ethnic parties and the creation of a new centrist liberal party with no prewar ancestry. The articulation of class identities within the context of competitive party politics was more fluid and open to reinterpretation in 1945 than standard theory has led us to believe.[18] Continuity held only in Sweden—the only country studied to remain neutral between 1939 and 1945—and there too all parties introduced new programs by the end of the war or shortly afterward, and significant changes took place in the infrastructure of the interest groups. In all cases, organizational change and reform reflected the newfound importance of the state.

Institutional continuities, national integration of interest groups, and a new public philosophy about the balance between private and public obligations were part of the warfare state's endowment to the postwar era. Its institutional components were of great importance to the arrogation of responsibility by states for socially responsible economic development in the postwar years. They included, among other things, the development of new forecasting techniques, planners to man forecasting institutions, and a knowledge component. British budgeting policies had shown, for example, that fiscal policies could be tied to projections of future income rather the actual reporting of past incomes. The development of price indices allowed for planning of wages and prices. Employment registration could be redirected easily to facilitate manpower planning. Strikes could be regulated by means of joint regulation. The list of innovations proceeds from the specific to the ecumenical when we add trade union representation in management, agricultural subsidies, and national wage policy, all policies that were not the innovations of war but were greatly expanded and accepted in the war years. On this matter Robert Gilpin (1981, 19) wrote: "The nation-state in historical terms is a rather recent arrival; its success has been due to a peculiar set of historical circumstances, and there are no guarantees that these conditions will continue into the future. Yet it would be premature to suggest (much less declare, as many contemporary writers do) that the nation-state is dead or dying." Gilpin proceeds to treat the state in purely systemic terms, to the point of concluding that states have "no endogenous interests." The domestic underpinnings of sovereignty were given by war, fixed in terms of territoriality, authority, and national norms.

The problem is that on all accounts the "stateness" of states has changed in the past 50 years. Integrated product and capital markets based on monetary coordination and relaxed or absent bank controls have made territoriality a fuzzy concept. European integration has added multiple dimensions to authority. Norms have changed in ways that make the triumphant nationalism of postwar labor leaders look naive. The number of Cassandras has increased since Gilpin warned against the premature declaration of the end of the state. Susan Strange (1995) has argued that national policy choice has become so constricted by the internationalization of trade that politics has lost its meaning. Government controls over national economies have become emasculated to a point where neoliberal policies represent the only choice; there are no alternatives, she says. It is not the case, however, that we have arrived at the end of politics. There remains room for divergent national strategies. Strange also has defined internationalization as a mind-set, a reorientation in personal opportunity strategies that link the well-being of the individual to world markets. This, I think, is the more important issue to discuss.

Has economic openness created the conditions for a return to the politics of the Internationales? In the absence of political opportunity structures for international political organization, the state retains its hold on the political imagination of elites and voters. A small group of individuals may create international utility functions for their personal lives, but few can do this. Tied by language, culture, and family, people remain much less mobile than goods and capital. (One of the notable differences between the late nineteenth century and the late twentieth century is that immigration has remained low, even as product and capital markets have become internationalized.) Politics is still local in action, if not always in mind.

In a comparative and historical perspective, the state-centered order created by the Great War, World War II, and the Cold War stands out as an interregnum characterized by strong state and social, economic, and political enclosure. The postwar welfare state represented a compromise between nationalism and internationalism as well as one between statism and liberalism. It also contained the "seeds of its own destruction" because of the built-in dynamism released by economic growth (Mosca 1967). Growth was associated with an expansion in foreign trade, large-scale changes in the social composition of the national community, and a secular decline in class. The primacy of the national community after 1945 lent itself to holistic conceptualizations of political strategies as "national." The presumption of social unity was always problematic. It was convenient because it allowed for a realization of John Stuart Mill's political liberalism, of politics as a progressive elimination of privilege. It conflicted with the greater liberal vision of the principled equality of all humans to have access to opportunity. The challenge in a liberal world order is to make economic liberalism compatible with political liberalism.

State over Society: The War Legacy

This book has presented an explanation of the prominence of economic planning in postwar discussions of economic policy. The problem attracted my attention for two somewhat contradictory reasons. The first was the prevailing enthusiasm for economic planning, which in hindsight can be characterized only as naive. The second was that, even if we now think postwar debates naive, postwar economic policies included elements of planning—even if these did not live up to the planners' expectations—that worked to bring about rapid national economic development and a novel attention to the social dimensions of capitalist development. Planning tethered economic policy to social policy and vice versa. The coupling of economic and social objectives defined the welfare state and made it more than an accretion of generous social insurance programs. The present study was not designed to decide if planning encouraged or deterred growth. It was designed to explain the origins of economic planning philosophies and the sources of contention over planning. I have shown that planning failed before it succeeded, in part because of inaccurate forecasts of what the main postwar economic policy objectives would be (reflation in place of inflation control) and in part due to unanticipated resistance to allow planners to control certain decisions. Planning rarely worked as planners thought it would or should. Within the basic convergence with respect to means and objectives—and, we may add, policy adjustments timed to crises—we find much national variation in both thoughts regarding the purposes of planning and in the application of planning.

I have found that postwar planning derived principally from the strategic position of states as mediators of domestic relations with nonnationals; democratic planning built on the national integration of the main economic interests into cohesive class-based interest groups, sustained by a discipline and deference for group leaders that had decidedly nonliberal aspects; and balance-of-payments and currency crises put a premium on stabilization policies over, for example, industrial planning or decontrol.

This study also shows that elite enthusiasm for planning was nonessential to the actual application of state direction of economic activity. This point was driven home in different ways by both the British and the West German cases. In the former, planning failed despite near-universal enthusiasm for central planning. In the latter, government responsibility for economic development was presented as nonplanning, and planning thrived, one can say, in spite of itself. One conclusion is that planning was an intrinsic attribute of the postwar state, as is the corollary that a near-universal concern with the protection of group autonomy and privileges was a principal source of the controversy over how and what to plan. As for the role of group interests in shaping policy, the ambiguous conclusion is that they both upheld and assailed the role for the state in the determination of the key economic decisions ranging from investments to wages. Aside from farmers, whose support for government action was unwavering over time and across countries, the enthusiasm for planning among other social groups was contingent and inconsistent. Labor and business were generally not adverse to state action, as long as it did not lead to state encroachment on key liberties, such as the "right" to control wages or the "right" to make managerial decisions.

Because of the contingent nature of group responses to planning efforts, it is futile to try to base a generalized theory of the sources of postwar economic planning on societal interests. That does not mean that group interests were irrelevant to the capacity of states to plan. The creation of integrated national interest groups was one of the principal innovations of the war years, and one that had enduring consequences for state-society relations after 1945. International relations theory commonly presumes that war has certain specific consequences for domestic social relations. The common notion is that a relaxation of social ties takes place in peacetime, while war brings a return to integration. This is borne out also in the present study. War fixes the territorial aspects of states and makes the presumptive unity of the community a fact. The institutionalization of interests inevitably creates insiders and outsiders, and over the long haul economic and social change works to undermine fixed interest confederations (Lindbeck and Snower 1988). Despite the focus of comparative politics on "national" models of political action as basic variables, the fact remains that domestic political communities are "constructed" political phenomena (Hoffmann 1965, 14; Klausen and Tilly 1997). Social cohesion and citizenship have been discussed in greater detail earlier. For now it suffices to conclude that in the hierarchy of variables that can be used to explain the role of economic planning after 1945, group interests assumed a secondary role to the institutional and strategic amplification of the nation-state brought about by the war and by autarkic conditions during the war and in its aftermath.

The creation of a centralized infrastructure for interest representation allowed for a new social compact between government and labor and industry, but it was not the cause of national integration; state expansion was. Wartime state expansion had both a strategic-systemic and an institutional component. The former derived from the constriction of world trade, national near autarky, and the economic-structural prospects for the world economy, including the rapidly changing security aspects of the new world order. The latter derived from state expansion and the new competencies accumulated during the war years. The functional requirements of economic autarky and the corollary need for liberalization continued to buttress state power long after demobilization. The postwar welfare state rested on a functional totality of interrelated means and ends, protocols bequeathed to postwar policymakers by the warfare state. Planning was the imperfect result of party strategies and brokered compromises between highly organized groups responding in an ad hoc fashion to preexisting policies and contingent alternative solutions.

I have proposed a historical-institutional explanation of the postwar welfare state that also posits the state as the central organizing principle of politics and policy. The theory implies that, in the absence of the concentrating powers of another war, we would expect disintegration to set in as part of an "aging" process. The analogy intimates irrevocable processes, but as scientists recently have found, aging is a predisposition that does not by itself cause demise. Demise needs a concrete cause. Events in the social area, such as the student revolts and outbreaks of industrial militancy in 1968, subverted aspects of the functional totality of the postwar welfare state long before others gave way. We can construct a chronology of subversive events, beginning with the refusals of unions to accept extensions of wartime wage-price agreements between 1947 and 1951 and moving on to 1968 and the collapse of the fixed-rate Bretton Woods system in 1971 to 1973. In this perspective the relaxation or elimination of bank controls and the shift to monetarist stabilization policies in 1982–1983 was another step toward disintegration. A "thin thread" of history runs from the collapse of Bretton Woods and the U.S. gold standard in 1971 to the end of the Cold War in 1989, and in the near-future, the 1999 creation of a European Monetary Union that will allow a European currency to replace the dollar as an international reserve currency. In contrast to proclamations of the "End of History," no single event between 1947 and 1989 signals the demise the postwar welfare state. In this perspective, the end already began in 1947 when the failure of European planners' designs for state-centered planning—with the singular exception of France, which until 1952 and the atypical intervention of the Austrian Supreme Court—had to be modified to allow for the liberal ideas of associational autonomy.

Notes

Chapter 1

1. The subordinate role of social policy was a source of resentment for Gustav Möller, the minister of social affairs (1932–1951), who occasionally threatened to resign in protest over the lack of attention to social issues. Möller's advocacy of social spending put him in opposition to the finance minister, Ernst Wigforss. See Wigforss 1954, 389.

2. Even Keynes appears to briefly have considered central planning a good idea for a backward country like the Soviet Union. See Skidelsky 1995, 235.

3. Clause Four committed the Labour Party to "secure for the producers by hand or by brain the full fruits of their industry and the most equitable distribution thereof that may be possible, upon the basis of the Common Ownership of the Means of Production and the best obtainable system of popular administration of each industry and service." In 1929 distribution and retail were added. Sidney Webb has been credited with authorship. For a brief but excellent discussion of the evolution of the party's thinking about economic planning, as reflected in party programs, see Roger Eatwell 1979, 34–35. For a discussion of Andrew Gamble's revisionist interpretation of Hayek, see Skidelsky 1996, 4.

4. Hugh Gaitskell attempted without success to eliminate Clause Four in 1959.

5. According to Stanley Hoffmann, "the meaning of war is to be found in its historical functions" (1965, 263).

6. For a complete history, see *Industrial Mobilization for War,* Vol. I (1947/1969).

7. The EPU started officially in July 1950, coinciding with the start of the Korean War.

8. For a comprehensive cross-national history of incomes policy and indexation agreements, see Braun 1986.

9. Access to American consumer goods was important, but European consumers were in any case generally still deprived of such access until the mid-1960s. The critical issue in the early postwar years was access to goods needed for economic modernization and by European producers.

10. Elsewhere I have provided statistical evidence that contradicts Swenson's thesis regarding the dominant position of the interests of the export industries in shaping Swedish wage policy in the 1930s. See Klausen 1998.

Chapter 2

1. In 1950 Labour was reelected with a majority of less than ten seats. Although the party reaped a small gain in votes the next election in 1951, a change in government was necessary because the election produced a majority for the Conservative party caused by rural over-representation. The 1951 election also produced a return of middle-class voters to the Conservative fold in subsequent elections; a loss that Labour did not recover until 1997.

2. The designs for the controls and the service ministries dated back to the previous war and the works of the Committee of Imperial Defense, an organization of experts and civil servants permanently engaged in planning for war since 1909, see Hancock and Gowing 1949, 43. In 1923 to 1939 representatives of the military were added to the committee. In 1939 it was absorbed into the War Cabinet. The committee held the institutional memory of the inadequacies of the government machinery in the first war and acted as a conduit for continuity between the two wars.

3. The defense departments were the Admiralty, the War Office, the Air Ministry, and the Ministry of Supply.

4. J. M. Keynes published a series of articles in December 1939 that were published as a book, *How to Pay for War*, in 1940. Therein he explained the principles of income stabilization by means of forward estimates of the effects of government spending and fiscal policies.

5. House of Commons Debates [hereafter: H. C. Debates], April 7, 1941, cols. 1322–24. The speech was followed up by a government White Paper, *Price Stabilization and Industrial Policy*, also from 1941, which presented an outline of wage-price stabilization policy.

6. The first official estimation of the national income was published in 1941 as *An Analysis of the Sources of War Finance and an Estimate of the National Income and Expenditure in 1938 and 1940*. See Chester 1951.

7. In a radio broadcast on May 25, 1940, Bevin went as far as to claim that "drastic as these powers may appear on paper, they were brought about by the act of democracy itself" and by "the overwhelming consent of the people." See Bevin 1941, 64.

8. Herbert Morrison had overseen the creation of London's public transportation system and a member of London's local government prior to entering the government in 1940. He was identified with what has been called "municipal socialism," and had a steadfast belief in the good of public ownership. In 1945 he, Stafford Cripps, and Hugh Dalton became the critical players in shaping economic policy. As head the Ministry of Health, Aneurin Bevan became responsible for the national health plan and much of the social reform legislation. He resigned from the cabinet in 1951 in protest against the government's economic policies. A list of the members of the two Labour cabinets between July 1945 and October 1951 is contained in Morgan 1984, appendix I.

9. Bevin was not a member of Parliament in 1940, and a vacant seat had to be found for him. In June 1940 he became M. P. for Central Wandsworth.

10. The next generation was waiting in the wings. Harold Wilson took over from Cripps at the Board of Trade in 1947. When Cripps resigned from the Treasury in 1950 for health reasons, he was succeeded by Hugh Gaitskell.

11. Hartley Shawcross, the new government's attorney-general, bragged on the occasion of a repeal act eliminating Tory trade union legislation that "[w]e are the masters of the moment, and not only at the moment, but for a very long time to come." Butler and Sloman 1975, 227.

12. James Chuter Ede, a junior Labour minister from 1940 to 1945, recorded a 67–35 split within the Labour Party against the government. The vote caused the leadership to threaten to resign from the coalition government. See Brooke 1992, 80; Jefferys 1987, 30.

13. A 1942 report from the National Council for Civil Liberties presented a comprehensive catalog of wartime administrative orders regulating industrial labor based on the 1940 Emergency Powers (Defense) Acts. See Tuckett 1942.

14. The TUC's annual report from 1945 listed 36 unions with a total of 543 representatives on wage councils. All appears to have been reformatted trade boards. The Tailor's and Garment Workers' Union was in the lead with 115 representatives, followed by the GMWU with 86 and the TGWU with 79 representatives. Twenty-five unions had less than ten nominees. In 1947 the creation of new councils in hairdressing and retail industries was proposed. See *TUC Report 1945,* 96–98, and 1947, 172.

15. They were the National Association of Local Government Officers (NALGO) and the National Association of Teachers.

16. The three most important organizations were the National Union of Manufacturers, the British Federation of Employers, and the FBI. The latter two collaborated closely and even shared the same building for offices and top officials. Rogow 1955, 90–96. After failed merger attempts in 1943 and 1947, they finally merged in 1965 to become the Confederation of British Industries (CBI).

17. Some statements by Labour leaders read on the BBC between September 1939 and June 1940 are contained in a pamphlet, "Labour's Aims in War and Peace," ca. 1940.

18. Two key verses read:

> England! awake! awake! awake!
> Jerusalem thy sister calls!
> Why wilt thou sleep the sleep of death
> And close her from thy ancient walls?
>
> . . .
>
> And now the time returns again:
> Our souls exult, & London's towers
> Retrieve the Lamb of God to dwell
> In England's green & pleasant bowers.

19. D. N. Chester, who worked for the War Cabinet, reflected later on "the remoteness of all this policy-making machinery from the everyday life of the people and therefore the effects of many of its decisions" and how the planners spoke only with each other and spend their time reading memoranda or reports of other committees. Chester 1972 [orig. 1951], 29–31.

20. In May 1943 Beveridge went on a speaking tour in the United States to present the Beveridge Report to an American audience. The Rockefeller Foundation had invited him and paid for the trip. See Harris 1977, 427.

21. The most important trade unions represented, with their general-secretaries listed in parenthesis, were: Amalgamated Union of Engineering Workers (J. Tanner), Electrical Trades Union (F. Foulkes), National Union of General and Municipal Workers (T. Williamson), National Union of Mineworkers (A. Horner), Transport and General Workers Union (A. Deakin). The latter was Bevin's old union. Foulkes and Horner were both Communists. In discussions with the government, the TUC General Council was represented during the war and immediately after by Walter Citrine, and after his retirement by Joseph Hallsworth, supplemented by Williamson and Deakin.

22. When Cripps introduced the survey in the House of Commons, he promised not to apply coercive measures against manpower but to control "raw materials, capital, investment, machinery allocation, taxation, and so on." H. C. Debates, March 10, 1947, col. 964.

23. The economists working on the paper included James Meade, D. N. Chester, J. Jewkes, Evan Durbin, and Lionel Robbins. Hubert Henderson and J. M. Keynes commented on it.

Chapter 3

1. In 1942 in response to the Beveridge Report, Churchill warned in 1942 that "A dangerous optimism is growing up about the conditions it will be possible to establish here after the war," and "the question steals across the mind whether we are not committing our forty-five million people to tasks beyond their compass, and laying upon them burdens beyond their capacity to bear." Churchill 1951, 861–862.

2. The government's delayed reaction to the 1949 currency crisis has been blamed on Cripps' absence in a Swiss sanatorium.

3. For a discussion of the visits of Labour leaders to Sweden, see Francis 1997, 229. Hugh Dalton was much inspired by the Swedish Social Democrats and their innovative policies.

4. After the Communists created their own Third International, the Second and the Two-and-a-half Internationals merged in 1923. For all practical purposes it was a joint organization of the SPD and the Labour Party. Its headquarters was in London, and it was run under Labour's auspices.

5. Attlee (1954, 232) later explained that: "There was [also] not much real opposition to our nationalization policy. It was realized on all sides that the

problem of the coal industry had been shockingly mishandled in the past and that if men were to be got to work in the pits a new start was necessary. Electricity and gas had already to a large extent passed into public ownership. . . . It was perhaps surprising, in view of the fury the banks had caused in the past, that nationalization of the Bank of England went through with a minimum of opposition. Of all our nationalization proposals, only iron and steel roused much feeling, perhaps because hopes of profit were greater here than elsewhere."

6. William Wallace, a staff member in the Ministry of Reconstruction and later director in the Ministry of Food during the war and an executive at Rowntree, the large food company, wrote a vehement protest against the *National Policy for Industry* group, arguing instead for self-regulation. See Wallace 1946, 45–48.

7. The legislation was included in the 1950 King's Speech as an "Economic Planning and Full Employment Bill." Rollings contends that when the necessity for new legislation was relieved by another extension of the emergency powers act, political concerns caused its demise. Rollings 1992, 25. The Conservatives exploited public weariness in the 1950 and 1951 electoral campaigns, which were fought on the theme of "setting the people free."

8. This passage was brought to my attention by Middlemas 1991, 49.

9. Even Keynes' acumen faltered, it appears. Richard Clarke, a close associate of Keynes, reported that Keynes on July 9, 1945, brushed away objections to the continuation of a strategy of Anglo-American cooperation after the war, saying "I do not think that there is any serious risk of an overall shortage of gold and dollars in the first three years." See Clarke 1982, 58. Even Keynes may have banked on a postwar depression to help the postwar government meet its foreign obligations.

10. Corelli Barnett's (1995) disparagement of the postwar government's policies as the cause of subsequent British ills has been criticized for inappropriate second-guessing, but his argument that the "right" policy at the time would have been a course of "little Britain" austerity resonates with general economic wisdom with respect to the need, at the time, for a radical restructuring of the British economy.

11. Food rationing ended officially on July 3, 1954, but a few goods still were subject to consumer rationing, such as coal, which remained rationed until July 1958. In some cases goods were decontrolled and then recontrolled again in 1947 and again in 1949 in response to balance-of-payment difficulties.

12. Lord Beaverbrook's crusade for an Imperial Free Trade zone, and even Lloyd George's publication of a quasi-Keynesian platform in 1929, *We Can Conquer Unemployment,* also had worked to reorient policy in protectionist directions. Between 1929 and 1931 the minority Labour government had introduced the first Agricultural Marketing Act, which permitted agricultural price-fixing schemes, even cartels. From 1931 to 1933 import

quotas and subsidies were added on certain products, such as bacon, sugar (beet), and milk.

13. The Ministry of Food was responsible for price controls and rationing, while that of Agriculture was in charge of increasing output and overseeing the industry. The two ministries were merged in 1951, in part fulfilling of a Conservative campaign promise to "set the people free." The reorganization did not imply a return to liberal principles, however.

14. Sixty-eight members of Parliament pledged themselves to the NFU in the 1910 election. Beer 1965, 111.

15. The British tradition of absentee owners and the general poor state of agriculture made family farming the less significant type of ownership. The presence of an agricultural proletariat consisting of roughly 645,000 workers and their families never seemed to matter much to Labour.

16. The major share of postwar subsidies went to price guarantees, a system of deficiency payments in which British farmers received compensation for the price difference between domestic goods and imported goods. Rather than have the market establish prices, the government negotiates a price list with the NFU published as the *Annual Review and Determination of Guarantees*. Farm subsidies were paid out by the Exchequer and financed by means of income taxation, in effect making the farm program a redistributive program for farmers.

17. The template of the worker-farmer alliance was still recognizable in the policies associated with the 1947 act. Land tribunals molded on industrial relations tribunals were created to mediate between tenant farmers and owners. In addition, the government and local authorities embarked on a program for providing agricultural workers with their own smallholdings, "as an avenue of 'promotion' within the industry," as it was put.

18. Only Welsh nationalists have challenged the organization's monopoly status. The organizational structure sustained the dominant position of larger farmers within the farm lobby. According to one study, the chief officials of the organization are not representative of the membership in sociological terms, and the organization is dominated by larger farmers, defined as those with holdings over 200 acres. Wilson 1977, 37.

19. Amalgamation of the Miners' Federation with several independent miners' unions in 1945 produced the National Union of Mineworkers (NUM).

20. Dalton was proud of his role in pushing for steel nationalization, which had become a test of allegiance of principle: "I made a row and asked whether we were a Socialist Government or not." Dalton 1962, 138 and 248–252.

21. Morgan (1984, 113) describes the conflict within the government on the question of steel nationalization. Morrison was against, arguing that economic efficiency would be better served by keeping the industry in private hands. Bevin, although in principle in favor, supported Morrison. Dalton and Bevan were avidly in favor, as were Cripps and Ellen Wilkinson, who then was chair of the party's National Executive Committee. The

result was that the nationalization measure was repeatedly delayed and the interim board allowed to continue for five years.

22. Sir Frederick Bain, Presidential Address to the FBI Annual Meeting, April 14, 1948.

23. Barbara Castle, one of a handful of Labour women in Parliament, also made a fiery speech denouncing the dissolution as "doctrinaire destructiveness." "The creation of the freedoms they talk about," she continued, meaning the Conservative government, "is the creation of freedom to stagnate, to stand still, freedom to do nothing about producing inside the industry, and inside the distribution, the maximum efficiency in the interests of consumers . . ." H. C. Debates, December 16, 1952, col. 1348.

24. Hugh Dalton's self-described reaction to the news of the cancellation of the Lend-Lease program.

25. Dalton circulated a bluntly pessimistic memo from Keynes on August 14, 1945, the day of Japanese surrender, on "Our Overseas Financial Prospects." Dalton 1962, 69. Corelli Barnett uses the lack of official response to Keynes' memo as evidence for the ineptitude of the government. Barnett 1995, 2–3.

26. The loan of $3.75 million was to be repaid by the end of 1951 at an interest rate of 2 percent per year.

27. A long-term plan, published as a White Paper, Cmd. 7572, which was prepared for the Organization for European Economic Co-operation (OEEC) in October 1948, went even further in stressing stabilization policy and macroeconomic balance as the core objectives of policy. Apparently the government at first had not planned to make the long-range "plan" public at home.

28. Not much has been written about this experiment, which had a parallel in Sweden where, on the urgings of Gunnar Myrdal, the government also tried to prevent an anticipated postwar depression by boosting the money supply through "cheap money" policies.

29. The act had made it illegal for trade unions to collect a levy for the Labour Party from the membership, except when members had expressly agreed, or "contracted-in." The question of the levy to the Labour Party reappeared in the 1980s, as did other aspects of the 1927 act, when the automatic deduction was once again prohibited by Conservative legislation.

30. One large union, the National Union of General and Municipal Workers, favored extension of compulsory arbitration. See TUC Report 1946, 369. The union organized approximately 30 percent of its potential base, mostly in the public sector.

31. The first was when a strike by 1,700 gas maintenance workers against a contract signed by their union interrupted the supply of gas. Ten unionists were given prison sentences. The punishment was later reduced to a fine. In the second incident, a few months later in February 1951, seven members of the transport workers union (TGWU) were arrested for

inciting dock workers to strike. See Allen 1960, 268–270, and TUC Report 1951, 233.

32. The Social Democratic Party/Liberal Party formed an alliance and won 25.4 percent of the vote in 1983 but got only 23 seats in Parliament. Labour won 27.6 percent but got 209 seats. The Conservative Party received a higher share of votes in the 1955 election (49.7 percent) but got the largest margin of seats ever after the 1983 election, 4 more seats even than Labour got in the 1945 "landslide" election. See Butler 1989, Appendix 1.

33. Walter Citrine, wartime general secretary of the TUC, complained of Attlee's reticence and recounted how members of the TUC General Council talked about him as "Clam Attlee." Citrine 1964, 367.

Chapter 4

1. In his autobiography, Ernst Wigforss described the confused opinion in the early war years: "It was difficult in the first war months not to get the impression that the majority of Swedish opinion both expected and hoped a Russian defeat which in the foreseeable future would secure Finland and therefore also Sweden against the danger in the East." He acknowledged that this view clouded the ability of many to consider the possible implications of Nazi domination in the West for Sweden's future. See Wigforss 1954, 233.

2. The administrative and constitutional issues associated with the war controls can be found in an official history by Karl Åmark, upon which this account builds. Sweden 1952.

3. The unions regarded the old system as a tool for strike-breaking employers and wanted to assert trade union influence on the boards. The rule changes prohibited the boards from assigning the unemployed to take the jobs of striking workers, for example. Wage rates for relief work were raised, and union rates paid at new public works projects.

4. A study of administrative employment in wartime control agencies carried out by Gunnar Myrdal's Committee on Postwar Economic Planning showed a high proportion of women among the employees, often in part-time positions. The report also noted that three-fourths of the male employees were married while three-fourths of the women were unmarried. See Sweden 1944b.

5. It was composed by the chief executive officers of five large companies: Asea, Electrolux, LME, SKF, and Seperator. A sixth joined later. See Söderpalm 1976.

6. The calculation of membership contributions was a subject of much friction. Until 1961, dues were calculated on the basis of the number of employees, penalizing smaller employers in low-paid occupations. After that dues were calculated as 2 percent of the total wage sum.

7. The Liberal Party, with which the Social Democrats shared a favorable view of free trade, was considered the natural alliance partner. There was no discussion of the possibility of working with the Agrarians before party leaders initiated secret negotiations, and the agreement with the protectionist party came as a surprise. Therborn 1992, 22.

8. Lundberg defended his dissertation in 1937 and became a charter member of the Stockholm School. He later became director of the government-financed but independent Swedish Economic Research Institute, which began issuing biannual economic evaluations of the inflationary gap in 1943. See Lundberg 1957.

9. A list of some of the most important memoranda and supplements accompanying the main reports, and their authors, is contained in Wadensjö 1991. For a discussion, see also Gustafsson 1973.

10. Anders Johansson has interpreted the same passages in the final report to imply a strong recommendation that wages be kept low. My reading of the final report and the reports it summarizes leads to a different conclusion. See Johansson 1989, 120–122. See also Sweden 1931b, 16 and Wadensjö 1991, 104.

11. For nearly 20 years Sweden subscribed to flexible, or rather variable, rate policies. With the decision to join the European Union, Swedish policy-makers have once again committed themselves to a fixed currency policy, this time with the aim of removing the shield against the effects of international competition and international business cycles that an independent monetary policy can provide.

12. The party's radicalism was put in doubt as early as in 1941, when Herbert Tingsten, a Swedish political scientist, published a study of the Social Democrats' ideological evolution in which he argued that the party had abandoned its socialist heritage. Tingsten 1941, 1973. In 1946 Tingsten became editor-in-chief of the influential Liberal paper, *Dagens Nyheter.*

13. Leif Lewin argues that Ernst Wigforss already had realized that government ownership would put a wedge between a Social Democratic government and workers, when the inevitable moment came and the government had to lay off workers or step in to control wages. See Lewin 1967, 286.

14. In 1938 speech to the Bourse Society in Göteborg, Wigforss had struck a similar note when he invited business to enter regular consultation with the government by suggesting that the Social Democrats were there to stay and business leaders had better get used to it. Reprinted in Wigforss 1941.

15. In 1938 it became the National Conservative Organization, Högern's riksorganisation. In 1969 the party changed its name to Moderata samlingsparti, the "moderate unified party." For reasons of simplicity, it is referred to throughout this book as the Conservative Party for the entire period.

16. In 1990 the party was renamed the Liberal Party, Folkspartiet Liberalerna. In this book it is consistently referred to as the Liberal Party.

17. In 1943 the party changed its name to the Village Party-Peasant Alliance, Landsbygdspartiet-Bondeförbundet.
18. Prior to the 1932 election, Ernst Wigforss wrote in his diary, "Now I want to fight and I want to govern." He expressed great frustration after the election, when it became clear the party was still short of the votes needed to govern. See Wigforss 1954, 9.
19. In 1944 the Social Democrats received only 46.7 percent of the vote, down from 53.8 percent in 1940. The Communist Party was the big winner, with 10.5 percent of the national vote. The trade unions and the Social Democratic left-wing saw the result as a rebuke to the Social Democrats for their wartime economic policy, the wage policy in particular, and responded by stepping up demands for radicalization.
20. Numbers illustrate the bias of the electoral system. With 46.7 percent of the vote, the Social Democrats controlled exactly half of the seats in parliament. The lack of true proportionality reflected a variation in the size of electoral districts, which in this case benefited the Social Democrats. Britain's Labour Party received 47.8 percent of the vote in 1945, also short of an absolute majority, but ended up controlling 61.4 percent of the seats in Parliament.
21. The geopolitical tensions in 1947–1948 of the escalating Cold War placed Sweden in a very uncomfortable position. The Soviet Union retained control over a Danish island, Bornholm, directly south of Sweden until 1948, and since the Finno-Russian War the Soviet Union also held a large part of what used to be Finnish territory. Soviet occupation of the Baltic states, across the Botnic Sea and to the east of Sweden, completed the nation's encroachment on three sides.
22. It was the practical details that caused difficulties: storage, safe transportation, quality control during transit, the politics of foreign trade. Swedish products competed on quality, not on price. No money was spend on advertising. Sixty percent of the businesses in the survey reported that their products were more expensive than those of their competitors in foreign markets. Surprisingly, large companies with more than 100 employees were overrepresented in the survey. Part of the explanation of this somewhat amateurish picture of the engagement of Swedish business with export markets is that the more important export industries were "nonproduct" industries, raw materials or semifinished products, and finished products that typically were produced by small or medium-size firms accounted only for a small part of overall exports. While as much as 80 percent (and periodically more) of the raw paper and paper pulp industry went for export markets, at most between one-fifth and one-fourth of finished goods (various industries) were exported at the time. The survey is contained in Strömbom 1964, 151.
23. The absence of controversy in connection with this change is highlighted by the controversy that arose on other issues; for example, foreign policy. See SAP 1944, 200–232.

Chapter 5

1. The old generation included Gustav Cassel, Eli Heckscher, and Gösta Bagge.
2. The debate was the biggest and most intensive public policy controversy in Sweden in the postwar period, matched only by the wage-earners' funds debate. See Elvander 1972, 37.
3. The Social Democrats have received most credit for creating the postwar welfare state. See Esping-Andersen and Korpi 1984; Olsson 1990. The Social Democratic delegation to the enabling legislative committee split on the issue, with a minority voting with the Agrarian and Conservative parties, which were arguing for the elimination of means-testing and for making the old-age pensions conform to the universalist "social citizenship" design idolized by T. H. Marshall. See also Baldwin 1988. Similar pension reforms took place in 1956 in Denmark and in 1957 in Norway, also with support from centrist-Conservative parties.
4. With the help of the Communists, the Social Democrats held 112 votes. The Liberals and the Conservatives together had 100 votes. With the Agrarian party's additional 19 seats, the center-right held a majority.
5. Göran Therborn cites Tage Erlander for having discussed, at a meeting of the party leadership, a secret poll taken in Stockholm in 1956 that showed that voters would turn down a pension reform presented as "obligatory" but vote for one that presented the new pensions as "a legal right." See Therborn 1992, 23.
6. The ATP pension reform originated with the trade unions. The LO wanted to equalize pensions across industries and trade, hoping to provide blue-collar workers with the same additional pension benefits that white-collar unions had obtained. Unable to extract concessions from employers, the unions asked for legislation. The party initially was not enthusiastic, afraid to alienate the growing white-collar unions that already exhibited a proclivity for aligning with the Liberals. The center-right parties and employers were united in their opposition to publicly controlled pension funds. See Esping-Andersen 1992, 47–51.
7. This was Hjalmar Adiels from *Pappers*. Herman Blomgreen represented railroad workers, Axel Johansson the agricultural workers, S. A. Larsson the clerical workers, Gunnar Mohlne the unskilled workers, and Charles Winroth the lumber workers. The discussion can be found in *Fackföreningsrörelsen*, 42, 1949, 253–273.
8. Strand retired in 1956 and was replaced by Arne Geijer.
9. For the follow-up debate, see *Fackföreningsrörelsen*, nos. 44–46, 1949.
10. A metalworkers' local from Göteborg, long a Communist stronghold, proposed motion no. 29, which asked the congress to condemn the LO for its acquiescence to stabilization policy and demand that the confederation conduct wage policy "independent" of the government. It also called for the socialization of "extra profits" in the export industries. An almost

identical resolution (no. 42) was put forward by a construction workers' local, a union that also historically had had a large Communist membership. LO 1951, 130 and 210.

11. The unions' positions are determined on the basis of an analysis of resolutions proposed at the 1946 and 1951 congresses. LO 1946, 1951. In contrast to the British TUC, the LO did not utilize a bloc vote; in contrast to the German trade union confederation, the DGB, the LO generally did not try to muzzle the opposition. When voting, hand votes were rare and never done by roll call. Consequently, we cannot link votes to particular unions. Speakers, however, are identified by name and by union, which makes it possible to identify particular unions with sponsorship of specific resolutions.

12. Notably, SAF also praised the 1951 Rehn-Meidner report. See *Industria,* November 1951, ii.

13. Employers in these industries had agreed to allow union shop or "closed shop"; this prevented their entrance into SAF, which in its statutes prohibited such agreements. Hence these industries were excluded from assistance from SAF's strike funds. See De Geer 1986, 125.

14. A summary of the centrally negotiated contracts is contained in LO 1986.

15. One study asserts that the solidaristic principle never amounted to much in any case, because most of the observed wage compression can be explained primarily by demographic changes and not by policy. Klevmarken 1983.

16. All figures based on Flora, Kraus, and Pfenning, chapter 8. Growth rates are averaged over several years to control for cyclical fluctuations, corrected for inflation, and measured in the 1933 exchange rates to correct for exchange rate changes.

17. One delegation mentioned that what impressed members most was, "the size of things in that big country: the unending streets, the huge buildings, the gigantic department stores, and the huge factories." See *Aktuella Frågor,* 14, 1950, 17.

18. Trade union publications dedicated whole issues to explaining the new ideas to unionists. See *Aktuella Frågor,* 16, 1951.

19. Johansson lists two prewar strikes and a strike in 1944 involving 700 workers caused by disagreements over piece rates. He also ascribes the 1945 metalworkers' strike, which normally is interpreted as a protest against wartime wage control, to a 1943 agreement between VF and Metall that piece rate changes should not result in wage reductions that was struck down by the labor court. See Johansson 1989, 322. Johansson's account is supported by an attack on Taylorism by Albin Lind, a leading champion of the solidarity principle. *Fackföreningsrörelsen,* 1945, 372.

20. Resolution no. 47, Andra Kammaren, and no. 211, Första Kammaren.

21. The LO's embrace of Taylorism was unconditional. "It is increasingly clear to workers that one of the preconditions for a higher standard of living is that the production process is made more efficient. Workers are also cog-

nizant that it is in their interests that piece rates are calibrated in as equal and fair a fashion as possible." Quoted in Johansson 1989, 343; author's translation.

22. *Aktuella Frågor,* 25, 1960. A second LO guide, *Aktuella Frågor,* 27, 1961, curiously legitimized MTM studies by comparing the system to work "valuation" and pitched MTM as means for greater wage equity. Basic pay schedules were fixed by gender and by age, but MTM systems did not discriminate.

23. The Danish LO resolution set the tone: "The labor movement can no longer tolerate that capital, the existence of which we recognize is necessary for future investment and production, is accumulated in such a manner that considerable inequality with respect to the distribution of wealth and capital persists. . . . Wage earners demand a part in the accumulation of capital which they by means of their work contribute to create." Author's translation.

24. In political-strategic terms, codetermination reform and other industrial relations reforms, which included white-collar workers, were part of a Social Democratic reform offensive that aimed to bring the radical unions back to the Social Democratic camp and reconcile blue-collar and white-collar workers. Several laws were passed in conjunction with the reform: (1) the Act on Co-Determination (MBL); (2) an act giving unions representation on corporate boards; (3) new provisions in the job security act requiring management to negotiate restructuring plans with local unions; (4) increased job protection for trade union representatives; and (5) work environment legislation that gave unions a say in the organization of work and safety regulation. For a discussion, see Pontusson 1992.

25. During the Social Democrats' opposition period, the LO called a strike involving 100,000 workers that, with the help of an employer lockout, ballooned to 750,000 workers.

26. A Swedish newspaper caught the Social Democratic finance minister, Kjell-Olof Feldt, scribbling on a piece of paper during the parliamentary debates on the wage-earner fund proposal: "Employee funds are junk, okay, but now we have dragged them all this way." See Lewin 1988, 297. On Palme's dislike for the proposal, see Åsard 1981, 51.

27. The tradition of bipartisan collaboration and *samverkan* had been broken. In the 1988 election campaign, the opposition parties vowed to abolish the funds if returned to power. Again in 1991, the new Conservative government promised to abolish the funds. *Svenska Dagbladet,* October 5, 1988, and *New York Times International,* October 6, 1991, 3.

28. The breakup was presaged by an attack, in 1986, by the general secretary of the metalworkers' union on the high salaries of public employees. He accused them of being like cuckoo chicks that push the parents out of the nest. See Pontusson and Swenson 1996; Swenson 1992, 52.

29. For a comparative discussion of Social Democratic retrenchment in Scandinavia, see Mjøset 1996.

Chapter 6

1. The multiplicity of German states complicates out terminology. Two German states emerged from the conflicts between the former allies, the Federal Republic and the German Democratic Republic. Here I use both "German" and "West German" to designate the Federal Republic. Between 1933 and 1945, the terms "German" and "Germany" refer to the Nazi state, while between 1918 and 1933, they refer to the Weimar Republic. After reunification in 1990, the terms refer to the expanded Federal Republic.

2. Austria relied on compulsory membership rules to sustain the "social partners" representative framework.

3. The CDU cooperates with a Bavarian party, the Christian Social Union (Christlich-Soziale Union, or CSU). The CDU does not contest in Bavarian elections.

4. President Roosevelt apparently had been more or less persuaded to support the Morgenthau plan as a blueprint for postwar reconstruction. A map of the proposed new German states is included in Morgenthau 1945, 160.

5. Upon arrival Clay and Murphy were more vexed by French intransigence and conflicts with Washington than by the prospects of collaborating with Soviet representatives in the Allied Control Council. Their complaints illustrate how unanticipated U.S.-Soviet conflict was at the time and the lack of appreciation of what the future would bring. Robert Murphy observed later that "The evolution of the West German state, and of American relations to it, were a totally unforeseen result of the peacemaking after World War II." Murphy 1964, 84.

6. Kindleberger referred to Clay as "not a little scary to talk to for us State Department types whom he regards as very unreasonable." See Kindleberger 1989, letter no. 2.

7. This was illustrated by the fate of Fritz Schäffer. An ultra-conservative nationalist, Schäffer was one of the founders of the Bavarian Christlisch-Soziale Union. As a representative for the Bavarian People's Party, he had voted for the enabling act in 1933 that permitted Hitler to abolish democracy. The U.S. military appointed him Minister-President of Bavaria on May 28, 1945, but four months later he was arrested as a Nazi collaborator and then released again after Robert Murphy, the U.S. ambassador, intervened. Murphy describes the incident in his autobiography: "A subordinate Civil Affairs officer, who had been recruited from the history department of an American college, was convinced that Bavaria should be governed by the social democrats, notwithstanding that this socialist party had always been a small minority party in this predominantly Catholic state." Murphy 1964, 296. Murphy does not mention the officer by name, but a second source names him as Walter L. Dorn. See Institut für Zeitgeschichte 1993, xxvi.

8. The U.S. military government used a cumbersome questionnaire—*Fragebogen*—to screen candidates and applicants, and maintained lists of accept-

able (and unacceptable) persons who could be relied on for official positions. In the British and French zones, rules were more lenient.

9. In 1957 Agartz came under suspicion for unconstitutional activities when a courier from East Germany was apprehended by West German border guards carrying 21,000 German marks earmarked for him. Although never convicted of wrongdoing, Agartz's career came to an end. He died in 1964.

10. Erhard had been appointed Economics Minister in a SPD-led government in Bavaria by the military government there in October 1945 after the removal of Fritz Schäffer, a Christian Democrat whom the Allies could not agree on because of his vote for the Nazi enabling act in 1933. The 1946 election brought the CSU in control of the *Länder* government. Erhard was reappointed but forced to step down in January 1947. He was essentially party less and jobless until his appoint to the Economic Council.

11. Erhard's neoliberalism did not correspond with CDU policies at the time, yet he was appointed with the support of Adenauer. Arnold J. Heidenheimer concludes on the basis of party archives that Erhard's appointment was part of Adenauer's plan to "fix" the influence of pro-planning groups within the CDU, which were supported by the British zonal authorities. By supporting a non-CDU candidate to the post, Adenauer hoped to give it "a blow from which it could not recover." See Heidenheimer 1960, 136.

12. Describing his "profound concerns" about the European situation to President Truman, Churchill telegraphed him on May 12, 1945, that "an iron curtain is drawn upon their front." Truman responded by assuring Churchill of American intentions to stand firm and his presumption that with firm protests against Soviet actions in Poland, "we can hope to avoid a host of other similar encroachments," Churchill ranted afterward about U.S. deceit. The authorship of the "iron curtain" term apparently did not belong to Churchill but to a high-ranking officer in the German army who in the last days of the Reich surmised that Germany would be the West's bulwark against communism in Europe. See Gilbert ed. 1988, 5–8.

13. Situated deep inside the Soviet occupation zones, the city had no lines of communication with the West. For reasons that have variously been ascribed to blunder or naïveté, British and American diplomats and generals had failed to secure access to Berlin in the closing days of the war or, when given a second chance, at Potsdam.

14. At the SPD's 1949 annual meeting in Hannover, it voted for its own version of the Basic Law. Schumacher incurred Clay's strong disapproval when from his sickbed he instructed SPD representatives on the Parliamentary Council to vote as a bloc and follow the lead of the central party leadership (Schumacher) rather than take instructions from the *Länder* parties. See Edinger 1965, 167.

15. The SPD emerged as the leading party in Hamburg, Berlin, Bremen, and in Schleswig-Holstein, Niedersachsen, and Hessen. The CDU emerged as the majority party in the south, including Baden, Bayern, Nordrhein-Westfalen, Rheinland-Pfalz, and Württemberg-Hohenzollern. In Baden-Württemberg

the two parties each captured one-third of the vote, and the first government was based on a grand coalition of all parties, including the Communists.

16. The title of the program first contained the word *Gemeinwirtschaft* but was changed to *Die CDU zum Neuordnung der Wirtschaft*. Presumably Adenauer had tactical reasons for accepting the program, above all his desire to avoid the splintering of the newly formed party. See Narr 1966, 77–91.

17. Erhard had published his ideas in a series of newspaper articles published in *Die Neue Zeitung*. For an account of the neoliberal economic position, see also Müller-Arnack 1976.

18. The program's significance was confirmed at the SPD's third postwar congress in 1948, when party leaders complained that, when representatives spoke about the party's goals, they too often did so by referring to the old Erfurt program. SPD 1948, 138.

19. Statement made by Schumacher at the 1946 SPD congress, May 9–11, in Hannover. See also discussion on August 14–15, 1946, in the Advisory Council to the military government, where Schumacher lectures all present about the SPD's status as the only German democratic party prior to the arrival of the occupation troops. See "Quellen zur Geschichte des Parlamentarismus und der Politische Partein" 1993, Source VI.3, 708.

20. In German: "Allerdings unter der Voraussetzung: Sie und Ihre junge Partei, Herr Adenauer, müssen den Führungsanspruch der SPD anerkennen."

21. Either side can ask for general binding but this cannot take place before a vote in a parity committee consisting of representatives from employers and trade unions. This means that either side can block its application.

22. For a summary of U.S. labor relations policy in Germany, see Office of U.S. High Commissioner for Germany 1952. For the British perspective, see Great Britain 1950.

23. Adenauer's ire about American domination matched Schumacher's. In 1963 the then 90-year-old Adenauer could do nothing but complain about how the Allies had prejudiced German political development by permitting the SPD to control the unions when he met with the inculpable new ambassador to the FRG, George McGhee, who had come to plan President Kennedy's prospective visit to Berlin. See McGhee 1989, 33.

24. In original: "Trotz dieses Drucks blieb in der Deutsche Unternehmerschaft der Gedanke des Zusammenschlusses und der Zusammenarbeit lebendig."

25. Curiously, Braunthal (1965, 238) lists an identical catalog of objections raised by the BDI against the legislation but with private correspondence between Adenauer and Fritz Berg from late 1952 as the source. The time discrepancy is no puzzle, if the BDI's arguments changed little as the debate progressed.

26. It is not difficult to estimate accurately the number of rules and regulations retained, but Henry Wallich, a Yale economist who was enamored of Erhard's neoliberal program, found roughly 60 percent of multilateral trade to be decontrolled by the fall of 1950. See Wallich 1955, 236. Foreign trade liberalization was suspended again on February 22, 1951, as part of a pack-

age of anti-inflation measures and liberalization not resumed until January 1952, when 57 percent of imports were "set free." Agricultural imports were listed as "free" but were in fact wholly controlled by agricultural cartels. Discounting agricultural products, and using Wallich's figures, "free" imports added to about perhaps 40 percent of all imports.

27. "In der letzen zeit ist wieder der Vorschlag diskutiert worden, die Mitarbeit der Wirtschaft im Staat durch die Institution eines *Bundeswirtschaftsrates* [emphasis in original] festzulegen."

Chapter 7

1. Demarcation conflicts and disagreements over policy caused the American Federation of Labor to expel a number of industrial unions in 1936. They created the Committee (later Congress) on Industrial Organization, later changed to the Congress. Under the leadership of John L. Lewis, the CIO succeeded in organizing the steel and auto industries. Soon the United Auto Workers and the United Steel Workers had taken the lead in reshaping American industrial relations. The two confederations merged in 1955 to become the AFL-CIO.

2. Whereas the London Chamber of Commerce implied that the "dollar gap" was the result of discriminatory rules, and the problem could be fixed by a different set of rules, American economists preferred to believe the problem to be a "real" reflection of the U.S. economic position. In truth, it was both. The United States ran a positive balance of trade already in the 1920s, which in itself resulted in a "dollar gap." After 1945, the capacity to restore a stable equilibrium in the balance of payments hinged not only on the ability of a country to match exports with imports, but also its ability to do so in dollars. American economists did not always understand why Europeans sometimes would think that unfair. See Haberler 1948, 435.

3. William S. Knudsen, a Danish immigrant who had risen to become president of General Motors, and Sidney Hillman, the Jewish (and socialist) president of the Amalgamated Clothing Workers union, were among the appointees, as were New Dealers Leon Henderson and Chester Davis, the latter of whom had a farming background. Another member was Edward Stettinius, who was connected to U.S. Steel, J. P. Morgan, and DuPont. Harriet Elliot, a political science professor, was appointed to represent "the underprivileged." Donald M. Nelson, from Sears, Roebuck, was appointed coordinator of National Defense Purchases.

4. Merriam was the more important person. The aging Delano was often ill and reluctant to press his relationship with his nephew. Merriam regarded the NRPB as a presidential agency and resisted contacts with Congress. The president should, in his view, assume leadership and chart a planned approach to social and economic development. Merriam's view of planning was that it should be nonpartisan and express a commonsensical national

purpose. He was deaf to the elitist implications of his conception of planning. See Merriam 1944.

5. The reasons for the delay are not entirely clear. One reason could be that the president hoped to capitalize on the attention awarded to the Beveridge Report; another that he hoped to detract attention from a congressional report issued by the Truman Committee, which criticized the administration for inadequate planning of the war effort. See Clawson 1981, 138; Warken 1979, 295.

6. In 1979 Burns denied that she was a student of Beveridge's. See Clawson 1981, 137. Merriam rejected the notion of descent with the argument that the NRPB report preceded Beveridge's by several months, but his argument does actually prove that. The Beveridge Report was published some time after Beveridge had begun speaking about his ideas. Merriam 1944, 1083.

7. Merriam lists this "Second Bill of Rights" as one of the great accomplishments of the NRPB. See Merriam 1944, 1079.

8. The trade unions had almost ceased to exist as effective interest organizations by the time of the first New Deal legislation. They were nevertheless awarded a place in the Code Authorities created under the National Recovery Administration. NIRA exempted business from antitrust regulation, and the codes were allowed to fix wages and prices on an industrywide basis, much as wartime price and wage boards would a decade later. See Lyon et al. 1935.

9. Economic policies that advocate state activism are curiously designated as "liberal" policy in the United States.

10. The Taft-Hartley Act did not directly prohibit closed shops but allowed states to pass so-called right-to-work laws that prohibited such agreements between employers and unions.

11. Orren claims that labor has advocated high price supports even when it failed to receive reciprocity from rural Democrats on important legislative issues. One example is the vote of congressmen loyal to labor in favor of high price support after labor lost a vote on the provision of food stamps to striking workers. See Orren 1986, 226.

12. Victor Reuther describes his brother's goal of "social unionism" in the following way:

Under Walter's guidance, collective bargaining became more than the instrument with which workers could win economic equality and decent working conditions; it became a tool for the UAW to use in organizing the workers' power and strength so that they might reach out beyond the work place and gain for themselves and their families a larger measure of security and dignity. He knew that innovative patterns for collective bargaining negotiations, in an industry as large and influential as auto, could be copied by workers across the land and bring new benefits even to unorganized employees. Reuther 1976, 304.

13. Following on 12 preparatory conferences held around the country with economists, business representatives, labor, and state and local government

officials, President Ford called an "economic summit" meeting in Washington and ten days later announced an economic program. The program combined a package of measures intended to both curb inflation and inflationary consumption and boost investments.

14. One agreement that the chairman of COWPS, Alfred Kahn, conceded was in "probable noncompliance" with the federal wage guidelines, between United Airlines and the International Association of Machinists, was estimated to represent an increase over three years of 35 percent. COWPS subsequently accepted the contract, with reference to an "undue hardship" clause intended to protect employers against costly industrial conflict. See *Monthly Labor Review* (2) 1980, 13. A similar thing happened when the chairman of the Teamsters Union, Frank E. Fitzsimmon, proudly announced, upon settlement of the longest strike in the trucking industry in 15 years in spring 1979, that the union had won a settlement that broke the government's guidelines. See *Monthly Labor Review* (6) 1979, 47.

15. The Ford contract did represent a shift from take-home pay increases to increases in benefits and increased employer payments to the Supplementary Unemployment Payment funds. Take-home pay increases were spread out throughout the contract period by means of scheduled increases rather than concentrated at the beginning of the contract. Job protection arrangements, such as work-sharing by introducing a four-day work week (with pay for the extra day off), limits on subcontracting, and special protection of the rights of older workers were an important part of the contract. See *Monthly Labor Review* (12) 1976, 53–54.

16. Hoerr lists the wage concessions made by the McLouth local as the following: a 79 cent per hour wage cut, suspension of COLA, and a number of benefits. As a result, McLouth's wage costs were lowered to about $6 less per hour than what was paid by U.S. Steel and the major eight companies negotiating in CCSC.

17. Then Senator Bill Bradley (D-N.J.) and Representative Stan Lundine (D-N.Y.) tried to frame a joint House and Senate Banking Committee bill that would require the president to establish a "competitive exchange rate" for the dollar. See *Congressional Quarterly Weekly Report*, February 22, 1986, 460–464.

18. Sweden: *Arbetarrörelsens Efterkrigsprogram. De 27 Punkterna med Motivering* (1944); United Kingdom: TUC, *Interim Report on Post-War Reconstruction* (1944) and The Labour Party, *Let Us Face the Future* (1945); Federal Republic: SPD, *The Dürkheim Points* (1948 [1950]).

19. In Britain, a general strike in 1926 produced a loss of 1.114 days per 100 nonagricultural workers. In Sweden, a strike combined with employer lockouts in 1909 resulted in 1.268 days lost per 100 workers. In the absence of general strikes, the measure of high levels of industrial unrest in other countries can look more modest than they really are. In Germany, 1919 was the year with the highest incidence of striking: 254 days lost. In Austria, 1924: 174 days lost.

Chapter 8

1. Peter Katzenstein has contrasted Austrian social corporatism with Swiss liberal capitalism and noted that while the latter aimed to further adaptation to international capitalism, the former has aimed more at domestic stabilization, at the "mobilization of consent." See Katzenstein 1984, 255, 31.

2. The SPÖ returned to its old name in 1990 and is now again the Social Democratic Party of Austria.

3. Since the early 1980s the party system has been transformed by the shift of the FPÖ to the right, under Jürg Haider, and by the emergence of an ecology party.

4. Herbert Kitschelt has pointed out that the adaptation of party organizations to a "pillared" system of patronage further worked to discourage programmatic debate and change. See Kitschelt 1994, 244–249.

5. For an account of wage regulation in the immediate postwar years, see Edelman 1954.

6. Parity representation and consensual decision making are the central features of consociationalism, which is a political system based on group veto. See Lijphart 1975.

7. Even if mostly of symbolic importance, it is also noteworthy that the two systems formally subscribed to a "voluntarist" norm for entirely different reasons. In Austria, the bow to liberalism that voluntarism implied was made in response to a court decision which in turn responded to outside perceptions, that is, U.S. pressures. In Sweden, voluntarism reflected a concession to interest group autonomy. This variation, in turn, helps explain why Swedish trade unions have been able to sustain representation after the collapse of the "frame contract," while Austrian trade union representation (measured in terms of membership figures) has declined as the centralized system has weakened. For a comparison of trade union adjustment, see Klausen 1998.

8. The Anglo-American roots of the organization was revealed by Monnet's first choice of a name, the "High Commission" for planning.

9. Shonfield puzzled over the French lack of sophisticated statistical forecasting techniques and particularly the fact that countries less committed to planning, such as the United Kingdom and the United States possessed much more advanced capabilities in that respect. Shonfield 1965, 127. Had Shonfield reflected on the importance of war mobilization in shaping British and American capacities in this respect, he would not have been puzzled.

10. Pretax 1930 figures for Sweden and 1938 figures for Great Britain. Calculated from Flora, Kraus, and Pfenning 1987, 641–673.

11. In the German case, the acute need for foreign currency to pay for agricultural imports in the face of shortages has been used to explain the early emphasis on the restoration of export trade. See Wallich 1955. Then again,

the same was said about British economic policy constraint but without the same consequence. When is a "need" a "need"? As is always the case with functional explanation, we are confounded by our inability to determine the critical values for when a "constraint" becomes a "compulsion." Measured in terms of percentage of national consumption, British consumers were more dependent on imported food than German consumers.

12. In the case of inconsistencies, the 1995 IMF *Yearbook* has been used as the authoritative source. All figures have been converted to constant 1970 figures using the GDP deflator. All figures are in the national currency. Any GDP data not included in the IMF *Yearbook* is from Flora et al. 1987.

13. The adjusted R^2 is a cumulative measure showing the "boost" to the equation that the inclusion of an additional variable provides. The procedure enter variables according to their importance.

14. Whereas transfer payments originally were seen as a way to boost domestic growth when exports failed, the increased propensity of consumers to consume foreign goods complicated matters greatly.

15. For theoretical and methodological reasons, the analysis is based on year-to-year changes in national income and in domestic consumption and exports. In time-series studies such as the present one, autocorrelation or serial correlation can be an issue. The Durbin-Watson test was performed as a check for the presence of autocorrelation. Autocorrelation is a bias that derives from the possibility that an overestimation of the positive effects of exports for growth in one year leads to overestimation in successive years. In that case R^2 provides an overly optimistic picture of the particular relationship that we are investigating, and we may falsely conclude that an association exists. It may, of course, also lead to an underestimation of the true relationship. In that case, we would falsely rule out an association. Here, autocorrelation was ruled out except in the analysis of Swedish data from 1950 to 1994, when the Durbin-Watson statistic dropped into an indeterminate ranges, indicating that autocorrelation possibly biased the analysis. When the analysis of Swedish data was broken up into two separate periods, the Durbin-Watson statistic improved. It ranges between 0 and 4, with a value near 2 indicating the absence of autocorrelation. Positive serial correlation is associated with values below 2 and negative serial correlation with values above 2. With a total number of cases of 45 and 1 variable in the equation, the legitimate range for the Durbin-Watson statistic is 2.43 and 1.48. With 2 variables in the equation, it ranges between 2.38 and 1.43; with 3 variables between 2.33 and 1.38. With 22 cases and 1 variable, the legitimate range is between 2.57 and 1.24. With 2 variables, it is between 2.46 and 1.15; and with 3, 2.34 and 1.05. See Pindyck and Rubinfeld 1981, 611.

16. A second multiple regression analysis not reported in table sustained this conclusion. Private and government consumption was treated as a combined variable in order to take into account the possible contractive effect of spending policies and compare it against exports. In this case, exports

were entered first in the equation ahead of combined domestic demand. Exports were the more important source of national growth, with an adjusted R^2 of 41.8 percent.

17. The effect of second-wave welfare state expansion does not show up in the last period multiple regression coefficients. That does not necessarily mean that policy did not have the desired effect, only that welfare state expansion as a source of growth yielded significant results only in the long term.

18. Stein Rokkan and Seymour Martin Lipset expressed these ideas in their thesis regarding the "frozen" nature of postwar European party systems: The party systems of the 1960s were, it was argued, direct descendants of the party systems of the 1920s and were shaped by events preceding the formation of the parties themselves. See Lipset and Rokkan 1967.

Bibliography

Abendroth, Wolfgang. 1975. *Arbeiterklasse, Staat und Verfassung*. Frankfurt: Europäische Verlagsanstalt.

Abelshauser, Werner. 1983. *Wirtschaftsgeschichte der Bundesrepublik Deutschland, 1945–1980*. Frankfurt am Main: Suhrkamp.

Abel-Smith, Brian. 1994. "The Beveridge Report: Its Origins and Outcomes." *Beveridge and Social Security*. Eds. John Hill et al. Oxford: Clarendon Press.

Abraham, David. 1981. *The Collapse of the Weimar Republic*. Princeton, NJ: Princeton University Press.

Addison, Paul. 1982. *The Road to 1945*. London: Quartet Books.

Adeney, Martin, and John Lloyd. 1986. *The Miners' Strike 1984–85: Loss Without Limit*. London: Routledge & Kegan Paul.

Agartz, Viktor. n.d. [orig. 1959]. "Die Integration der gewerkschaften in das kapitalistischen System," WISO no. 9, 1959. Reprinted in *WISO. Dokumente über die Formierung des DGB, 1951–1961. Kritik einer arbeiterfeindlichen Gewerkschaftspolitik*. Dortmund: Rote Front Verlag.

Albert, Michel. 1993. *Capitalism Against Capitalism*. London: Whurr Publishers.

Alford, W. E. 1995. *British Economic Performance, 1945–1975*. Cambridge: Cambridge University Press.

Allen, Christopher S. 1989. "The Underdevelopment of Keynesianism in the Federal Republic of Germany." *The Political Power of Economic Ideas: Keynesianism Across Nations*. Ed. Peter A. Hall. Princeton, NJ: Princeton University Press.

Allen, V. L. 1960. *Trade Unions and the Government*. London: Longmans.

Anderson, Benedict. 1991. Rev. ed. *Imagined Communities*. London: Verso.

Astor, Viscount, and B. Seebohm Rowntree. 1938. *British Agriculture. The Principles of Future Policy*. London: Longmans, Greens and Co.

Attlee, Clement R. 1946. *Purpose and Policy. Selected Speeches*. London: Hutchinson and Co.

———. 1954. *As It Happened*. New York: Viking.

Ausubel, Nathan, ed. 1945. *Voices of History, 1944–45*. New York: Franklin Watts, Inc.

Bailey, Stephen K. 1950. *Congress Makes a Law*. New York: Columbia University Press.

Baldwin, Peter. 1988. "How Socialist Is Solidaristic Social Policy? Swedish Postwar Reform as a Case in Point." *International Review of Social History* 33 (2):121–147.

————. 1990. *The Politics of Social Solidarity: Class Bases of the European Welfare State.* New York: Cambridge University Press.

Ball, George W. 1982. *The Past Has Another Pattern: Memoirs.* New York: Norton.

Barnett, Corelli. 1986. *The Audit of War.* London: Macmillan.

————. 1995. *The Lost Victory. British Dreams, British Realities, 1945–1950.* London: Macmillan.

Batstone, Eric. 1984. *Working Order: Workplace Industrial Relations Over Two Decades.* London: Basil Blackwell.

Bundesverband der Deutschen Industrie. (BDI, Federal Republic of Germany). 1951. *Kartellverbot oder Kartellaufsicht? Zur gesetzlichen Behandlung des Wettbewerbs in the Marktwirtschaft.* Bericht über die Diskussionsveranstaltung des Bundesverbandes der Deutschen Industrie in Unkel/Rhein am 2 juli 1951. Stuttart: Forkel-Verlag.

————. 1952. *Jahresbericht des BDI.* 1 Juni 1951 bis 30 April 1952. Vorgelegt an der dritte ordentliche Mitgliederversammlung in Hamburg an 6. Mai 1952. (No publisher.)

————. 1954. *Fünf Jahre BDI. Aufbau und Arbeitziele des industriellen Spitzenverbandes.* Bergisch Gladbach: Heider-Verlag.

————. 1956. *Der Weg zum Industriellen Spitzenverband.* Frankfurt am Main: Frankfurter Societäts-Druckerei GmbH.

Beer, Samuel H. 1965. *British Politics in the Collectivist Age.* New York: Knopf.

Benn, Tony. 1990. *Against the Tide: Diaries 1973–1976.* London: Huchinson.

Bensel, Richard F. 1984. *Sectionalism and American Political Development, 1880–1980.* Madison: University of Wisconsin Press.

Berger, Suzanne and Ronald Dore, eds. 1996. *National Diversity and Global Capitalism.* Ithaca, NY: Cornell University Press.

Berghahn, Volker R. 1986. *The Americanization of West German Industry, 1945–1973.* Leamington: Berg.

Bergström, Villy. 1973. *Kapitalbildning och industriell demokrati.* Stockholm: Tiden.

Beveridge, Sir William H. 1942. *Social Insurance and Allied Services.* Inter-Departmental Committee on Social Insurance and Allied Services. New York: Macmillan.

————. 1943. *The Pillars of Security and Other War-Time Essays and Addresses.* New York: Macmillan.

————. 1945. *Full Employment in a Free Society.* New York: W. W. Norton.

Bevin, Ernest. 1941. "Broadcast, May 25, 1940." *The Balance Sheet of the Future.* New York: Robert McBride and Company.

Bischof, Gunter, and Antony Pelinka, eds. 1996. *Austro-Corporatism: Past, Present, Future.* New Brunswick, NJ: Transaction.

Blackaby, F.T. 1964. "Economic Policy in the United Kingdom, 1949 to 1961." *Economic Policy in Our Time. Vol. II.* Chicago: Rand McNally.

Boltho, Andrea, ed. 1982. *The European Economy. Growth and Crisis.* Oxford: Oxford University Press.

Borkin, Joseph, and Charles A. Welsh. 1943. *Germany's Master Plan. The Story of Industrial Offensive.* New York: Duell, Sloan, and Pearce.

Bowles, Samuel, David M. Gordon, and Thomas E. Weisskopf. 1983. *Beyond the Wasteland: A Democratic Alternative to Economic Decline.* Garden City, NY: Anchor Press, Doubleday.

Braun, Anne Romanis. 1986. *Wage Determination and Incomes Policy in Open Economies.* Washington, D.C.: International Monetary Fund.

Braunthal, Gerard. 1965. *The Federation of German Industry in Politics.* Ithaca, NY: Cornell University Press.

Brinkley, Alan. 1995. *The End of Reform. New Deal Liberalism in Recession and War.* New York: Alfred A. Knopf.

Brooke, Stephen. 1992. *Labour's War. The Labour Party During the Second World War.* Oxford: Clarendon Press.

Brown, Henry Phelps. 1986. *The Origins of Trade Union Power.* Oxford: Oxford University Press.

Brown, Michael K. 1998. "Bargaining for Social Rights: Unions and the Reemergence of Welfare Capitalism." *Political Science Quarterly* 112 (4):645–674.

Bryant, Ralph C. 1987. *International Financial Intermediation.* Washington, D.C.: The Brookings Institution.

Bührer, Werner. 1989. "Unternehmerverbände." *Die Geschichte der Bundesrepublik Deutschland. Wirtschaft.* Ed. Wolfgang Benz. Frankfurt am Main: Fischer.

Bullock, Alan. 1960. *The Life and Times of Ernest Bevin.* 2 vols. London: Heinemann.

Butler, David. 1989. *British General Elections Since 1945.* London: Basil Blackwell.

Butler, David, and Anne Sloman. 1975. 4th ed. *British Political Facts, 1900–1975.* London: Macmillan.

Butler, David, and Dennis Kavanagh. 1984. *The British General Election of 1983.* New York: St. Martin's Press.

Cairncross, Alec. 1978. "Keynes and the Planned Economy." *Keynes and Laissez-Faire.* Ed. A. P. Thirlwall. London: Macmillan.

———. 1985. *Years of Recovery. British Economic Policy 1945–51.* London: Methuen.

———. 1992. *The British Economy Since 1945.* Oxford: Blackwell.

———. 1994. "Economic Policy and Performance, 1945–1964." *The Economic History of Britain Since 1700, Vol. 3: 1939–1992.* Ed. Roderick Floud and Donald McCloskey. Cambridge: Cambridge University Press.

Cameron, David. 1978. "The Expansion of the Public Economy: A Comparative Analysis." *American Political Science Review* 72 (4):1243–1261.

———. 1988. "Distributional Coalitions and Other Sources of Economic Stagnation: On Olson's Rise and Decline of Nations." *International Organization* 42 (4):561–603.

Carew, Anthony. 1987. *Labour Under the Marshall Plan. The Politics of Productivity and the Marketing of Management Science.* Detroit, MI: Wayne State University Press.

Carlin, Wendy, and David Soskice. 1990. *Macroeconomics and the Wage Bargain. A Modern Approach to Employment, Inflation, and the Exchange Rate.* Oxford: Oxford University Press.

Calmfors, Lars, ed. 1990. *Wage Formation and Macroeconomic Policy in the Nordic Countries.* Oxford: Oxford University Press and SNS Förlag.

Calmfors, Lars, and John Driffill. 1988. "Bargaining Structure, Corporatism and Macroeconomic Performance." *Economic Policy* 6:14–61.

Catton, Bruce. 1948. *The War Lords of Washington*. New York: Harcourt, Brace.

Chandler, Alfred D. Jr. 1990. *Scale and Scope: The Dynamics of Industrial Capitalism*. Cambridge, MA: Harvard University Press.

Chester, D. N., ed. 1972 (orig. 1951). *Lessons of the British War Economy*. Westport, CT: Greenwood Press.

Charmley, John. 1993. *Churchill: The End of Glory. A Political Biography*. New York: Harcourt, Brace.

Churchill, Winston S. 1951. *The Second World War. Vol. IV. The Hinge of Fate*. London: Cassel.

Citrine, Walter. 1964. *Men and Work, An Autobiography*. Westwood, CT: Greenwood Press.

Clarke, Richard. 1982. *Anglo-American Economic Collaboration in War and Peace, 1942–1949*. Oxford: Clarendon Press.

Clawson, Marion. 1981. *New Deal Planning. The National Resources Planning Board*. Baltimore, MD: Johns Hopkins University Press.

Clay, Lucius D. 1950. *Decision in Germany*. Garden City, NY: Doubleday.

Clegg, Hugh A. 1994. *A History of British Trade Unions Since 1889. Vol. III. 1934–1951*. Oxford: Clarendon Press.

Coates, David. 1975. *The Labour Party and the Struggle for Socialism*. Cambridge: Cambridge University Press.

———. 1989. *The Crisis of the Labour Party*. Oxford: Phillips Allen.

Coates, David, and Tony Topham. 1986. *Trade Unions and Politics*. Oxford: Basil Blackwell.

Cohen, Stephen S. 1977. *Modern Capitalist Planning: The French Model*. Berkeley: University of California.

Cole, G. D. H. 1935. *Economic Planning*. New York: Alfred A. Knopf.

Cole, Taylor. 1953. "Labor Relations." *Governing Postwar Germany*. Ed. Edward H. Litchfield. Ithaca, NY: Cornell University Press.

Congressional Quarterly Weekly Report. Various years. Washington, D.C.: Congressional Quarterly.

Conservative Party (Great Britain). 1947. *The Industrial Charter. A Statement of Conservative Industrial Policy*. Conservative and Unionist Central Office.

Cooke, Colin. 1957. *The Life of Richard Stafford Cripps*. London: Hodder and Stoughton.

Cooper, Andrew Fenton. 1989. *British Agricultural Policy, 1912–36. A Study in Conservative Politics*. Manchester: Manchester University Press.

Cosgrave, Patrick. 1992. *The Strange Death of Socialist Britain*. London: Constable.

Council on Foreign Relations. 1944, July. *American Interests in the War and the Peace. Postwar Controls of the German Economy*. Confidential Paper. New York.

———. 1947. *American Policy Towards Germany*. Ed. Joseph Barber. New York: Council on Foreign Relations.

Courtauld, Samuel. 1949. *Ideals and Industry. War-Time Papers*. Cambridge: Cambridge University Press.

Crafts, N. F. R. 1995. "'You've Never Had It So Good?': British Economic Policy and Performance, 1945–60." *Europe's Post-War Recovery.* Ed. B. Eichengreen. Cambridge: Cambridge University Press.

Crepaz, Markus M. L. 1994. "From Semisovereignty to Sovereignty: The Decline of Corporatism and the Rise of Parliament in Austria." *Comparative Politics* 27 (2):45–65.

Crewe, Ivor, and Bo Särlvik. 1983. *Decade of Dealignment. The Conservative Victory of 1979 and Electoral Trends in the 1970s.* Cambridge: Cambridge University Press.

Cronin, James E. 1979. *Industrial Conflict in Modern Britain.* London: Croom Helm.

Crouch, Colin. 1977. *Class Conflict and the Industrial Relations Crisis: Compromise and Corporatism in the Policies of the British State.* London: Humanities Press.

———. 1993. *Industrial Relations and European State Traditions.* Oxford: Clarendon Press.

Crouch, Colin, and Alessandro Pizzorno, eds. 1978. *The Resurgence of Class Conflict in Western Europe Since 1968.* New York: Holmes and Meier.

Croucher, Richard. 1982. *Engineers at War.* London: Merlin Press.

Dahl, Robert A., and Charles Lindblom. 1976 (orig. 1953). *Politics, Economics and Welfare.* Chicago: Chicago University Press.

Dahrendorf, Ralph. 1959. *Class and Class Conflict in Industrial Society.* Stanford, CA: Stanford University Press.

———. 1967. *Society and Democracy in Germany.* New York: W. W. Norton.

———. 1980a. *After Social Democracy.* London: Weidenfeld and Nicolson.

———. 1980b. *Life Chances: Approaches to Social and Political Theory.* London: Weidenfeld and Nicolson.

Dalton, Hugh. 1962. *High Tide and After. Memoirs 1945–1960.* London: Frederick Muller, Ltd.

De Geer, Hans. 1986. *SAF i förhandlingar. Svenska Arbetsgivareföreningen och dess förhandlingsrelationer till LO och tjänstemannaorganisationerna, 1930–1970.* Stockholm: SAF.

Denton, Geoffrey, Murray Forsyth, and Malcolm Maclennan. 1968. *Economic Planning and Policies in Britain, France, and Germany.* Political and Economic Planning. (PEP). New York: Praeger.

Dewhurst, J. Frederick. 1947. *America's Needs and Resources.* New York: The Twentieth Century Fund.

———. 1961. *Europe's Needs and Resources. Trends and Prospects in Eighteen Countries.* New York: Twentieth Century Fund.

Die Quelle. Various issues. Dusseldorf.

Dornbusch, Rudiger, and Stanley Fischer. 1994. *Macroeconomics.* 6th ed. New York: McGrawHill.

Dow, J. C. R. 1970. 3rd ed. *The Management of the British Economy, 1945–60.* Cambridge: Cambridge University Press.

Downing, Brian M. 1992. *The Military Revolution and Political Change. Origins of Democracy and Autocracy in Early Modern Europe.* Princeton, NJ: Princeton University Press.

Downs, Anthony. 1964. *An Economic Theory of Democracy.* New York: Harper.

Duchêne, Francois. 1994. *Jean Monnet. The First Statesman of Interdependence*. New York: W. W. Norton.

Durbin, E. F. M. 1949. *Problems of Economic Planning. Papers on Planning and Economics*. London: Routledge & Kegan Paul.

Durbin, Elizabeth. 1985. *New Jerusalems. The Labour Party and the Economics of Democratic Socialism*. London: Routledge & Kegan Paul.

Durcan, J. W., et al. 1983. *Strikes in Post-War Britain: A Study of Stoppages of Work Due to Industrial Disputes, 1946–73*. London: George Allen & Unwin.

Eatwell, Roger. 1979. *The 1945–1951 Labour Government*. London: Batsford Academic.

Edelman, Murray J. 1954. *National Economic Planning: The Formation of Austrian Wage, Price, and Tax Policy after World War II*. Urbana, IL: University of Illinois. Institute of Labor and Industrial Relations.

Edgerton, David. 1992. "Whatever Happened to the British Warfare State? The Ministry of Supply, 1945–1951." *Labour Governments and Private Industry*. Eds. H. Mercer, N. Rollings, and J. D. Tomlinson. Edinburgh: Edinburgh University Press.

Edinger, Lewis J. 1965. *Kurt Schumacher. A Study in Personality and Political Behavior*. Stanford, CA: Stanford University Press.

Eichengreen, Barry. 1993. *Restructuring Europe's Trade and Payments. The European Payments Union*. Ann Arbor: University of Michigan Press.

———. 1996. *Globalizing Capital, A History of the International Monetary System*. Princeton, NJ: Princeton University Press.

Eichengreen, Barry, ed. 1995. *Europe's Post-War Recovery*. Cambridge: Cambridge University Press.

Elvander, Nils. 1966. *Interesseorganisationerna i dagens Sverige*. Lund: CWK Gleerup Bokförlag, 1966.

———. 1972. *Svensk skattepolitik, 1945–1970. En studie i partiers och organisationernes funktion*. Stockholm: Rabén och Sjögren.

———. 1990. "Incomes Policy in the Nordic Countries." *International Labour Review* 129 (1): 1–21.

Erhard, Ludwig. 1958. *Prosperity through Competition*. New York: Praeger.

Erlander, Tage. 1974. *1949–1954*. Stockholm: Tidens Förlag.

———. 1982. *1960-Talet. Samtal med Arvid Lagercrantz*. Stockholm: Tidens Förlag.

Eschenburg, Theodor, ed. 1983. *Geschichte der Bundesrepublik Deutschland. Jahre der Besatzung, 1945–1949*. University Press, Stuttgart: Deutsche Varlags-Anstalt GmbH.

Esping-Andersen, Gøsta. 1985. *Politics Against Markets. The Social Democratic Road to Power*. Princeton, NJ: Princeton University Press

———. 1990. *The Three Worlds of Welfare Capitalism*. Princeton, NJ: Princeton University Press.

———. 1992. "The Making of a Social Democratic Welfare State." *Creating Social Democracy. A Century of the Social Democratic Labor Party in Sweden*. Eds. Klaus Misgeld et al. University Park, Penn.: Pennsylvania State University Press, 1992.

Esping-Andersen, Gøsta, and Walter Korpi. 1984. "Social Policy as Class Politics in Post-War Capitalism: Scandinavia, Austria, and Germany." Ed. John D.

Goldthorpe. *Order and Conflict in Contemporary Capitalism.* Oxford: Clarendon Press.

Fackföreningsrörelsen. Various years. Stockholm: Landsorganisationen.

Fearon, James D. 1991. "Counterfactuals and Hypothesis Testing in Political Science." *World Politics* 43 (2):169–196.

FBI. (Federation of British Industries, Great Britain). 1942. *Reconstruction.* London.

———. 1944a. *The Organization of British Industry.* Report of the FBI Organization of Industry Committee. October.

———. 1944b. *International Trade Policy.* February. London.

———. 1945. *Report on Reconstruction.* London.

Feldt, Kjell-Olof. 1985. *Den Tredje Vägen.* Stockholm: Tiden.

Fels, Allan. 1972. *The British Prices and Incomes Board.* Cambridge: Cambridge University Press.

Fielding, Steven, Peter Thompson, and Nick Tiratsoo. 1995. *"England Arise!" The Labour Party and Popular Politics in 1940s Britain.* Manchester: Manchester University Press.

Flanders, Allen. 1950. *A Policy for Wages.* Fabian Tract no. 281. London: Gollancz.

———. 1952. "Great Britain." *Comparative Labor Movements.* Ed. Walter Galenson. New York: Prentice-Hall.

Flora, Peter, et al. 1983. *State, Economy, and Society in Western Europe, 1815–1975: a Datahandbook.* Vol. 1. Frankfurt: Campus Verlag.

Flora, Peter, Franz Kraus, and Winfred Pfenning. 1987. *State, Economy, and Society in Western Europe, 1815–1975: a Datahandbook.* Vol. 2. Frankfurt: Campus Verlag.

Folkpartiet (Sweden). 1955. *Efterkrigstidens Samhälle. Några ekonomiska och sociala riktlinjer framförda inom Folkpartiet.* Stockholm.

Forschung und Quellen zur Zeitgeschichte. 1986. *Adenauer: "Es mußte alles neu gemacht werden." Die Protokolle des CDU-Bundesverstandes, 1950–1953.* Vol. 8. By Günter Buchstab. Stuttgart: Emil Klett Verlag.

———. 1988. *Die CDU in der britischen Zone, 1945–1949. Gründung, Organization, Program, und Politik.* Vol. 12. By Horstweiler Heitzer. Düsseldorf: Droste.

Francis, Martin. 1997. *Ideas and Policies Under Labour, 1945–1951.* Manchester: Manchester University Press.

Frederiksson, Karl. 1947. "Efterkrigsprogrammet förverkligas." *Vår politik.* SAP. Stockholm.

Friberg, Lennart. 1973. *Styre i kristid. Studier i krigsförvaltnings organisation och structur, 1939–1945.* Stockholm: Allmänna Förlaget.

Frieden, Jeffry A. 1996. "The Impact of Goods and Capital Market Integration on European Monetary Politics." *Comparative Political Studies* 29 (2):193–222.

Från Riksdag & Departement. Various issues. Stockholm.

Fukuyama, Francis. 1995. *Trust. The Social Virtues and the Creation of Prosperity.* New York: Free Press.

Fulcher, James. 1991. *Labour Movements, Employers, and the State: Conflict and Co-Operation in Britain and Sweden.* New York: Oxford University Press.

Fyrth, Jim, ed. 1995. *Labour's Promised Land? Culture and Society in Labour Britain, 1945–1951.* London: Lawrence and Wishart.

Galbraith, John K. 1946. *Recovery in Europe.* Washington D.C.: National Planning Association.

———. 1948. "The German Economy." *Foreign Economic Policy for the United States.* Ed. Seymour E. Harris. Cambridge, MA: Harvard University Press.

Gamble, Andrew. 1996. *Hayek: The Iron Cage of Liberty.* Boulder, CO: Westview.

Gardner, Richard M. 1969 (orig. 1956). *Sterling-Dollar Diplomacy in Current Perspective.* New York: Columbia University Press.

Garrett, Geoffrey, and Peter Lange. 1996. "Internationalization, Institutions, and Political Change." *Internationalization and Domestic Politics.* Eds. Robert O. Keohane and Helen Milner. Cambridge, MA: Cambridge University Press.

Gerlich, Peter. 1992. "A Farewell to Corporatism." *West European Politics* 1:132–146.

Giavazzi, Francesco, and Alberto Giovanni. 1987. *Limiting Exchange Rate Flexibility.* Cambridge, MA: MIT Press.

Gilbert, Martin, ed. 1988. *Winston S. Churchill: Never Despair, 1949–1965.* Vol. 8 Boston: Houghton Mifflin.

Gillingham, John. 1993. "From Morgenthau Plan to Schuman Plan: America and the Organization of Europe." *American Policy and the Reconstruction of West Germany, 1945–1955.* Eds. Hartmut Lehmann and the German Historical Institute. New York: Cambridge University Press.

Gilpin, Robert. 1981. *War and Change in World Politics.* Cambridge, MA: Cambridge University Press.

Gollancz, Victor. 1946. *Leaving Them to Their Fate.* London: Gollancz.

Goodin, Robert E. 1996. "Institutionalizing the Public Interests: The Defense of Deadlock and Beyond." *American Political Science Review* 90 (2):331–344.

Gourevitch, Peter, et al. 1984. *Unions and Economic Crisis: Britain, West Germany, and Sweden.* London: Allen & Unwin.

Gourevitch, Peter. 1986. *Politics in Hard Times: Comparative Responses to International Economic Crises.* Ithaca, NY: Cornell University Press.

Grant, Wyn. 1995. *Pressure Groups. Politics and Democracy in Britain.* 2nd ed. New York: Harvester, Wheatsheaf.

Great Britain. Parliament. House of Commons. Various years. *House of Commons Debates* (cited as H.C. Debs.). Hansard Series. London: HMSO.

Great Britain. 1941. *Price Stabilization and Industrial Policy.* Cdm. 6294. London: HMSO.

———. 1942. *Coal.* Board of Trade. Cmd. 6364. London: HMSO.

———. 1944a. *A National Health Service.* Minister of Health. Cmd. 6502. London: HMSO.

———. 1944b. *Employment.* Minister of Reconstruction. Cmd. 6527. London: HMSO.

———. 1944c. *Industrial Relations Handbook.* Ministry of Labour and National Service. London: HMSO.

———. 1944d-e. *Social Insurance I-II.* Chancellor of the Exchequer. Cmd. 6550–6551. London: HMSO.

———. 1947a. *Economic Survey for 1947.* Chancellor of the Exchequer. Cmd. 7046. London: HMSO.

————. 1947b. *Staffs Employed in Government Departments.* Financial Statement to the Treasury. Cmd. 7027. London: HMSO.

————. 1947c. *Statement on the Economic Considerations Affecting Relations between Employers and Workers.* Minister of Labour and National Service. Cdm. 7018. London: HMSO.

————. 1948a. *Economic Survey.* Chancellor of the Exchequer. Cmd. 7344. London: HMSO.

————. 1948b. *Statement on Personal Incomes, Costs, and Prices.* Cmd. 7321. London: HMSO.

————. 1949. *Economic Survey for 1949.* Chancellor of the Exchequer. Cmd. 7647. London: HMSO.

————. 1950. *Industrial Relations in Germany, 1945–1949.* Cmd. 7923. London: HMSO.

————. 1965. *National Plan.* Cmd. 2764. London: HMSO.

Greenstone, J. David. 1977. 2nd ed. *Labor in American Politics.* Chicago: University of Chicago Press.

Griffiths, Richard T. ed. 1993. *Socialist Parties and the Question of Europe in the 1950s.* Leiden: E. J. Brill.

Grove, J. W. 1962. *Government and Industry in Britain.* London: Longmans.

Guger, Alois, 1992. "Corporatism: Success or Failure? Austrian Experiences." *Social Corporatism: A Superior Economic System?* Eds. Jukka Pekkarinen, Matti Pohjola, and Bob Rowthorn. Oxford: Clarendon Press.

Guger, Alois, and Wolfgang Polt. 1994. "Corporatism and Incomes Policy in Austria: Experiences and Perspectives." *The Return to Incomes Policy.* Ed. Ronald Dore. London: Pinter Publishers.

Gustafsson, Bo. 1973. "A Perennial of Doctrinal History. Keynes and the "Stockholm School." *Economy and History* 16 (2):114–28.

Haberl, Othmar Nikola, and Lutz Niethammer, eds. 1986. *Der Marshall-Plan und die Europäische Linke.* Frankfurt am Main: Europäische Verlagsanstalt.

Haberler, Gottfried. 1948. "Dollar Shortage?" *Foreign Economic Policy for the United States.* Ed. Seymour E. Harris. Cambridge, MA: Harvard Univesity Press.

Hadenius, Alex. 1976. *Facklig Organisationsutveckling. En studie av landsorganisationen in Sverige.* Statsvitenskapliga foreningen i Uppsala. Skrifter. vol. 75. Uppsala.

Hahn, Erich J. 1993. "U.S. Policy on a West German Constitution, 1947–1949." *American Policy and the Reconstruction of West Germany, 1945–1955.* Ed. Hartmut Lehmann and the German Historical Institute. New York: Cambridge University Press.

Hall, Peter A. 1986. *Governing the Economy. The Politics of State Intervention in Britain and France.* New York: Oxford University Press.

Hall, Peter A. ed. 1989. *The Political Power of Economic Ideas. Keynesianism Across Nations.* Princeton, NJ: Princeton University Press.

Hammond, R. J. 1954. *Food and Agriculture in Britain, 1939–45.* Stanford, CA: Stanford University Press.

Hancock, W. K., and M. M. Gowing. 1949. *British War Economy.* History of the Second World War. United Kingdom Civil Series. London: HMSO.

Hansson, Per Albin. 1935. "Land Skall Med Lag Byggas." *Demokrati*. Stockholm: Tidens Förlag.

Hardach, Karl. 1976. *The Political Economy of Germany in the Twentieth Century*. Berkeley: University of California Press.

Harris, José. 1977. *William Beveridge. A Biography*. Oxford: Clarendon Press.

———. 1990. "Society and State in Twentieth-Century Britain." *The Cambridge Social History of Britain 1750–1950*. Ed. F. M. L. Thompson. Vol. 3. Cambridge: Cambridge University Press.

Harris, Seymour E., ed. 1948. *Foreign Economic Policy for the United States*. Cambridge, MA: Harvard University Press.

Harrison, Martin. 1960. *Trade Unions and the Labour Party Since 1945*. London: George Allen & Unwin.

Heckscher, Gunnar. 1946. *Staten och organisationerna*. Stockholm: KFs Bokförlag.

Hedlund, Stefan, and Mats Lundahl. 1985. *Beredskap eller protektionism? En studie av beredskapsmålet i svensk jordbrukspolitik*. Stockholm: Liber Förlag.

Heidenheimer, Arnold J. 1960. *Adenauer and the CDU. The Rise of the Leader and the Integration of the Party*. The Hague: Martinus Nijhoff.

Helleiner, Eric. 1994. *States and the Reemergence of Global Finance. From Bretton Woods to the 1990s*. Ithaca, NY: Cornell University Press.

Hesselbach, Walter. 1984. "Tarifpolitik—Stand und Perspektive." *Beiträge zur sozialdemokratischen Wirtschaftspolitik*. Eds. Georg Kurlbaum and Uwe Jens. Bonn: Verlag Neue Gesellschaft.

Hibbs, Douglas A. Jr. 1990. "Wage Dispersion and Trade Union Action in Sweden." *Generating Equality in the Welfare State: The Swedish Experience*. Ed. Inga Persson. Oslo: Norwegian University Press.

Hibbs, Jr., Douglas A., and Håkan Locking. 1996. "Wage Compresion, Wage Drift and Wage Inflation in Sweden." *Labour Economics* 3 (Sept.):109–141.

Hirsch, Fred. 1976. *Social Limits to Growth*. Cambridge, MA: Harvard University Press.

Hirsch, Fred, and John H. Goldthorpe, eds. 1978. *The Political Economy of Inflation*. London: Martin Robertson, 1978.

Hobsbawm, Eric J. 1964. "The Labour Aristocracy in Nineteenth-Century Britain." *Labouring Men. Studies in the History of Labour*. New York: Basic Books.

———. 1982. "The Retreat Into Extremism." *The Forward March of Labour Halted?* Eds. Martin Jacques and Francis Mulhern. London: Verso.

———. 1994. *The Age of Extremes. A History of the World, 1914–1991*. New York: Pantheon Books.

Hoffmann, Stanley. 1965. *The State of War. Essays on the Theory and Practice of International Politics*. New York: Frederick A. Praeger.

Hogan, Michael J. 1987. *The Marshall Plan. America, Britain, and the Reconstruction of Western Europe, 1947–1952*. Cambridge, MA: Cambridge University Press.

House of Commons Debates (cited as H.C. Debs.). Various years. See Great Britain. Parliament. House of Commons. Parliamentary Debates. Hansard. London: HMSO.

Howarth, T. E. B. 1985. *Prospects and Reality: Great Britain, 1945–55*. London: Collins.

Howell, David. 1989. *The Politics of the NUM. A Lancashire View.* Manchester: Manchester University Press.

Howson, Susan. 1994. "Money and Monetary Policy in Britain, 1945–1990." *The Economic History of Britain Since 1700, Vol. 3: 1939–1992.* Eds. Roderick Floud and Donald McCloskey. Cambridge: Cambridge University Press.

Huber, Evelyne, and John D. Stephens. 1996, March 14–17. "Internationalization and the Social Democratic Welfare State: Crisis and Future Prospects." Paper presented at the Tenth Conference of Europeanists. Chicago.

Högerns Riksorganisation (Sweden). 1944. *Fri företagsamhet och fråmatskridande.* Stockholm.

———. 1945. *Framtidens svenska ekonomiska samhälle.* Föredrag å Stockholm-Högerns diskussions möte i Borgerskolan den 24 maj 1945. By Gustaf Söderlund. Stockholm.

———. 1946. *Frihet och framsteg.* Stockholm.

IMF (International Monetary Fund). Various years. *International Financial Statistics Yearbook.* Washington, D.C.

Industria. Various years. SAF (Svenska Arbetsgivareföreningen). Stockholm.

Industrial Mobilization for War. History of the War Production Board and the Predecessor Agencies, 1940–1945. Vol. I. Program and Administration. 1969 (orig. 1947). New York: Greenwood Press.

Industriens Utredningsinstitut (Sweden). 1944, February. *Industriens sysselsättning under åren närmast efter kriget.* International Trade Policy. Stockholm.

Ingham, Geoffrey. 1974. *Strikes and Industrial Conflict: Britain and Scandinavia.* London: Macmillan.

Inman, P. 1957. *Labour in the Munitions Industries. History of the Second World War. United Kingdom Civil Series.* Ed. Sir Keith Hancock. London: HMSO.

Institut für Zeitgeschichte. 1993. *Die CSU, 1945–48. Protokolle und materialen zur Frühgeschichte der Christlich-Sozialer Union.* Vol. 1. Munich: Oldenburg Verlag.

Jefferys, Kevin, ed. 1987. *Labour and the Wartime Coalition. From the Diary of James Chuter Ede, 1941–1945.* London: The Historians' Press.

Jenson, Jane, and Rianne Mahon. 1993. "Representing Solidarity: Class, Gender and the Crisis in Social Democratic Sweden." *New Left Review* 201:76–100.

Johansson, Alf W., and Torbjörn Norman. 1992. "Sweden's Security and World Peace." *Creating Social Democracy. A Century of the Social Democratic Labor Party in Sweden.* Eds. Klaus Misgeld et al. University Park, PA: Pennsylvania State University Press.

Johansson, Anders L. 1989. *Tillväxt och klassamarbete. En studie of den svenska modellens uppkomst.* Stockholm: Tidens Forlag.

Johansson, Mat. 1985. *Svensk industri, 1930–1950. Production, produktivitet, sysselsättning.* Lund: Skrifter utgivna av ekonomisk-historiska föreningen.

Johnstone, Harry W. 1951. *The Restraint of Competition in the Austrian Economy.* Vienna: Office of the U.S. High Commissioner for Austria.

Jonasson, Gustaf. 1976. *Per Edvin Sköld, 1946–1951.* Stockholm: Almquist and Wiksell.

Jonasson, Gustaf. 1981. *I väntan på uppbrott? Bondeförbundet/Centerpartiet i regeringskoalitionens slutskede 1956–57.* Acta Universitatis Upsaliensis 118. Uppsala.

Jones, Jack. 1986. *Union Man. The Autobiography of Jack Jones.* London: Collins.

Jonung, Lars. 1994. "The Rise and Fall of Credit Controls: The Case of Sweden, 1939–1989." *Monetary Regimes in Transition.* Eds. Michael D. Bordo and Forrest Capie. Cambridge: Cambridge University Press.

Josephy, Berthold. 1945. *Program och verklighet. Arbeterrörelsens efterkrigsprogram skärskådas.* Stockholm: Hugo Gebers Förlag.

Katzenstein, Peter J. 1978. *Between Power and Plenty. Foreign Economic Policies of Advanced Industrial States.* Madison: University of Wisconsin Press.

———. 1984. *Corporatism and Change. Austria, Switzerland and the Politics of Industry.* Ithaca, NY: Cornell University Press.

———. 1985. *Small States in World Markets: Industrial Policy in Europe.* Ithaca, NY: Cornell University Press.

———. 1987. *Policy and Politics in West Germany. The Growth of a Semisovereign State.* Philadelphia: Temple University Press.

Katznelson, Ira, Kim Geiger, and Daniel Kryder. 1993. "Limiting Liberalism: The Southern Vote in Congress, 1933–1950." *Political Science Quarterly* 108 (2):283–307.

Kelly, Gavin, Dominic Kelly, and Andrew Gamble, eds. 1997. *Stakeholder Capitalism.* Basingstoke: Macmillan.

Keohane, Robert O., and Joseph Nye, Jr. 1977. *Power and Interdependence: World Politics in Transition.* Boston: Little, Brown.

Keohane, Robert O., Gary King, and Sidney Verba. 1994. *Designing Social Inquiry. Scientific Inference in Qualitative Research.* Princeton, NJ: Princeton University Press.

Keohane, Robert O., and Helen Milner, eds. 1996. *Internationalization and Domestic Politics.* Cambridge: Cambridge University Press.

Kesselman, Louis Coleridge. 1948. *The Social Politics of FEPC. A Study in Reform Pressure Movements.* Chapel Hill: University of North Carolina Press.

Keynes, James Maynard. 1940. *How to Pay for the War: A Radical Plan for the Chancellor of the Exchequer.* New York: Harcourt, Brace.

———. 1973. *The General Theory of Employment, Interest and Money. The Collected Writings of John Maynard Keynes.* Vol. 3. London: Macmillan.

Kindleberger, Charles P. 1966. *Europe and the Dollar.* Cambridge, MA: MIT Press.

———. 1987. *Marshall Plan Days.* Boston: Allen & Unwin.

———. 1989. *The German Economy, 1945–1947. Charles P. Kindleberger's Letters from the Field.* Westport, CT: Meckler.

———. 1993. *A Financial History of Western Europe.* 2 ed. New York: Oxford University Press.

Kitschelt, Herbert. 1994a. "Austrian and Swedish Social Democrats in Crisis: Party Strategy and Organization in Corporatist Regimes." *Comparative Political Studies* 27 (1):3–39.

———. 1994b. *The Transformation of European Social Democracy.* New York: Cambridge University Press.

Klausen, Jytte. 1998. "The Declining Significance of Male Workers: Trade Union Responses to Changing Labor Markets, 1970–1990." *Change and Continuity in Contemporary Capitalism.* Eds. Herbert Kitschelt et al. New York: Cambridge University Press.

Klausen, Jytte, and Louise A. Tilly, eds. 1997. *European Integration as a Social and Historical Process, From 1850 to the Present.* Boulder, CO: Rowman and Littlefield.

Klevmarken, Anders N. 1983. *Lönebildning och lönestruktur. En jämförelse mellan Sverige och USA.* Stockholm: Industriens Utredningsinstitut, Almquist & Wiksell.

Kluge, Ulrich. 1993. "West German Agriculture and the European Recovery Program, 1948–1952." *American Policy and the Reconstruction of West Germany, 1945–1955.* Eds. Hartmut Lehmann and the German Historical Institute. New York: Cambridge University Press.

Kocka, Jürgen. 1994. rev. ed. "1945: Neubeginn oder Restoration?" *Wendepunkte Deutsche Geschichte, 1848–1945.* Eds. Carola Stern and Heinrich A. Winkler. Frankfurt am Main: Fischer-Taschenbuch-Verlag.

Kogan, David, and Maurice Kogan. 1982 (1983, 2 ed.). *The Battle for the Labour Party.* London: Kegan Paul.

Korpi, Walter. 1978. *The Working Class in Welfare Capitalism: Work, Unions, and Politics in Sweden.* London: Routledge & Kegan, Paul.

———. 1982. *Från undersåte till medborgare. Om fonder och ekonomisk demokrati.* Tidens Debatt 3. Stockholm: Tidens Forlag.

———. 1983. *The Democratic Class Struggle.* London: Routledge & Kegan Paul.

———. 1989. "Power Politics and State Autonomy in the Development of Social Citizenship: Social Rights During Sickness in Eighteen OECD Countries Since 1930." *American Sociological Review* 54 (3):309–320.

Korpi, Walter, and Michael Shalev. 1979. "Strikes, Industrial Relations and Class Conflict in Capitalist Societies." *British Journal of Sociology* 30 (2):164–187.

Korpi, Walter, and Michael Shalev. 1980. "Strikes, Power and Politics in Western Nations, 1900–76." *Political Power and Social Theory* (1). Greenwich, CT: JAI Press.

Krammer, Josef. 1991. "Interessenorganisation der Landwirtschaft." *Handbuch des Politische Systems Österreichs.* Wein: Manzsche Verlags- und Universitätsbuchhandlung.

Krasner, Stephen D. 1978. *Defending the National Interest.* Princeton, NJ: Princeton University Press.

———. 1982. "Structural Causes and Regime Consequences: Regimes as Intervening Variables." *International Regimes.* Ed. Stephen Krasner. Ithaca, NY: Cornell University Press.

Kravis, Irving B. 1948, January. "Prices and Wages in the Austrian Economy, 1938–47." *Monthly Labor Review* 20–27.

Kreuger, Anne O. 1996. *The Political Economy of American Trade Policy.* Chicago: University of Chicago Press.

Krugman, Paul. 1992. *Currencies and Crises.* Cambridge, MA: MIT Press.

Kurzer, Paulette. 1993. *Business and Banking. Political Change and Economic Integration in Western Europe.* Ithaca, NY: Cornell University Press.

Kärre, Bo. 1954. *Sverige och det internationella ekonomiska samarbetetet.* Stockholm: Utenrikspolitiska Instituttet.

Labour Party (Great Britain). ca. 1940. *Labour's Aims in War and Peace.* Welwyn Garden City, U.K.: Lincolns-Prager.

———. 1942 (reissued 1943). *"The Old World and the New Society": Reconstruction in War and Peace. Interim Report of the National Executive Committee of the British Labour Party.* New York: League for Industrial Democracy.

———. 1944. *Full Employment and Financial Policy.* Report by the National Executive Committee of the Labour Party. London.

———. 1945. *Let Us Face the Future.* London.

———. 1948. *Labour Party Year Book, 1947–8.* London: Transport House.

Lange, Peter. 1984. "Unions, Workers, and Wage Regulation: the Rational Bases of Consent." *Order and Capitalism in Contemporary Capitalism.* Ed. John H. Goldthorpe. Oxford: Clarendon Press.

League for Industrial Democracy. 1943. *British Labour on Reconstruction in War and Peace.* LID Pamphlet Series. New York.

Lemke, Christiane. 1997. "Crossing Borders and Building Barriers: Migration, Citizenship, and State Building in Germany." *European Integration in Social and Historical Perspective.* Eds. Jytte Klausen and Louise A. Tilly. Lanham, MD: Rowman and Littlefield.

Lewin, Leif. 1967. *Planhushållningsdebatten.* Stockholm: Almquist and Wiksell.

———. 1977. *Hur styrs facket? Om demokratin inom fackföreningsrörelsen.* Stockholm: Rabén & Sjögren.

———. 1988. *Ideology and Strategy: A Century of Swedish Politics.* Boston: Cambridge University Press.

Lewis-Beck, Michael. 1988. *Economics and Elections. The Major Western Democracies.* Ann Arbor: University of Michigan Press.

Lichtenstein, Nelson. 1982. *Labor's War At Home.* Cambridge, MA: Cambridge University Press.

———. 1989. "From Corporatism to Collective Bargaining: Organized Labor and the Eclipse of Social Democracy in the Postwar Era." *The Rise and Fall of the New Deal Order, 1930–1980.* Eds. Steve Fraser and Gary Gerstle. Princeton, NJ: Princeton University Press.

———. 1995. *The Most Dangerous Man in Detroit. Walter Reuther and the Fate of American Labor.* New York: Basic Books.

Lijphart, Arend. 1975. *The Politics of Accommodation.* Berkeley: University of California Press.

———. 1977. *Democracy in Plural Societies.* New Haven, CT: Yale University Press.

Lindbeck, Assar. 1974. *Swedish Economic Policy.* Berkeley: University of California Press.

Lindbeck, Assar, and Dennis J. Snower. 1988. *The Insider-Outsider Theory of Employment and Unemployment.* Cambridge, MA: MIT Press.

Lindberg, Leon N., and Charles S. Maier, eds. 1985. *The Politics of Inflation and Economic Stagnation.* Washington, D.C.: Brookings Institution, 1985.

Lipset, Seymour Martin. 1959. *Agrarian Socialism: The Cooperative Commonwealth Federation in Saskatchewan.* Berkeley, CA: University of California Press.

———. 1967. "Cleavage Structures, Party Systems, and Voter Alignments." *Party Systems and Voter Alignments: Cross-National Perspectives.* Eds. S. M. Lipset and S. Rokkan. New York: Free Press.

Litchfield, Edward H. 1953. "Emergence of German Government." *Governing Postwar Germany.* Ed. Edward H. Litchfield. Ithaca, NY: Cornell University Press.

Ljunggren, Stig-Björn. 1992. *Folkhemskapitalismen. Högerns programutveckling under efterkrigstiden.* Stockholm: Tiden.

Landsorganisationen. (LO, Sweden.) 1941. *Fackföreningsrörelsen och näringslivet.* Landsorganisationens 15-mammakommitteé. Stockholm: Tiden.

———. Various years. *Aktuella Frågor.* Stockholm.

———. Various years. *Fackföreningsrörelsen.* Stockholm.

———. Various years. *LO Kongress-Protokoll.* Stockholm.

———. Various years. *LO Verksamhetsberättelse.* Stockholm.

———. 1953. *Trade Unions and Full Employment.* Stockholm.

———. 1973. *Steg för steg, 1945–1973.* Stockholm: Prisma.

———. 1977a. *Co-determination on the Foundation of Solidarity.* A Report to the 1976 Congress of the Swedish Trade Union Confederation. Stockholm.

———. 1977b. *Vilda strejker inom LO-området 1974 och 1975.* Stockholm.

———. 1978. *Samordning och solidarisk lönepolitik.* [By Rudolf Meidner.] Stockholm: Prisma and LO, 1974. [In English. *Employee Investment Funds. An Approach to Collective Capital Formation.* London: George Allen & Unwin.]

———. 1981. *Lönepolitik för 80-talet.* Stockholm: Tiden.

———. 1982. *Näringspolitik för 80-Talet.* Stockholm.

———. 1984. *Lontägarfonder är. . . .* Stockholm: Nordstedt.

———. 1986a. *De centrala överenskommalserna mellan LO och SAF, 1952–1987.* Stockholm.

———. 1986b. *Fackföreningsrörelsen och välfärdsstaten.* Rapport till 1986 års LO-kongress från LOs utredning om den offentliga sektorn. Stockholm.

London Chamber of Commerce (Great Britain). 1944. *Report of the London Chamber of Commerce on the Government White Paper on "Employment Policy."* October. London.

———. 1947, September 30. *Report on the Economic Crisis.* London.

Longstreth, Frank, Sven Steinmo, and Kathleen Thelen, eds. 1992. *Structuring Politics. Historical Institutionalism in Comparative Politics.* New York: Cambridge University Press.

Lovell, John, and B. C. Roberts. 1968. *A Short History of the T.U.C.* London: Macmillan.

Luebbert, Gregory M. 1991. *Liberalism, Fascism, or Social Democracy: Social Classes and the Political Origins of Regimes in Interwar Europe.* New York: Oxford University Press.

Lundberg, Erik. 1957. *Business Cycles and Economic Policy.* Cambridge, MA: Harvard University Press.

Lyon, Leverett S., et al. 1935. *The NRA. An Analysis and Appraisal.* Washington, D.C.: The Brookings Institution.

Maier, Charles S. 1975. *Recasting Bourgeois Europe: Stabilization in France, Germany, and Italy in the Decade After World War I.* Princeton, NJ: Princeton University Press.

———. *The Origins of the Cold War and Contemporary Europe.* New York: New Viewpoints.

———. 1987. "The Politics of Productivity: Foundations of American International Economic Policy After World War II." *In Search of Stability. Explorations in Historical Political Economy.* Cambridge: Cambridge University Press.

———. 1997. *Dissolution: The Crisis of Communism and the End of East Germany.* Princeton, NJ: Princeton University Press.

Mann, Michael. 1988. "Ruling Class Strategies and Citizenship." *States, War and Capitalism. Studies in Political Sociology.* Oxford: Basil Blackwell.

Mann, Siegfried. 1994. *Mackt und Ohnemackt der Verbände. Das Beispiel des BDI aus empirische-analytischer Sicht.* Baden-Baden: Nomos Verlaggesellschaft.

Marshall, T. H. 1950. *Citizenship and Social Class and Other Essays.* London: Cambridge University Press.

Martin, Andrew. 1984. "Trade Unions in Sweden: Strategic Responses to Change and Crisis." *Unions and Economic Crisis: Britain, West Germany, and Sweden.* Eds. Peter A. Gourevitch, Christopher H. Allen, and Andrew Martin. London: Allen & Unwin.

Martin, Ross M. 1980. *TUC: The Growth of a Pressure Group, 1868–1976.* Oxford: Clarendon Press.

Mathis, Franz. 1995. "Between Regulation and Laissez Faire: Austrian State Industries after World War II." *Austria in the Nineteen Fifties. Contemporary Austrian Studies.* Eds. Günter Bischof, Anton Pelinka, and Rolf Steininger. New Brunswick, NJ: Transaction Publisher.

McCrone, Gavin. 1962. *The Economics of Subsidizing Agriculture. A Study of British Policy.* London: George Allen & Unwin.

McGhee, George. 1989. *At the Creation of a New Germany. From Adenauer to Brandt. An Ambassador's Account.* New Haven, CT: Yale University Press.

McKeown, Timothy J. 1991. "A Liberal Trade Order: The Long-Run Patterns of Imports to Advanced Capitalist States." *International Studies Quarterly* 35 (2):151–172.

———. 1998. " Untitled." *Change and Conflict in Contemporary Capitalism.* Eds. Peter Lange, Gary Marks, Herbert Kitschelt, and John D. Stephens. Cambridge: Cambridge University Press.

Meadows, P. 1978. "Planning." *British Economic Policy, 1960–74.* Ed. F. T. Blackaby. Cambridge: Cambridge University Press.

Meidner, Rudolf. 1974. *Samordning och solidarisk lønepolitik.* Stockholm: Prisma.

Mendell, Marguerite, and Daniel Salee, eds. 1993. *The Legacy of Karl Polanyi. Markets, States and Society at the End of the Twentieth Century.* New York: St. Martin's Press.

Merriam, Charles E. 1944. "The National Resources Planning Board: A Chapter in American Planning Experience." *American Political Science Review* 38 (6): 1075–1088.

Metall (Sweden).Various years. *Metallarbetaren*. Stockholm.

Metcalf, David. 1988. "Water Notes Dry Up:The Impact of the Donovan Reform Proposal and Thatcherism at Work on Labour Productivity in British Manufacturing Industry." *British Journal of Industrial Relations* 26 (2): 246–274.

Micheletti, Michele. 1990. *The Swedish Farmers' Movement and Government Agricultural Policy.* New York: Praeger.

Middlemas, Keith. 1986. *Power, Competition and the State. Vol. 1: Britain in Search of Balance, 1940–61.* London: Macmillan.

———. 1990. *Power, Competition and the State.Vol. 2:Threats to the Postwar Settlement Britain, 1961–74.* London: Macmillan.

———. 1991. *Power, Competition and the State. Vol. 3: The End of the Postwar Era: Britain Since 1974.* London: Macmillan.

Miliband, Ralph. 1961. *Parliamentary Socialism:A Study in the Politics of Labour.* London: Allen & Unwin.

Mill, John Stuart. 1949 (orig. 1843). *A System of Logic, Ratiocinative and Inductive.* London: Longmans, Green.

Miller, Marcus H., and John Williamson. 1988. "The International Monetary System. An Analysis of Alternative Regimes." *European Economic Review* 32:1031–1054.

Miller, Susanne. 1986. "The SPD from 1945 to the Present." *A History of German Social Democracy. From 1848 to the Present.* By Susanne Miller and Heinrich Potthoff. Leamington, U.K.: Berg Publishers.

Miller, Susanne, and Heinrich Potthoff. 1986. *A History of German Social Democracy From 1848 to the Present.* Leamington, U.K.: Berg.

Milward, Alan S. 1965. *The German Economy at War.* London: Athlone Press.

———. 1979. *War, Economy, and Society, 1939–1945.* Berkeley: University of California Press, 1979.

———. 1984, 2 ed. *The Economic Effects of the Two World Wars on Britain.* Studies in Economic and Social History. London: Macmillan.

———. 1984. *The Reconstruction of Western Europe, 1945–51.* London: Methuen.

———. 1992. *The European Rescue of the Nation-State.* London: Routledge.

Minkin, Lewis. 1991. *The Contentious Alliance.Trade Unions and the Labour Party.* Edinburgh: Edinburgh University Press.

Mjøset, Lars. 1996, March 14–16. "Nordic Economic Policies in the 1980s and 1990s."Tenth International Conference of Europeanists. Chicago.

Moene, Karl-Ove, and Michael Wallerstein. 1995. "How Social Democracy Worked: Labor Market Institutions." *Politics and Society* 23 (2):187–227.

Monnet, Jean. 1978. *Memoirs.* New York: Doubleday and Co.

Monthly Labor Review. Various issues.

Morgan, Kenneth O. 1984. *Labour in Power, 1945–1951.* Oxford: Clarendon Press.

Morgenthau, Henry, Jr. 1945. *Germany Is Our Problem.* New York: Harper & Brothers.

Mosca, Gaetano. 1967. *The Ruling Class.* [Elimenti di Scienza politica.] New York: McGraw-Hill.

Müller-Arnack, Alfred. 1966. *Wirtschaftsordnung and Wirtschaftspolitik.* Freiburg: Rombach.

Murphy, Robert. 1964. *Diplomat Among Warriors.* Garden City, NY: Doubleday.

Murray, Keith A. H. 1955. *Agriculture.* The History of the Second World War. United Kingdom Civil Series. London: HMSO.

Myrdal, Gunnar. 1938. *Jordbrukspolitiken Under Omläggning.* Stockholm.

———. 1944. *Varning För Fredsoptimismen.* Stockholm: Bonnier.

———. 1946, December. *The Reconstruction of World Trade and Swedish Trade.* Policy Supplement B to Svenska Handelsbanken's Index.

———. 1960. *Beyond the Welfare State.* New Haven, CT: Yale University Press.

Narr, Wolf-Dieter. 1966. *CDU-SPD. Programm und Praxis Seit 1945.* Stuttgart: W. Hohlhammer Verlag.

National Union of Manufacturers (Great Britain). ca. 1944. *Observations by the National Union of Manufacturers on the Government White Paper, Cmd. 6527.* London.

Nelson, Donald M. 1946. *Arsenal of Democracy. The Story of American War Production.* New York: Harcourt, Brace.

Nettl, J. P. 1965, February "Consensus or Elite Domination: The Case of Business." *Political Studies* 22–44.

North, Douglass C. 1990. *Institutions, Institutional Change, and Economic Performance.* Cambridge, MA: Cambridge University Press.

Nyman, Olle. 1947. *Svensk parlementarisme, 1932–36. Från minoritetsparlementarisme till majoritetskoalition.* Uppsala och Stockholm: Almquist & Wiksell.

Odhner, Clas-Erik. 1992. "Workers and Farmers Shape the Swedish Model: Social Democracy and Agricultural Policy." *Creating Social Democracy.* A Century of the Social Democratic Labor Party in Sweden. Eds. Klaus Misgeld et al. University Park, PA: Pennsylvania State University Press.

Ohlin, Bertil G. 1972. *Ung man blir politiker.* Stockholm: Bonnier.

Okun, Arthur M. 1975. *Equality and Efficiency. The Big Tradeoff.* Washington, D.C.: The Brookings Institution.

Olson, Mancur. 1965. *The Logic of Collective Action.* Cambridge: Cambridge University Press.

———. 1982. *The Rise and Decline of Nations. Economic Growth, Stagflation, and Social Rigidities.* New Haven, CT: Yale University Press.

Olsson, Sven E. 1990. *Social Policy and Welfare State in Sweden.* Lund: Arkiv.

Orren, Karen. 1986. "Union Politics and Postwar Liberalism in the U.S., 1946–1979." *Studies in American Political Development* 1: 215–252.

Oschilewski, Walther G., and Arno Scholz, eds. 1954. *Turmwächter der Demokratie. Ein Lebensbild von Kurt Schumacher. Sein Weg durch die Zeit.* Vol. 1. Berlin: Arani.

Panitch, Leo. 1976. *Social Democracy and Industrial Militancy. The Labour Party, the Trade Unions and Incomes Policy, 1945–1974.* Cambridge: Cambridge University Press.

———. 1981. "Trade Unions and the Capitalist State." *New Left Review* 125: 21–43.

Parker, H. M. D. 1957. *Manpower. A Study of War-Time Policy and Administration.* History of the Second World War. United Kingdom Civil Series. Ed. Sir Keith Hancock. London: HMSO.

Political and Economic Planning. (PEP). 1945. *Planning: Government and Trade Associations.* Broadsheet No. 240. London.

————.1957. *Industrial Trade Associations. Activities and Organization.* London: George Allen & Unwin.

————. 1968. *Economic Planning and Policies in Britain, France, and Germany.* New York: Praeger.

Pelling, Henry. 1963. *A History of British Trade Unionism.* London: Macmillan.

Pindyck, Robert S., and Daniel L. Rubinfeld. 1981. *Econometric Models and Economic Forecasts.* New York: McGraw-Hill.

Piore, Michael J. 1995. *Beyond Individualism. How Social Demands of the New Identity Groups Challenge American Political and Economic Life.* Cambridge, MA: Harvard University Press.

Piore, Michael J., and Charles F. Sabel. 1984. *The Second Industrial Divide: Possibilities for Prosperity.* New York: Basic Books.

Poggi, Gianfranco. 1990. *The State. Its Nature, Development, and Prospects.* Stanford, CA: Stanford University Press.

Polanyi, Karl. 1944. *The Great Transformation.* Boston: Beacon Press.

Polenberg, Richard. 1972. *War and Society. The United States, 1941–1945.* Westport, CT: Greenwood Press.

Pontusson, Jonas. 1987. "Radicalization and Retreat in Swedish Social Democracy." *New Left Review* 165: 5–33.

————. 1988. *Swedish Social Democracy and British Labour: Essays on the Nature and Conditions of Social Democratic Hegemony.* Ithaca, NY: Center for International Studies, Cornell University.

————. 1992. *The Limits of Social Democracy.* Ithaca, NY: Cornell University Press.

————. 1995. "From Comparative Public Policy to Political Economy. Putting Political Institutions in Their Place and Taking Interests Seriously." *Comparative Political Studies* 28 (1):117–147.

Pontusson, Jonas, and Peter Swenson. 1996. "Labor Markets, Production Strategies, and Wage Bargaining Institutions. The Swedish Employer Offensive in Comparative Perspective." *Comparative Political Studies* 29 (2):223–250.

Postan, M. M. 1952. *British War Production. History of the Second World War. United Kingdom Civil Series.* London: HMSO.

Priestly, John Boynton. 1941. *Out of the People.* New York: Harper & Brothers

Protokoll. See: Socialdemokratiska Arbetareparti. (SAP, Sweden). Various years. *Protokoll.* Stockholm.

Protokoll. See: Sozialdemokratischen Partei Deutschland. (SPD, Federal Republic of Germany). Various years. *Protokoll der Verhandlungen des Parteitages der Sozialdemokratischen Partei Deutschland.* Berlin: Verlag J.H.W. Diez Nachf. GmbH.

Przeworski, Adam, and Henry Teune. 1970. *The Logic of Comparative Social Inquiry.* New York: Wiley.

Przeworski, Adam, and John Sprague. 1986. *Paper Stones: A History of Electoral Socialism.* Chicago: University of Chicago Press.

Quellen zur Geschichte des Parlamentarismus und der Politische Partein. Vierte Reihe (4th series). Deutschland Seit 1945. 1984. Vol. 4. *Montanmitbestimmung. Das Gesetz über die Mitbestimmung der Arbeitnehmer in der Aufsichtsräten und*

*Vorständen der Unternehmer des Bergbahn und der Eisen und Stahl erzeugenden In-
dustries vom 21 Mai 1951.* Düsseldorf: Droste Verlag.

————. 1985. Vol. 3. *Auftakt zur Ära Adenauer: Koalitionsverhandlungen und
Regierungsbildung.* Ed. Udo Wengst. Dusseldorf: Droste Verlag.

————. 1993.Vol. 9. (1) *Zonenbeirat. Zonal Advisory Council, 1946–1948.* Protokolle
und anlagen 1–11 sitzung, 1946–47. Düsseldorf: Droste Verlag.

Reed, David, et al. 1985. *Miners' Strike 1984–85: People Versus the State.* London:
Larkin Publishers.

Reed, Merl E. 1991. *Seedtime for the Modern Civil Rights Movement. The President's
Committee on Fair Employment, 1941–1946.* Baton Rouge, LA: Louisiana State
University Press.

Reich, Robert. 1991. *The Work of Nations: Preparing Ourselves for the 21st-Century.*
New York: Knopf.

Reich, Simon. 1990. *The Fruits of Fascism. Postwar Prosperity in Historical Perspective.*
Ithaca, NY: Cornell University Press.

Renner, Karl. 1978. "The Development of the National Idea." *Austro-Marxism.* Eds.
Tom Bottomore and Patrick Goode. Oxford: Oxford University Press.

Report. See: Trades Union Congress. (TUC, Great Britain). Various years. *Report.*
London.

Reuther, Victor G. 1976. *The Brothers Reuther and the Story of the UAW.* Boston:
Houghton Mifflin.

Riksdagsprotokollen See: Sweden. Various year. *Riksdagsprotokollen.* Stockholm.

Ritschel, Daniel. 1997. *The Politics of Planning. The Debate on Economic Planning in
the 1930s.* Oxford: Clarendon Press.

Robbins, Lionel R. 1947. *The Economic Problem in Peace and War: Some Reflections on
Objectives and Means.* London: Macmillan.

Rogow, A. A. 1955. *The Labour Government and British Industry, 1945–1951.* Ithaca,
NY: Cornell University Press.

Rollings, Neil. 1992. "'The Reichstag Method of Governing?' The Attlee Governments and Permanent Economic Controls." *Labour Governments and Private Industry.* Eds. H. Mercer, N. Rollings, and J. D. Tomlinson. Edinburgh: Edinburgh
University Press.

Roseman, Mark. 1992. *Recasting the Ruhr, 1945–1958. Manpower, Economic Recovery
and Labour Relations.* New York: Berg.

Rothstein, Bo. 1992a. *Den korporativa staten.* Stockholm: Norstedt.

————. 1992b. "Explaining Swedish Corporatism: The Formative Moment." *Scandinavian Political Studies* 15 (3):173–191.

————. 1996. *The Swedish Model and the Bureaucratic Problem of Social Reform.* Pittsburgh, PA: University of Pittsburgh Press.

Rueschemeyer, Dietrich, Evelyne Huber Stephens, and John D. Stephens. 1992.
Capitalist Development and Democracy. Chicago: University of Chicago Press.

Ruggie, John G. 1983. "International Regimes, Transactions, and Change: Embedded Liberalism in the Postwar Economic Order." *International Regimes.* Ed.
Stephen D. Krasner. Ithaca, NY: Cornell University Press.

Ruin, Olof. 1968. *Mellan samlingsregering och tvåpartisystem. Den svenska regeringsfrågan, 1945–1960.* Stockholm: Bonnier.

Svenska Arbetsgivareföreningen. (SAF, Sweden).Various years. *Industria.* Stockholm.

Sandlund, Elisabeth. 1984. *Svenska Dagbladets Historia. Del III. Svenska Dagbladet Under Ivar Andersons Tid, 1940–1955.* Stockholm: Svenska Dagbladet.

Socialdemokratiska Arbetareparti. (SAP, Sweden.) Various years. *Protokoll.* Stockholm.

———. 1944. *Arbetarrörelsens efterkrigsprogram. De 27 punkterna med motivering.* Stockholm.

———. 1945. *SAP Information.* Stockholm.

SAP/LO. 1983. *Ett svensk sätt at lösa svenska problem.* [A Swedish Way to Solve Swedish Problems.] Stockholm.

Scharpf, Fritz W. 1991. *Crisis and Choice in European Social Democracy.* Ithaca, NY: Cornell University Press.

Schattschneider, E. E. 1960. *The Semi-Sovereign People.* New York: Holt, Rinehart and Winston.

Schmidt, Eberhard. 1970. *Verhinderte Neuordnung 1945 bis 1952.* Frankfurt: Europäische Verlagsanstalt.

Schmidt, Vivien A. 1996. *From State to Market? The Transformation of French Business and Government.* New York: Cambridge University Press.

Schmitter, Philippe C. 1974. "Still the Century of Corporatism?" *Journal of Politics* 36:85–131.

Scholliers, Peter, ed. 1989. *Real Wages in 19th and 20th Century Europe: Historical and Comparative Perspectives.* New York: Berg.

Scholz, Arno, and Walter G. Oschilewski. 1953. *Kurt Schumacher. Reden und Schriften.* Vol. 2. Berlin: Arani.

Schriften des Bundesarchiv. 1964. *Westdeutschland 1945–1950. Der Aufbau von Verfassungs- und Verwaltungseinrichtungen über den Ländern der drei westliche Besatzungszonen.* Vol. 2. Ed. Walter Vogel. Boppard am Rhein: Harald Boldt Verlag.

Schwarz, Hans-Peter. 1981. *Die ära Adenauer. Grundungjahre der Republik, 1949–1957.* Geschichte der Bundesrepublik Deutschlands, vol. 1. Stuttgart: Deutsche Verlags-Anstalt.

Schumpeter, Joseph A. 1950. *Capitalism, Socialism and Democracy.* New York: Harper and Row.

Scott, J. D., and Richard Hughes. 1955. *The Administration of War Production. History of the Second World War. United Kingdom Civil Series.* Ed. Sir Keith Hancock. London: HMSO.

Self, Peter, and Herbert J. Storing. 1963. *The State and the Farmer. British Agricultural Policies and Politics.* Berkeley: University of California Press.

Seyd, Patrick. 19987. *The Rise and Fall of the Labour Left.* New York: St. Martin's Press.

Shaw, Eric. 1988. *Discipline and Discord in the Labour Party.* Manchester: Manchester University Press.

Shonfield, Andrew. 1965. *Modern Capitalism. The Changing Balance of Public and Private Power.* London: Oxford University Press.

Simon, Walter. 1976. *Macht und Herrschaft der Unternehmerverbände. BDI, BDA und DIHT im ökonomischen und politischen System der BRD.* Cologne: Pahl-Rugenstein.

Skidelsky, Robert. 1995. *John Maynard Keynes. The Economist as Savior, 1920–1937.* New York: Penguin Books.

———. 1996, 20 September. "After Serfdom." *Times Literary Supplement.*

Skocpol, Theda. 1985. "Bringing the State Back In: Strategies of Analysis in Current Research." *Bringing the State Back In.* Eds. Peter B. Evans, Dietrich Rueschemeyer, and Theda Skocpol. New York: Cambridge University Press.

Skowronek, Stephen. 1982. *Building a New American State: The Expansion of National Administrative Capacities, 1877–1920.* Cambridge, MA: Cambridge University Press.

Sohn-Rethel, Alfred. 1978. *Aufstieg und Krise der Deutschen Sozialdemokratie.* Köln: Pahl-Rugenstein.

Sombart, Werner. 1976 (orig. 1906). *Why Is There No Socialism in the United States?* White Plains, NY: M. E. Sharpe.

Sozialdemokratischen Partei. (SPD, Federal Republic of Germany). Various years. *Protokoll der Verhandlungen des Parteitages der Sozialdemokratischen Partei Deutschland.* Berlin: Verlag J.H.W. Dietz Nachf. GmbH.

———. 1950. *The Dürkheim Points.* Jahrbuch der SPD 1948/49. Bonn, 1950.

———. 1952, Sept. *Action Program of the Social Democratic Party of Germany.* Adopted by the Party Conference at Dortmund. 1952. English translation.

Stein, Herbert. 1969. *The Fiscal Revolution in America.* Chicago: University of Chicago Press.

Stepan, Alfred C., and Cindy Skach. 1993, October. "Constitutional Frameworks and Democratic Consolidation: Parliamentarism versus Presidentialism." *World Politics* 46: 1–22.

Stephens, John D. 1986. *The Transition from Capitalism to Socialism.* Urbana: University of Illinois Press.

Stockholms Kommunistiska Arbetarkommun. 1947. *Årsberättelse 1946.* Stockholm.

Stone, Richard. 1972 (orig. 1951). "The Use and Development of National Income and Expenditure Estimates." *Lessons of the British War Economy.* Ed. D. N. Chester. Westport, CT: Greenwood Press.

Strachey, John. 1939. *How Socialism Works.* New York: Modern Age Books.

———. 1941. *A Faith to Fight For.* London: V. Gollanz.

———. 1956. *Contemporary Capitalism.* New York: Random House.

Strange, Susan. 1971. *Sterling and British Policy.* London: Oxford University Press.

———. 1996. *The Retreat of the State. The Diffusion of Power in the World Economy.* Cambridge: Cambridge University Press.

Strikwerda, Carl. 1993. "The Troubled Origins of Euroepan Economic Integration: International Iron and Steel and Labor Migration in the Era of World War I." *American Historical Review* 98: 1106–1142.

———. 1997. "Reinterpreting the History of European Integration: Business, Labor, and Social Citizenship in Twentieth-Century Europe." *European Integra-*

tion in Social and Historical Prespective. 1850 to the Present. Eds. Jytte Klausen and Louise A. Tilly. Boulder, CO: Rowman & Littlefield.

Sturmthal, Adolf. 1989. *Democracy Under Fire. Memoirs of a European Socialist.* Durham, NC: Duke University Press.

Strömbom, Bo. 1964. *Svensk marknadsföring på Europamarknaden.* Handelshögskolan i Göteborg Skriften (1).

Svenning, Olle. 1972. *Socialdemokratin och näringslivet.* Stockholm: Tidens Förlag.

Sweden. Various years. *Riksdagsprotokollen.* Stockholm.

Sweden. 1931a. Socialdepartementet. Arbetslöshetsutredningens betänkande. *Arbetslöshetens omfattning, karaktär och orsaker.* SOU 1931:20. Stockholm.

———. 1931b. Socialdepartementet. Arbetslöshetsutredningens betänkande. 1. Bilagor. Vol. 1. *Orsaker till arbetslöshet.* By Gösta Bagge. [Med bilaga: P. M. ang. arbetsmarknaden och de faktorer, som bestämma dess utveckling. By Gunnar Huss.] SOU 1931:21. Stockholm.

———. 1931c. Socialdepartementet. Arbetslöshetsutredningens betänkande. 1. Bilagor. Vol. 2. *Om den industriella rationaliseringen och dess verkningar särskilt beträffande arbetarsysselsättningen.* By Gustaf Åkerman. SOU 1931:42. Stockholm.

———. 1933a. Jordbruksdepartementet. *Betänkande met förslag ang. åtgärder för ett bättre utnyttjande av landets skogstillgångar.* Avg. den 4 jan. 1933 av 1931 års skogssakkunniga. SOU 1933:2. Stockholm.

———. 1933b. Socialdepartementet. Arbetslöshetsutredningens betänkande. 2. Bilagor. Vol. 1. *Konjunkturspridningen. En teoretisk och historisk undersökning.* By Dag Hammarskjöld. SOU 1933:29. Stockholm.

———. 1934a. Socialdepartementet. Arbetslöshetsutredningens betänkande. 2. Bilagor. Vol. 2. *Finanspolitikens ekonomiska verkningar.* By Gunnar Myrdal. SOU 1934:1. Stockholm.

———. 1934b. Socialdepartementet. Arbetslöshetsutredningens betänkande. 2. Bilagor. Vol. 3. *Löneutvecklingen och arbetslösheten.* By Alf Johansson. SOU 1934:2. Stockholm.

———. 1934c. Socialdepartementet. Arbetslöshetsutredningens betänkande. 2. Bilagor. Vol. 4. *Penningpolitik, offentliga arbeten, subventioner och tullar som medel mot arbetslöshet. Bidrag till expansionens teori.* By Bertil Ohlin. SOU 1934:12. Stockholm.

———. 1934d. Socialdepartementet. *Betänkande med förslag till lag ang. vissa ekonomiska stridsåtgärder m. m. Avg. den 4 maj 1934 an en inom socialdepartementet tilsatt kommission* [trettonmannakommissionen]. SOU 1934:16. Stockholm.

———. 1935a. Socialdepartementet. Arbetslöshetsutredningens betänkande. *Åtgärder mot arbetslöshet.* [Med bilaga: P. M. ang. vissa grenar av den svenska ekonomiska statistiken. By Einar Dahlgren.] SOU 1935:6. Stockholm.

———. 1935b. Socialdepartementet. *Betänkande om folkförsörjning och arbetsfred.* Vol. 1. Förslag. By Torsten Nothin, Elof Ericsson, and Frans Severin. SOU 1935:65. Stockholm.

———. 1935c. Socialdepartementet. *Betänkande om folkförsörjning och arbetsfred.* Vol. 2. Specialutredningar. SOU 1935:66. Stockholm.

————. 1944a. Folkhushållningsdepartementet. *Statsmakterna och folkhushållningen under den till följd av stormaktskriget 1939 indträdde krisen, Juli 1943-June 1944.* SOU 1944:11. Stockholm.

————. 1944b. Finansdepartementet. Utredningar ang. ekonomisk efterkrigs-planering. *Krigsorganens personel.* Vol. 6. SOU 1944:36. Stockholm.

————. 1944c. Finansdepartementet. Utredningar ang. ekonomisk efterkrigs-planering. Vol. 7. *Framställningar och utlåtanden från kommissionen för ekonomisk efterkrigsplanering.* SOU 1944:57. Stockholm.

————. 1944d. Kommissionen för Ekonomisk Efterkrigsplanering. *P.M. ang. de konjunkturbestämmande faktorererna inom det svenska näringslivet, June 15, 1944.* Stockholm.

————. 1944e. Kommissionen för Ekonomisk Efterkrigsplanering. *Konjunktur-rörelserna hos det svenska näringslivet under mellenkrigsperioden.* September 20. Stockholm.

————. 1945. Socialdepartementet. *Socialpolitikkens ekonomiska verkningar. Frågeställ-ningar och riktlinjer.* SOU 1945:14. Stockholm.

————. 1952a. Handelsdepartementet. *Kristidspolitik och kristidshushållning i Sverige under och efter andra världskriget. Översikt på offentligt uppdrag under medverkan av fackmän utarb.* [By Karl Åmark.] 2 vols. SOU 1952:49–50. Stockholm.

————. 1954. Finansdepartementet. *Yrkesutbildningen. Betänkande av 1952 års yrke-sutbildningssakkunniga.* SOU 1954:11. Stockholm.

Swenson, Peter. 1989. *Fair Shares. Unions, Pay, and Politics in Sweden and West Germany.* Ithaca, NY: Cornell University Press.

————. 1991. "Bringing Capital Back In, Or Social Democracy Reconsidered." *World Politics* 43 (4):69–96.

————. 1992. "Union Politics, the Welfare State, and Intraclass Conflict in Sweden and Germany." *Bargaining for Change. Union Politics in North America and Europe.* Eds. Miriam Golden and Jonas Pontusson. Ithaca, NY: Cornell University Press.

————. 1997, March. "Arranged Alliance: Business Interests in the New Deal." *Politics and Society* 25: 66–116.

Söderpalm, Sven Anders. 1976. *Direktörsklubben. Storindustrin i Svensk Politik under 1930- och 40-talen.* Stockholm: Zenith-Rabén Sjögren.

Tálos, Emmerich. 1991. "Sozialpartnerschaft. Kooperation-Konzertierung-politische Regulierung." *Handbuch des Politische Systems Österreichs.* Wein: Manzsche Ver-lags- und Universitätsbuchhandlung.

Tew, J. H. B. 1978. "Monetary Policy—Part I." *British Economic Policy, 1960–74.* Ed. F. T. Blackaby. Cambridge: Cambridge University Press.

Thelen, Kathleen A. 1991. *Union of Parts. Labor Politics in Postwar Germany.* Ithaca, NY: Cornell University Press.

Thelen, Kathleen, and Sven Steinmo. 1992. "Historical Institutionalism in Comparative Politics." *Structuring Politics: Historical Institutionalism in Comparative Analysis.* Eds. Sven Steinmo, Kathleen Thelen, and Frank Longstreth. Cambridge, MA: Cambridge University Press.

Therborn, Göran. 1992. "A Unique Chapter in the History of Democracy." *Creating Social Democracy. A Century of the Social Democratic Labor Party in Sweden.* Eds.

Klaus Misgeld, Karl Molin, and Klas Åmark. University Park, PA: Pennsylvania State University Press.

Tilly, Charles. 1975. "Reflections on the History of European State-Making." *The Formation of National States in Western Europe*. Ed. Charles Tilly. Princeton, NJ: Princeton University Press.

————. 1984. *Big Structures, Large Processes, Huge Comparisons*. New York: Russell Sage Foundation.

————. 1985. "War Making and State Making as Organized Crime." *Bringing the State Back In*. Eds. Peter Evans, Dietrich Rueschemeyer, and Theda Skocpol. Cambridge, MA: Cambridge University Press.

————. 1989. "Cities and States in Europe, 1000–1800." *Theory and Society* 18. 563–584.

Tilton, Tim. 1992. "The Role of Ideology." *Creating Social Democracy. A Century of the Social Democratic Labor Party in Sweden*. Ed. Klaus Misgeld. University Park, PA: Pennsylvania State University Press.

Tinbergen, Jan. 1956. *Economic Policy: Principles and Design*. Amsterdam: North Holland Publishing Co.

————. 1964. *Central Planning*. New Haven, CT: Yale University Press.

Tingsten, Herbert. 1973 (Sw. orig. 1941.) *The Swedish Social Democrats. Their Ideological Development*. Totowa, NJ: Bedminster Press.

Tiratsoo, Nick, ed. 1991. *The Attlee Years*. London: Pinter.

Titmuss, Richard D. 1950. *Problems of Social Policy*. History of the Second World War. United Kingdom Civil Series. London: HMSO.

————. 1976. 3rd ed. "War and Social Policy." *Essays on "The Welfare State."* London: George Allen & Unwin.

Tomlins, Christopher L. 1986. *The State and The Unions. Labor Relations, Law, and the Organized Labor Movement in America, 1880–1960*. New York: Cambridge University Press.

Tomlinson, Jim. 1987. *Employment Policy. The Crucial Years, 1939–1955*. Oxford: Clarendon Press.

————. 1990. *Public Policy and the Economy Since 1900*. Oxford: Clarendon Press.

————. 1991. "The Labour Government and the Trade Unions, 1945–1951." *The Attlee Years*. Ed. N. Tiratsoo. London: Pinter.

————. 1992. "Productivity Policy." *Labour Governments and Private Industry*. Eds. H. Mercer, N. Rollings, and J. D. Tomlinson. Edinburgh: Edinburgh University Press.

————. 1994a. *Government and The Enterprise Since 1900*. Oxford: Clarendon Press.

————. 1994b. "British Economic Policy Since 1945." *The Economic History of Britain Since 1700, Vol. 3: 1939–1992*. Eds. Roderick Floud and Donald McCloskey. Cambridge: Cambridge University Press.

————. 1997. *Democratic Socialism and Economic Policy. The Attlee Years, 1945–1951*. Cambridge, MA: Cambridge University Press.

Tranøy, Bent Sofus. 1996a, March 1–3. "Monetary Surrender in Norway: External Pressure and Domestic Analysis Beyond Economic Approaches." Graduate Student Workshop on "The Distributive Dimensions of Political Economy:

European Politics and Society in the High Unemployment Age." Center for European Studies, Harvard University.

———. 1996b, Aug. 29–Sept. 1. "The Underrated Financial Dimension of Social Democracy." Paper Presented at the Annual Meeting of the American Political Science Association. San Francisco.

Traxler, Franz. 1986. *Interessevernverbände der Unternehmer*. Frankfurt: Campus Verlag.

———. 1991. "Gewerkschaften und Unternehmerverbände in Österreichs politischem System." *Handbuch des Politische Systems Österreichs*. Wein: Manzsche Verlags- und Universitätsbuchhandlung.

Troy, Leo, and Neil Sheflin. 1985. *U.S. Union Sourcebook. Membership, Finances, Structure, Directory*. West Orange, NJ: Industrial relations Data and Information Services.

Trades Union Congress. (TUC, Great Britain.) Various years. *Report*. London.

———. 1944. *Interim Report on Post-War Reconstruction*. Blackpool.

———. 1946. *Trade Union Structure and Closer Unity*. Final Report. An Examination by the TUC of the Present Structure and Functions of Trade Unions. Suggestions for Improved Machinery and Notes on Progress Achieved. London.

Tuckett, Angela. 1942. *Civil Liberties and the Industrial Worker*. London: National Council for Civil Liberties.

Turner, Frederick Jackson. 1920. *The Frontier in American History*. New York: Henry Holt.

Turner, Henry Ashby, Jr. 1985. *German Big Business and the Rise of Hitler*. New York: Oxford University Press.

Unga, Nils. 1976. *Socialdemokratin och arbetslöshetsfrågan, 1912–1934*. Stockholm: Arkiv för studier i arbetarrörelsens historia.

United Nations. Economic Commission for Europe. Various years. *Economic Survey of Europe*. Geneva.

U.S. Congress. 1943a. *Security, Work, and Relief Policies*. Report of the Committee on Long-Range Work and Relief Policies to the National Resources Planning Board. Washington, D.C.: Government Printing Office.

———. 1943b. Rev. ed. National Resources Planing Board. *After the War—Full Employment. Post-War Planning*. By Alvin H. Hansen. (Rev. ed.) Washington, D.C.: Government Printing Office.

U.S. Economic Cooperation Administration. n.d. [1948?] *Long Term Program for the United States and United Kingdom Occupied Areas in Germany*. European Recovery program. Program Submitted to the Economic Cooperation Administration in Washington, D.C.

———. n.d. [1949?]. *Western Germany. Country Study*. European Recovery Program. Washington, D.C.

U.S. Department of State. 1947. *Occupation of Germany. Policy and Process, 1945–46*. Washington, D.C.: Government Printing Office.

———. Various years. The European Recovery Program. *Country Studies*. Washington, D.C.

———. 1964, June. Bureau of Intelligence and Research. External Research Staff. *Cartellization in Western Europe*. By Corwin D. Edwards. Policy Research Study.

———. Office of the U.S. High Commissioner to Germany. (HICOG). 1949. *1st Quarterly Report, September 21-December 31.* Washington, D.C.

———. 1950a. *2nd Quarterly Report, January 1-March 31.* Washington, D.C.

———. 1950b. *3rd Quarterly Report, April 1-June 30.* Washington, D.C.

———. 1952. "Political Influence of German Labor." *Report on Germany.* Summary Report. September 31, 1949-July 31.

———. Office of Military Government of the United States. (OMGUS). 1948, October. Manpower Division. Visiting Expert Series no. 2. *Labor Relations in Western Germany.* By K. Taylor Cole. Washington, D.C.

Veckans affärer. Various issues. Stockholm.

Visser, Jelle. 1990. "In Search of Inclusive Unionism." *Bulletin of Comparative Labour Relations* (18).

Wade, Robert. 1990. *Governing the Market. Economic Theory and the Role of Government in East Asian Industrialization.* Princeton, NJ: Princeton University Press.

Wadensjö, Eskil. 1991. "The Committee on Unemployment and the Stockholm School." *The Stockholm School of Economics Revisited.* Ed. Lars Jonung. Cambridge: Cambridge University Press.

Wala, Michael. 1993. "'Ripping Holes in the Iron Curtain': The Council on Foreign Relations and Germany, 1945–1950." *American Policy and the Reconstruction of West Germany, 1945–1955.* Ed. Hartmut Lehmann and the German Historical Institute. New York: Cambridge University Press.

Wallace, William. 1946. *Enterprise First. The Relationship of the State to Industry, With Particular Reference to Private Enterprise.* London: Longmans, Green.

Wallich, Henry C. 1955. *Mainsprings of the German Revival.* New Haven, CT: Yale University Press.

Ward, J. T., and W. Hamish Fraser, eds. 1980. *Workers and Employers. Documents on Trade Unions and Industrial relations in Britain Since the Early Nineteenth Century.* Hamden, CT: Archon Books.

Warken, Philip W. 1979. *A History of the National Resources Planning Board, 1933–1943.* New York: Garland.

Wege in die Neue Zeit. 1946. Berliner Tagung der Union. 15 bis 17 juni, 1946. Berlin, SW68: Union-verlag GMBH.

Weir, Margaret. 1992. *Politics and Jobs. The Boundaries of Employment Policy in the United States.* Princeton, NJ: Princeton University Press.

Weir, Margaret, and Theda Skocpol. 1985. "State Structures and the Possibilities for 'Keynesian' Responses to the Great Depression in Sweden, Great Britain and the United States." *Bringing the State Back In.* Eds. Peter B. Evans, et al. Cambridge, MA: Cambridge University Press.

Whiteley, Paul. 1983. *The Labour Party in Crisis.* London: Methuen.

Wigforss, Ernst. 1941. *Från Klasskamp till samverkan* [From Class Struggle to Collaboration]. Stockholm: Tidens Förlag.

———. 1954. *Minnen, 1932–1949.* Stockholm: Tidens Förlag.

Williamson, Oliver E. 1985. *The Economic Institutions of Capitalism.* New York: Free Press.

Willgerodt, Hans. 1976. "Planning in West-Germany: The Social Market Economy." *The Politics of Planning: A Review and Critique of Centralized Economic Planning.* Ed. B. Bruce Briggs et al. San Francisco: Institute for Contemporary Studies.

Wilson, Graham K. 1977. *Special Interests and Policy-Making. Agricultural Policies and Politics in Britain and the United States of America, 1956–70.* London: Wiley and Sons.

Winch, Donald. 1969. *Economics and Policy. A Historical Study.* New York: Walker and Co.

———. 1989. "Keynes, Keynesianism, and State Intervention." *The Political Power of Economic Ideas. Keynesianism Across Nations.* Ed. Peter Hall. Princeton, NJ: Princeton University Press.

Wolfe, Alan, and Jytte Klausen. 1997. "Identity Politics and the Welfare State." *The Welfare State.* Eds. Ellen Frankel Paul, Fred D. Miller, Jr., and Jeffrey Paul. New York: Cambridge University Press.

Woolton, The Earl of. 1959. *The Memoirs of the Rt. Hon. The Earl of Woolton.* London: Cassel.

Wootton, Barbara. 1955. *The Social Foundations of Wage Policy.* New York: W. W. Norton.

Worswick, G. D. N. and P. H. Ady, eds. 1962. *The British Economy in the Nineteen-Fifties.* Oxford: Clarendon Press.

Wunderlich, Frieda. 1961. *Farm Labor in Germany, 1810–1945.* Princeton, NJ: Princeton University Press.

Zolberg, Aristide R. 1986. "How Many Exceptionalism?" *Working-Class Formation: Nineteenth-Century Patterns in Western Europe and the United States.* Eds. Ira Katznelson and Aristide R. Zolberg. Princeton, NJ: Princeton University Press.

Zysman, John. 1983. *Governments, Markets, and Growth: Financial Systems and the Politics of Industrial Challenge.* Ithaca, NY: Cornell University Press.

Åmark, Karl. 1952 a and b. *Kristidspolitik och kristidshushållning i Sverige under och efter andra världskriget.* Sweden. Handelsdepartementet. Statens Offentliga Utredningar. (SOU) 50–51.

Åsard, Erik. 1981. *Kampen om löntagarfonderna.* Stockholm: Norstedts.

Index

(Numerals in italics represent pages with tables or figures)